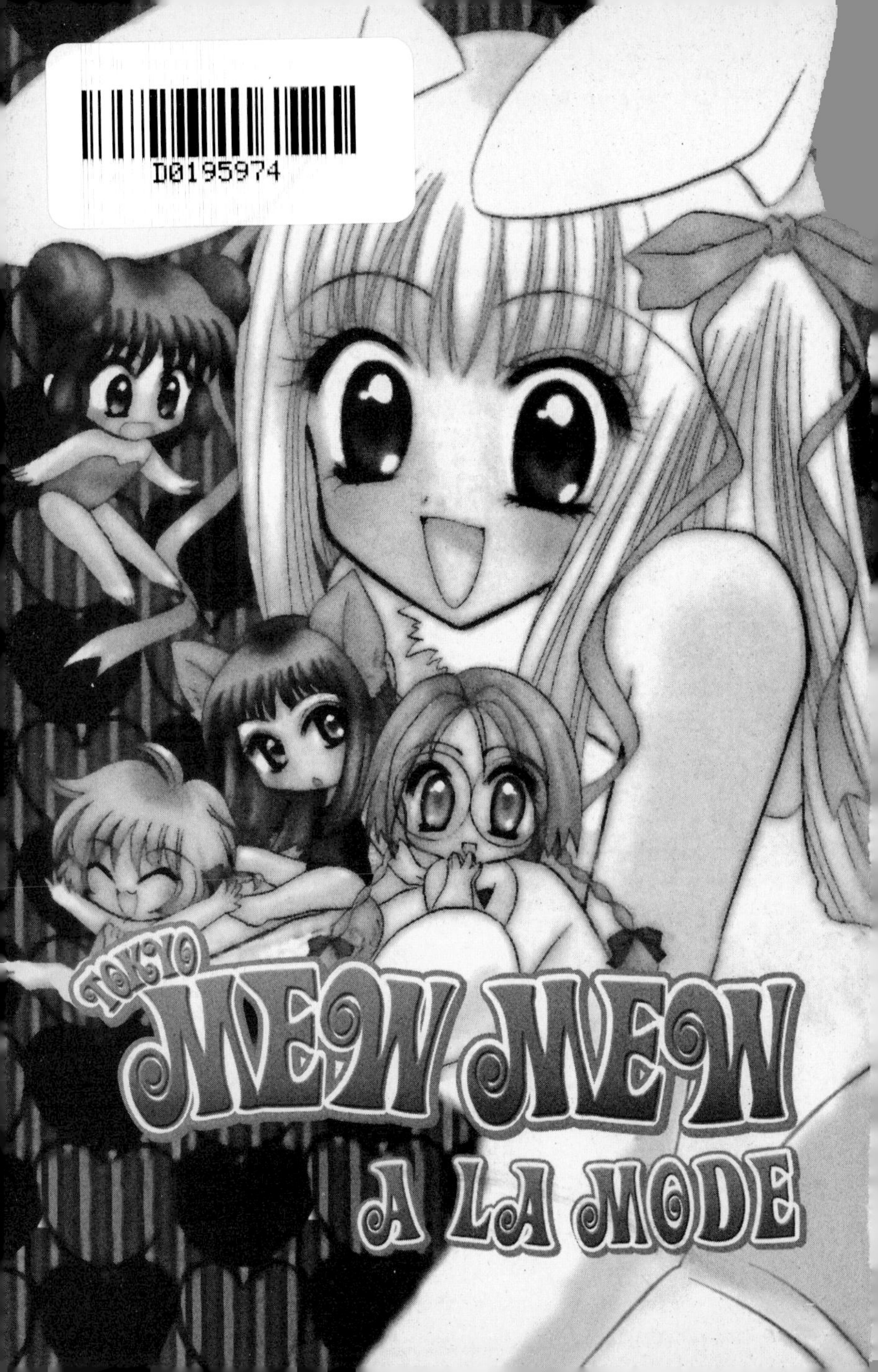
TOKYO
MEW MEW
A LA MODE

Tokyo Mew Mew a la Mode Vol. 1
Art by Mia Ikumi
Original Concept by Kodansha

Translation - Yoohae Yang
English Adaptation - Stuart Hazleton
Associate Editor - Peter Ahlstrom
Retouch and Lettering - Irene Woori Choi
Production Artist - Jason Milligan
Cover Design - Steven Chao

Editor - Carol Fox
Digital Imaging Manager - Chris Buford
Pre-Press Manager - Antonio DePietro
Production Managers - Jennifer Miller and Mutsumi Miyazaki
Art Director - Matt Alford
Managing Editor - Jill Freshney
VP of Production - Ron Klamert
Editor-in-Chief - Mike Kiley
President and C.O.O. - John Parker
Publisher and C.E.O. - Stuart Levy

A **TOKYOPOP** Manga

TOKYOPOP Inc.
5900 Wilshire Blvd. Suite 2000
Los Angeles, CA 90036

E-mail: info@TOKYOPOP.com
Come visit us online at www.TOKYOPOP.com

ISBN: 1-59532-789-4

First TOKYOPOP printing: June 2005
10 9 8 7 6 5 4 3
Printed in Canada

TOKYO MEW MEW A LA MODE™

ART BY MIA IKUMI
ORIGINAL CONCEPT BY KODANSHA

VOLUME 1

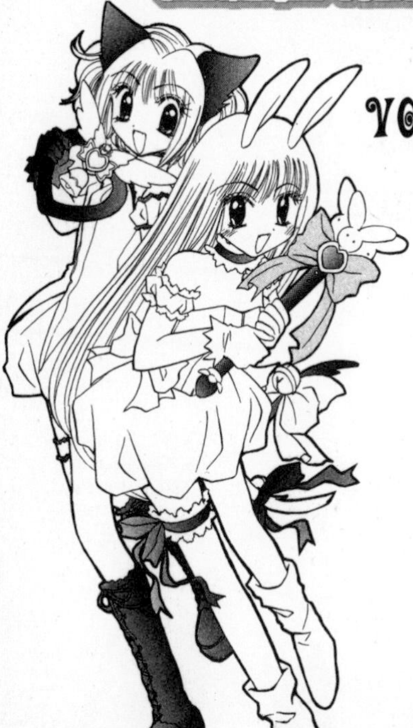

TOKYOPOP®

HAMBURG // LONDON // LOS ANGELES // TOKYO

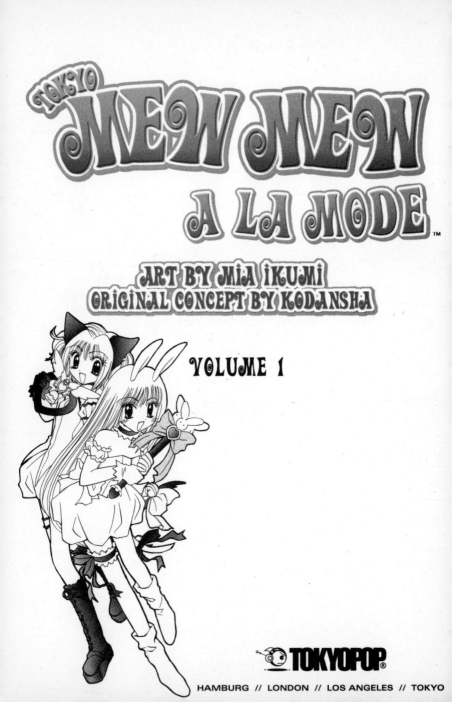

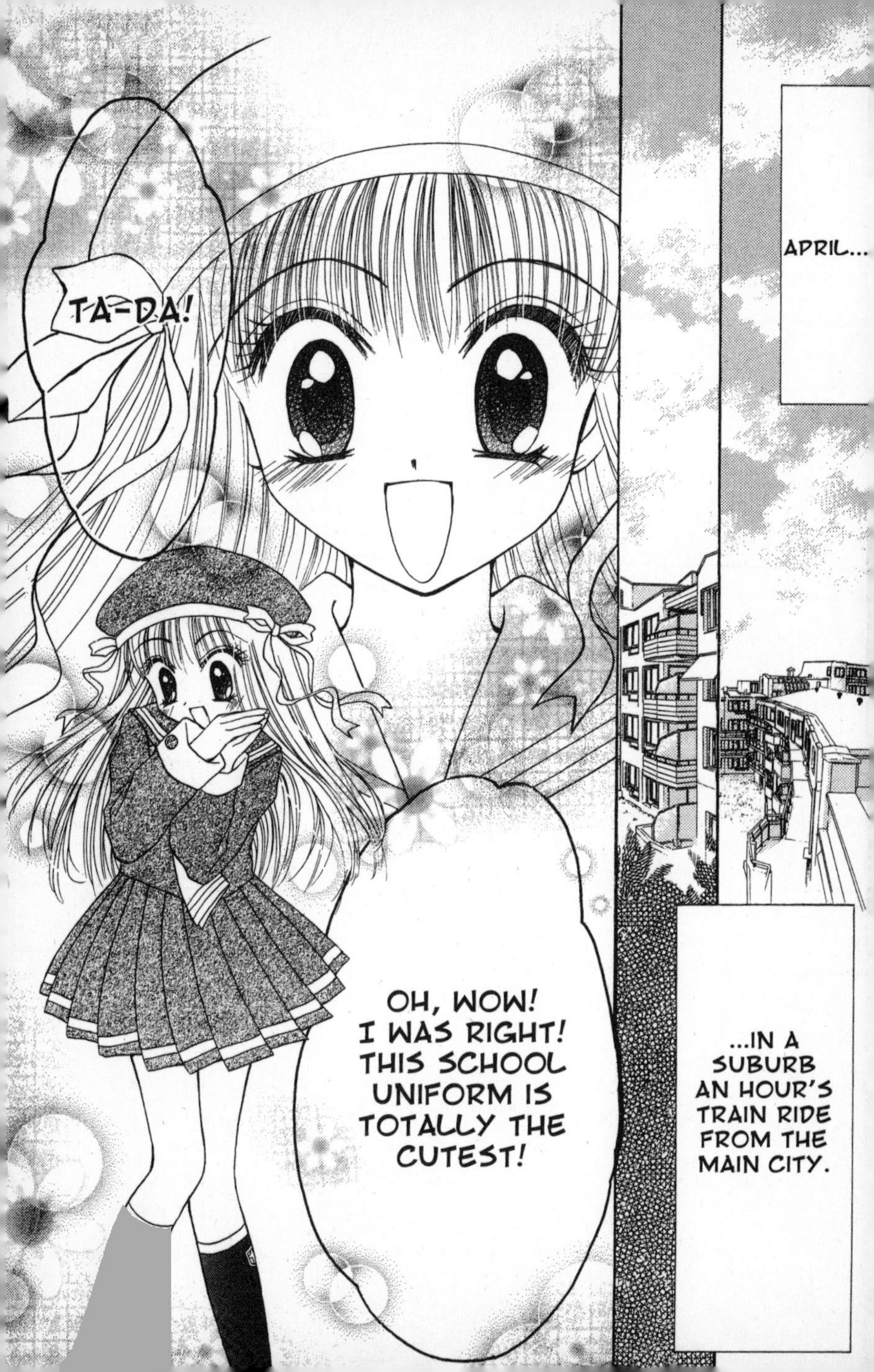
APRIL...
...IN A SUBURB AN HOUR'S TRAIN RIDE FROM THE MAIN CITY.
TA-DA!
OH, WOW! I WAS RIGHT! THIS SCHOOL UNIFORM IS TOTALLY THE CUTEST!

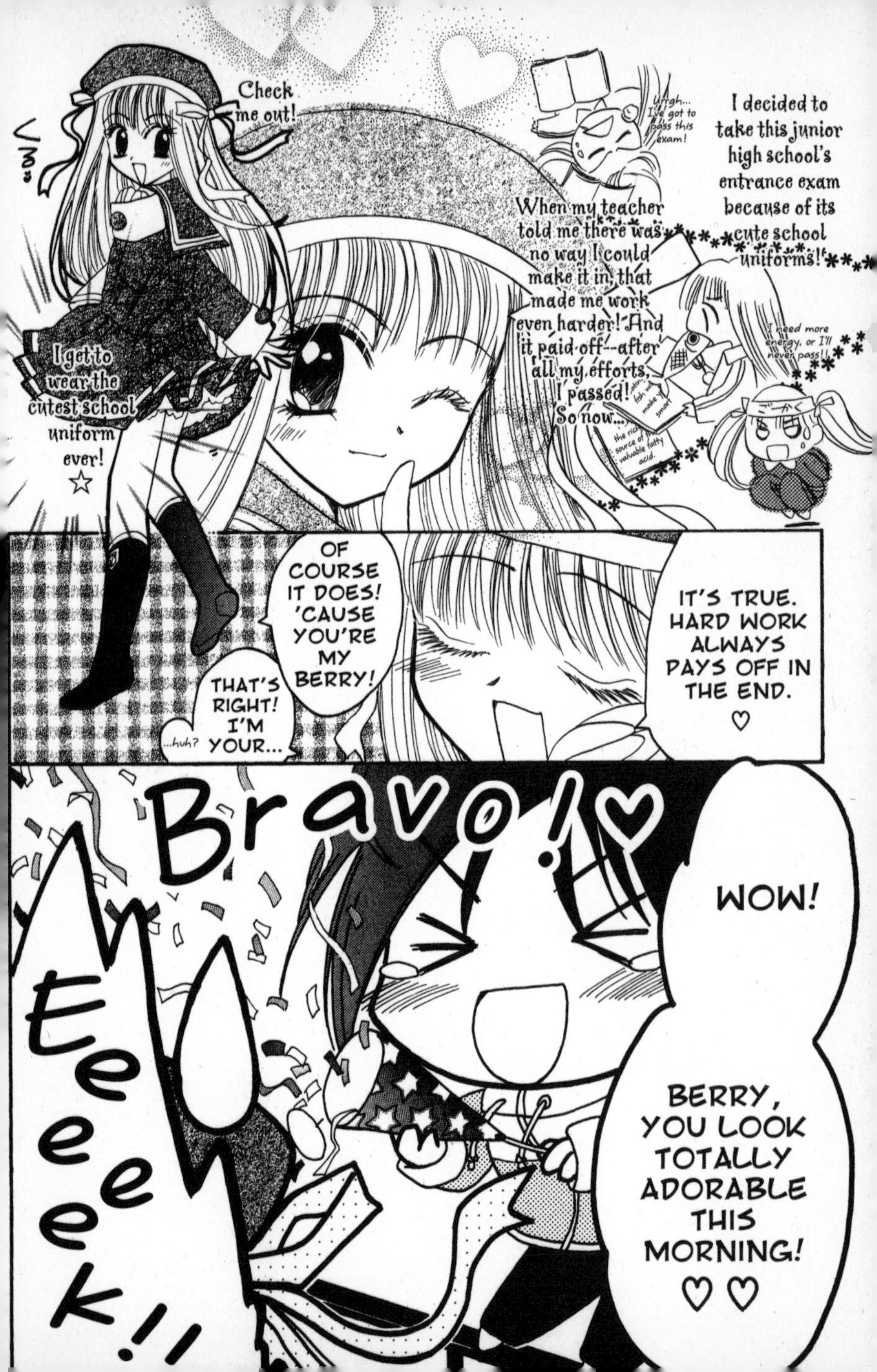
I decided to take this junior high school's entrance exam because of its cute school uniforms!
Urrgh... I've got to pass this exam!
I need more energy, or I'll never pass!!
When my teacher told me there was no way I could make it in, that made me work even harder! And it paid off--after all my efforts, I passed! So now...
Check me out!
I get to wear the cutest school uniform ever! ☆
IT'S TRUE. HARD WORK ALWAYS PAYS OFF IN THE END. ♡
OF COURSE IT DOES! 'CAUSE YOU'RE MY BERRY!
THAT'S RIGHT! I'M YOUR...
...huh?
WOW!
BERRY, YOU LOOK TOTALLY ADORABLE THIS MORNING! ♡ ♡
Bravo!♡
Eeeeek!!

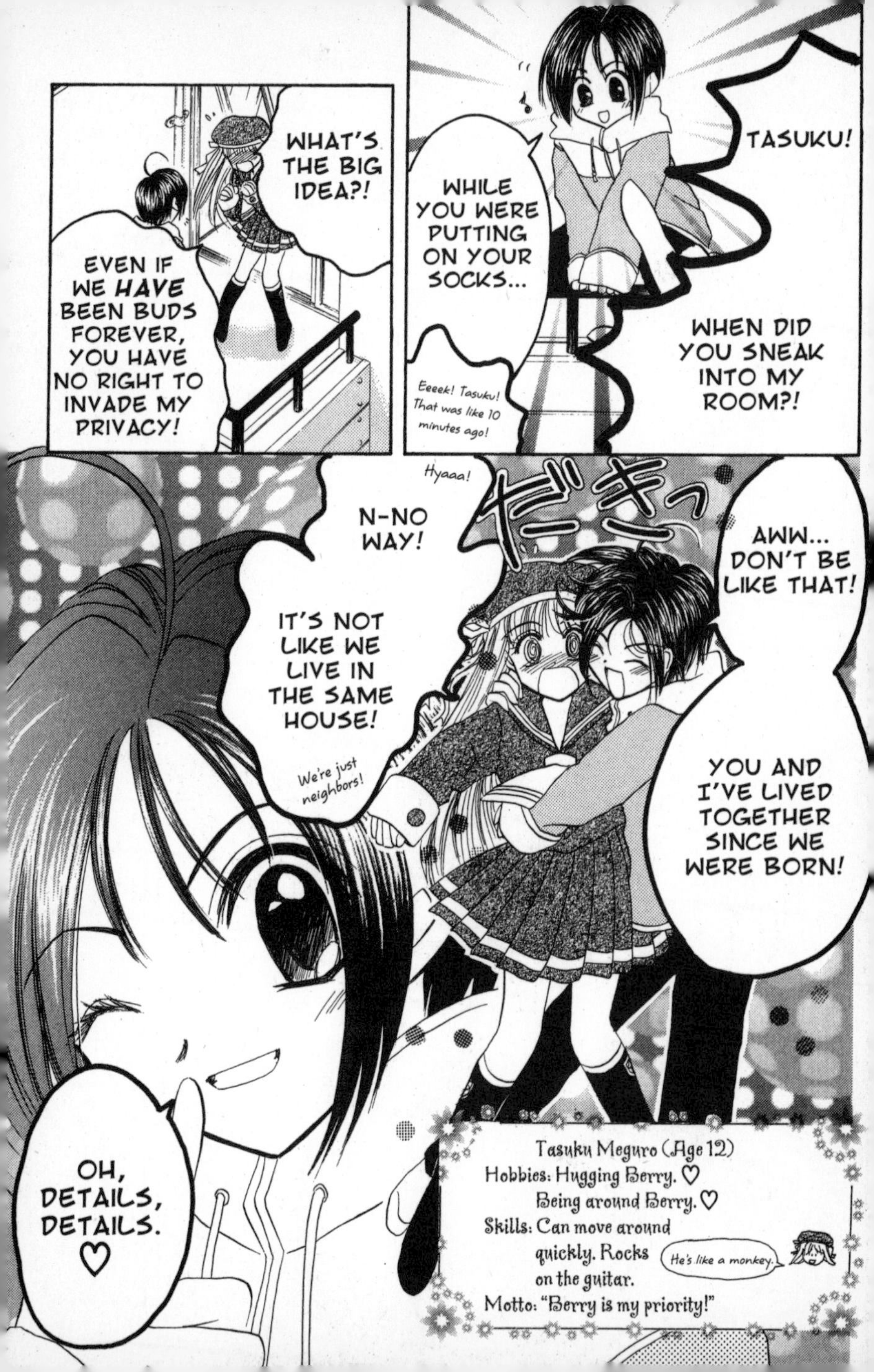
TASUKU!
WHEN DID YOU SNEAK INTO MY ROOM?!
WHILE YOU WERE PUTTING ON YOUR SOCKS...
Eeeek! Tasuku! That was like 10 minutes ago!
WHAT'S THE BIG IDEA?!
EVEN IF WE *HAVE* BEEN BUDS FOREVER, YOU HAVE NO RIGHT TO INVADE MY PRIVACY!
AWW... DON'T BE LIKE THAT!
YOU AND I'VE LIVED TOGETHER SINCE WE WERE BORN!
Hyaaa!
N-NO WAY!
IT'S NOT LIKE WE LIVE IN THE SAME HOUSE!
We're just neighbors!
OH, DETAILS, DETAILS. ♡
Tasuku Meguro (Age 12)
Hobbies: Hugging Berry. ♡ Being around Berry. ♡
Skills: Can move around quickly. Rocks on the guitar.
He's like a monkey.
Motto: "Berry is my priority!"

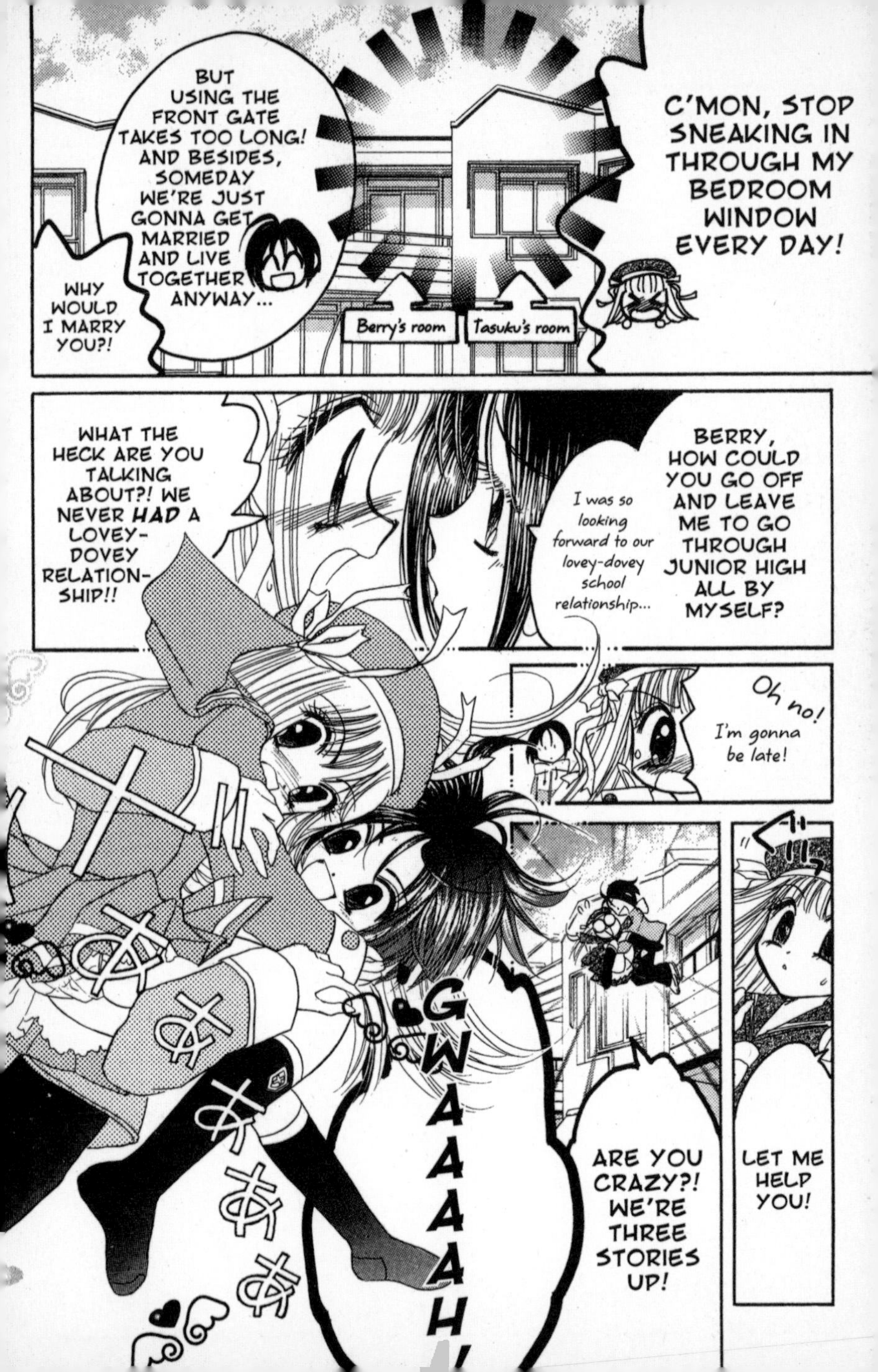
C'MON, STOP SNEAKING IN THROUGH MY BEDROOM WINDOW EVERY DAY!
Tasuku's room
Berry's room
BUT USING THE FRONT GATE TAKES TOO LONG! AND BESIDES, SOMEDAY WE'RE JUST GONNA GET MARRIED AND LIVE TOGETHER ANYWAY...
WHY WOULD I MARRY YOU?!
BERRY, HOW COULD YOU GO OFF AND LEAVE ME TO GO THROUGH JUNIOR HIGH ALL BY MYSELF?
I was so looking forward to our lovey-dovey school relationship...
WHAT THE HECK ARE YOU TALKING ABOUT?! WE NEVER HAD A LOVEY-DOVEY RELATION-SHIP!!
Oh no!
I'm gonna be late!
LET ME HELP YOU!
ARE YOU CRAZY?! WE'RE THREE STORIES UP!
GWAAAAH!

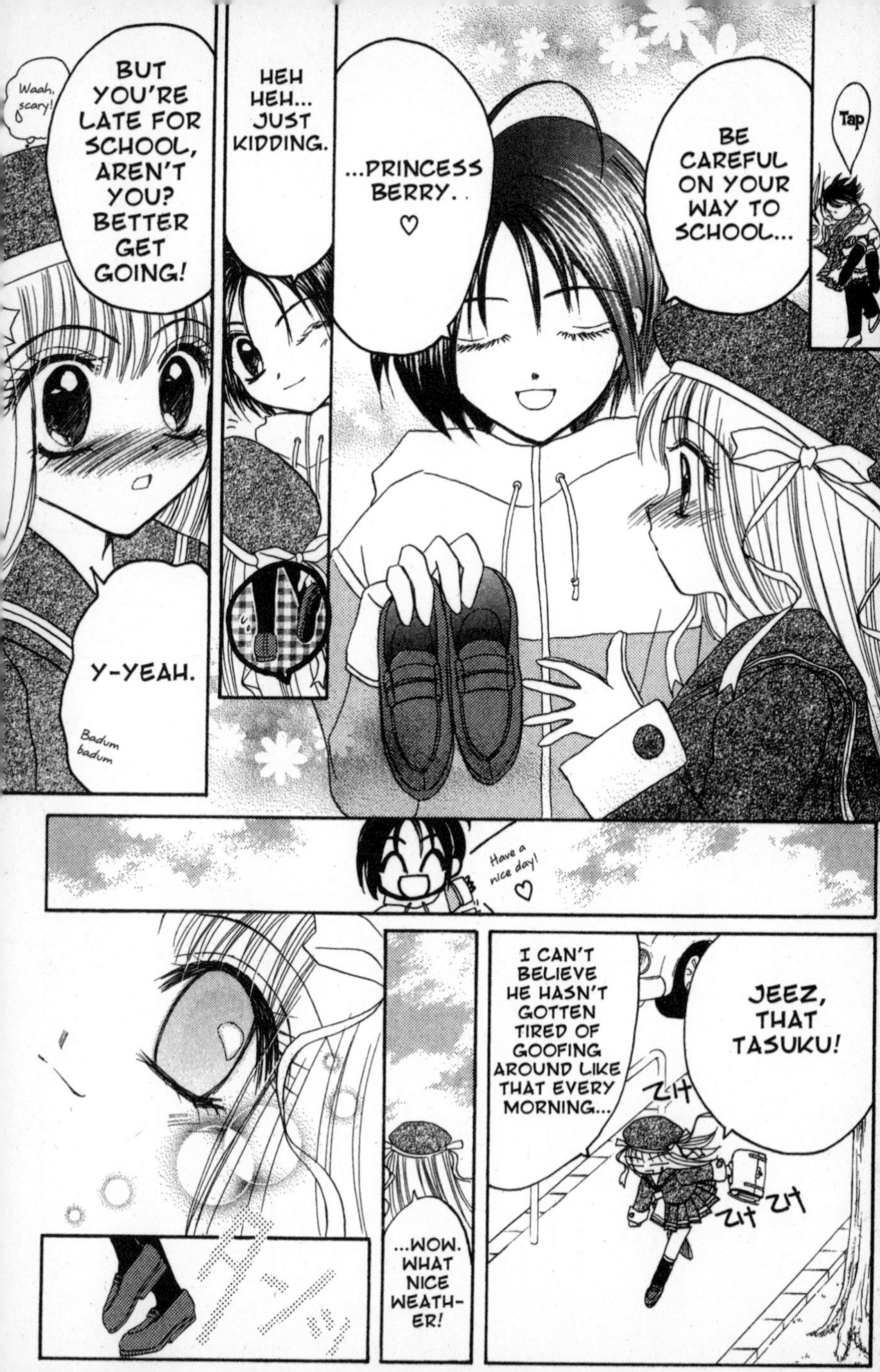
Tap
BE CAREFUL ON YOUR WAY TO SCHOOL...
...PRINCESS BERRY. ♡
HEH HEH... JUST KIDDING.
BUT YOU'RE LATE FOR SCHOOL, AREN'T YOU? BETTER GET GOING!
Waah, scary!
Y-YEAH.
Badum badum
Have a nice day! ♡
JEEZ, THAT TASUKU!
I CAN'T BELIEVE HE HASN'T GOTTEN TIRED OF GOOFING AROUND LIKE THAT EVERY MORNING...
...WOW. WHAT NICE WEATHER!

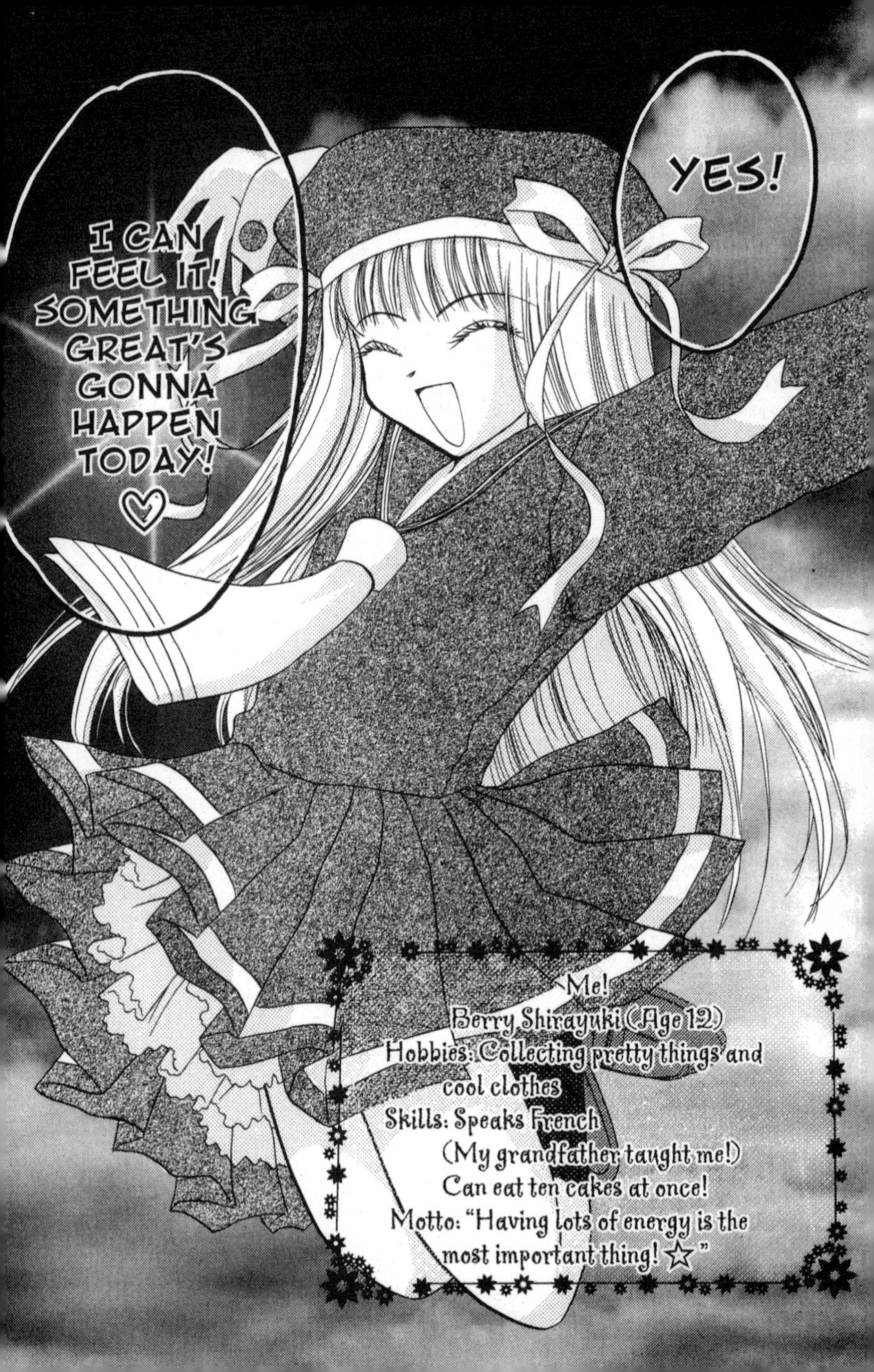
YES!
I CAN FEEL IT! SOMETHING GREAT'S GONNA HAPPEN TODAY! ♡
Me!
Berry Shirayuki (Age 12)
Hobbies: Collecting pretty things and cool clothes
Skills: Speaks French
(My grandfather taught me!)
Can eat ten cakes at once!
Motto: "Having lots of energy is the most important thing! ☆"

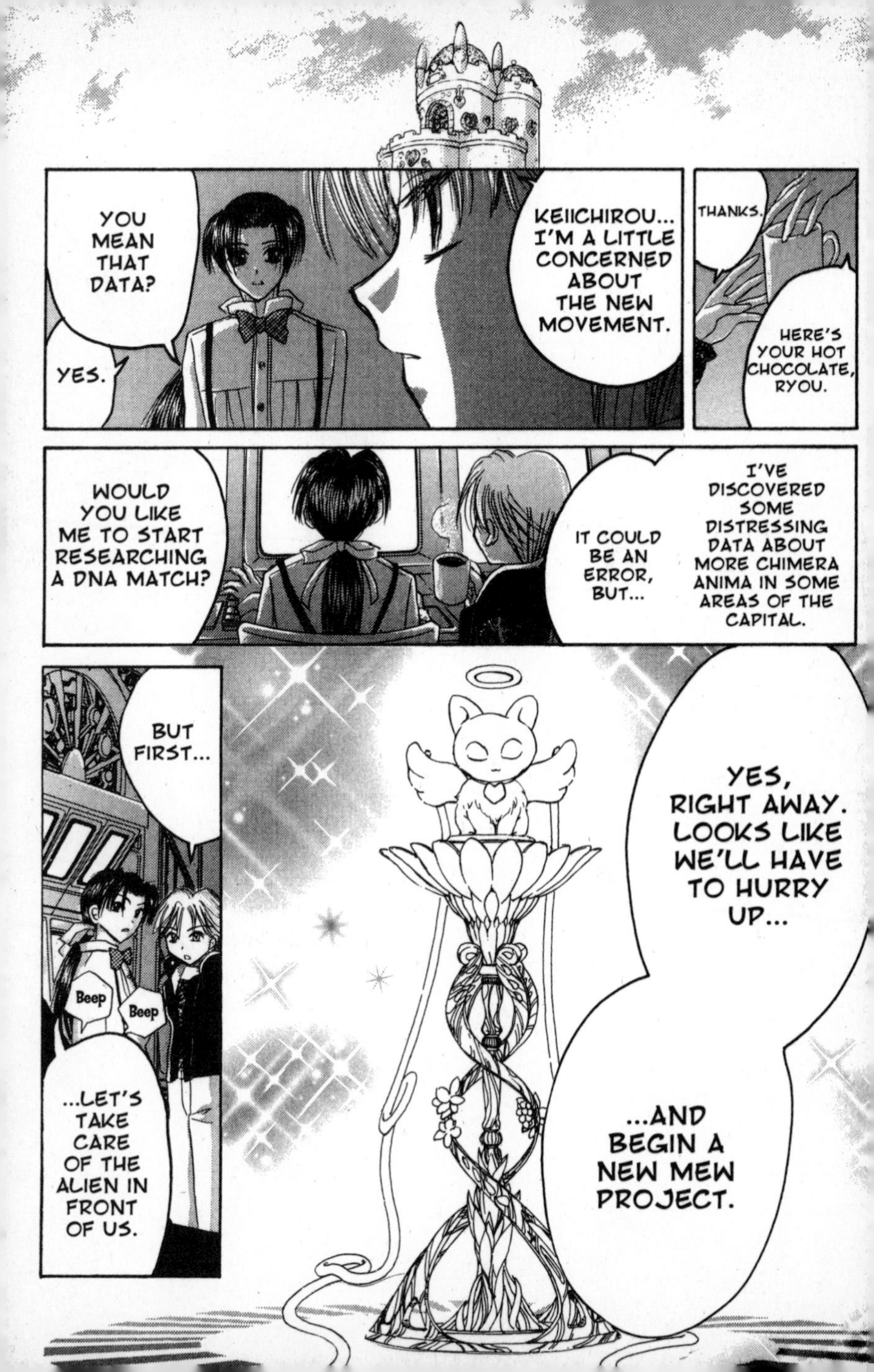
HERE'S YOUR HOT CHOCOLATE, RYOU.
THANKS.
KEIICHIROU... I'M A LITTLE CONCERNED ABOUT THE NEW MOVEMENT.
YOU MEAN THAT DATA?
YES.
I'VE DISCOVERED SOME DISTRESSING DATA ABOUT MORE CHIMERA ANIMA IN SOME AREAS OF THE CAPITAL.
IT COULD BE AN ERROR, BUT...
WOULD YOU LIKE ME TO START RESEARCHING A DNA MATCH?
YES, RIGHT AWAY. LOOKS LIKE WE'LL HAVE TO HURRY UP...
...AND BEGIN A NEW MEW PROJECT.
BUT FIRST...
Beep
Beep
...LET'S TAKE CARE OF THE ALIEN IN FRONT OF US.

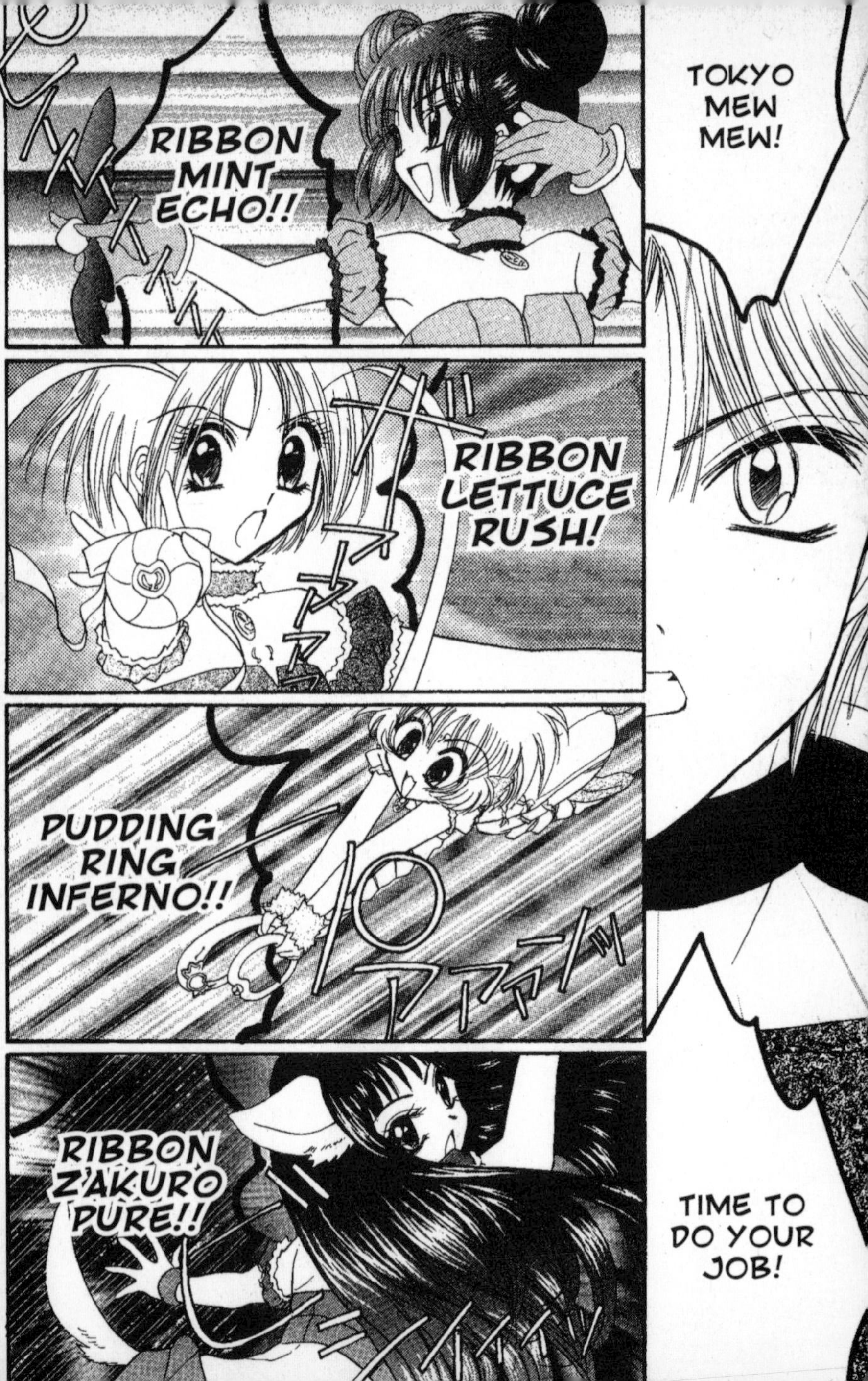
TOKYO MEW MEW!
TIME TO DO YOUR JOB!
RIBBON MINT ECHO!!
RIBBON LETTUCE RUSH!
PUDDING RING INFERNO!!
RIBBON ZAKURO PURE!!

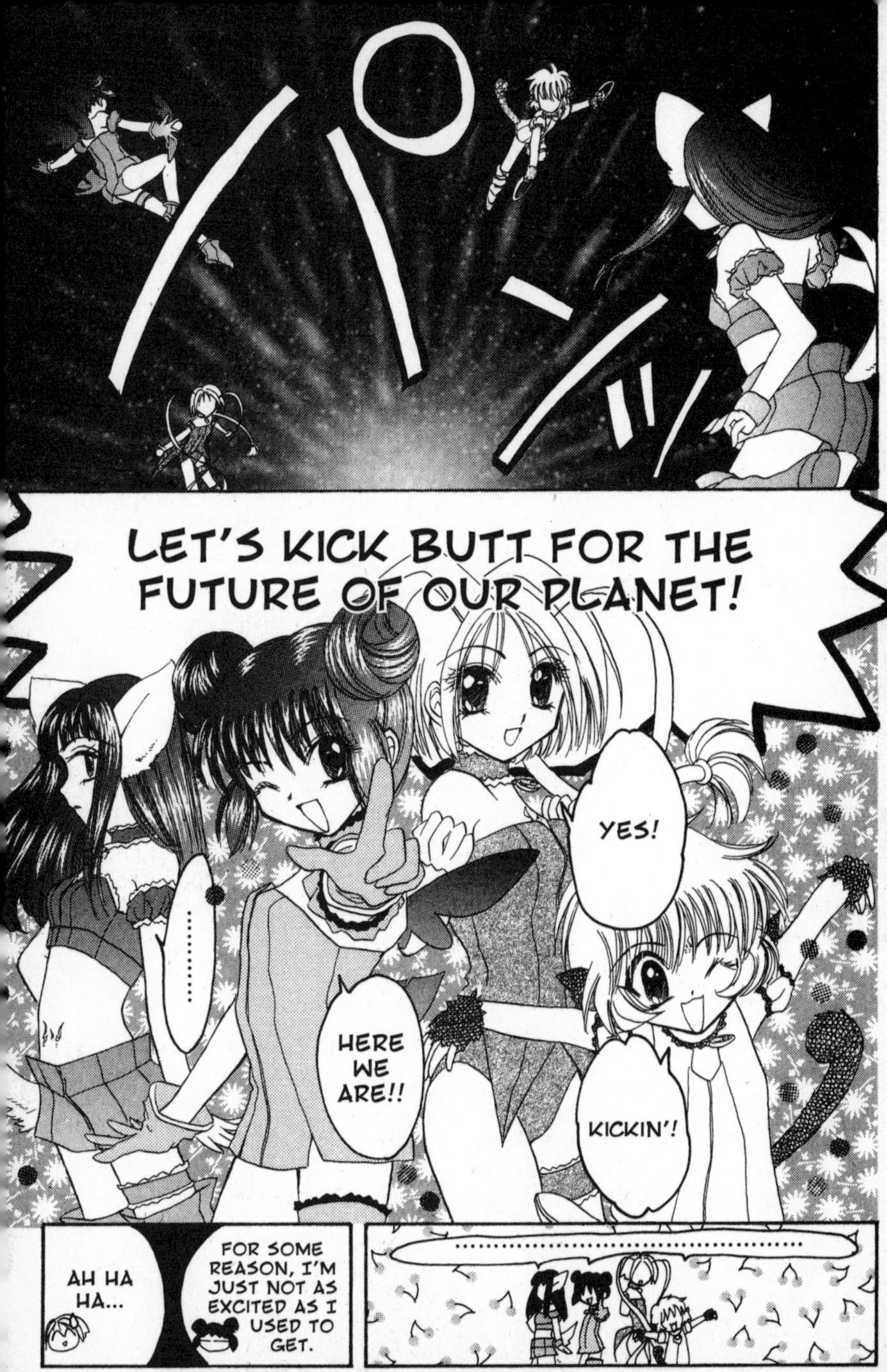

LET'S KICK BUTT FOR THE FUTURE OF OUR PLANET!
YES!
KICKIN'!
HERE WE ARE!!
....
....
FOR SOME REASON, I'M JUST NOT AS EXCITED AS I USED TO GET.
AH HA HA...

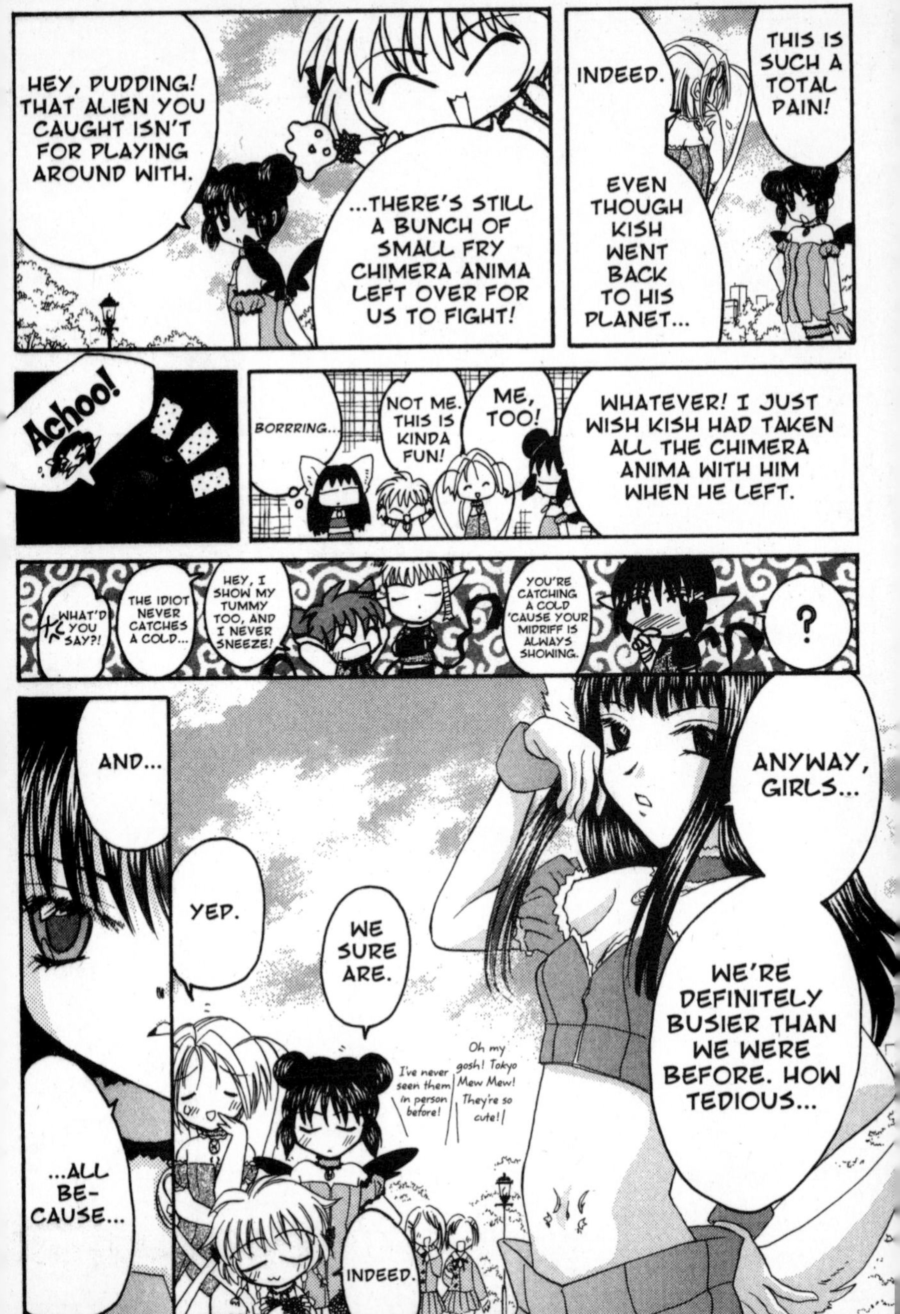
THIS IS SUCH A TOTAL PAIN!
INDEED.
EVEN THOUGH KISH WENT BACK TO HIS PLANET...
...THERE'S STILL A BUNCH OF SMALL FRY CHIMERA ANIMA LEFT OVER FOR US TO FIGHT!
HEY, PUDDING! THAT ALIEN YOU CAUGHT ISN'T FOR PLAYING AROUND WITH.
WHATEVER! I JUST WISH KISH HAD TAKEN ALL THE CHIMERA ANIMA WITH HIM WHEN HE LEFT.
ME, TOO!
NOT ME. THIS IS KINDA FUN!
BORRRING...
Achoo!
?
YOU'RE CATCHING A COLD 'CAUSE YOUR MIDRIFF IS ALWAYS SHOWING.
HEY, I SHOW MY TUMMY TOO, AND I NEVER SNEEZE!
THE IDIOT NEVER CATCHES A COLD...
WHAT'D YOU SAY?!
ANYWAY, GIRLS...
WE'RE DEFINITELY BUSIER THAN WE WERE BEFORE. HOW TEDIOUS...
Oh my gosh! Tokyo Mew Mew! They're so cute!
I've never seen them in person before!
WE SURE ARE.
YEP.
INDEED.
AND...
...ALL BE-CAUSE...

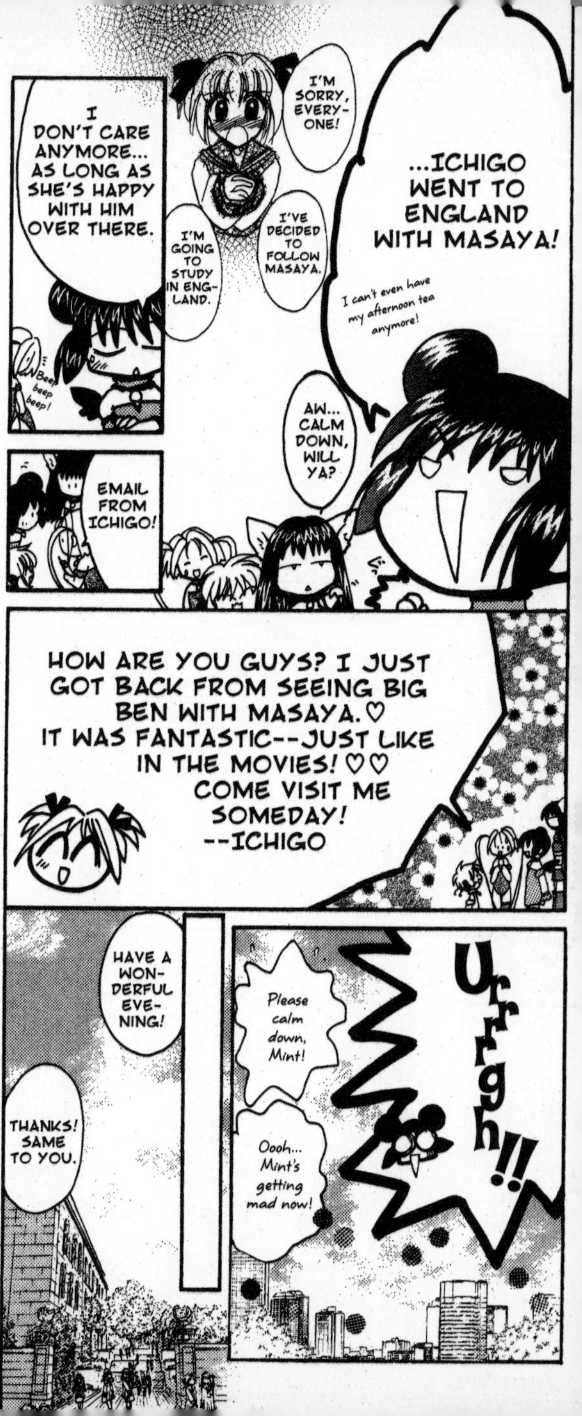
...ICHIGO WENT TO ENGLAND WITH MASAYA!
I can't even have my afternoon tea anymore!
AW... CALM DOWN, WILL YA?
I'M SORRY, EVERYONE!
I'VE DECIDED TO FOLLOW MASAYA.
I'M GOING TO STUDY IN ENGLAND.
I DON'T CARE ANYMORE... AS LONG AS SHE'S HAPPY WITH HIM OVER THERE.
Beep beep beep!
EMAIL FROM ICHIGO!
HOW ARE YOU GUYS? I JUST GOT BACK FROM SEEING BIG BEN WITH MASAYA.♡ IT WAS FANTASTIC--JUST LIKE IN THE MOVIES! ♡♡ COME VISIT ME SOMEDAY! --ICHIGO
Urrrgh!!
Please calm down, Mint!
Oooh... Mint's getting mad now!
HAVE A WONDERFUL EVENING!
THANKS! SAME TO YOU.

1

In this space, I'd like to show you some illustrations from the 2004 Tokyo Mew Mew Calendar. It's called "Big Edo Mew Mew" (Laugh). Unfortunately, the calendar has already sold out. So for those who couldn't get it, enjoy the pics!

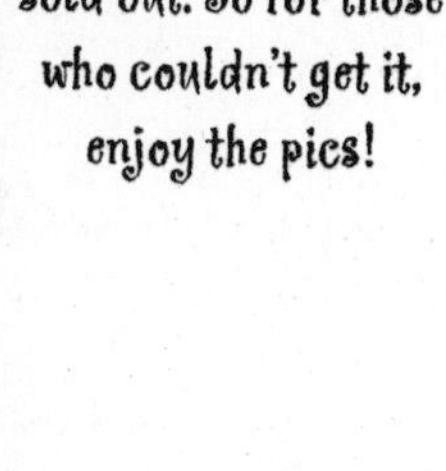

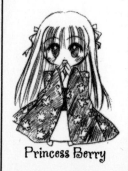

Princess Berry

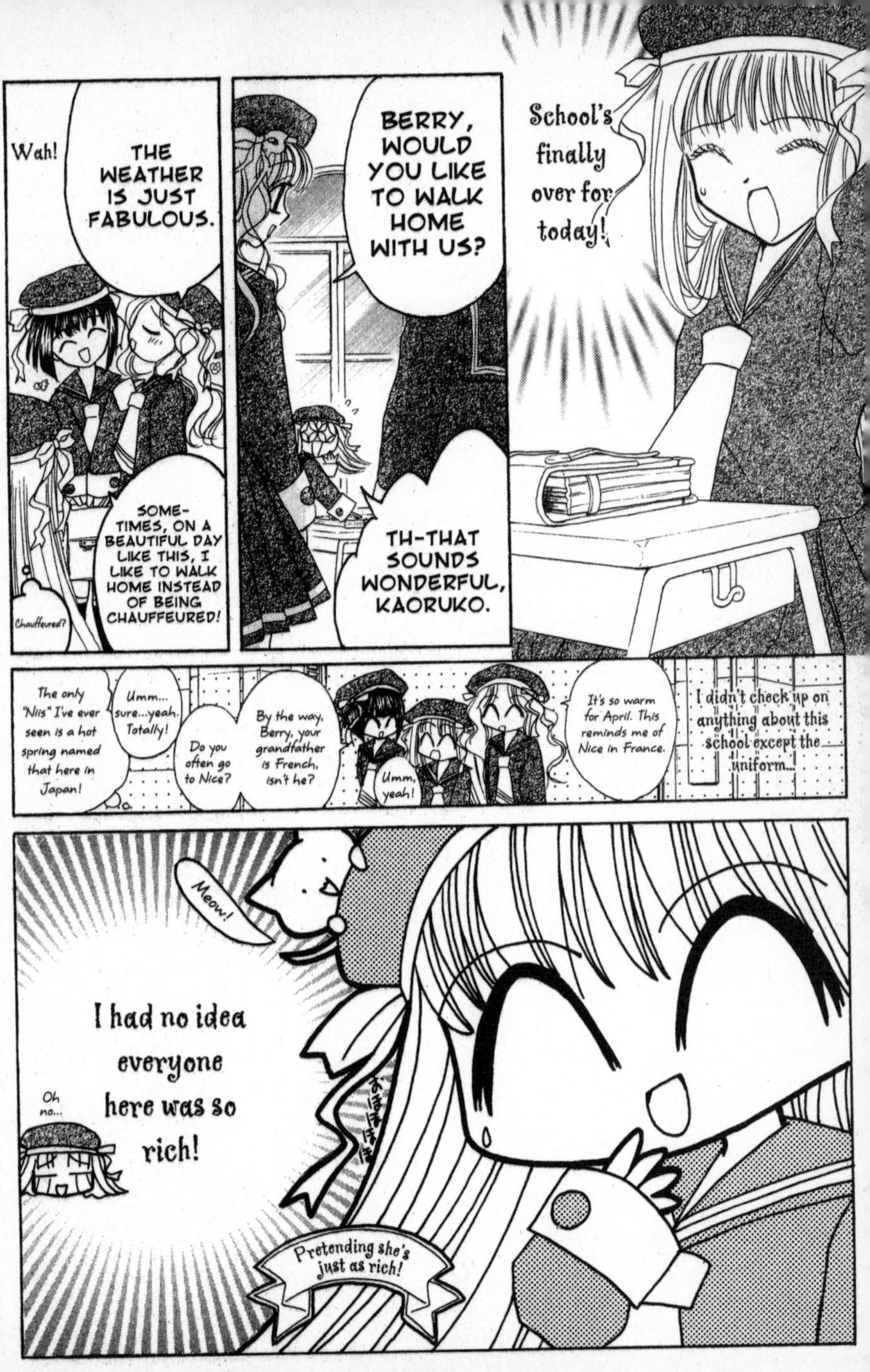
School's finally over for today!
Berry, would you like to walk home with us?
Th-that sounds wonderful, Kaoruko.
Wah!
The weather is just fabulous.
Sometimes, on a beautiful day like this, I like to walk home instead of being chauffeured!
Chauffeured?
I didn't check up on anything about this school except the uniform...
It's so warm for April. This reminds me of Nice in France.
Umm, yeah!
By the way, Berry, your grandfather is French, isn't he?
Do you often go to Nice?
Umm... sure...yeah. Totally!
The only "Niis" I've ever seen is a hot spring named that here in Japan!
Meow!
I had no idea everyone here was so rich!
Oh no...
Pretending she's just as rich!

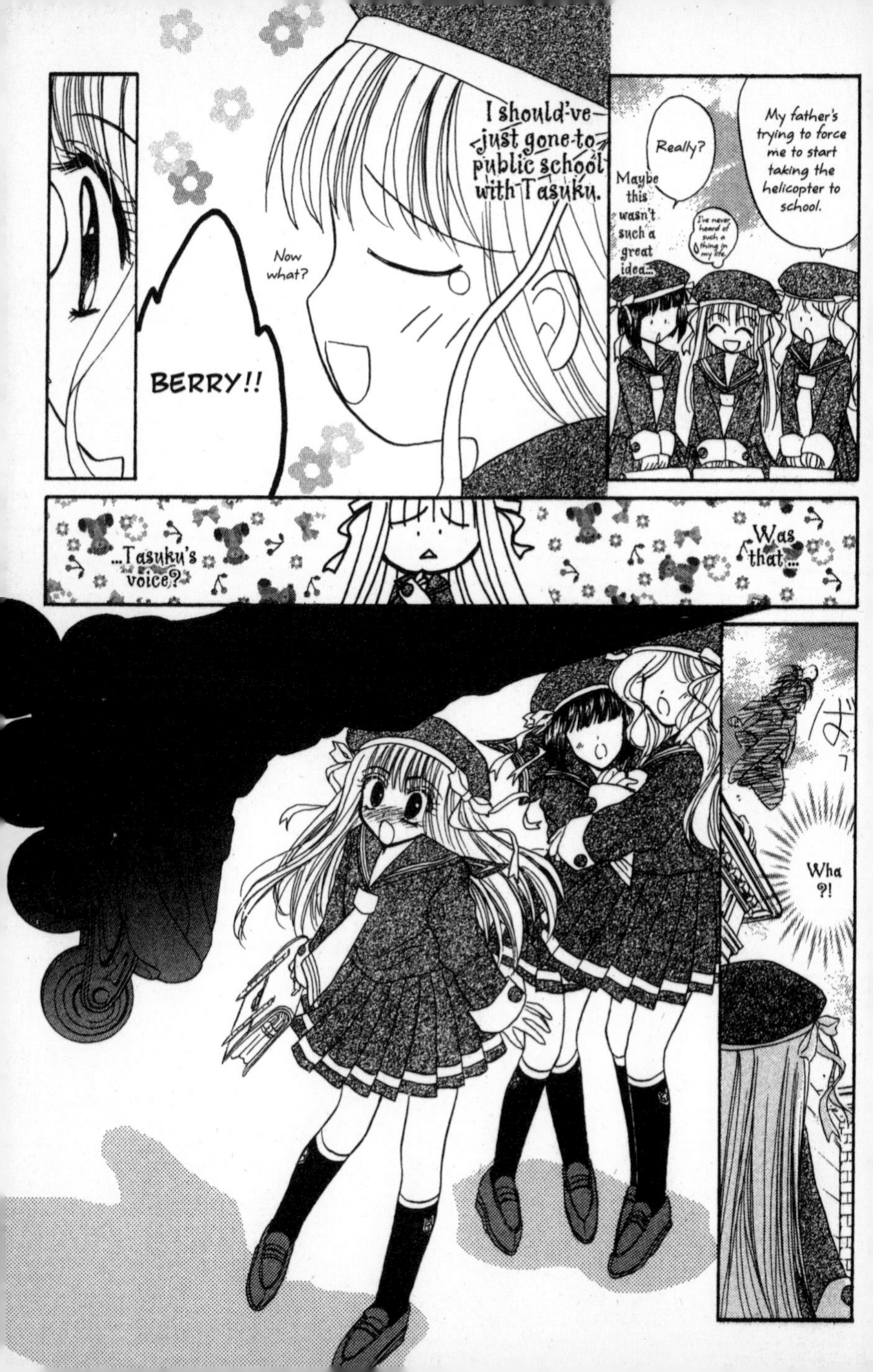
My father's trying to force me to start taking the helicopter to school.
Really?
I've never heard of such a thing in my life.
Maybe this wasn't such a great idea...
I should've just gone to public school with Tasuku.
Now what?
BERRY!!
Was that...
...Tasuku's voice?
ばっ
Wha ?!

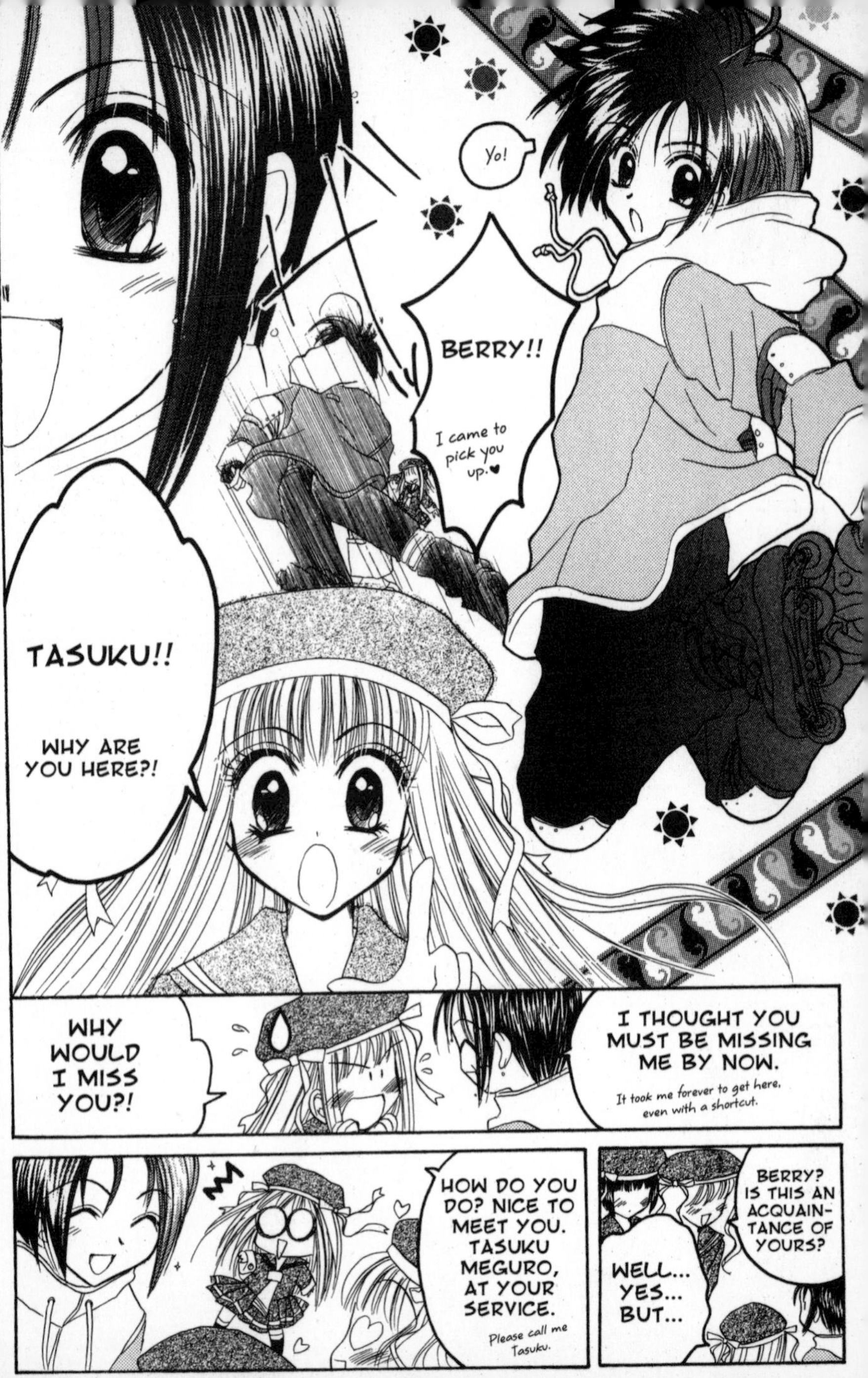
Yo!
BERRY!!
I came to pick you up.♥
TASUKU!!
WHY ARE YOU HERE?!
I THOUGHT YOU MUST BE MISSING ME BY NOW.
It took me forever to get here, even with a shortcut.
WHY WOULD I MISS YOU?!
BERRY? IS THIS AN ACQUAINTANCE OF YOURS?
WELL... YES... BUT...
HOW DO YOU DO? NICE TO MEET YOU. TASUKU MEGURO, AT YOUR SERVICE.
Please call me Tasuku.

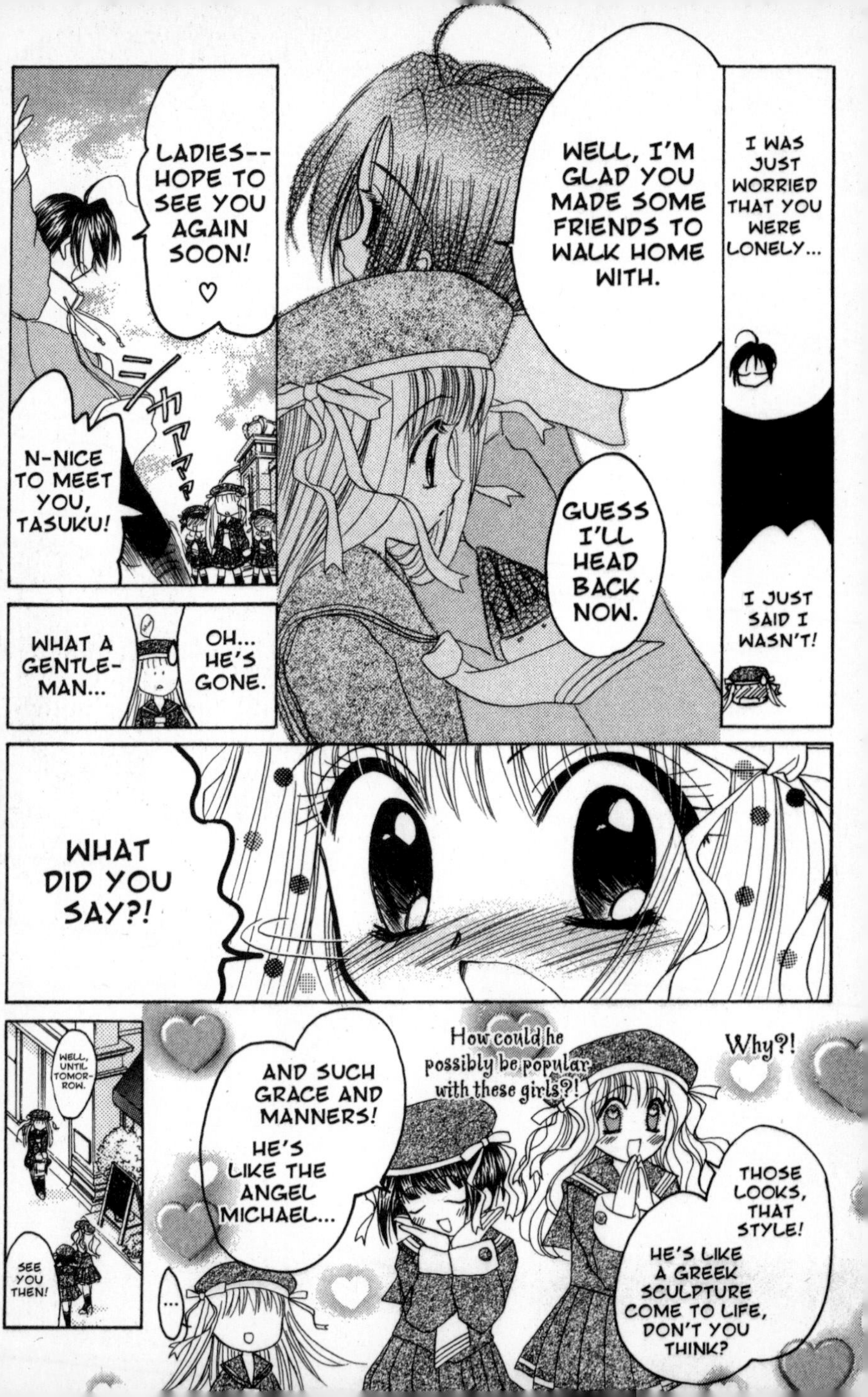
I WAS JUST WORRIED THAT YOU WERE LONELY...
I JUST SAID I WASN'T!
WELL, I'M GLAD YOU MADE SOME FRIENDS TO WALK HOME WITH.
GUESS I'LL HEAD BACK NOW.
LADIES-- HOPE TO SEE YOU AGAIN SOON! ♡
N-NICE TO MEET YOU, TASUKU!
OH... HE'S GONE.
WHAT A GENTLEMAN...
WHAT DID YOU SAY?!
Why?!
How could he possibly be popular with these girls?!
THOSE LOOKS, THAT STYLE!
HE'S LIKE A GREEK SCULPTURE COME TO LIFE, DON'T YOU THINK?
AND SUCH GRACE AND MANNERS!
HE'S LIKE THE ANGEL MICHAEL...
...
WELL, UNTIL TOMORROW.
SEE YOU THEN!

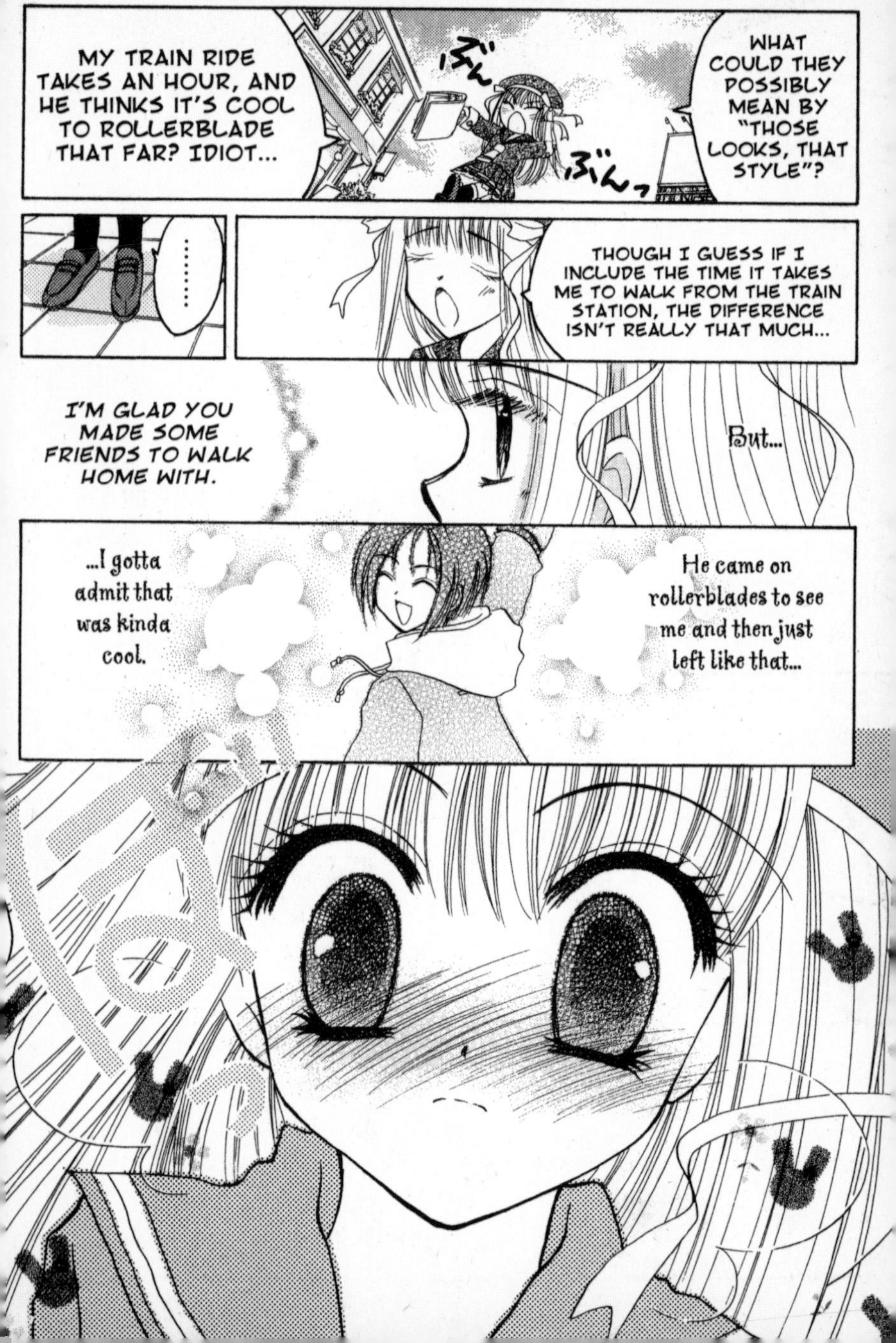
WHAT COULD THEY POSSIBLY MEAN BY "THOSE LOOKS, THAT STYLE"?
ぶんっ
ぶん
MY TRAIN RIDE TAKES AN HOUR, AND HE THINKS IT'S COOL TO ROLLERBLADE THAT FAR? IDIOT...
THOUGH I GUESS IF I INCLUDE THE TIME IT TAKES ME TO WALK FROM THE TRAIN STATION, THE DIFFERENCE ISN'T REALLY THAT MUCH...
......
But...
I'M GLAD YOU MADE SOME FRIENDS TO WALK HOME WITH.
He came on rollerblades to see me and then just left like that...
...I gotta admit that was kinda cool.

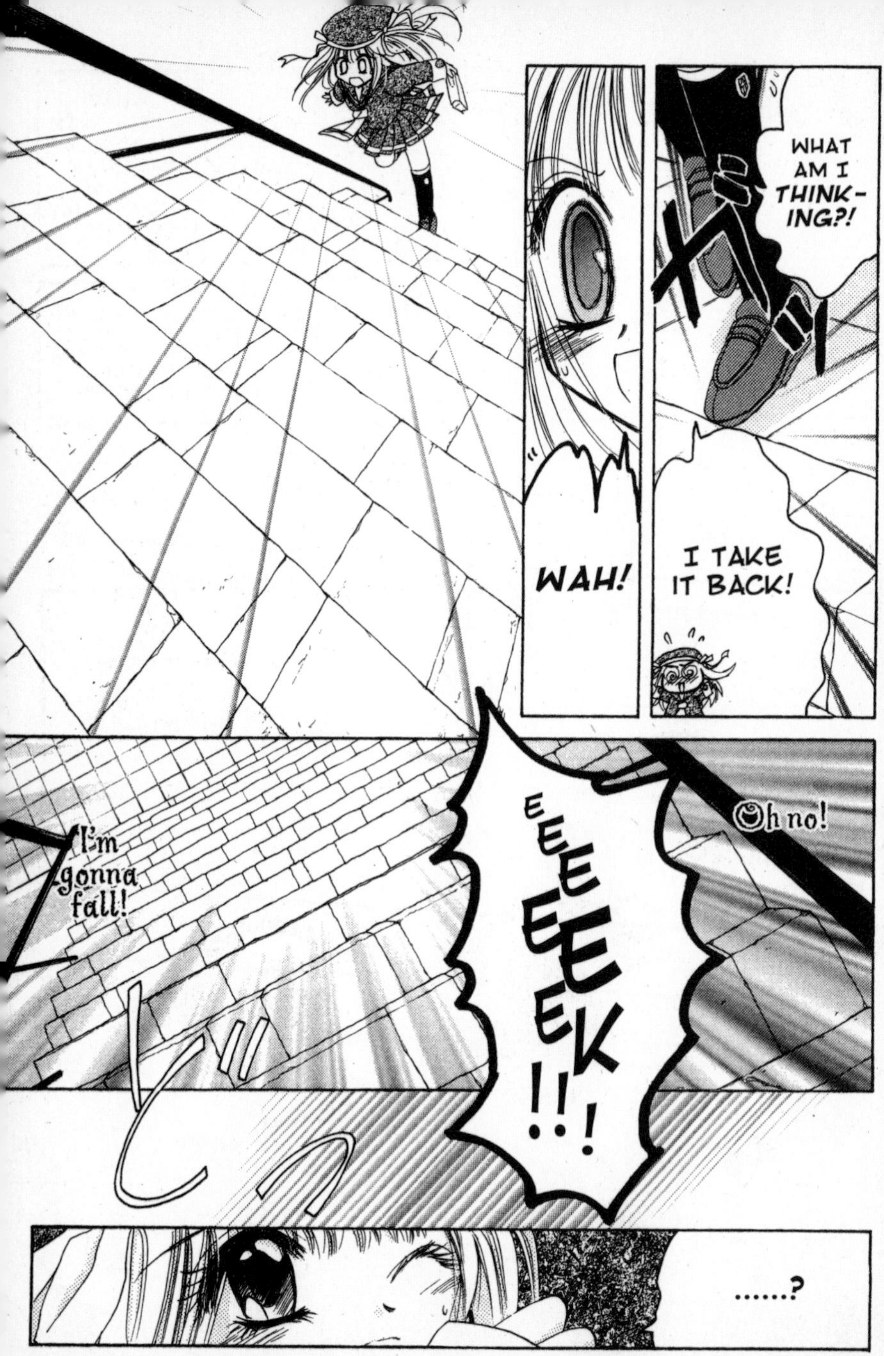

WHAT AM I THINKING?!
I TAKE IT BACK!
WAH!
Oh no!
EEEEEEEK!!!
I'm gonna fall!
......?

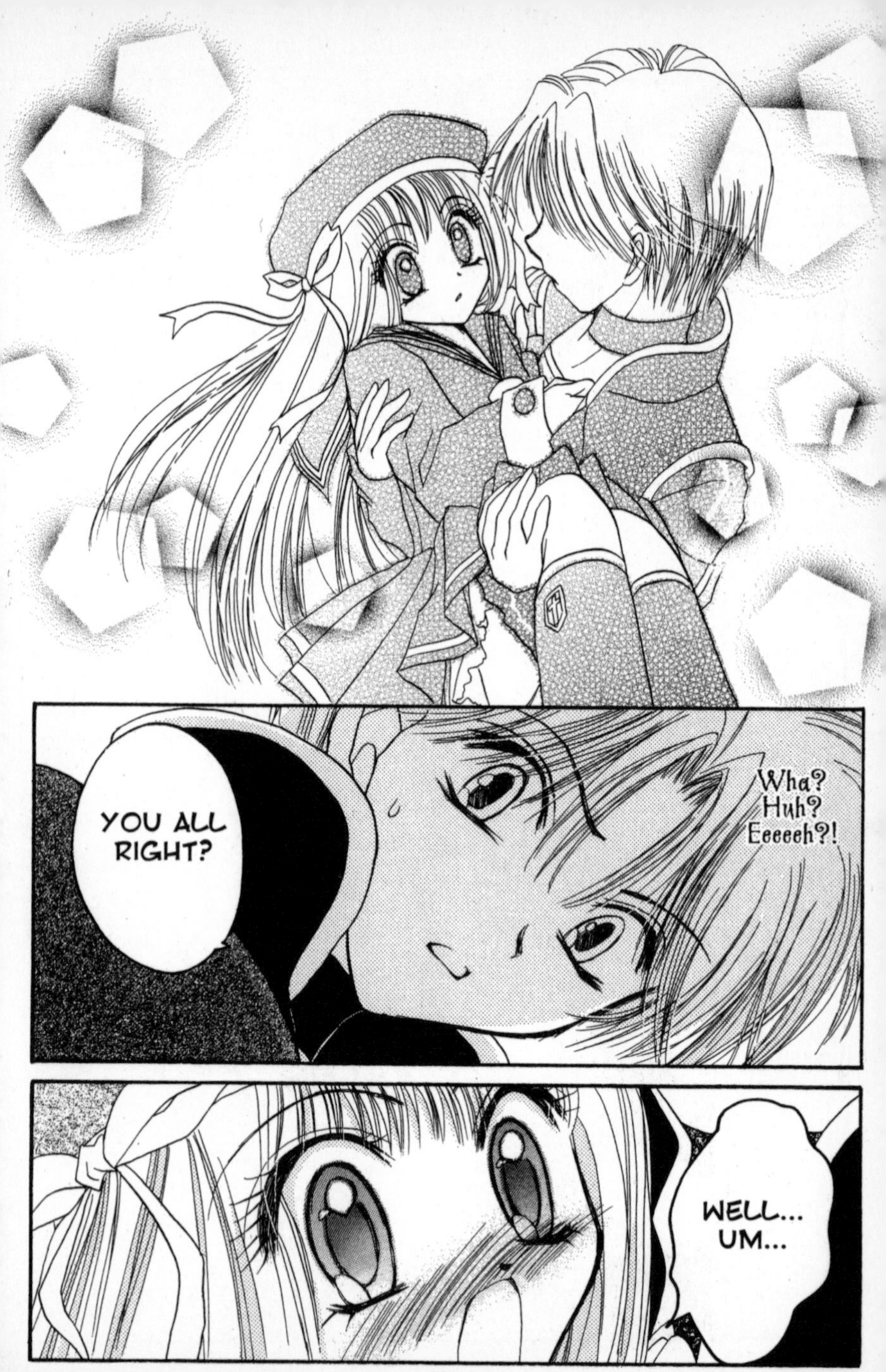
Wha? Huh? Eeeeeh?!
YOU ALL RIGHT?
WELL... UM...

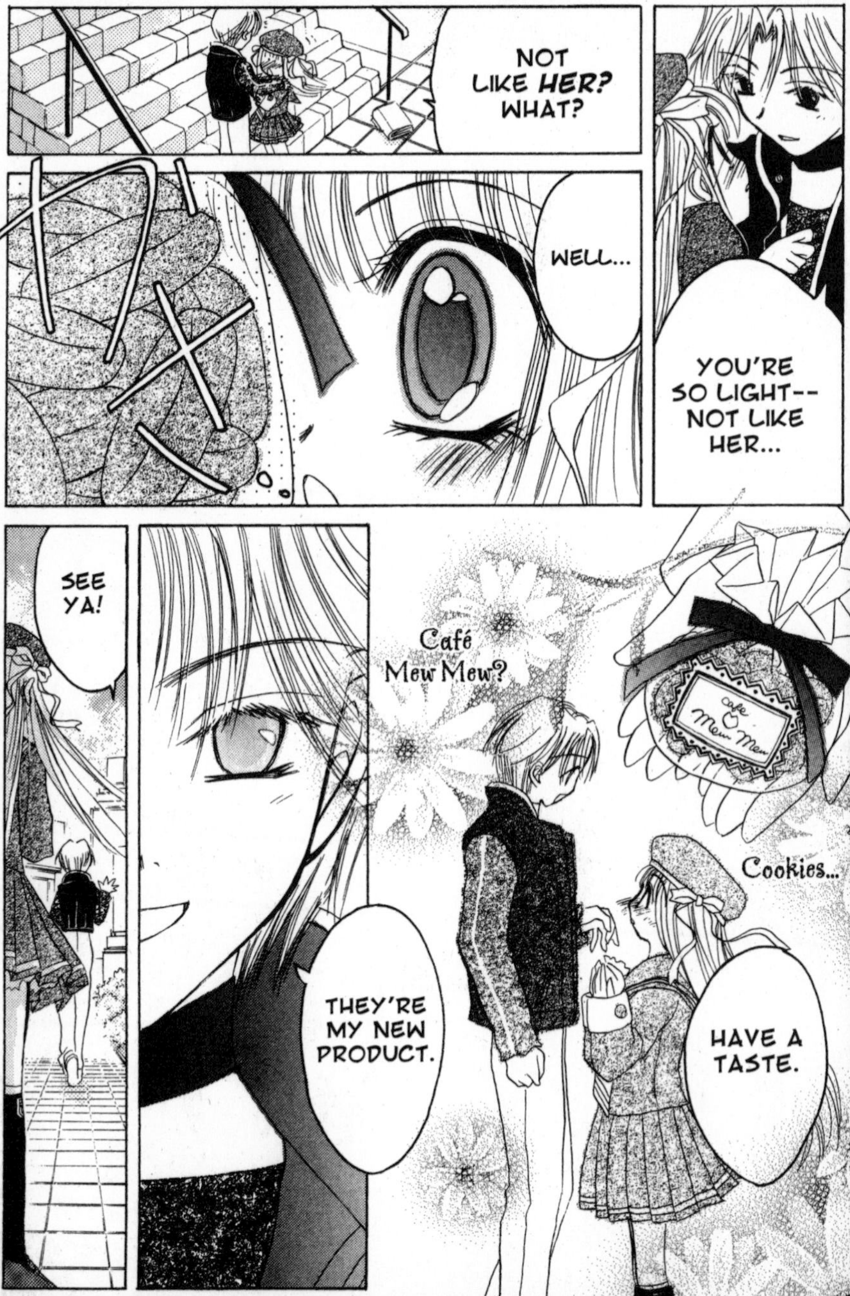
YOU'RE SO LIGHT-- NOT LIKE HER...
NOT LIKE **HER**? WHAT?
WELL...
Café Mew Mew?
Cookies...
HAVE A TASTE.
THEY'RE MY NEW PRODUCT.
SEE YA!

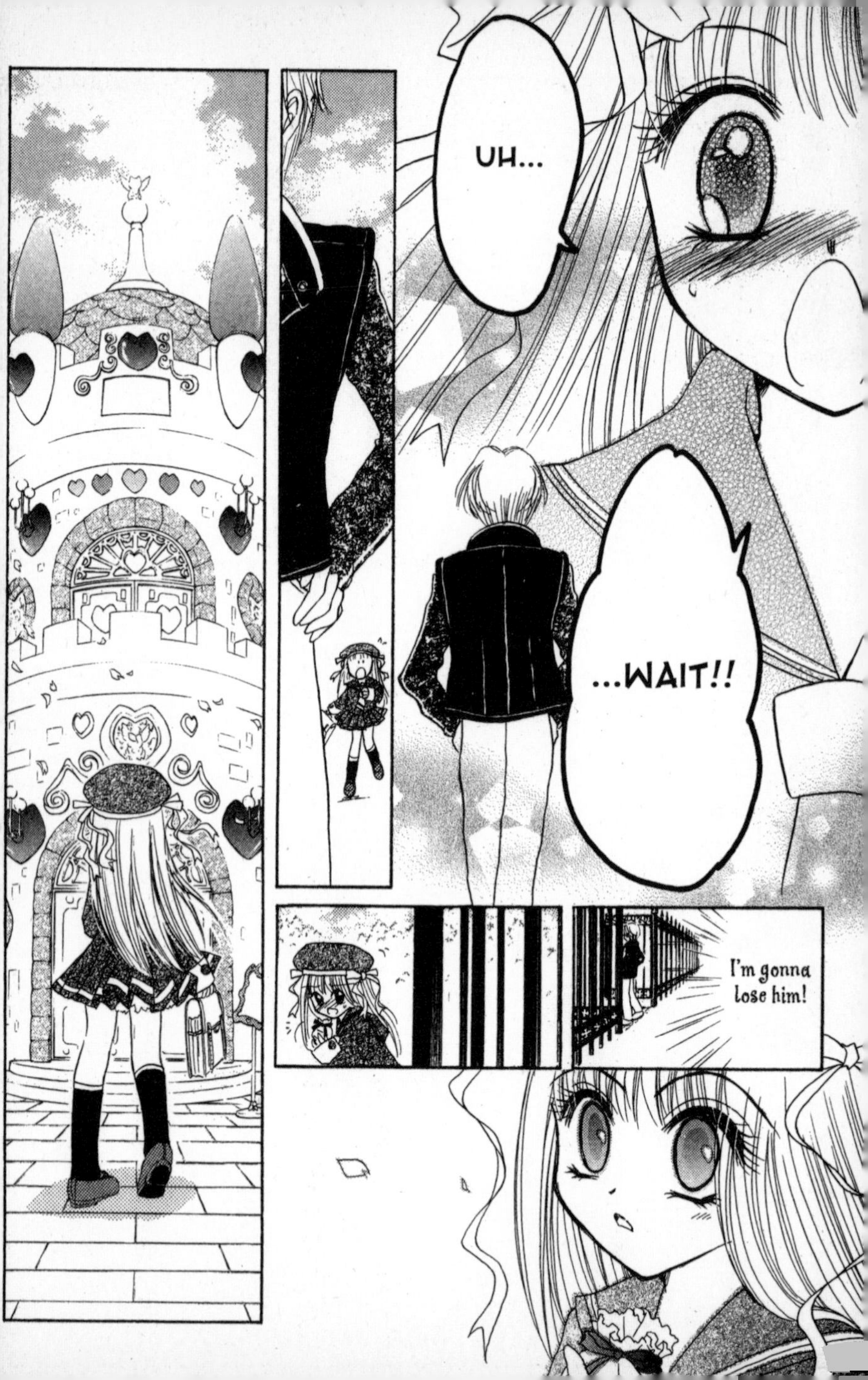
UH...
...WAIT!!
I'm gonna lose him!

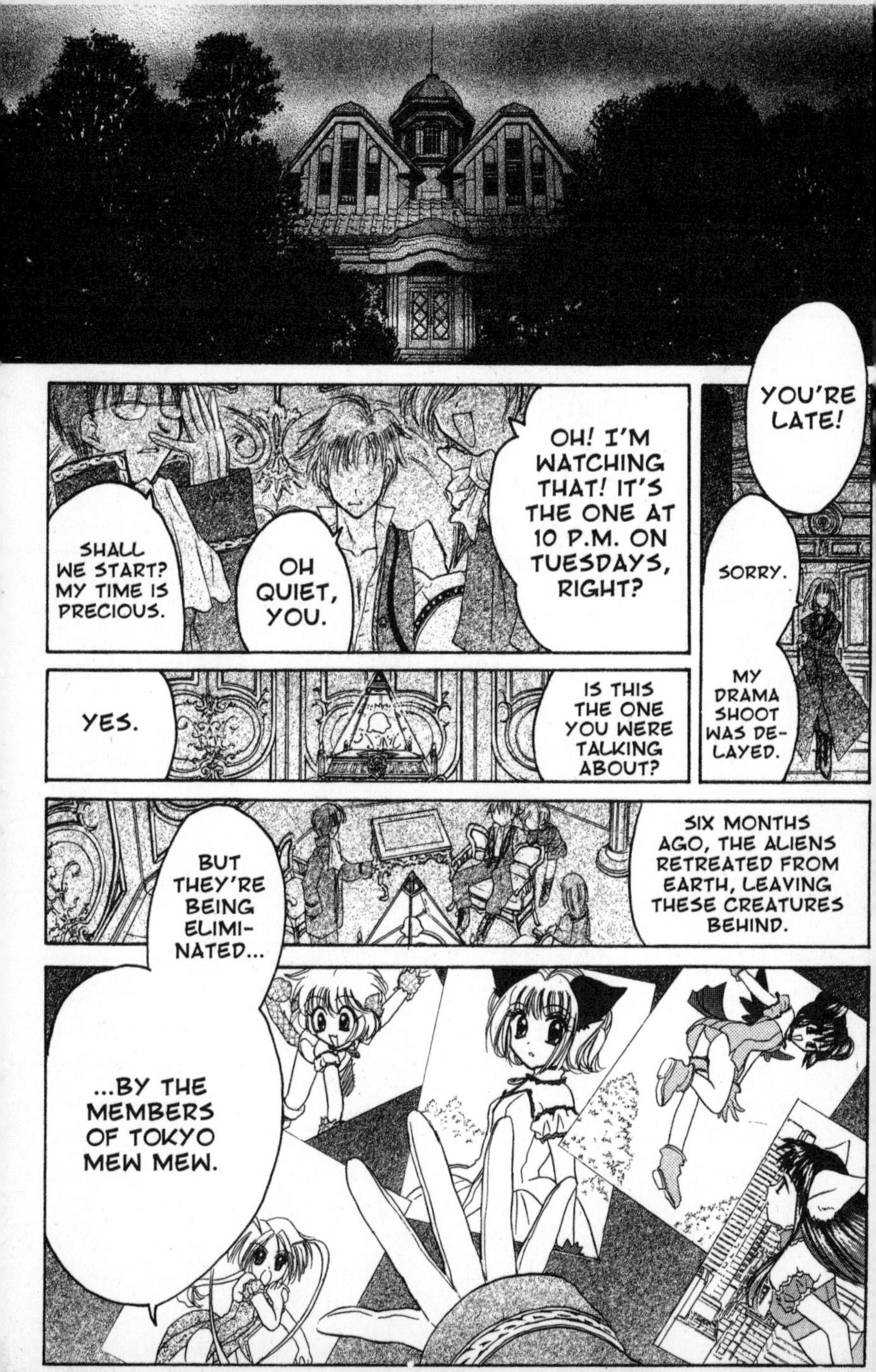
YOU'RE LATE!
SORRY.
MY DRAMA SHOOT WAS DE-LAYED.
OH! I'M WATCHING THAT! IT'S THE ONE AT 10 P.M. ON TUESDAYS, RIGHT?
OH QUIET, YOU.
SHALL WE START? MY TIME IS PRECIOUS.
IS THIS THE ONE YOU WERE TALKING ABOUT?
YES.
SIX MONTHS AGO, THE ALIENS RETREATED FROM EARTH, LEAVING THESE CREATURES BEHIND.
BUT THEY'RE BEING ELIMI-NATED...
...BY THE MEMBERS OF TOKYO MEW MEW.

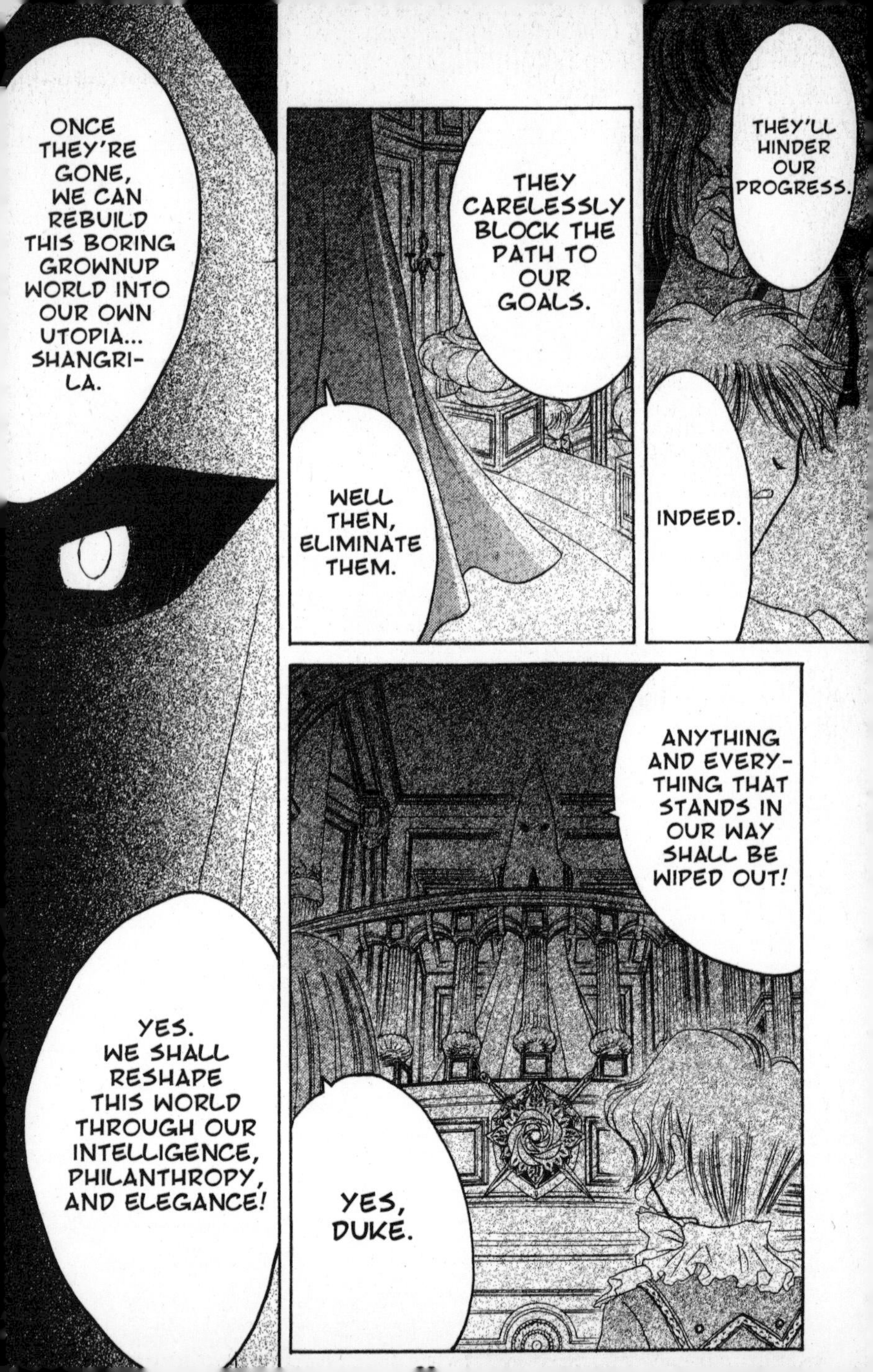
THEY'LL HINDER OUR PROGRESS.
INDEED.
THEY CARELESSLY BLOCK THE PATH TO OUR GOALS.
WELL THEN, ELIMINATE THEM.
ANYTHING AND EVERYTHING THAT STANDS IN OUR WAY SHALL BE WIPED OUT!
YES, DUKE.
ONCE THEY'RE GONE, WE CAN REBUILD THIS BORING GROWNUP WORLD INTO OUR OWN UTOPIA... SHANGRI-LA.
YES. WE SHALL RESHAPE THIS WORLD THROUGH OUR INTELLIGENCE, PHILANTHROPY, AND ELEGANCE!

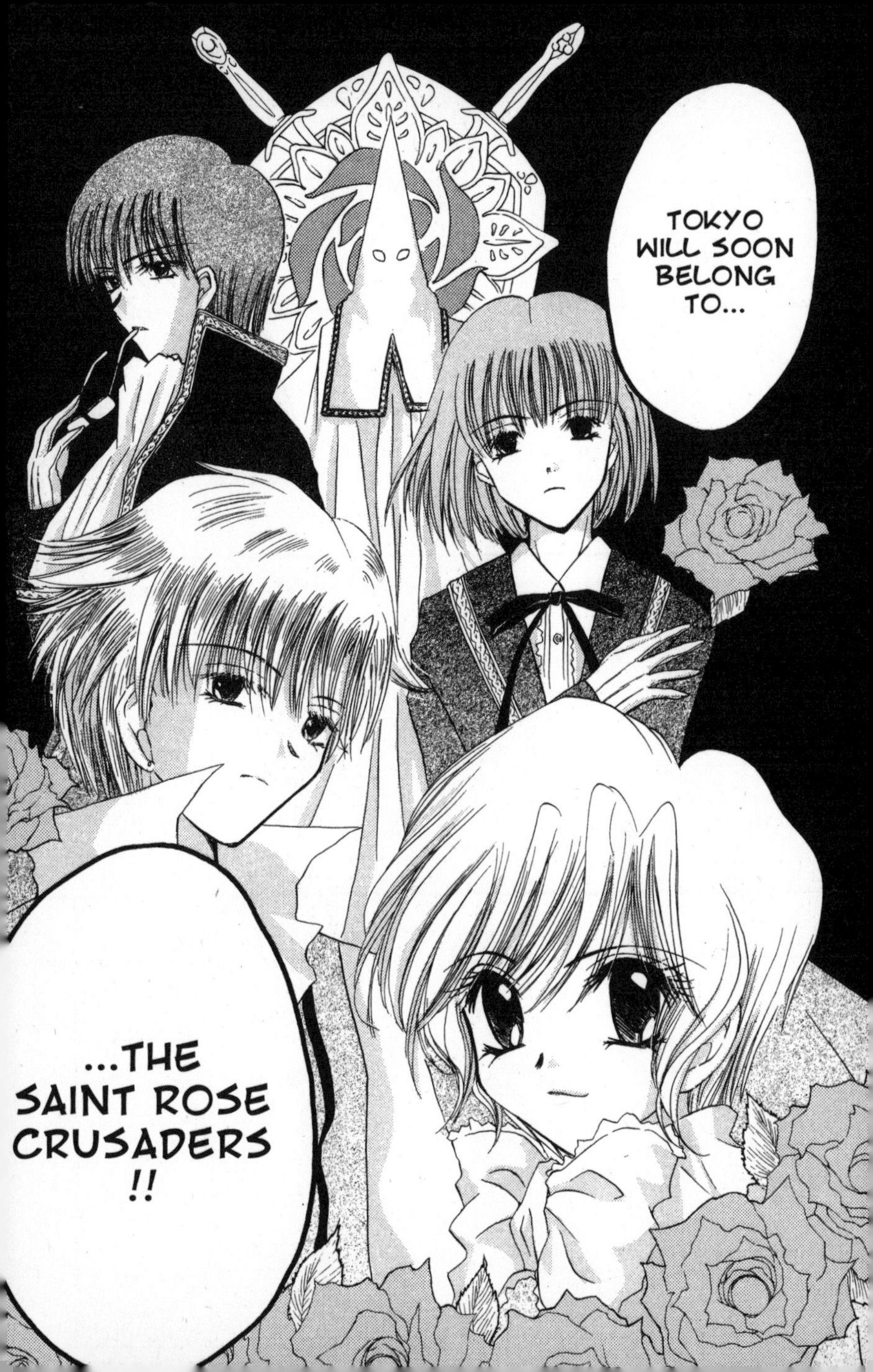
TOKYO WILL SOON BELONG TO...
...THE SAINT ROSE CRUSADERS !!

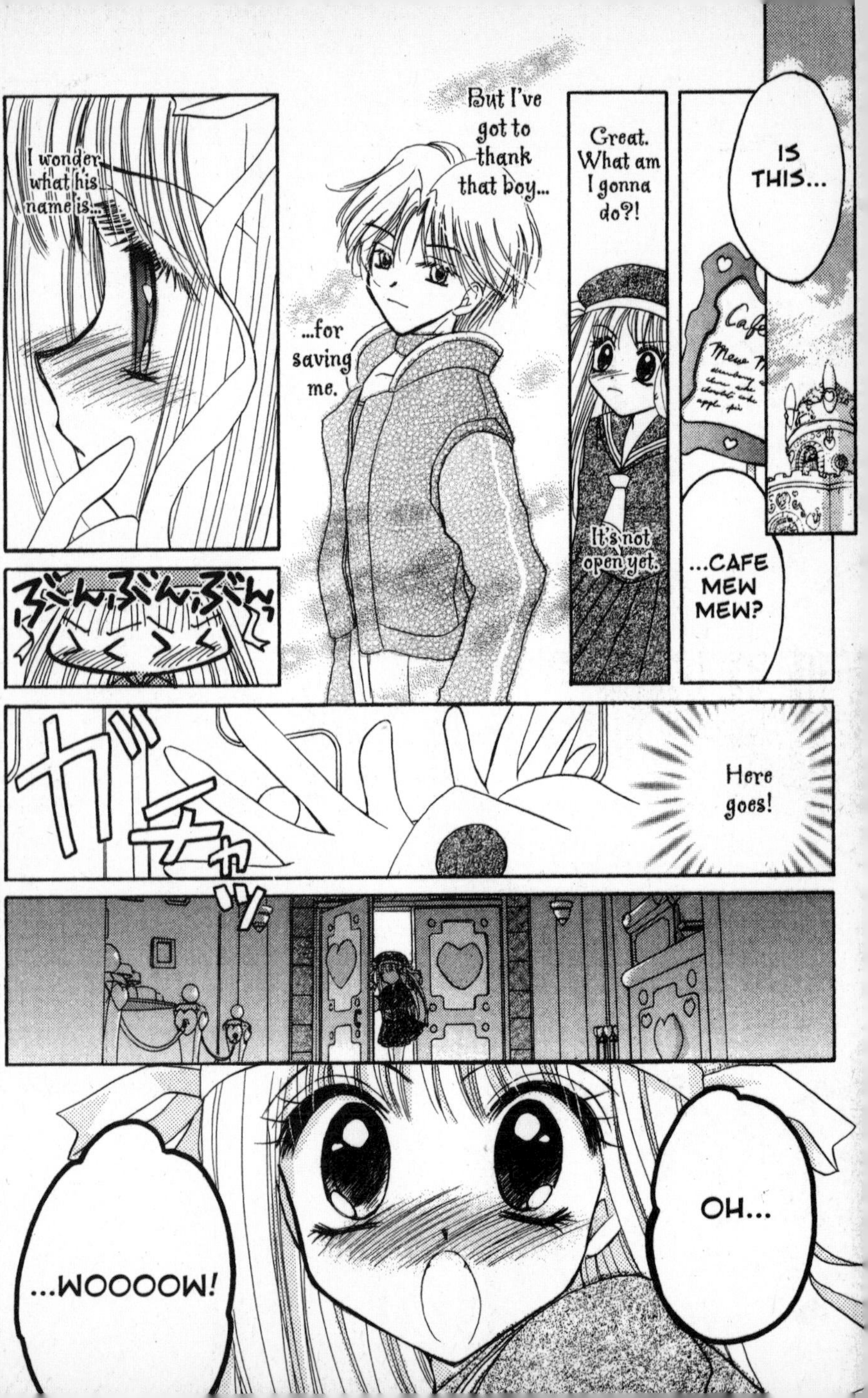
IS THIS...
...CAFE MEW MEW?
Great. What am I gonna do?!
It's not open yet.
But I've got to thank that boy...
...for saving me.
I wonder what his name is...
ぶんぶんぶん
Here goes!
ガチャッ
OH...
...WOOOOW!

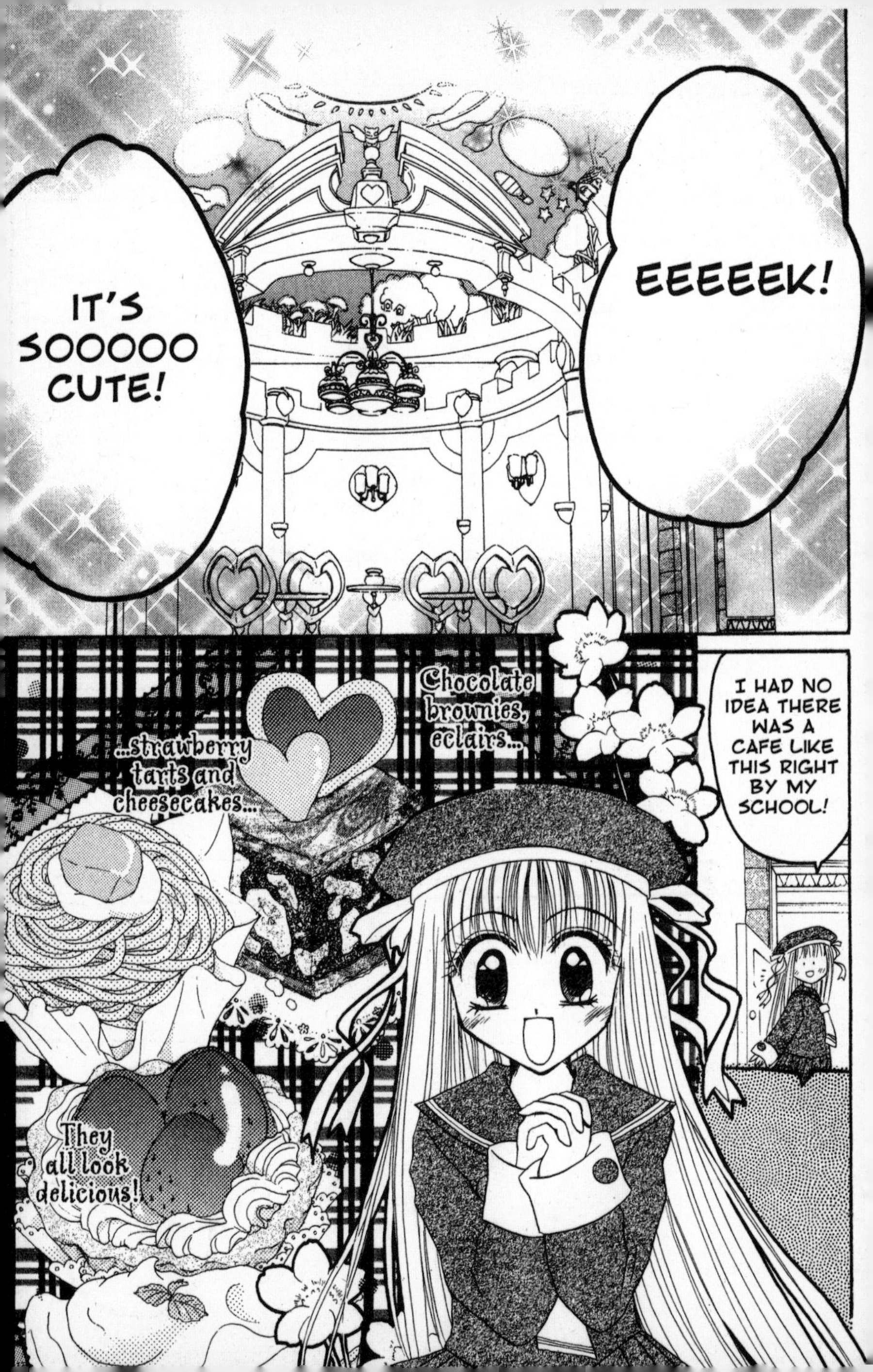
EEEEEK!
IT'S SOOOOO CUTE!
I HAD NO IDEA THERE WAS A CAFE LIKE THIS RIGHT BY MY SCHOOL!
Chocolate brownies, eclairs...
...strawberry tarts and cheesecakes...
They all look delicious!

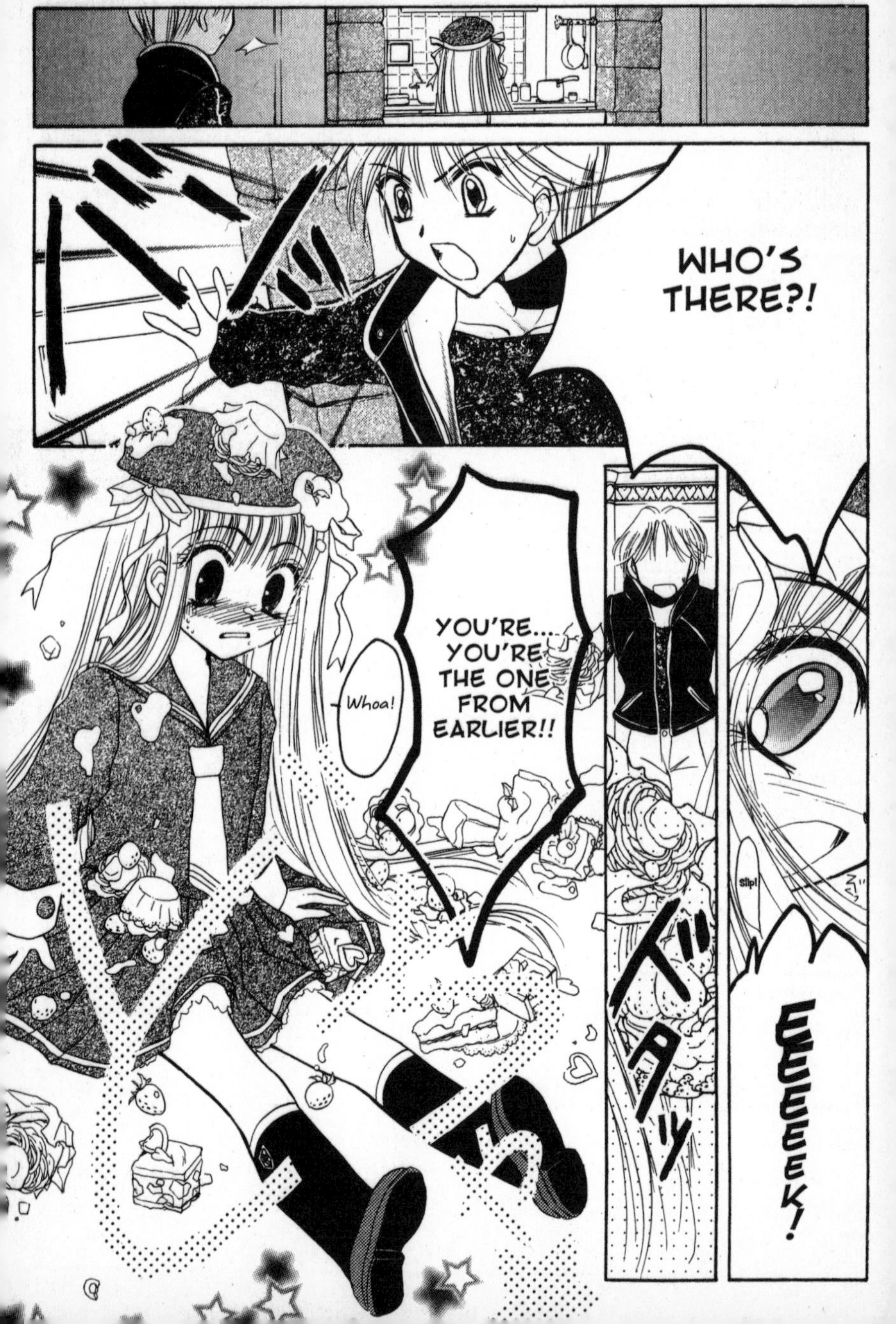
WHO'S THERE?!
Slip!
EEEEEEK!
YOU'RE... YOU'RE THE ONE FROM EARLIER!!
Whoa!

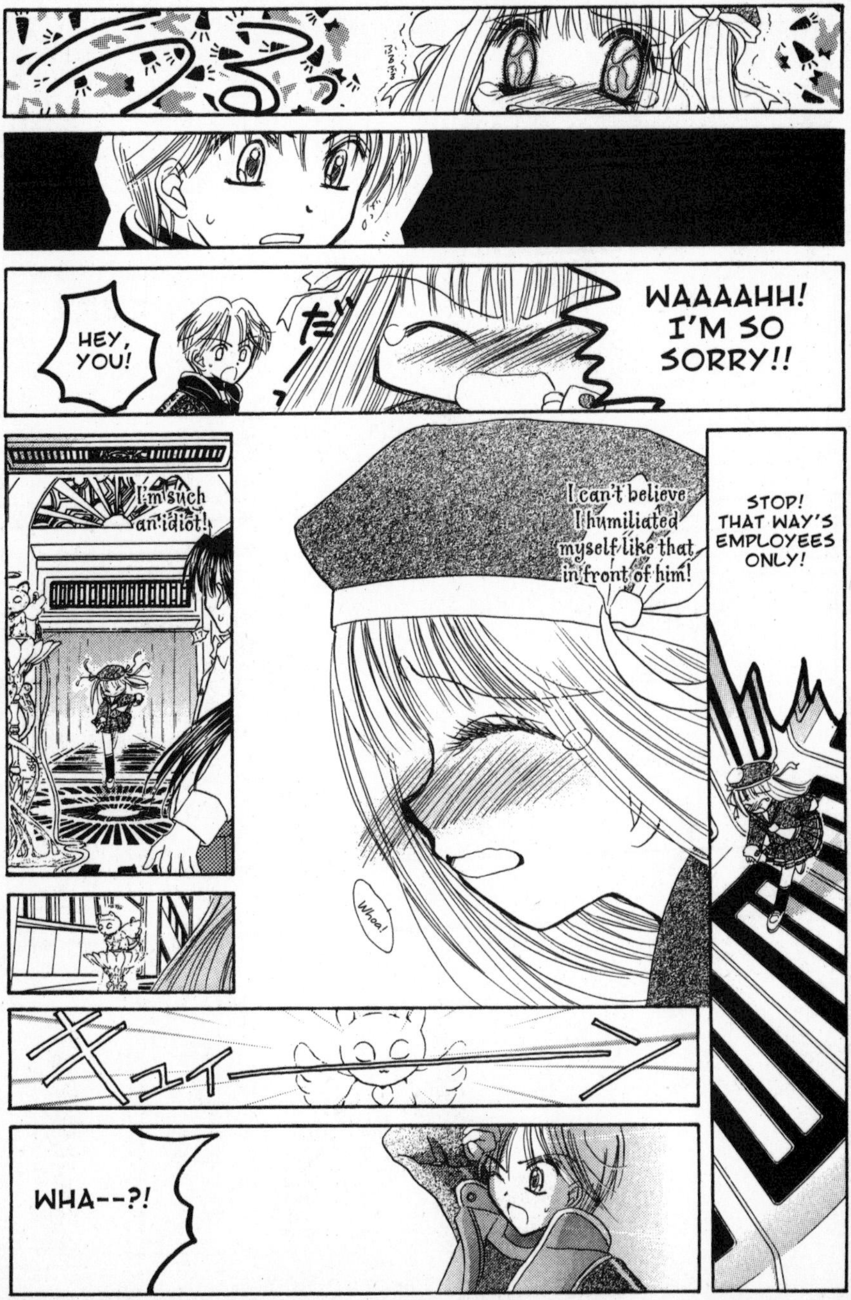
WAAAAHH! I'M SO SORRY!!
HEY, YOU!
STOP! THAT WAY'S EMPLOYEES ONLY!
I can't believe I humiliated myself like that in front of him!
Whoa!
I'm such an idiot!
キュイーン
WHA--?!

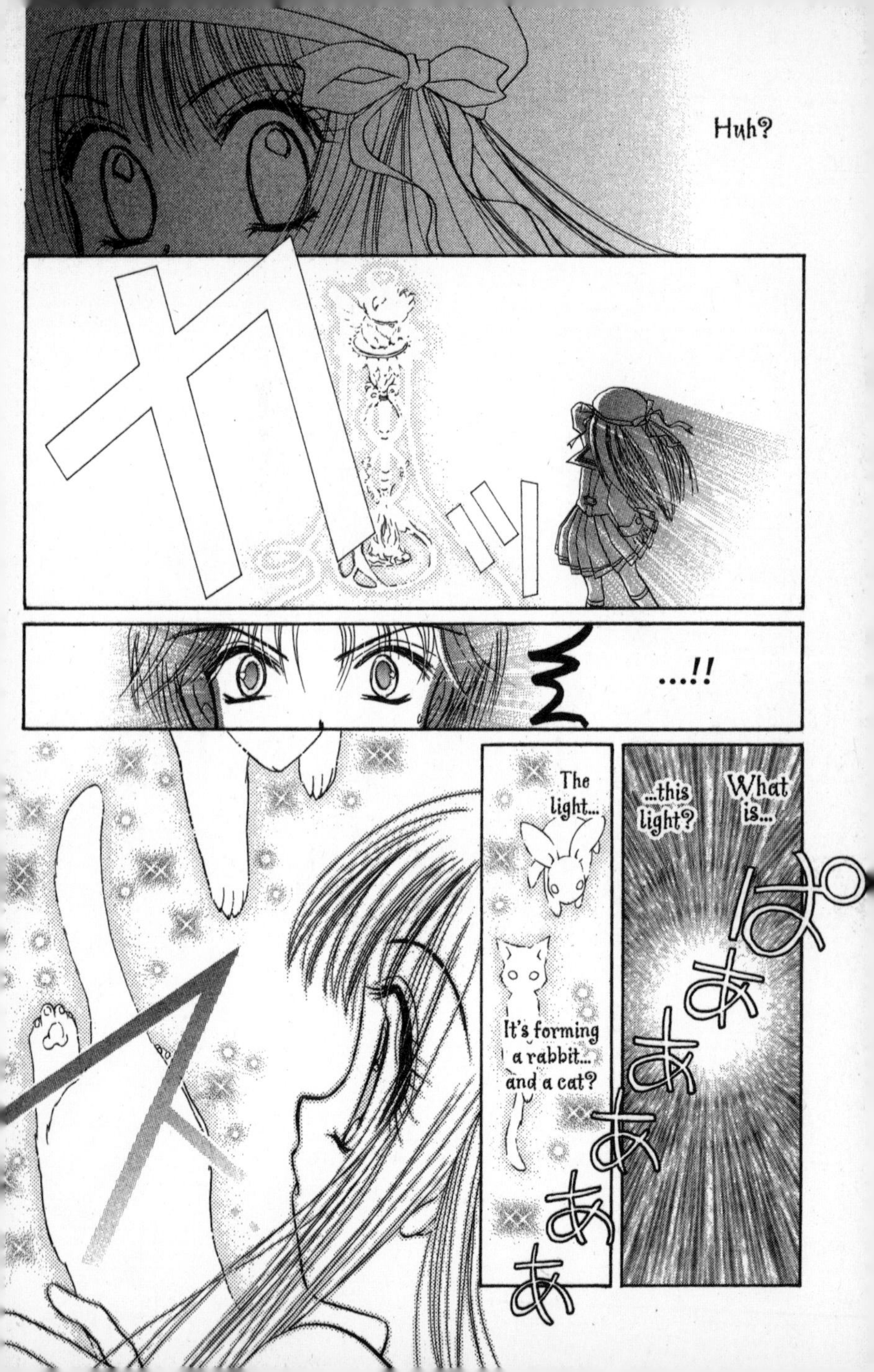
Huh?
カッ
...!!
What is...
...this light?
ぱあああああ
The light...
It's forming a rabbit... and a cat?

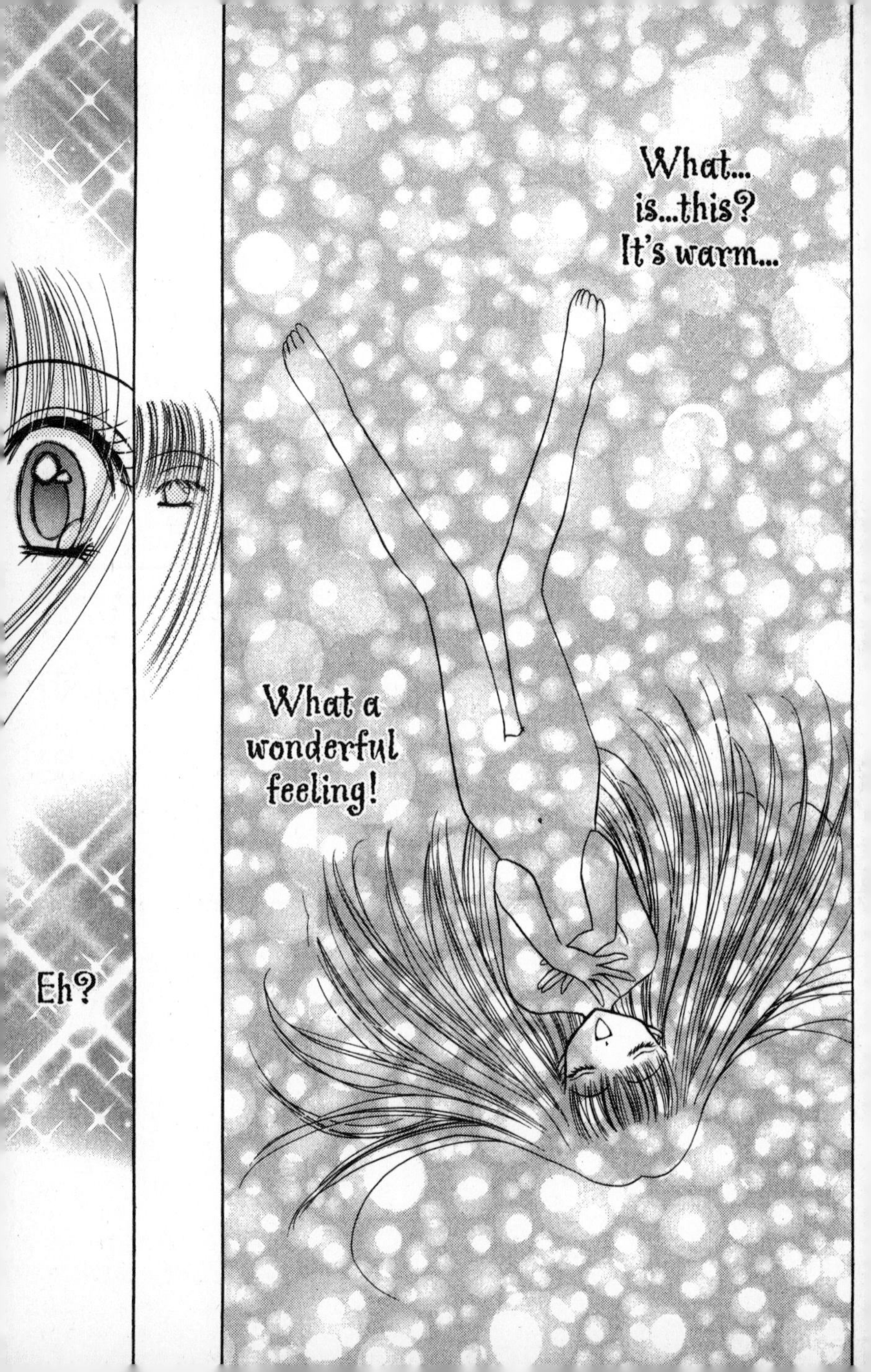
What... is...this? It's warm...
What a wonderful feeling!
Eh?

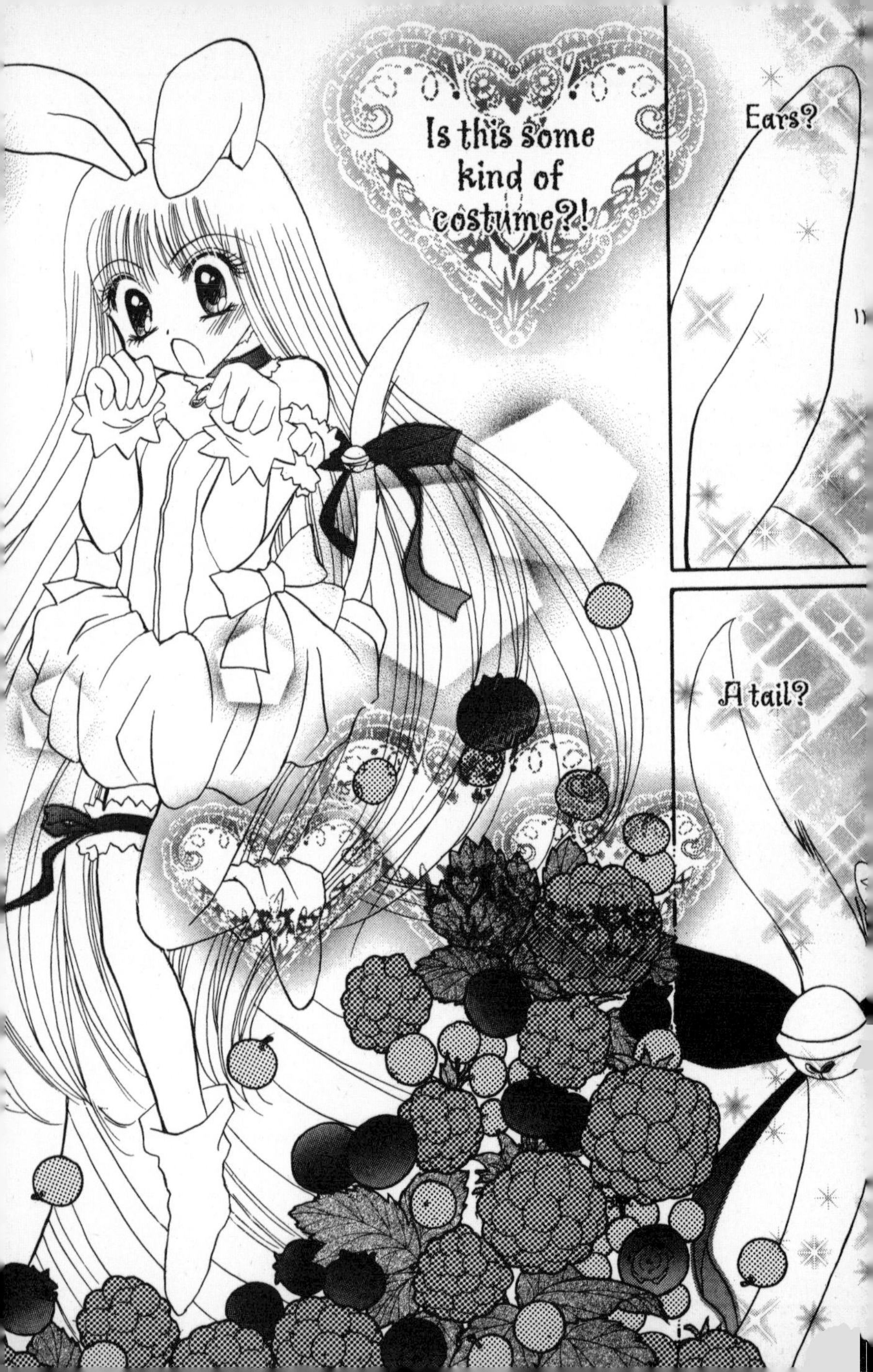
Ears?
A tail?
Is this some kind of costume?!

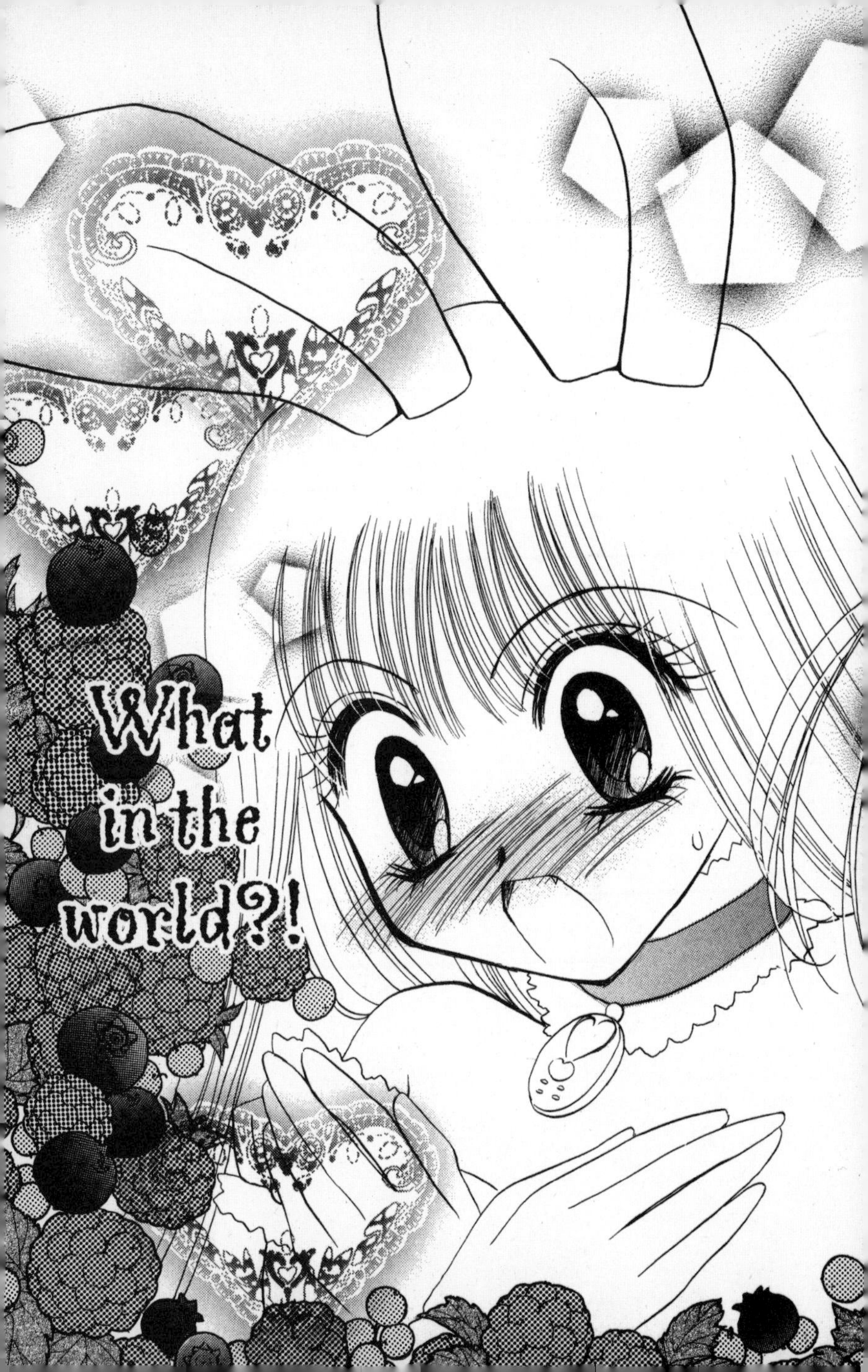
What in the world?!

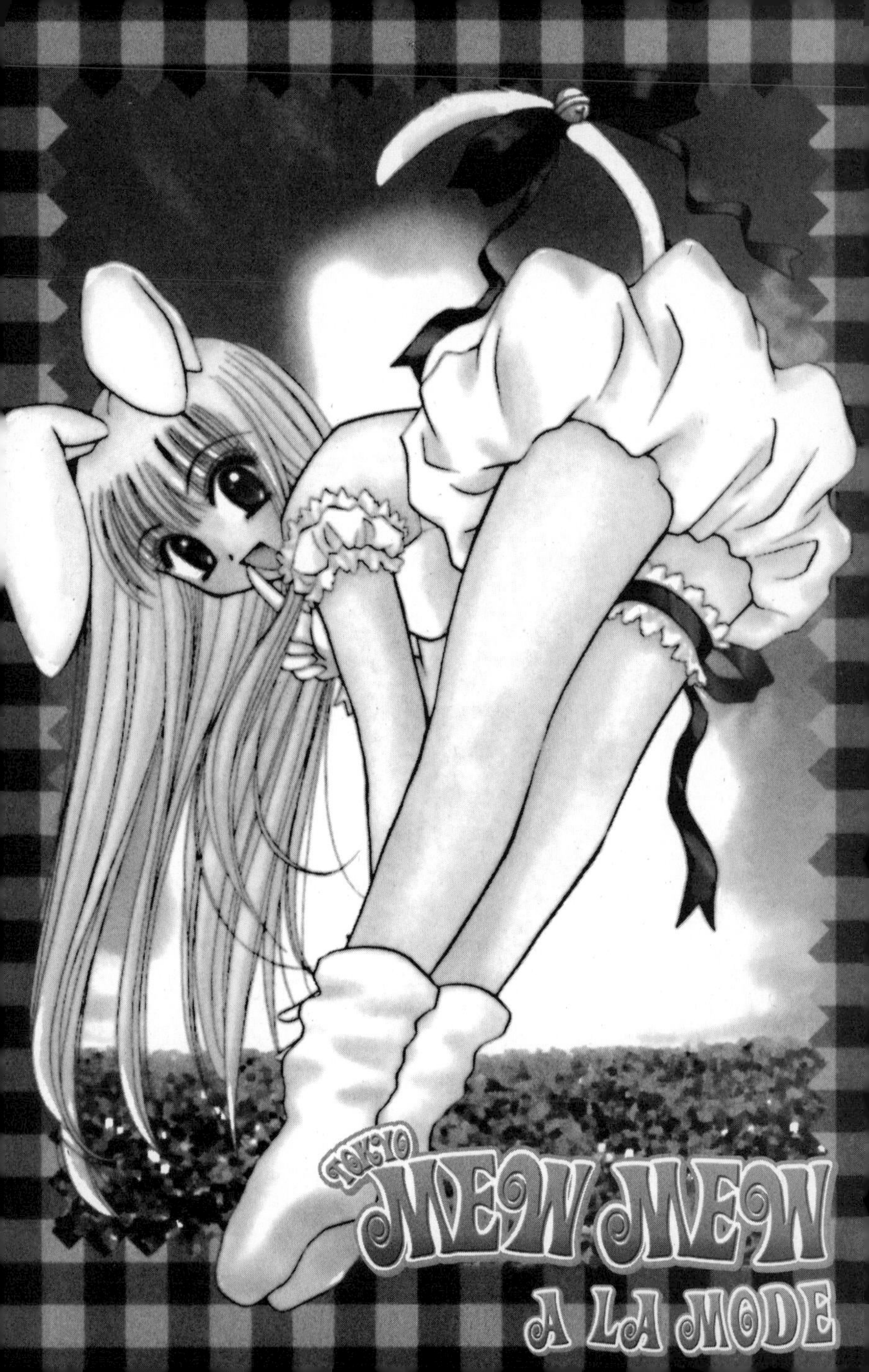
TOKYO
MEW MEW
A LA MODE

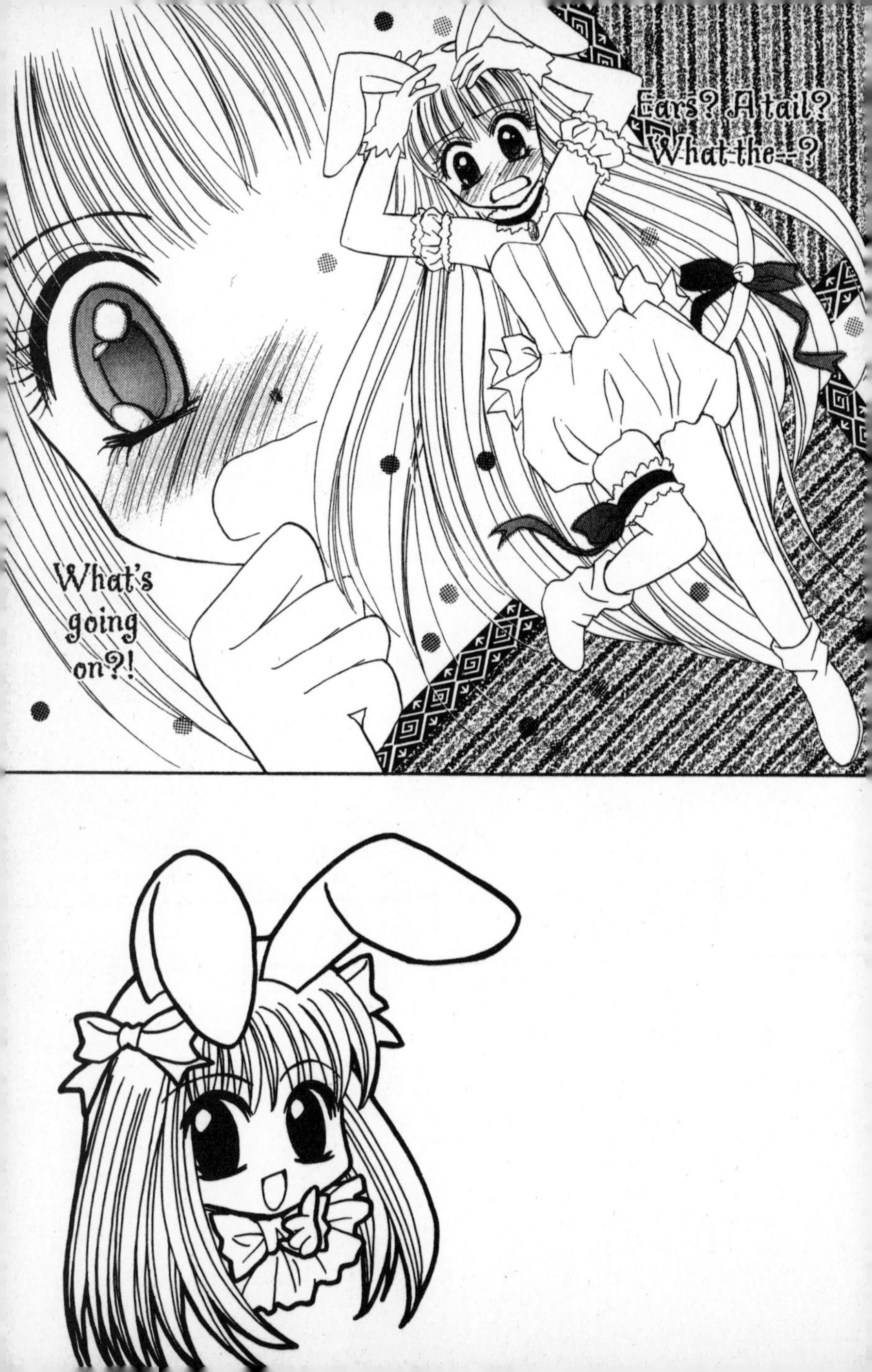
Ears? A tail? What the--?
What's going on?!

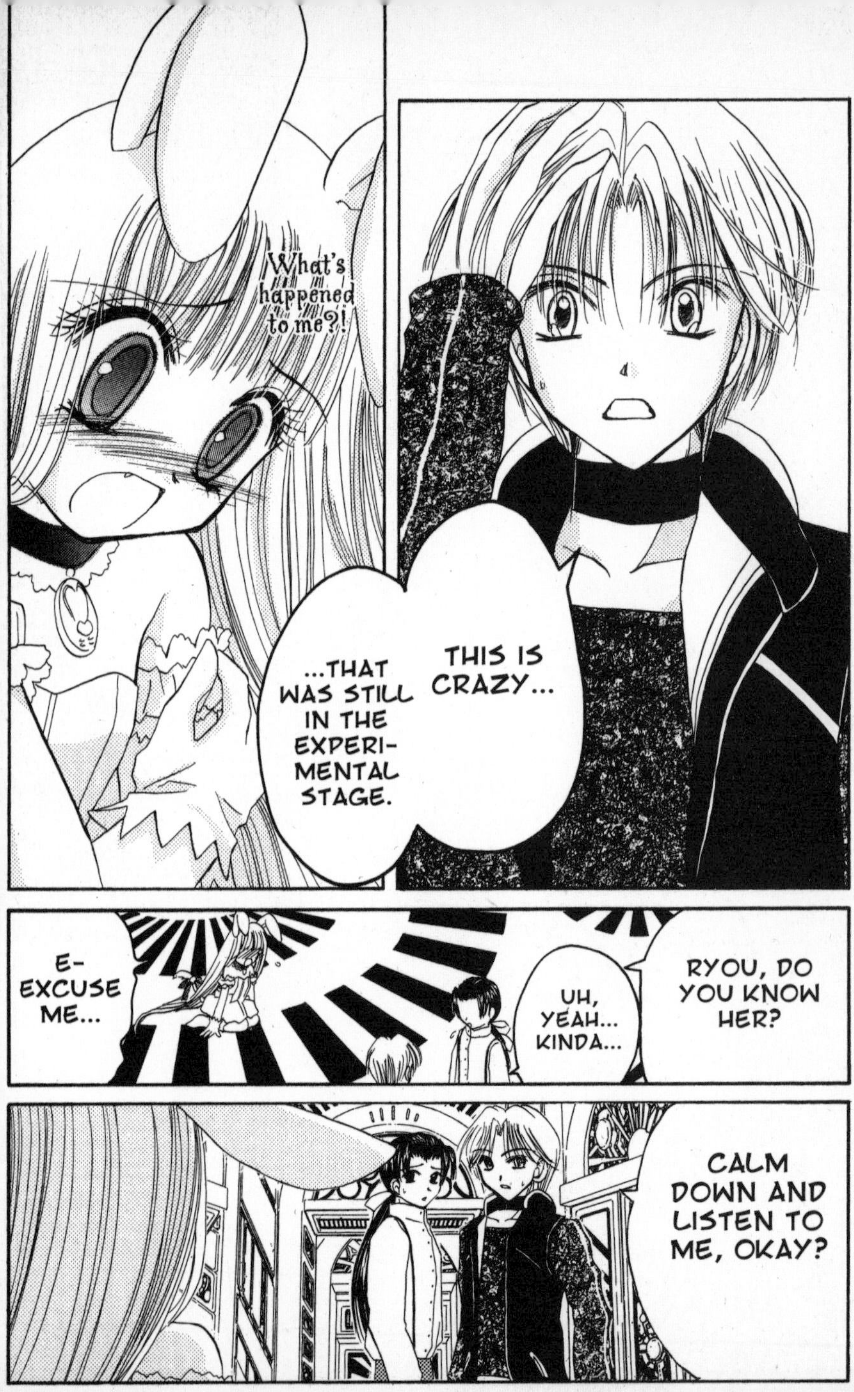
THIS IS CRAZY...
...THAT WAS STILL IN THE EXPERIMENTAL STAGE.
What's happened to me?!
RYOU, DO YOU KNOW HER?
UH, YEAH... KINDA...
E-EXCUSE ME...
CALM DOWN AND LISTEN TO ME, OKAY?

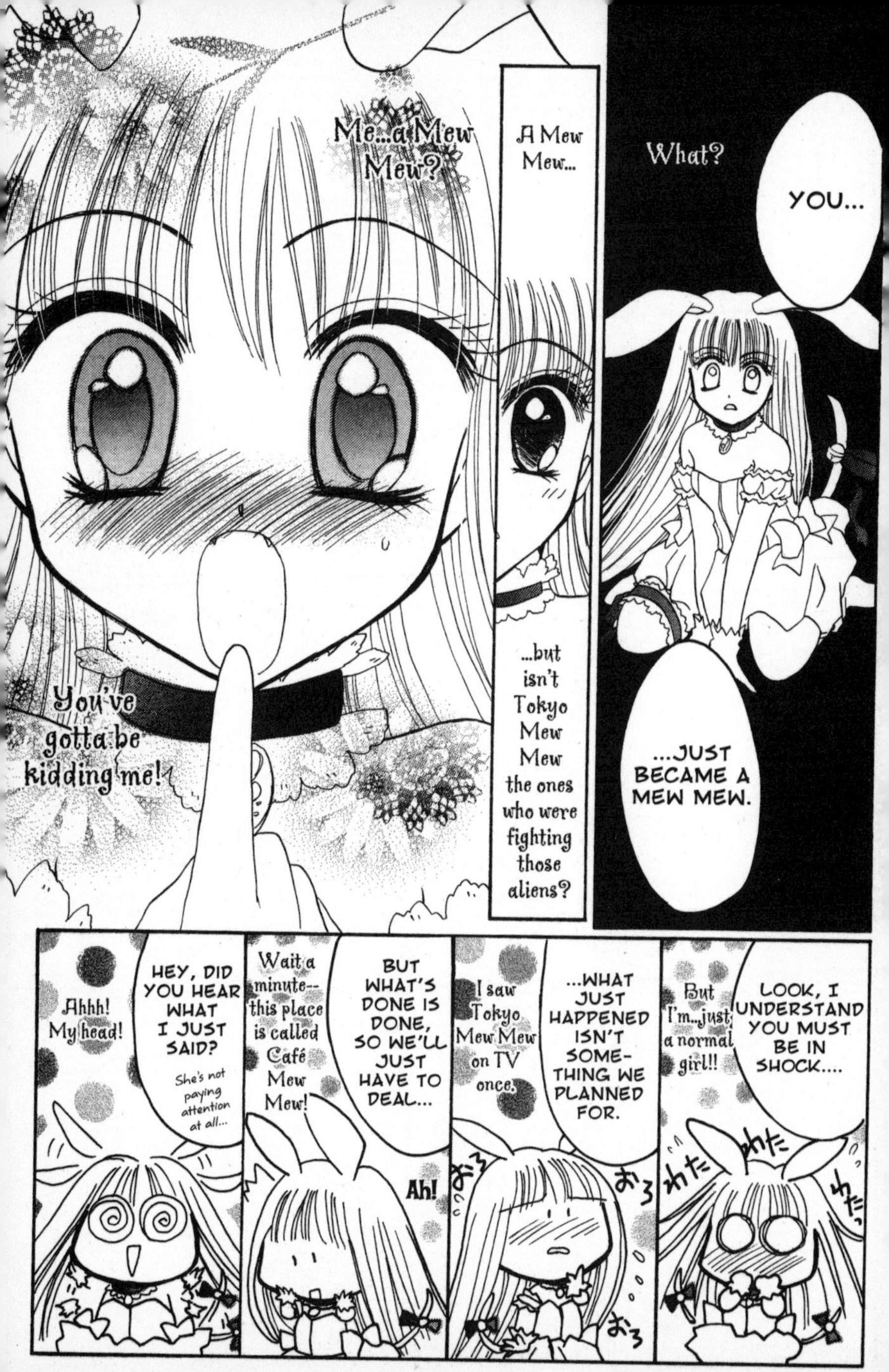
YOU...
What?
...JUST BECAME A MEW MEW.
A Mew Mew...
...but isn't Tokyo Mew Mew the ones who were fighting those aliens?
Me...a Mew Mew?
You've gotta be kidding me!
LOOK, I UNDERSTAND YOU MUST BE IN SHOCK....
But I'm...just a normal girl!!
わた
わた
...WHAT JUST HAPPENED ISN'T SOME-THING WE PLANNED FOR.
I saw Tokyo Mew Mew on TV once.
おろ
おろ
おろ
BUT WHAT'S DONE IS DONE, SO WE'LL JUST HAVE TO DEAL...
Wait a minute--this place is called Café Mew Mew!
Ah!
HEY, DID YOU HEAR WHAT I JUST SAID?
Ahhh! My head!
She's not paying attention at all...

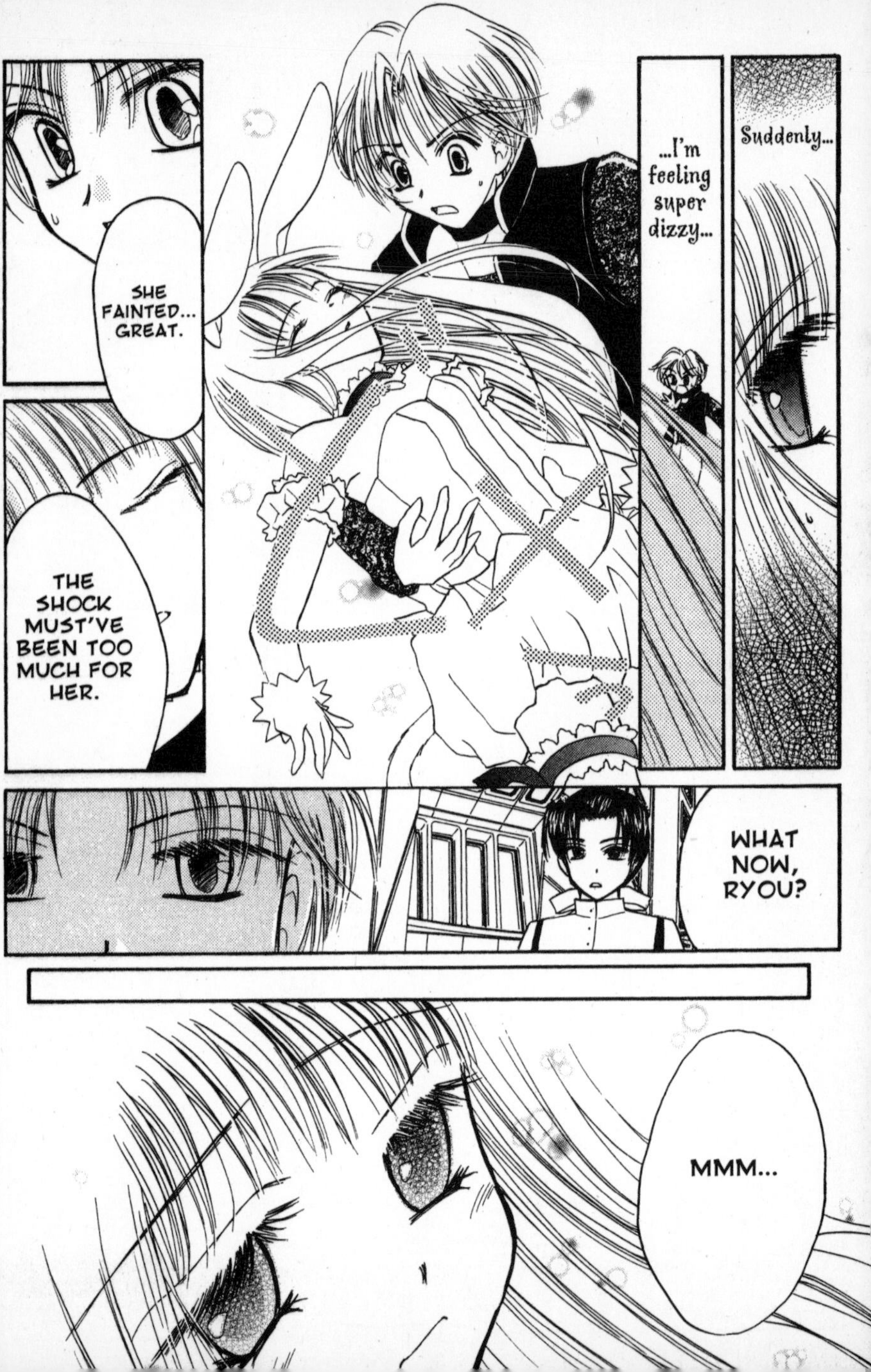
Suddenly...
...I'm feeling super dizzy...
SHE FAINTED... GREAT.
THE SHOCK MUST'VE BEEN TOO MUCH FOR HER.
WHAT NOW, RYOU?
MMM...

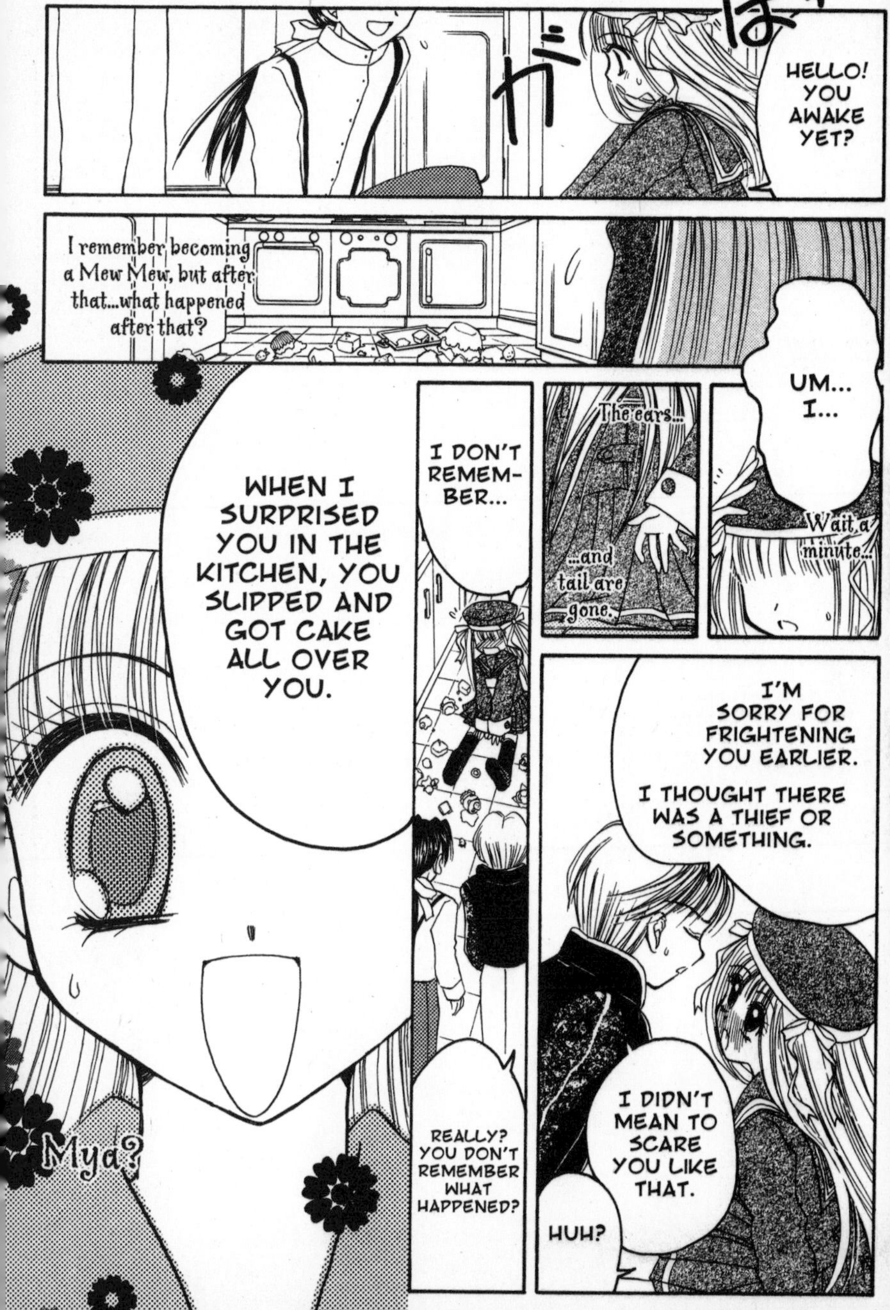
ばっ
ガ
HELLO! YOU AWAKE YET?
I remember becoming a Mew Mew, but after that...what happened after that?
UM... I...
Wait a minute...
The ears...
...and tail are gone.
I'M SORRY FOR FRIGHTENING YOU EARLIER.
I THOUGHT THERE WAS A THIEF OR SOMETHING.
I DIDN'T MEAN TO SCARE YOU LIKE THAT.
HUH?
I DON'T REMEMBER...
REALLY? YOU DON'T REMEMBER WHAT HAPPENED?
WHEN I SURPRISED YOU IN THE KITCHEN, YOU SLIPPED AND GOT CAKE ALL OVER YOU.
Mya?

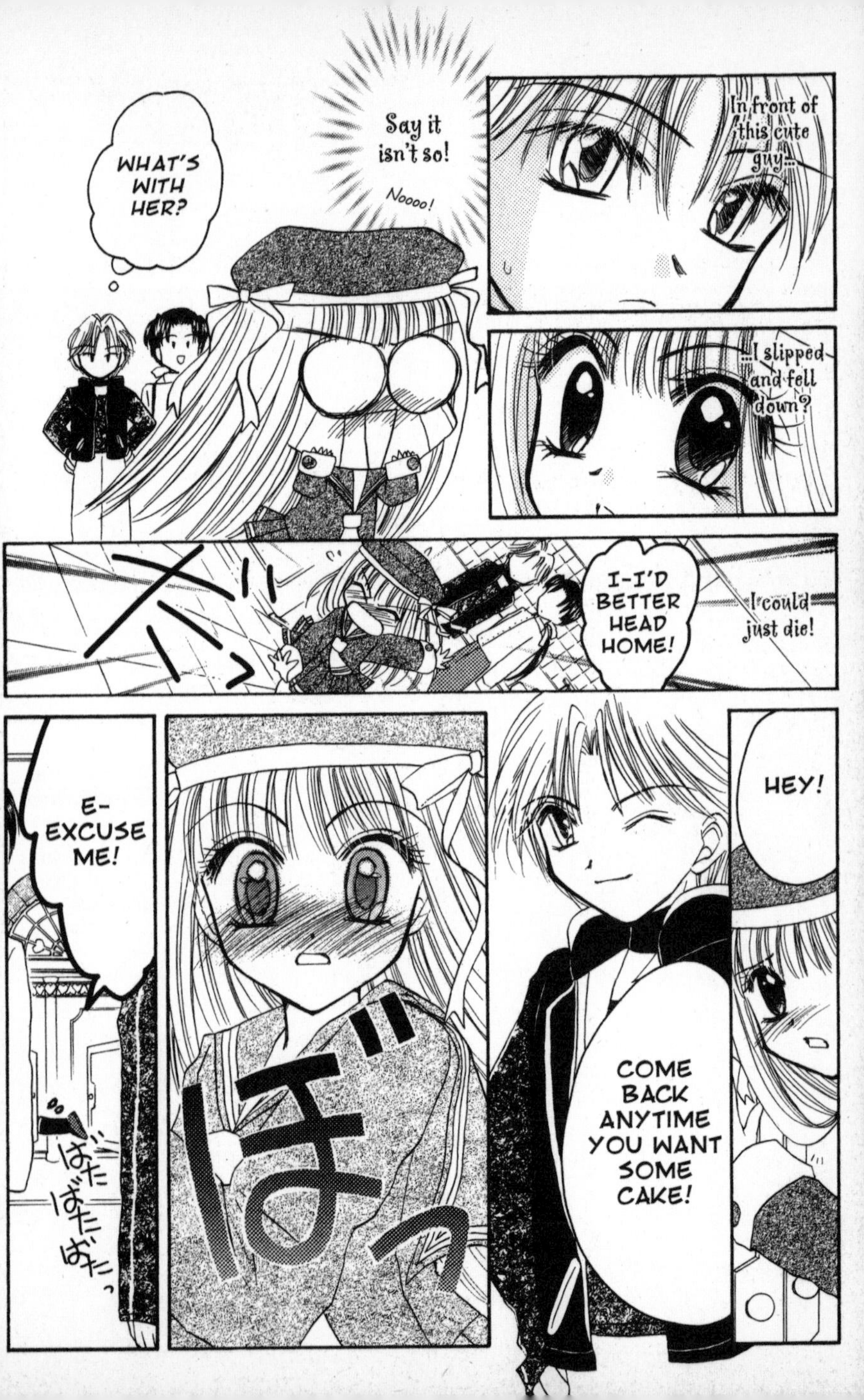
In front of this cute guy...
...I slipped and fell down?
Say it isn't so!
Noooo!
WHAT'S WITH HER?
I could just die!
I-I'D BETTER HEAD HOME!
HEY!
COME BACK ANYTIME YOU WANT SOME CAKE!
ぼっ
E-EXCUSE ME!
ばたばたばた

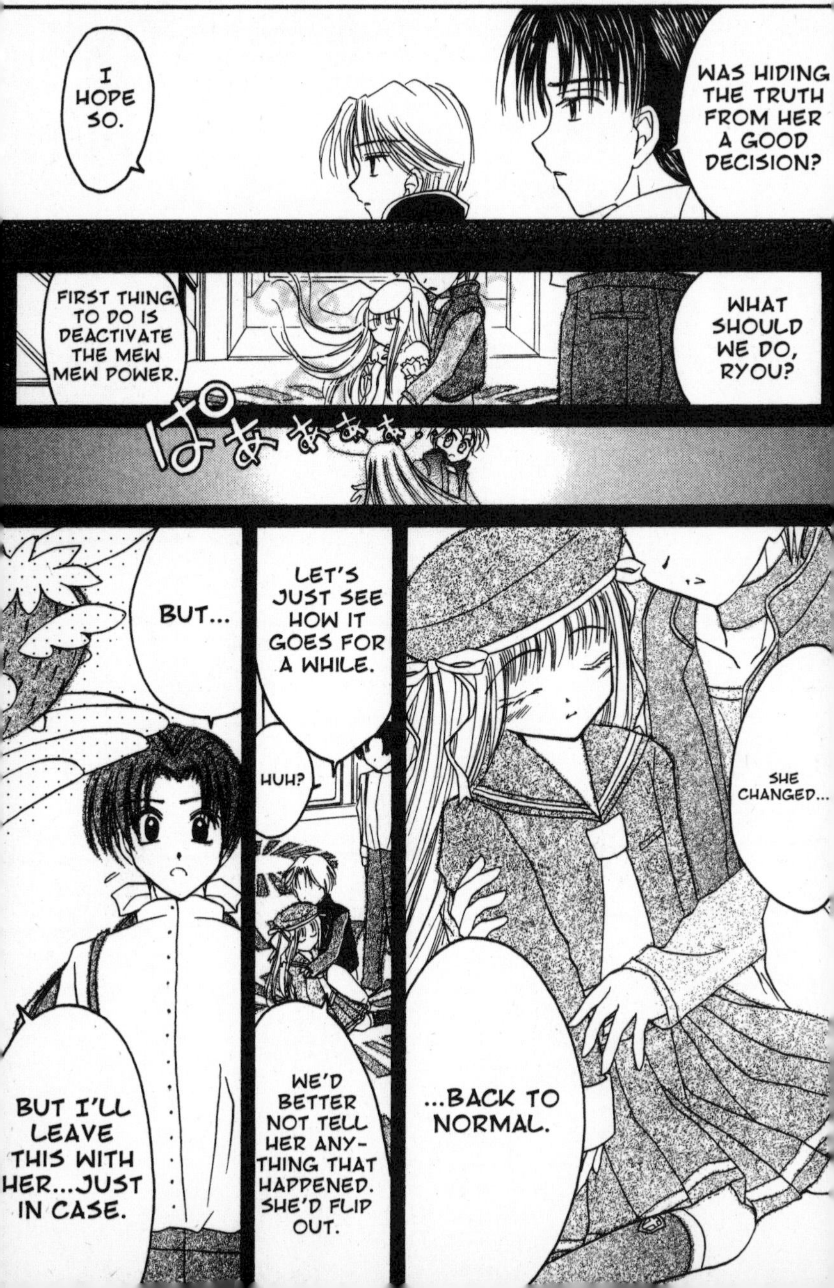
WAS HIDING THE TRUTH FROM HER A GOOD DECISION?
I HOPE SO.
WHAT SHOULD WE DO, RYOU?
FIRST THING TO DO IS DEACTIVATE THE MEW MEW POWER.
ぱあぁぁ
SHE CHANGED...
...BACK TO NORMAL.
LET'S JUST SEE HOW IT GOES FOR A WHILE.
HUH?
WE'D BETTER NOT TELL HER ANYTHING THAT HAPPENED. SHE'D FLIP OUT.
BUT...
BUT I'LL LEAVE THIS WITH HER...JUST IN CASE.

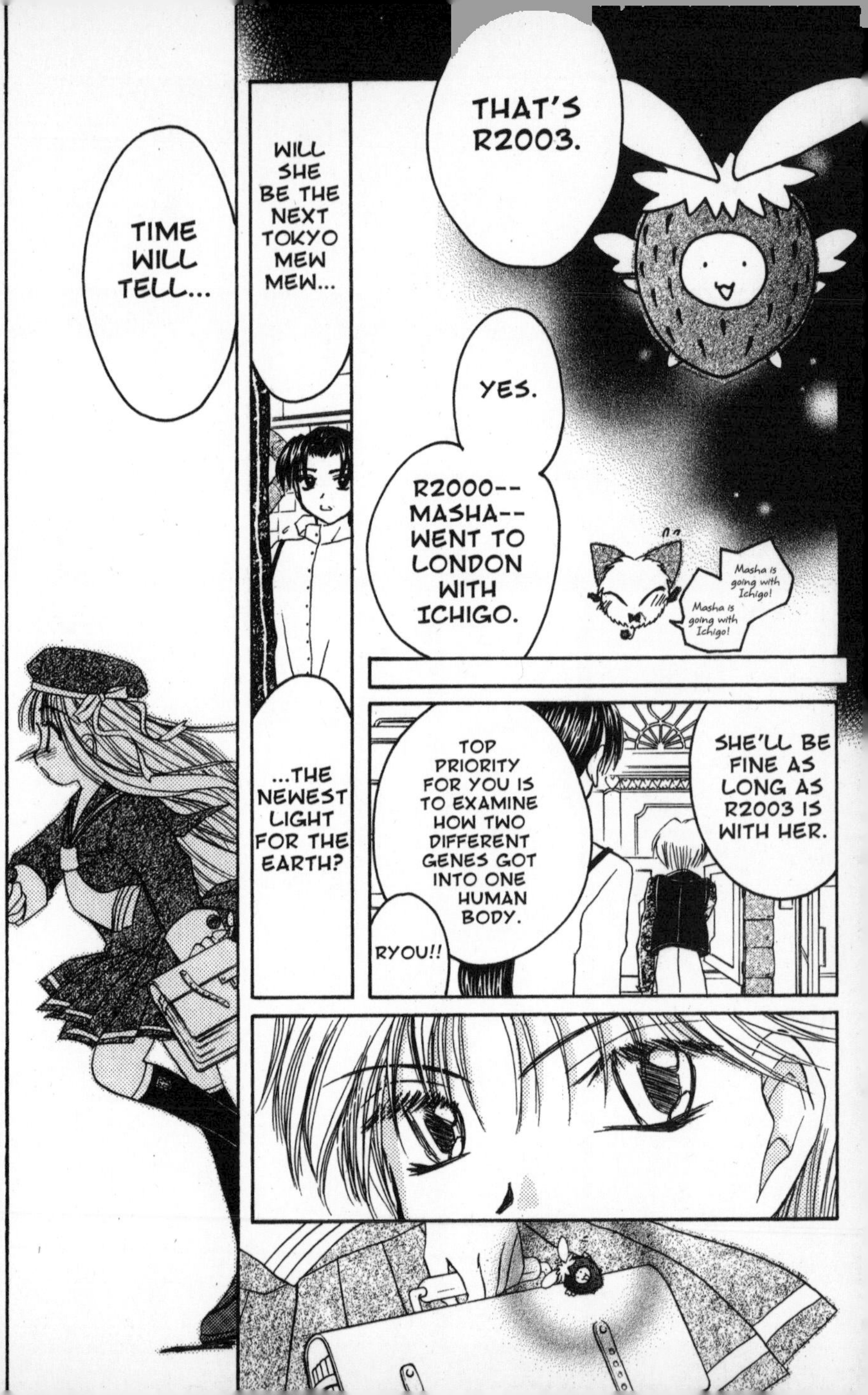
THAT'S R2003.
YES.
R2000--MASHA--WENT TO LONDON WITH ICHIGO.
Masha is going with Ichigo!
Masha is going with Ichigo!
SHE'LL BE FINE AS LONG AS R2003 IS WITH HER.
TOP PRIORITY FOR YOU IS TO EXAMINE HOW TWO DIFFERENT GENES GOT INTO ONE HUMAN BODY.
RYOU!!
WILL SHE BE THE NEXT TOKYO MEW MEW...
...THE NEWEST LIGHT FOR THE EARTH?
TIME WILL TELL...

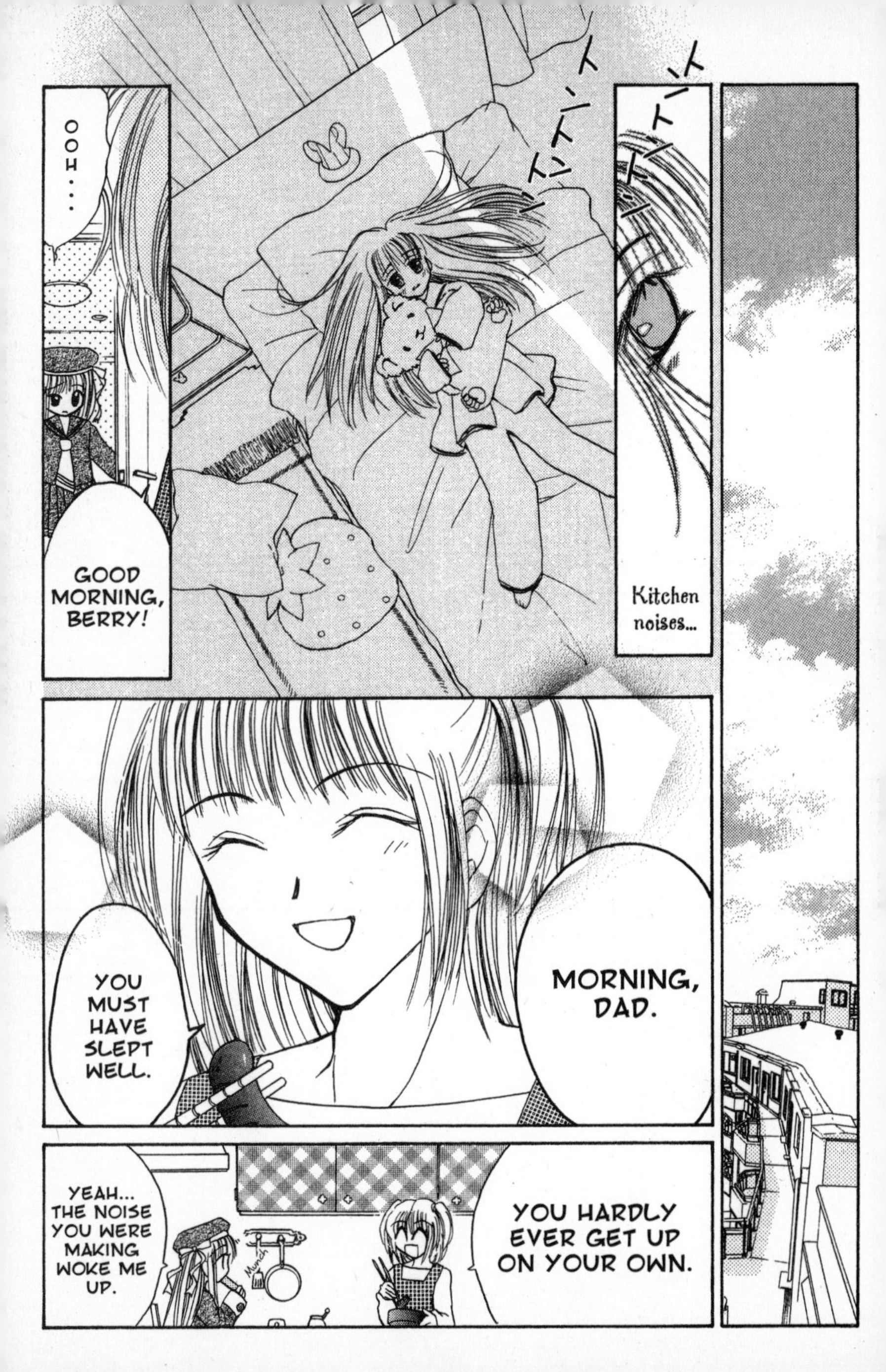
トントントン
トントントン
Kitchen noises...
OOH...
GOOD MORNING, BERRY!
MORNING, DAD.
YOU MUST HAVE SLEPT WELL.
YOU HARDLY EVER GET UP ON YOUR OWN.
YEAH... THE NOISE YOU WERE MAKING WOKE ME UP.
Munch

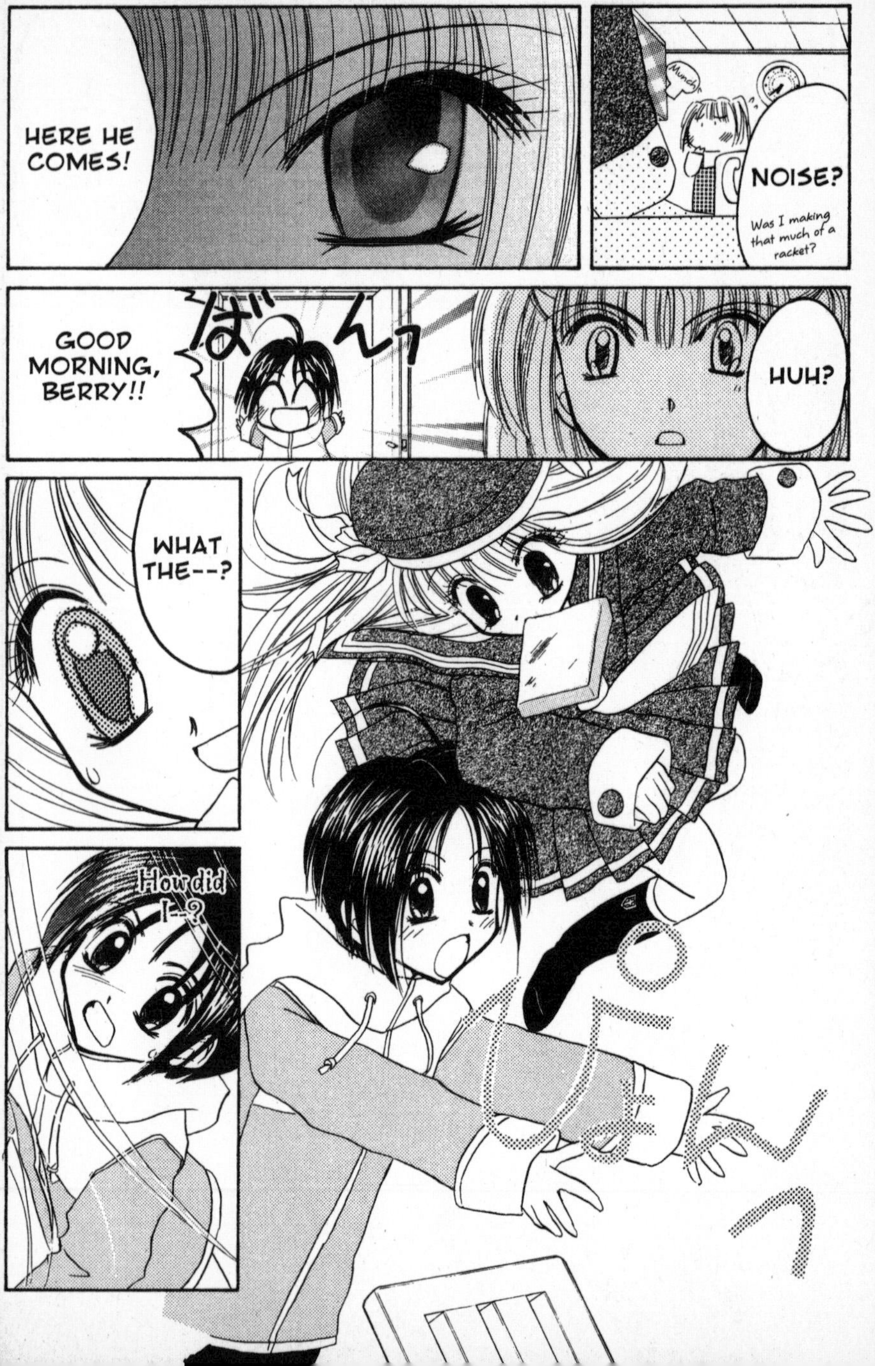
Munch
NOISE?
Was I making that much of a racket?
HERE HE COMES!
HUH?
GOOD MORNING, BERRY!!
ばん
WHAT THE--?
How did I--?

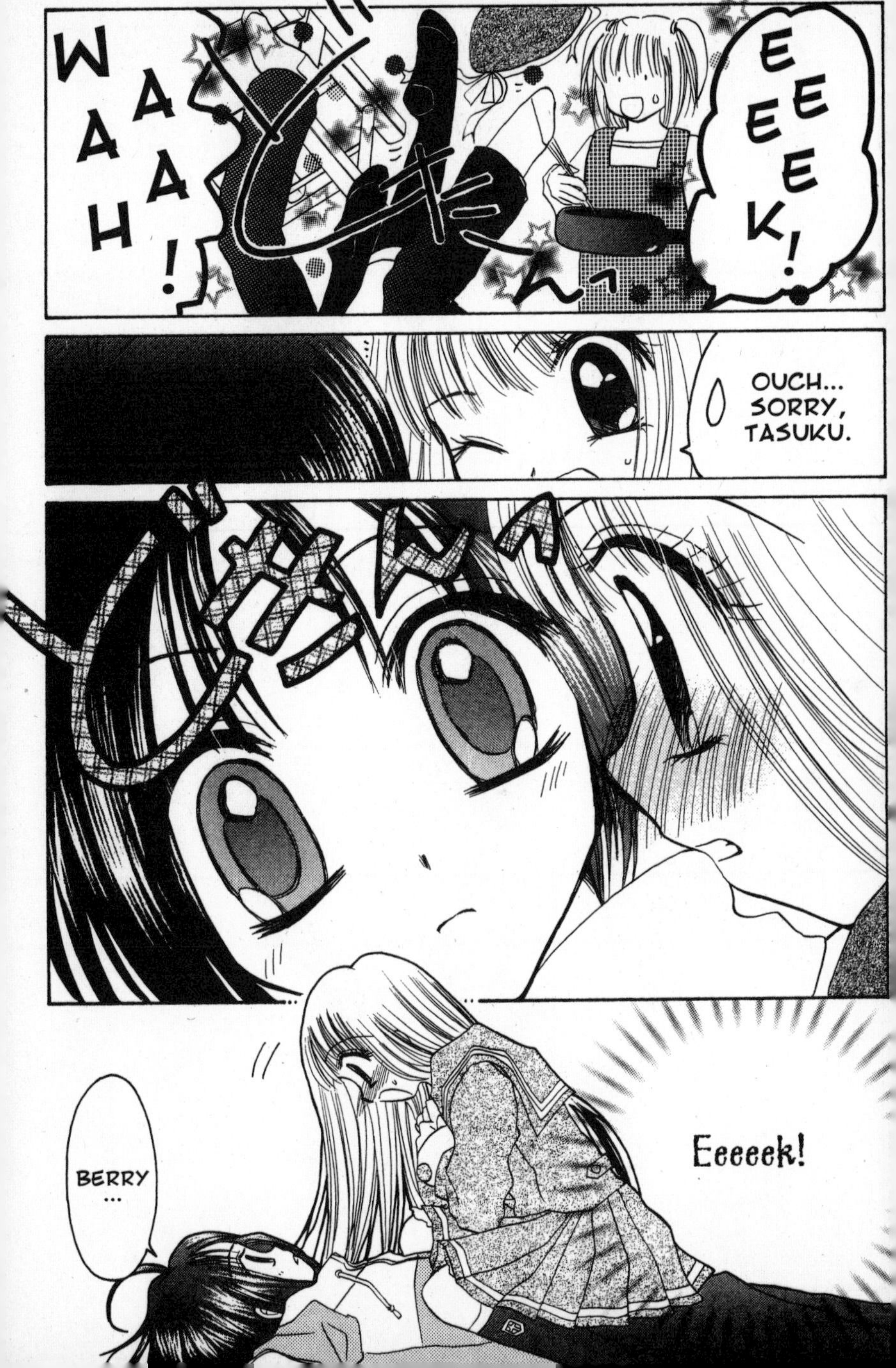
EEEEK!
WAAAH!
OUCH... SORRY, TASUKU.
Eeeeek!
BERRY...

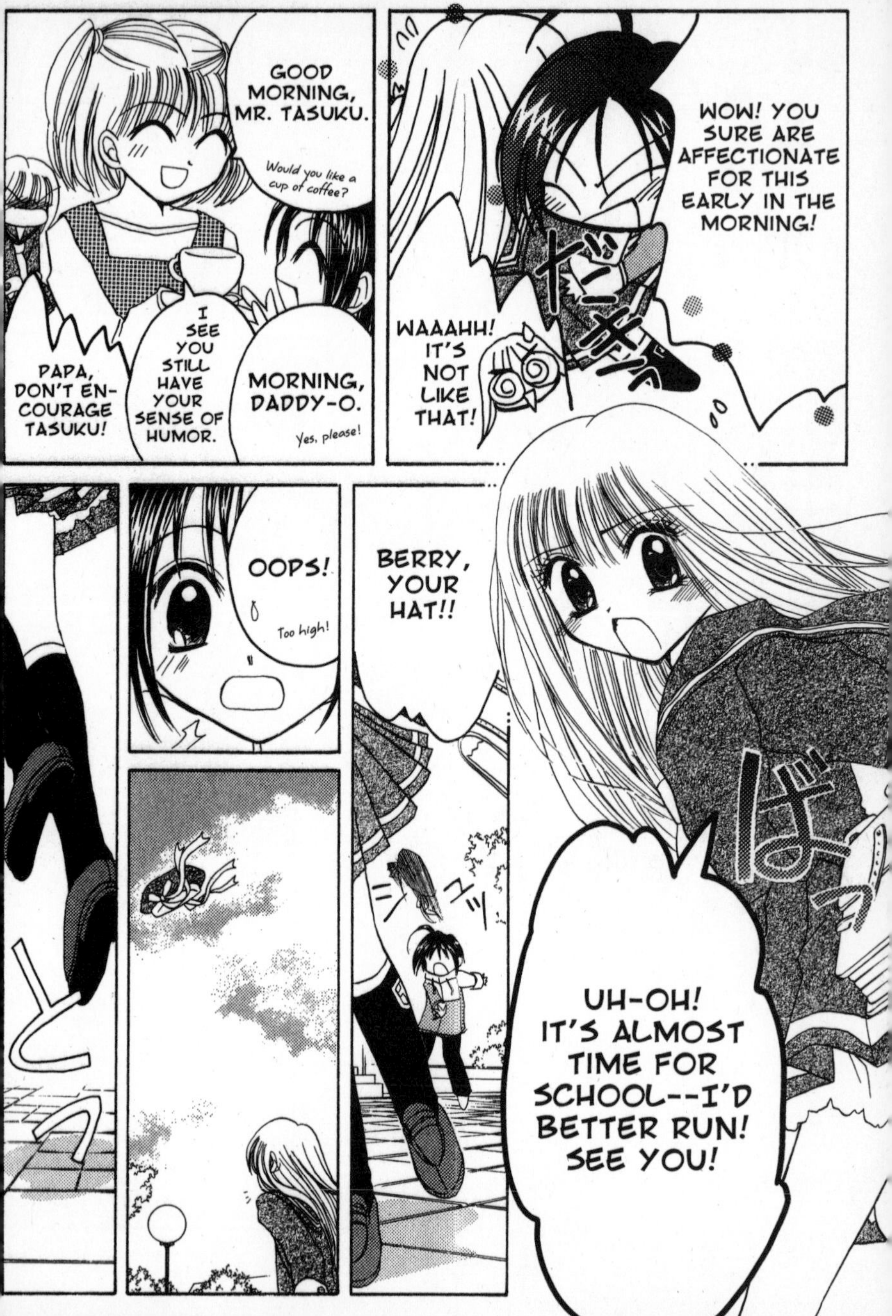
WOW! YOU SURE ARE AFFECTIONATE FOR THIS EARLY IN THE MORNING!
WAAAHH! IT'S NOT LIKE THAT!
GOOD MORNING, MR. TASUKU.
Would you like a cup of coffee?
MORNING, DADDY-O.
Yes, please!
I SEE YOU STILL HAVE YOUR SENSE OF HUMOR.
PAPA, DON'T EN-COURAGE TASUKU!
UH-OH! IT'S ALMOST TIME FOR SCHOOL--I'D BETTER RUN! SEE YOU!
BERRY, YOUR HAT!!
OOPS!
Too high!

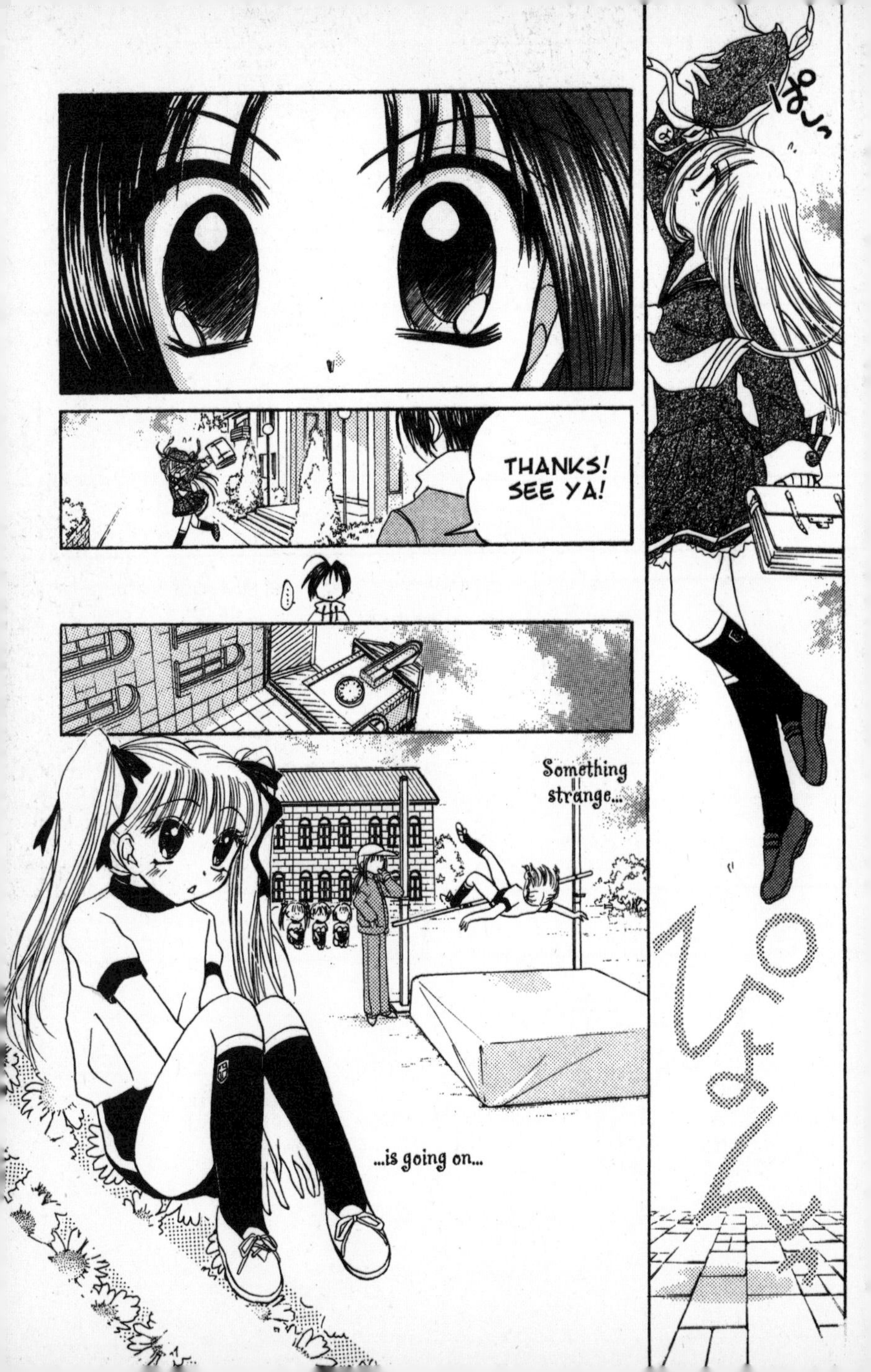
THANKS! SEE YA!
...
Something strange...
...is going on...

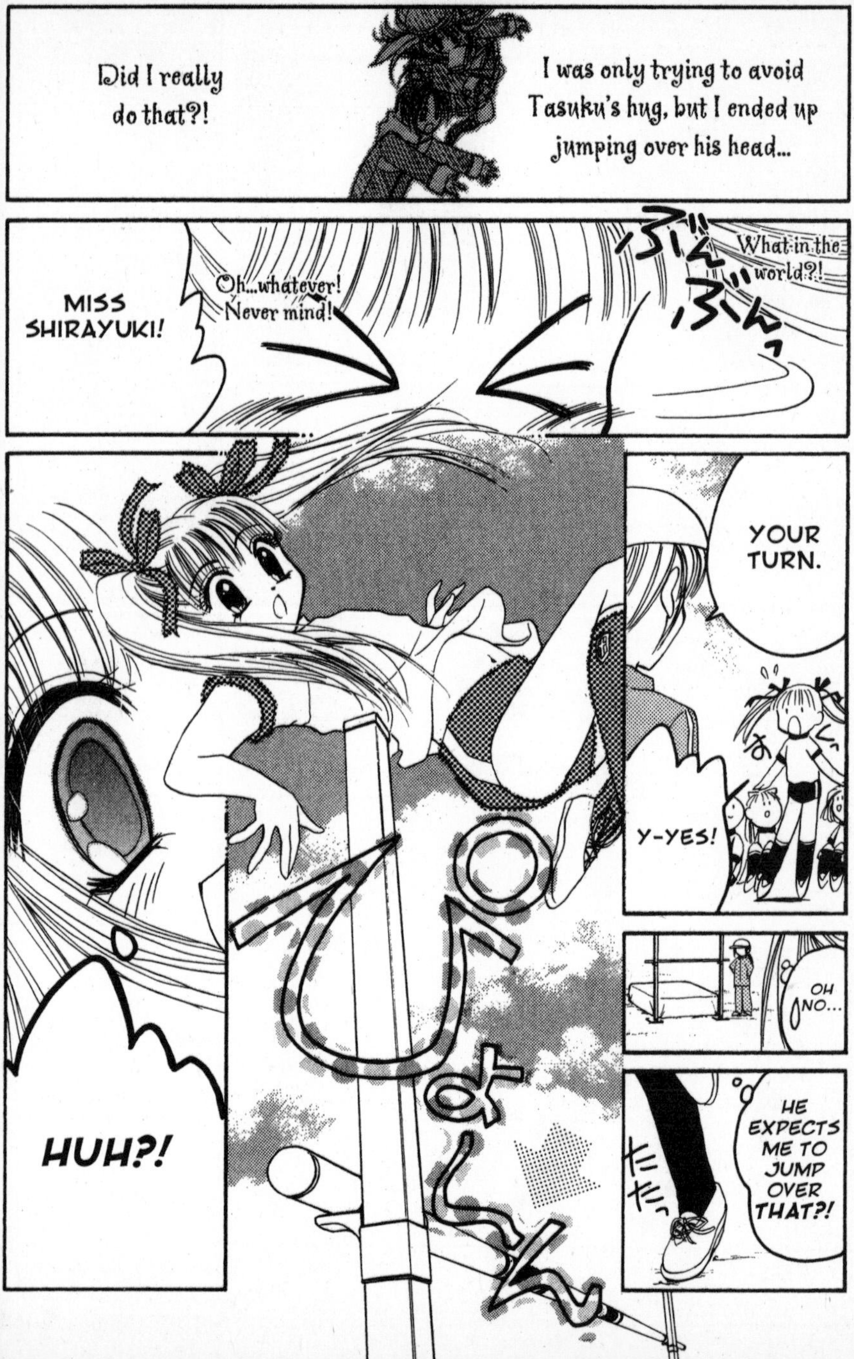
I was only trying to avoid Tasuku's hug, but I ended up jumping over his head...
Did I really do that?!
ぶん
ぶん
What in the world?!
Oh...whatever! Never mind!
MISS SHIRAYUKI!
YOUR TURN.
Y-YES!
OH NO...
HE EXPECTS ME TO JUMP OVER THAT?!
HUH?!

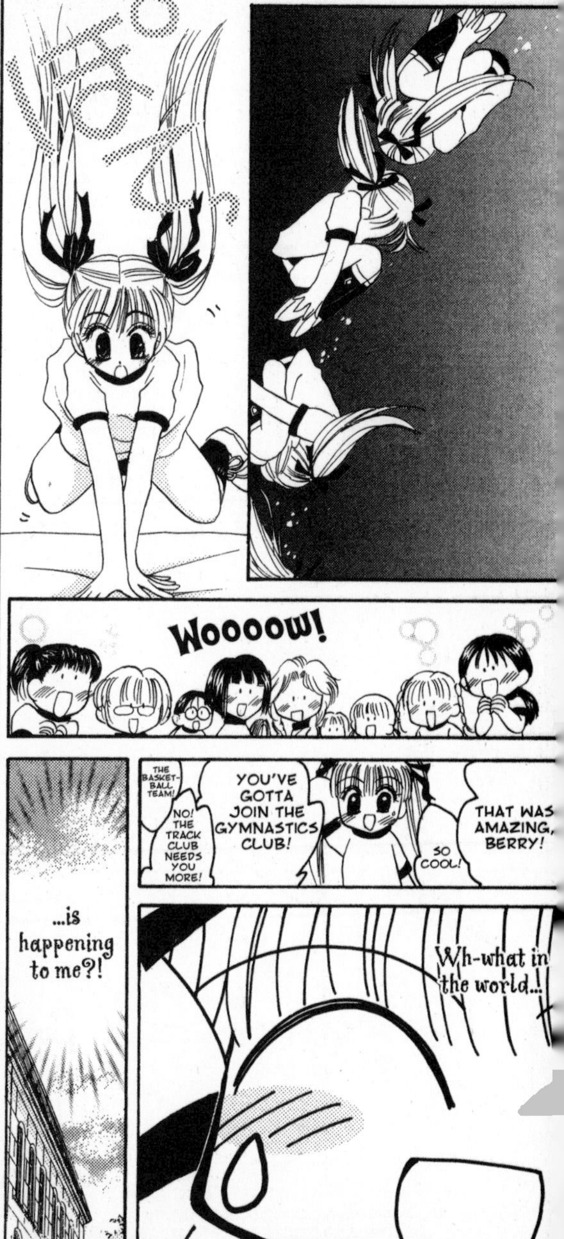
Wooooow!
THAT WAS AMAZING, BERRY!
SO COOL!
YOU'VE GOTTA JOIN THE GYMNASTICS CLUB!
NO! THE TRACK CLUB NEEDS YOU MORE!
THE BASKET-BALL TEAM!
Wh-what in the world...
...is happening to me?!

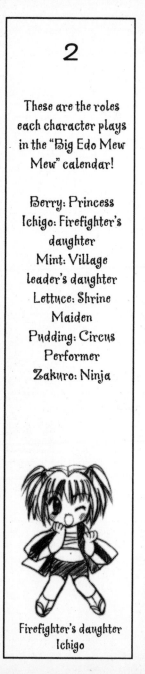

2

These are the roles each character plays in the "Big Edo Mew Mew" calendar!

Berry: Princess
Ichigo: Firefighter's daughter
Mint: Village leader's daughter
Lettuce: Shrine Maiden
Pudding: Circus Performer
Zakuro: Ninja

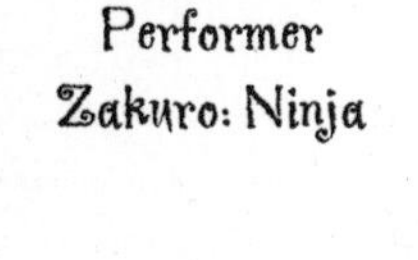

Firefighter's daughter Ichigo

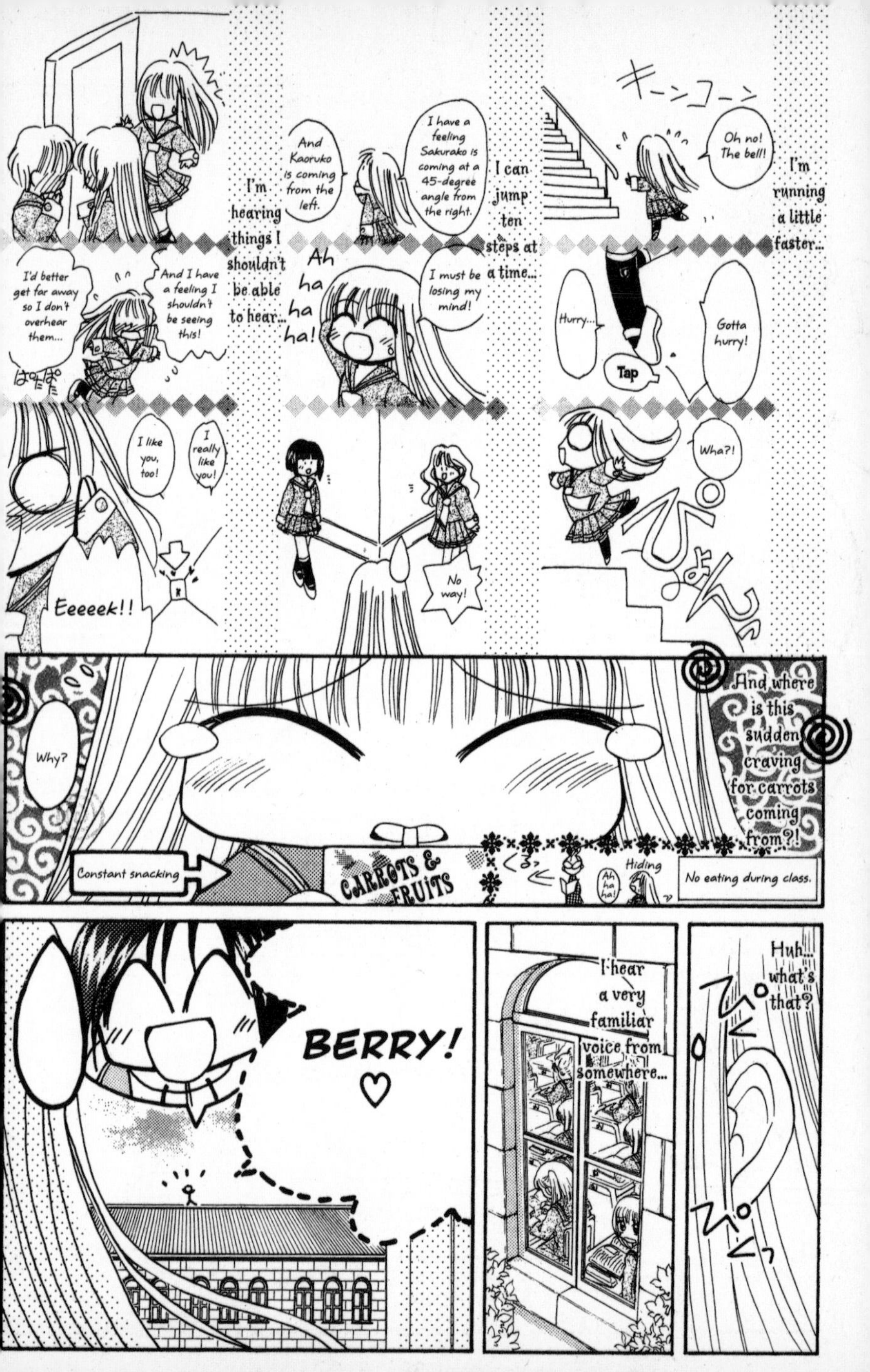

I'm running a little faster...
キーンコーン
Oh no! The bell!
Gotta hurry!
Hurry...
Tap
Wha?!
ぴょんっ
I can jump ten steps at a time...
I have a feeling Sakurako is coming at a 45-degree angle from the right.
And Kaoruko is coming from the left.
I must be losing my mind!
Ah ha ha ha!
No way!
I'm hearing things I shouldn't be able to hear...
And I have a feeling I shouldn't be seeing this!
I'd better get far away so I don't overhear them...
はたぱた
I really like you!
I like you, too!
Eeeeek!!
And where is this sudden craving for carrots coming from?!
Why?
No eating during class.
Hiding
Ah ha ha!
くるっ
CARROTS & FRUITS
Constant snacking
Huh... what's that?
ぴくっ
ぴくっ
I hear a very familiar voice from somewhere...
BERRY! ♡

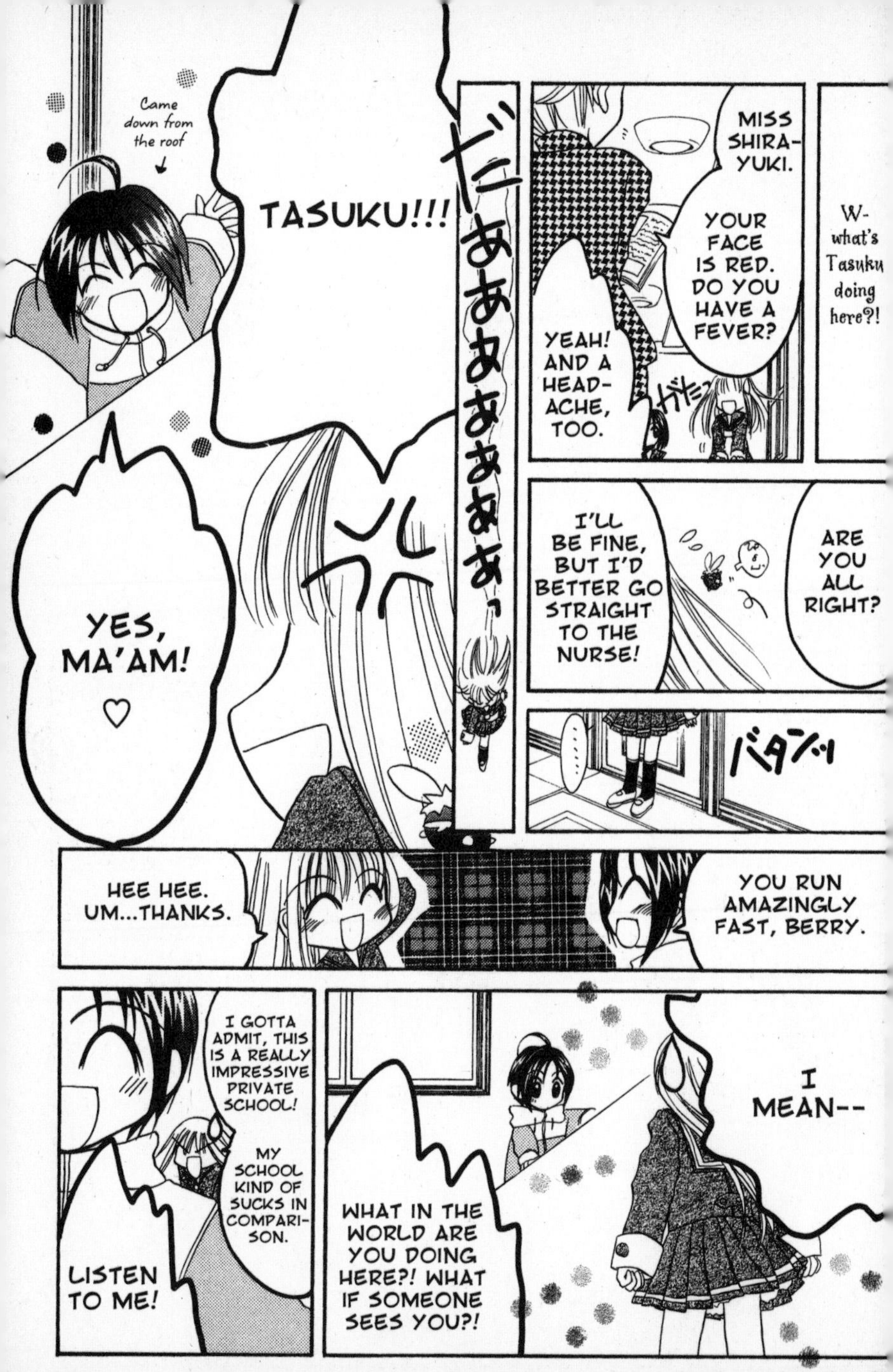
W- what's Tasuku doing here?!
MISS SHIRA-YUKI.
YOUR FACE IS RED. DO YOU HAVE A FEVER?
YEAH! AND A HEAD-ACHE, TOO.
ARE YOU ALL RIGHT?
I'LL BE FINE, BUT I'D BETTER GO STRAIGHT TO THE NURSE!
バタンッ
......
だあああああああっ
TASUKU!!!
Came down from the roof
YES, MA'AM! ♡
YOU RUN AMAZINGLY FAST, BERRY.
HEE HEE. UM...THANKS.
I MEAN--
WHAT IN THE WORLD ARE YOU DOING HERE?! WHAT IF SOMEONE SEES YOU?!
I GOTTA ADMIT, THIS IS A REALLY IMPRESSIVE PRIVATE SCHOOL!
MY SCHOOL KIND OF SUCKS IN COMPARI-SON.
LISTEN TO ME!

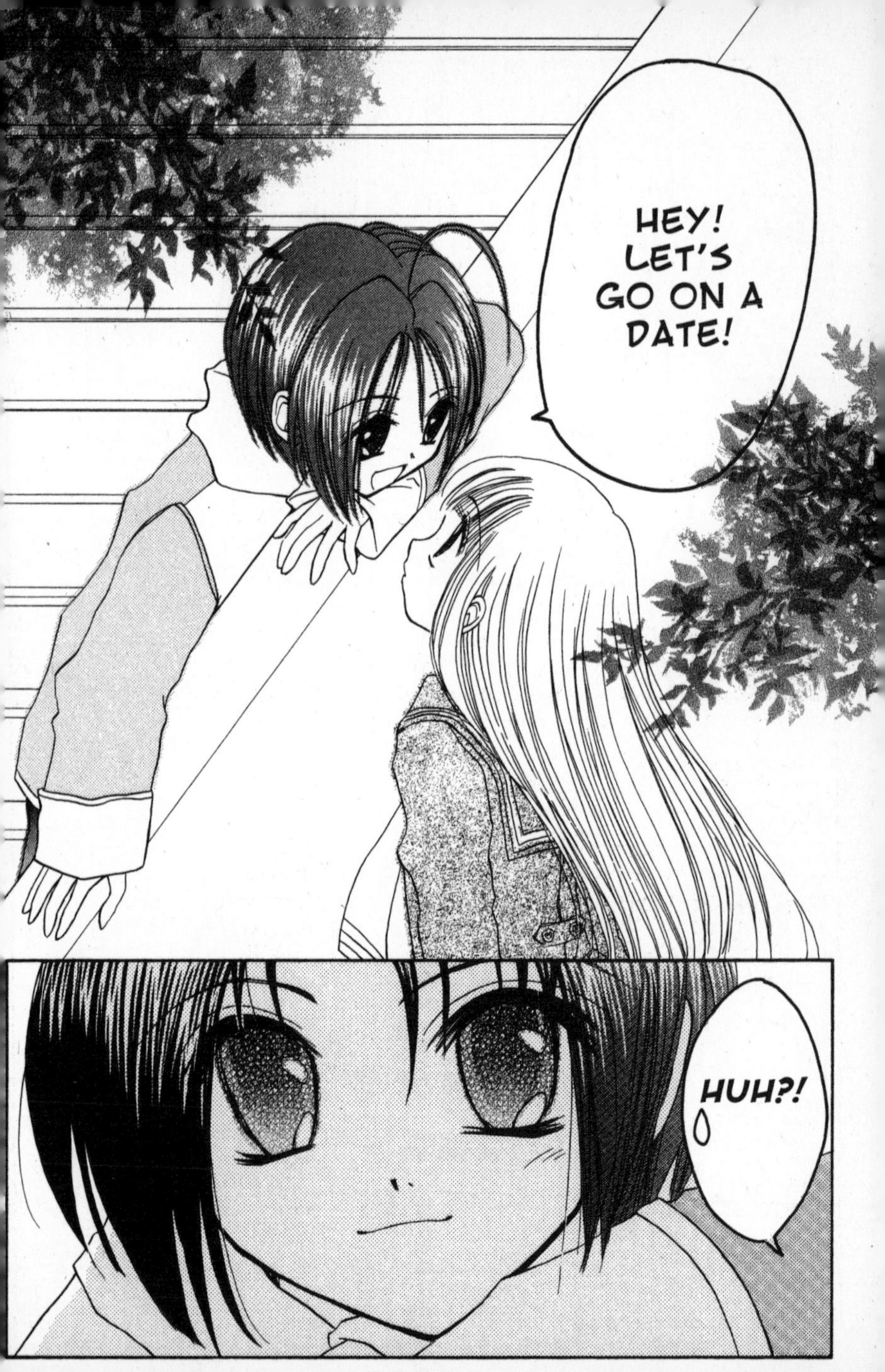
HEY! LET'S GO ON A DATE!
HUH?!

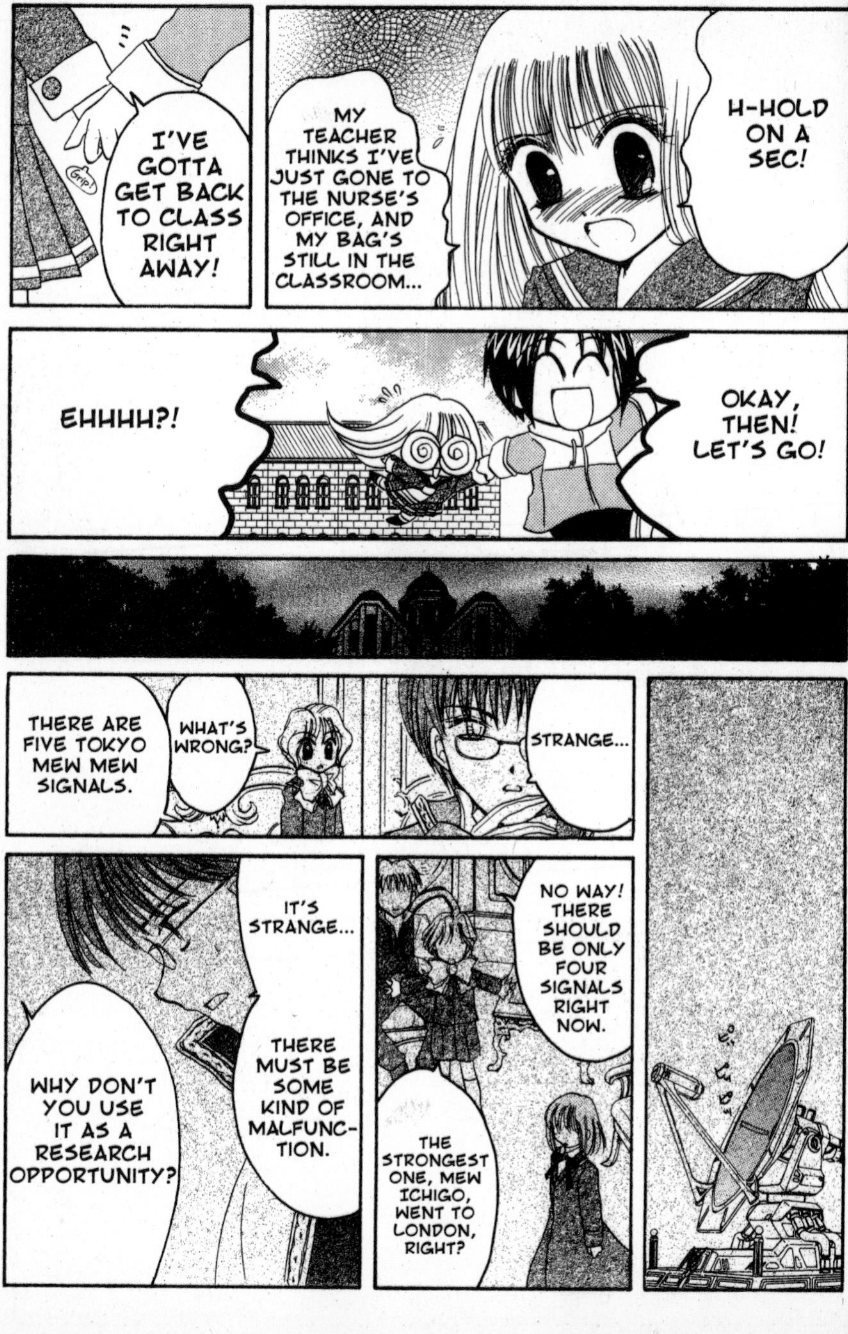
H-HOLD ON A SEC!
MY TEACHER THINKS I'VE JUST GONE TO THE NURSE'S OFFICE, AND MY BAG'S STILL IN THE CLASSROOM...
I'VE GOTTA GET BACK TO CLASS RIGHT AWAY!
Grip!
OKAY, THEN! LET'S GO!
EHHHH?!
STRANGE...
WHAT'S WRONG?
THERE ARE FIVE TOKYO MEW MEW SIGNALS.
NO WAY! THERE SHOULD BE ONLY FOUR SIGNALS RIGHT NOW.
THE STRONGEST ONE, MEW ICHIGO, WENT TO LONDON, RIGHT?
IT'S STRANGE...
THERE MUST BE SOME KIND OF MALFUNCTION.
WHY DON'T YOU USE IT AS A RESEARCH OPPORTUNITY?

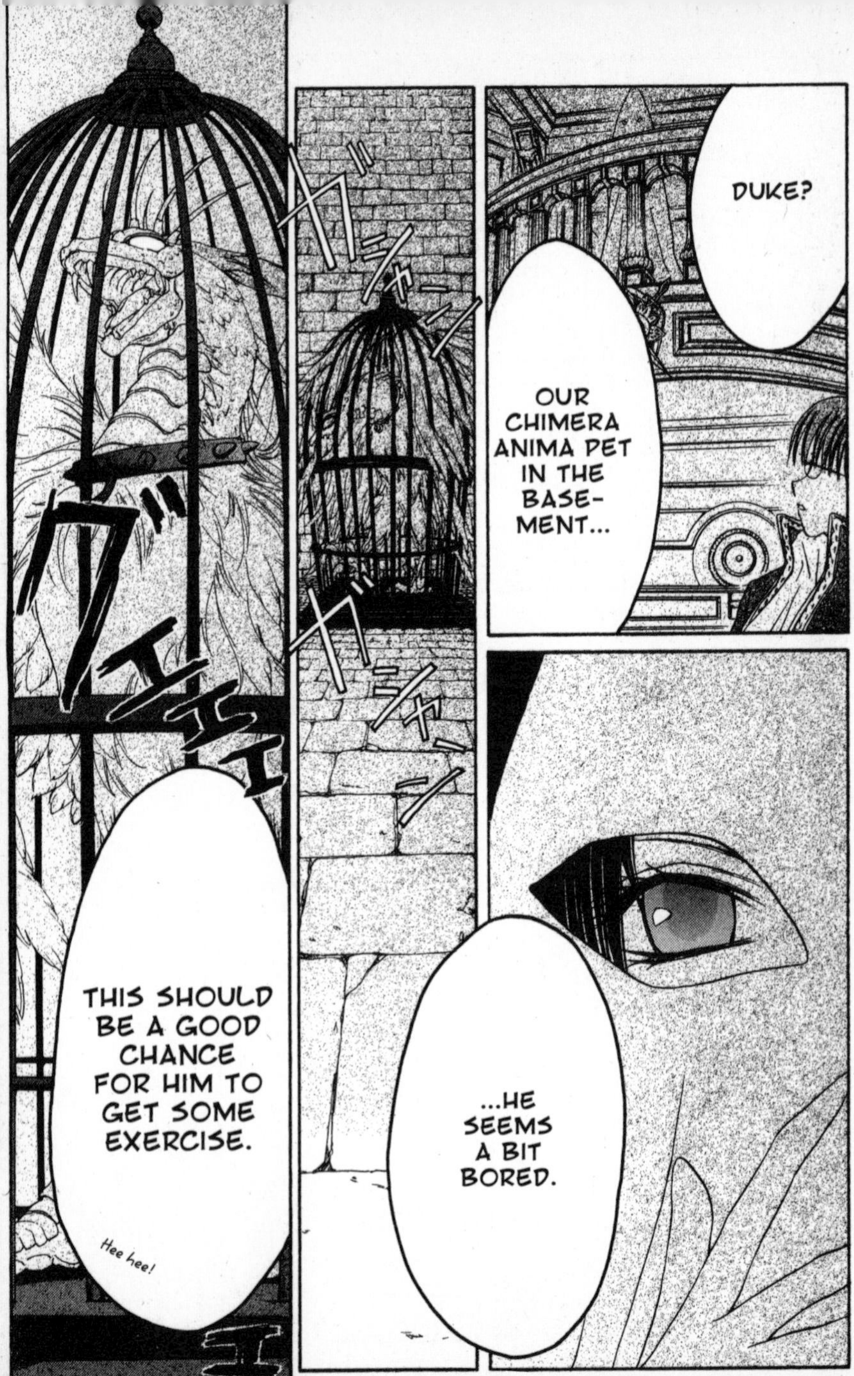
DUKE?
OUR CHIMERA ANIMA PET IN THE BASEMENT...
...HE SEEMS A BIT BORED.
THIS SHOULD BE A GOOD CHANCE FOR HIM TO GET SOME EXERCISE.
Hee hee!

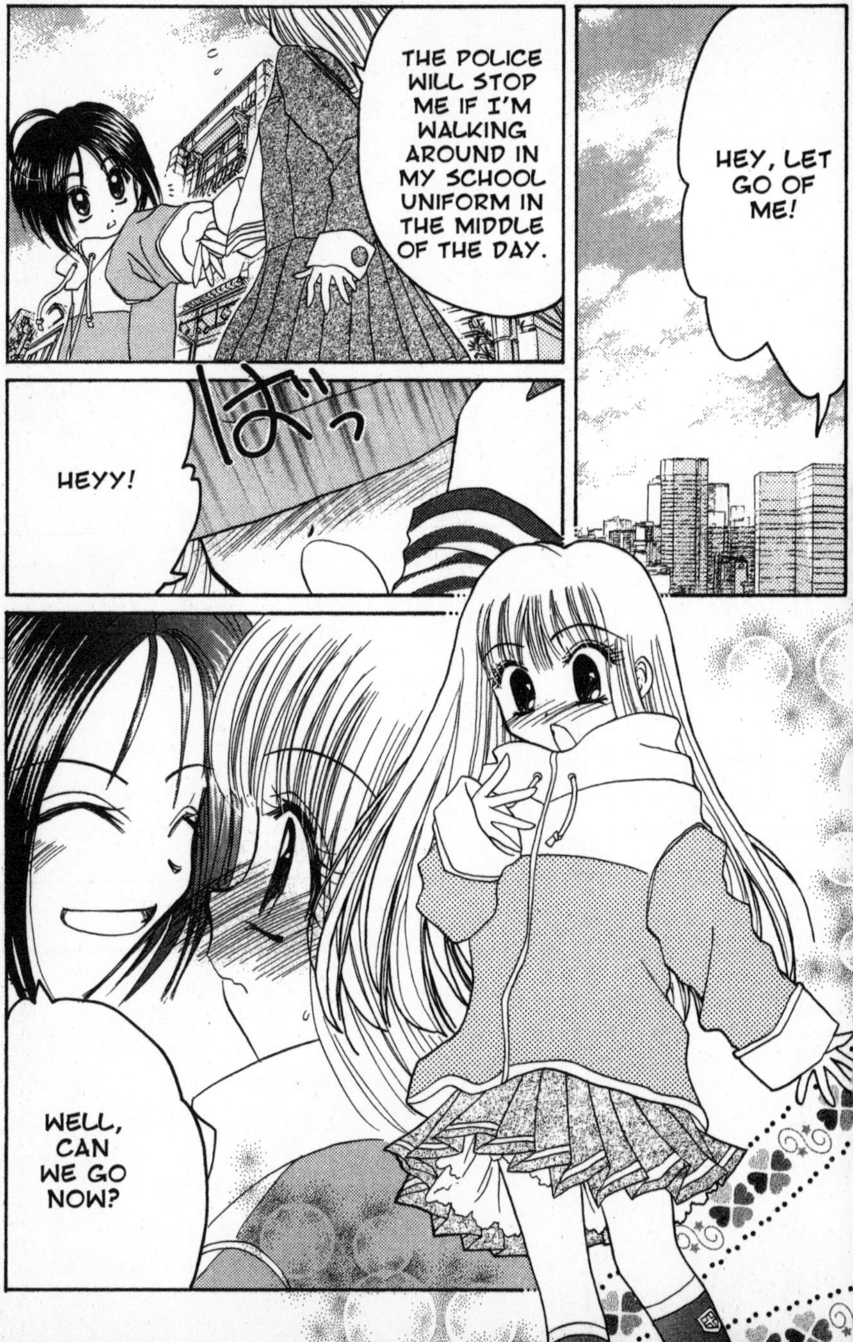
HEY, LET GO OF ME!
THE POLICE WILL STOP ME IF I'M WALKING AROUND IN MY SCHOOL UNIFORM IN THE MIDDLE OF THE DAY.
ばっ
HEYY!
WELL, CAN WE GO NOW?

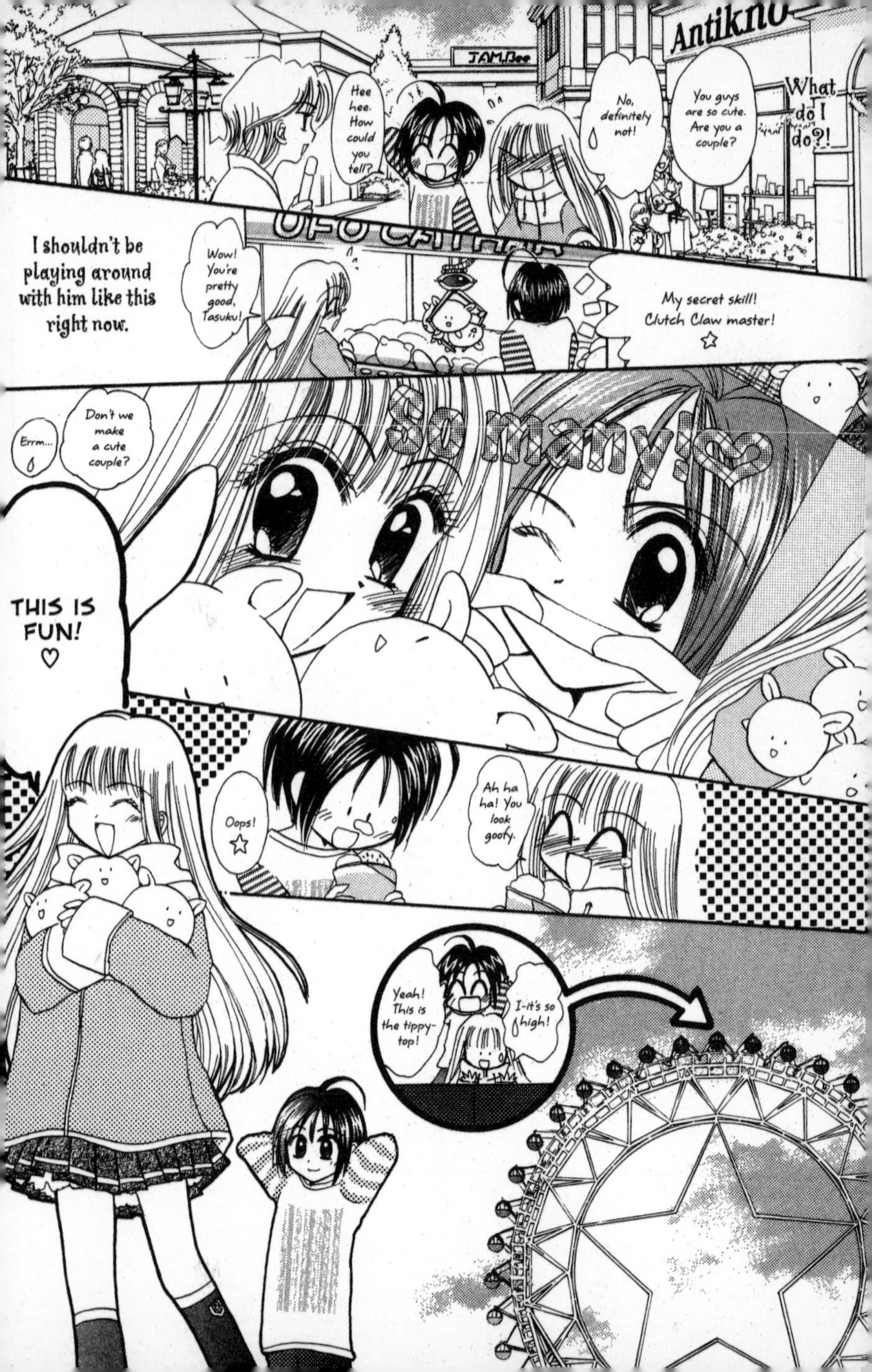
Antikno
What do I do?!
You guys are so cute. Are you a couple?
No, definitely not!
JAM.Bee
Hee hee. How could you tell?
My secret skill! Clutch Claw master! ☆
Wow! You're pretty good, Tasuku!
I shouldn't be playing around with him like this right now.
So many!♡
Don't we make a cute couple?
Errm...
Ah ha ha! You look goofy.
Oops! ☆
THIS IS FUN! ♡
I-it's so high!
Yeah! This is the tippy-top!

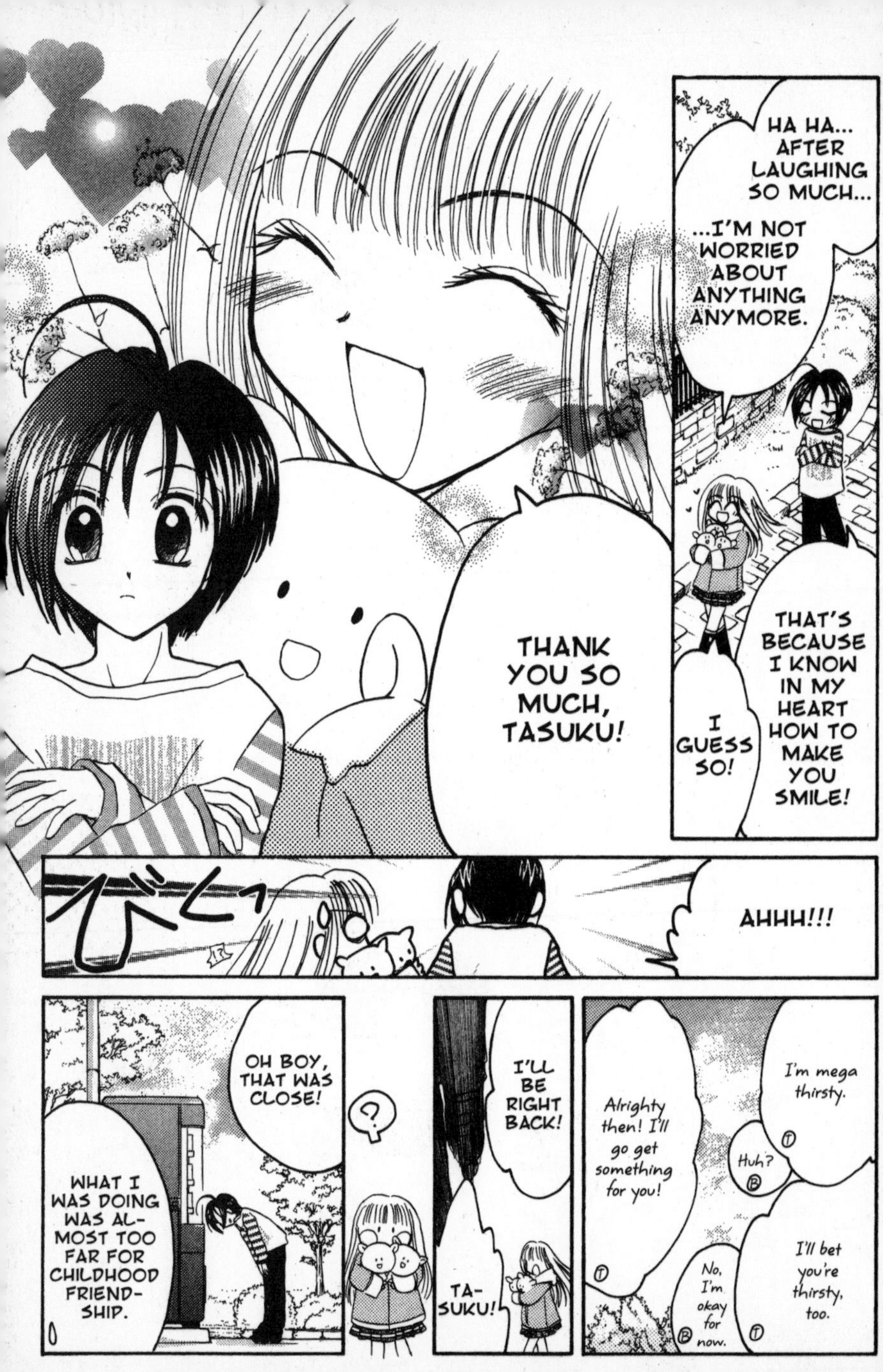
HA HA... AFTER LAUGHING SO MUCH...
...I'M NOT WORRIED ABOUT ANYTHING ANYMORE.
THAT'S BECAUSE I KNOW IN MY HEART HOW TO MAKE YOU SMILE!
I GUESS SO!
THANK YOU SO MUCH, TASUKU!
AHHH!!!
びくっ
I'm mega thirsty.
Huh?
I'll bet you're thirsty, too.
No, I'm okay for now.
Alrighty then! I'll go get something for you!
I'LL BE RIGHT BACK!
TA-SUKU!
?
OH BOY, THAT WAS CLOSE!
WHAT I WAS DOING WAS AL-MOST TOO FAR FOR CHILDHOOD FRIEND-SHIP.

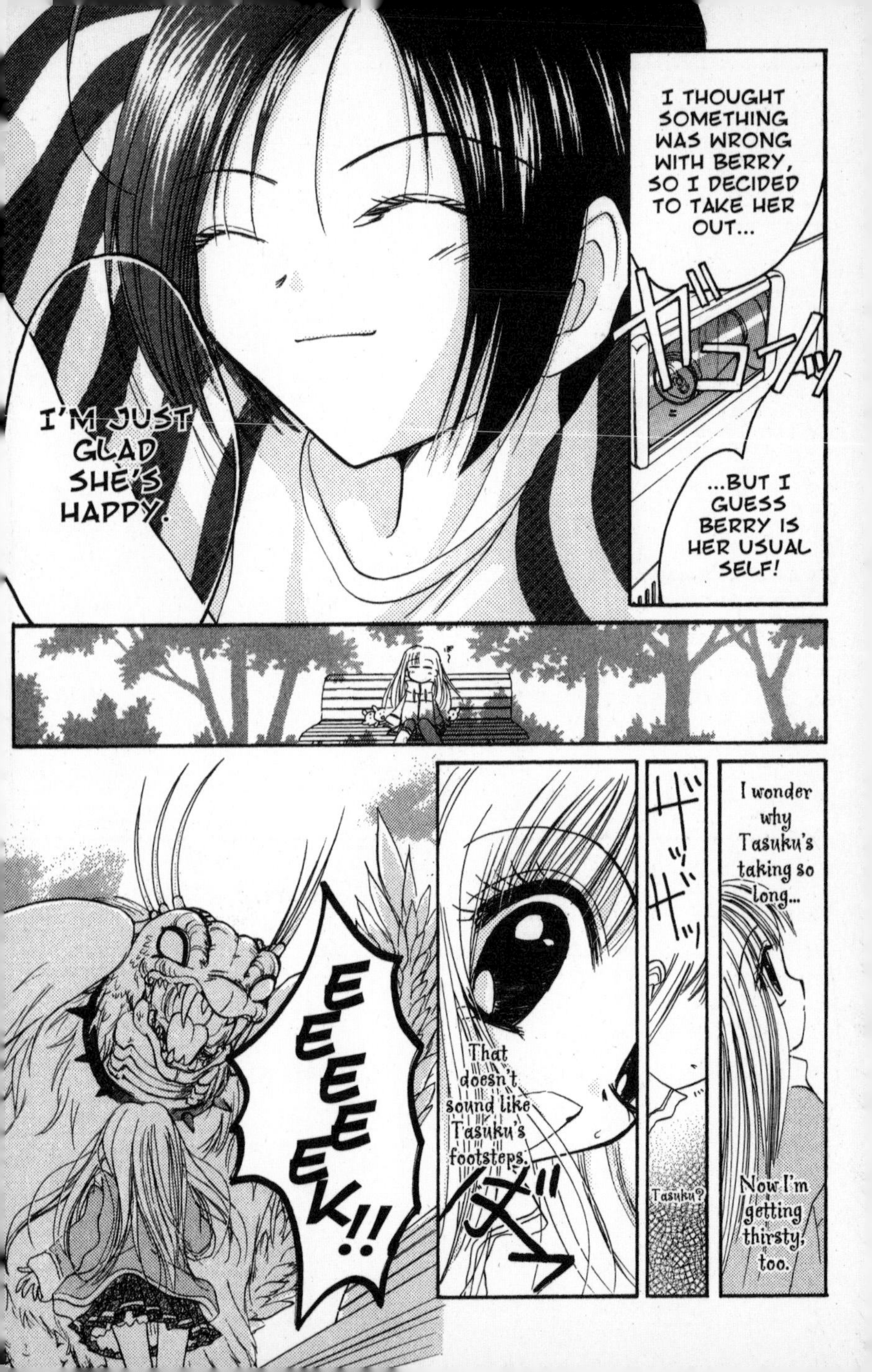

I THOUGHT SOMETHING WAS WRONG WITH BERRY, SO I DECIDED TO TAKE HER OUT...
ガコーンッ
...BUT I GUESS BERRY IS HER USUAL SELF!
I'M JUST GLAD SHE'S HAPPY.
I wonder why Tasuku's taking so long...
Now I'm getting thirsty, too.
ザッ ザッ
Tasuku?
That doesn't sound like Tasuku's footsteps.
EEEEEEK!!

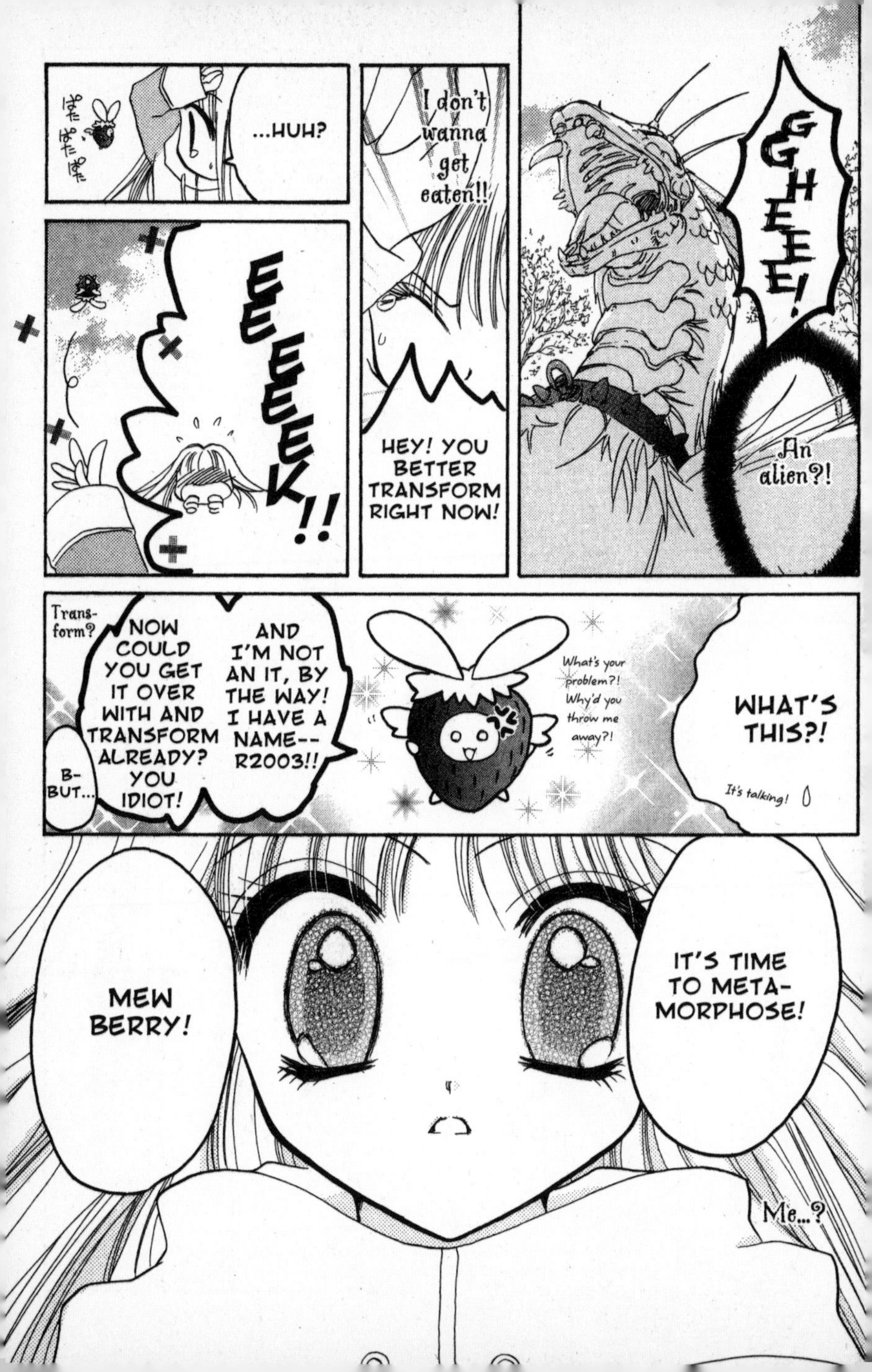
GGHEEEE!
An alien?!
I don't wanna get eaten!!
HEY! YOU BETTER TRANSFORM RIGHT NOW!
...HUH?
ぱたぱたぱた
EEEEEK!!
WHAT'S THIS?!
It's talking!
What's your problem?! Why'd you throw me away?!
AND I'M NOT AN IT, BY THE WAY! I HAVE A NAME-- R2003!!
NOW COULD YOU GET IT OVER WITH AND TRANSFORM ALREADY? YOU IDIOT!
Trans-form?
B-BUT...
IT'S TIME TO META-MORPHOSE!
MEW BERRY!
Me...?

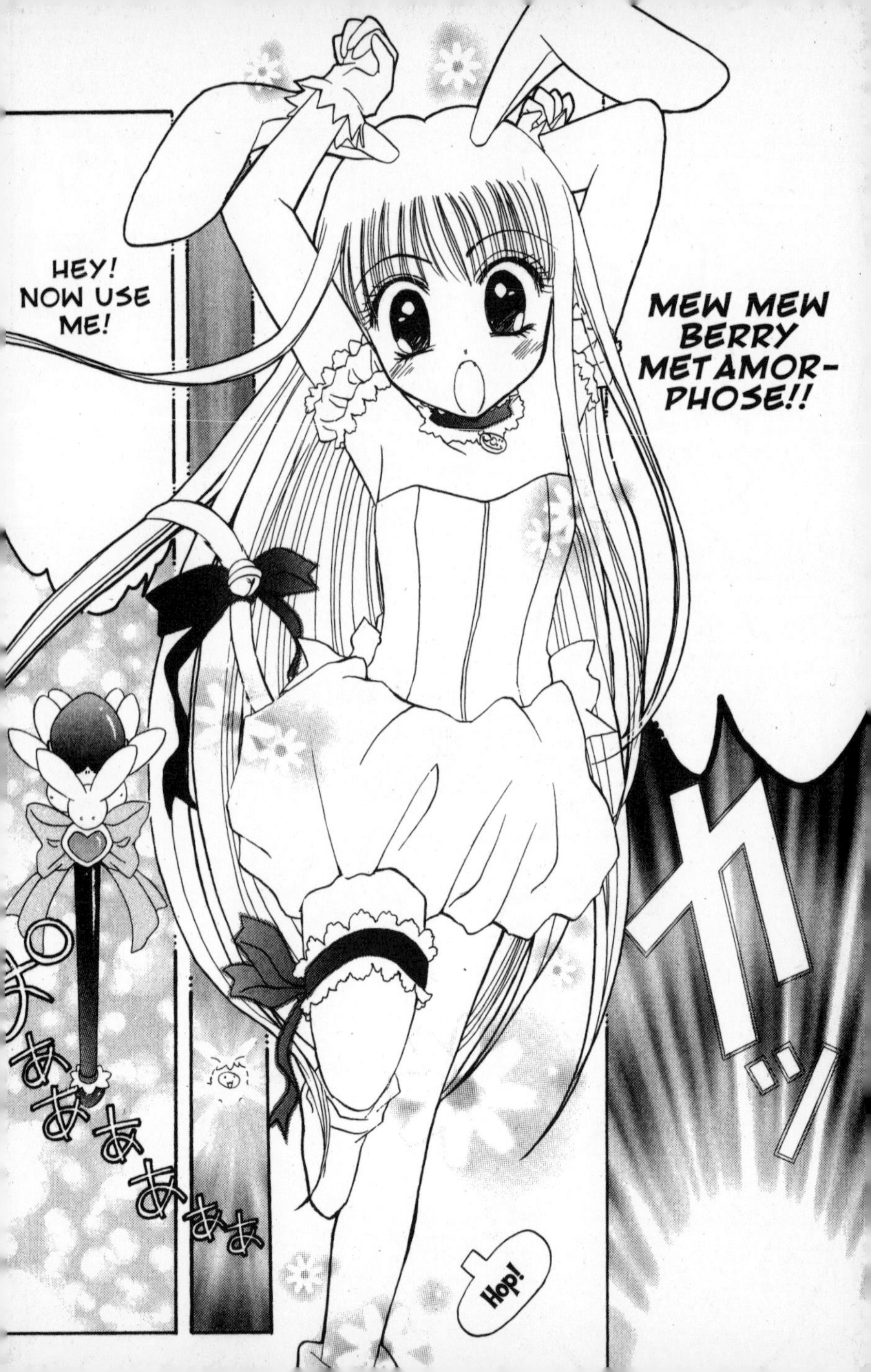
MEW MEW BERRY METAMOR-PHOSE!!
HEY! NOW USE ME!
Hop!

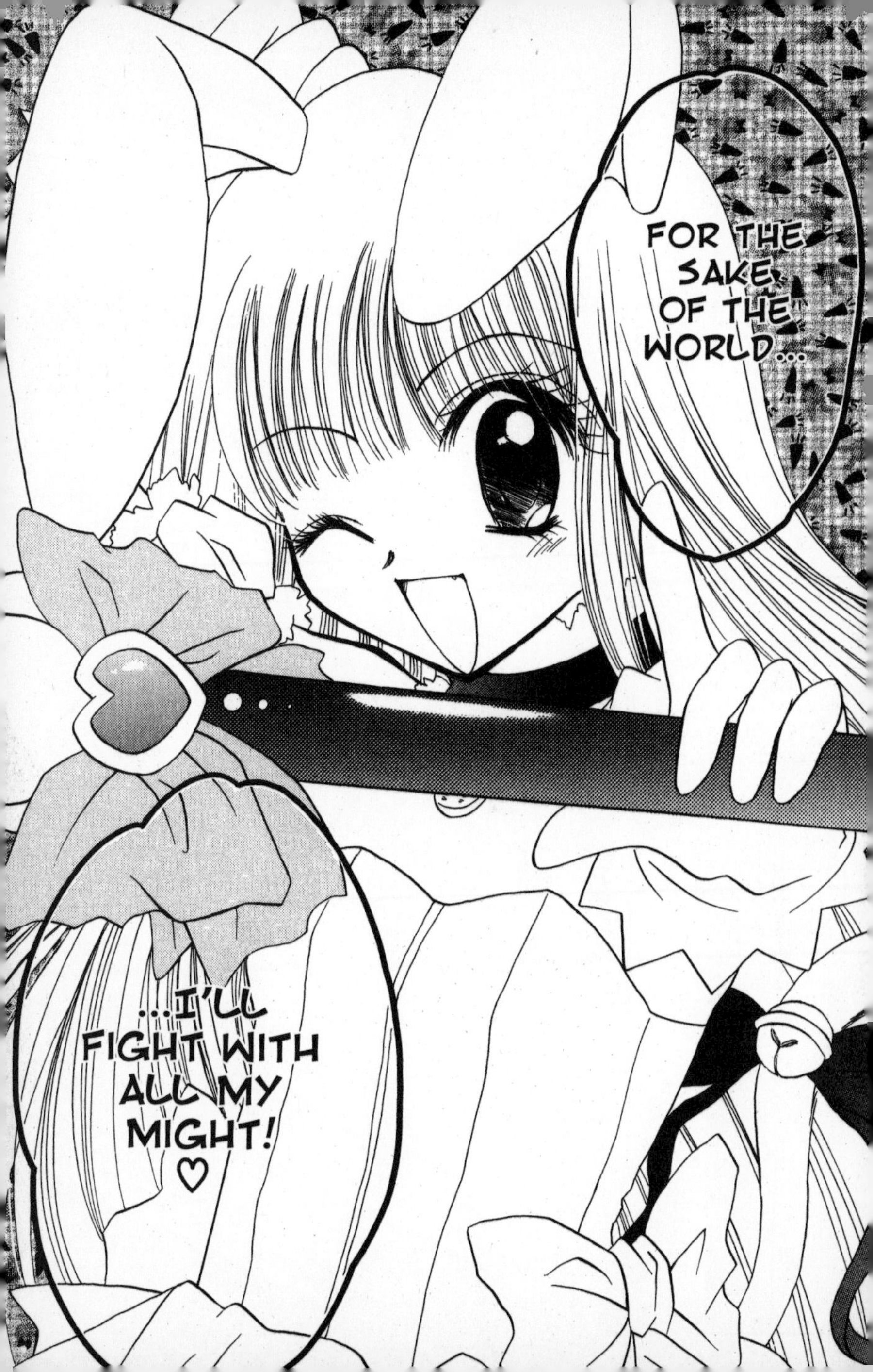
FOR THE SAKE OF THE WORLD...
...I'LL FIGHT WITH ALL MY MIGHT! ♡

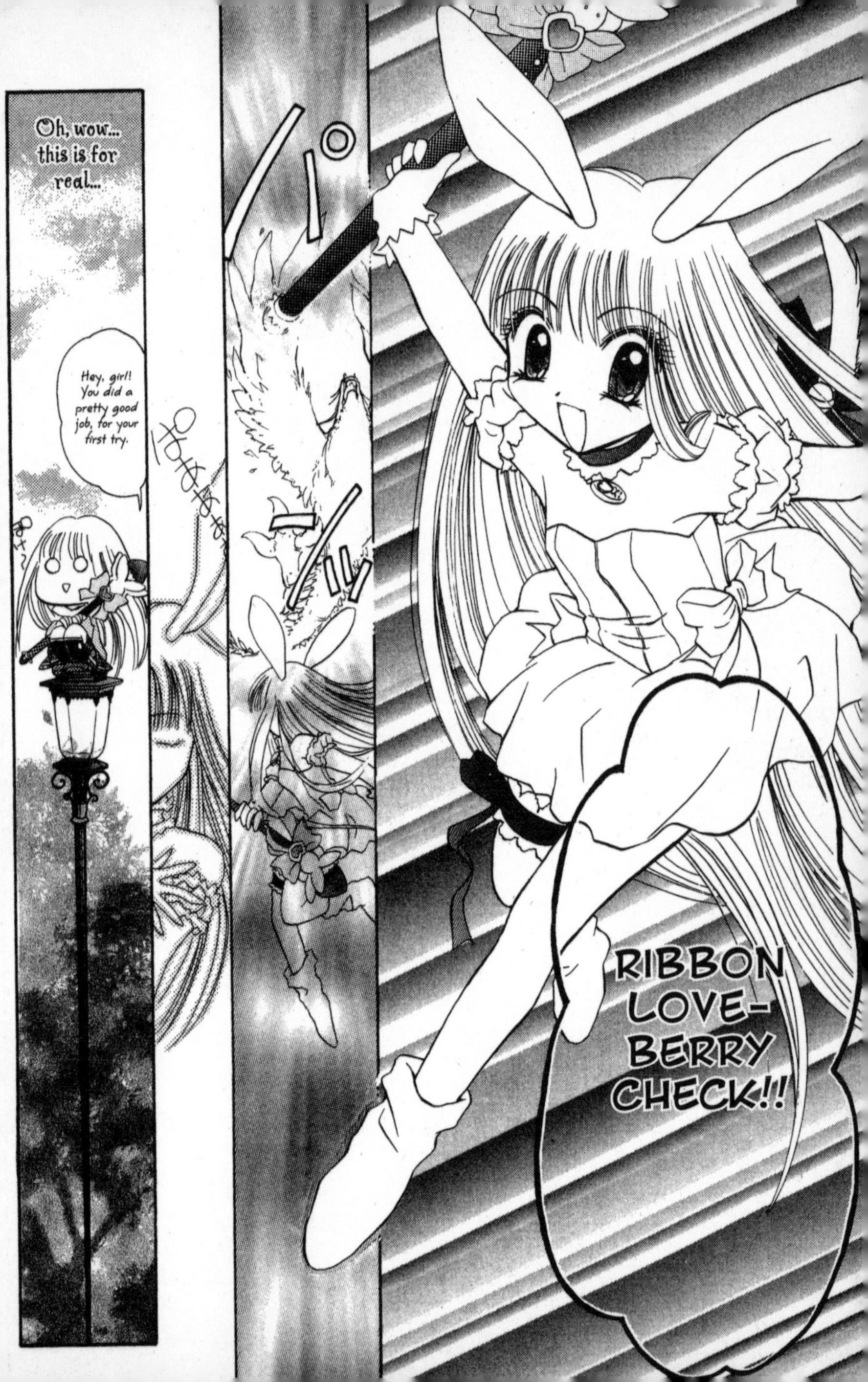
RIBBON LOVE-BERRY CHECK!!
Oh, wow... this is for real...
Hey, girl! You did a pretty good job, for your first try.

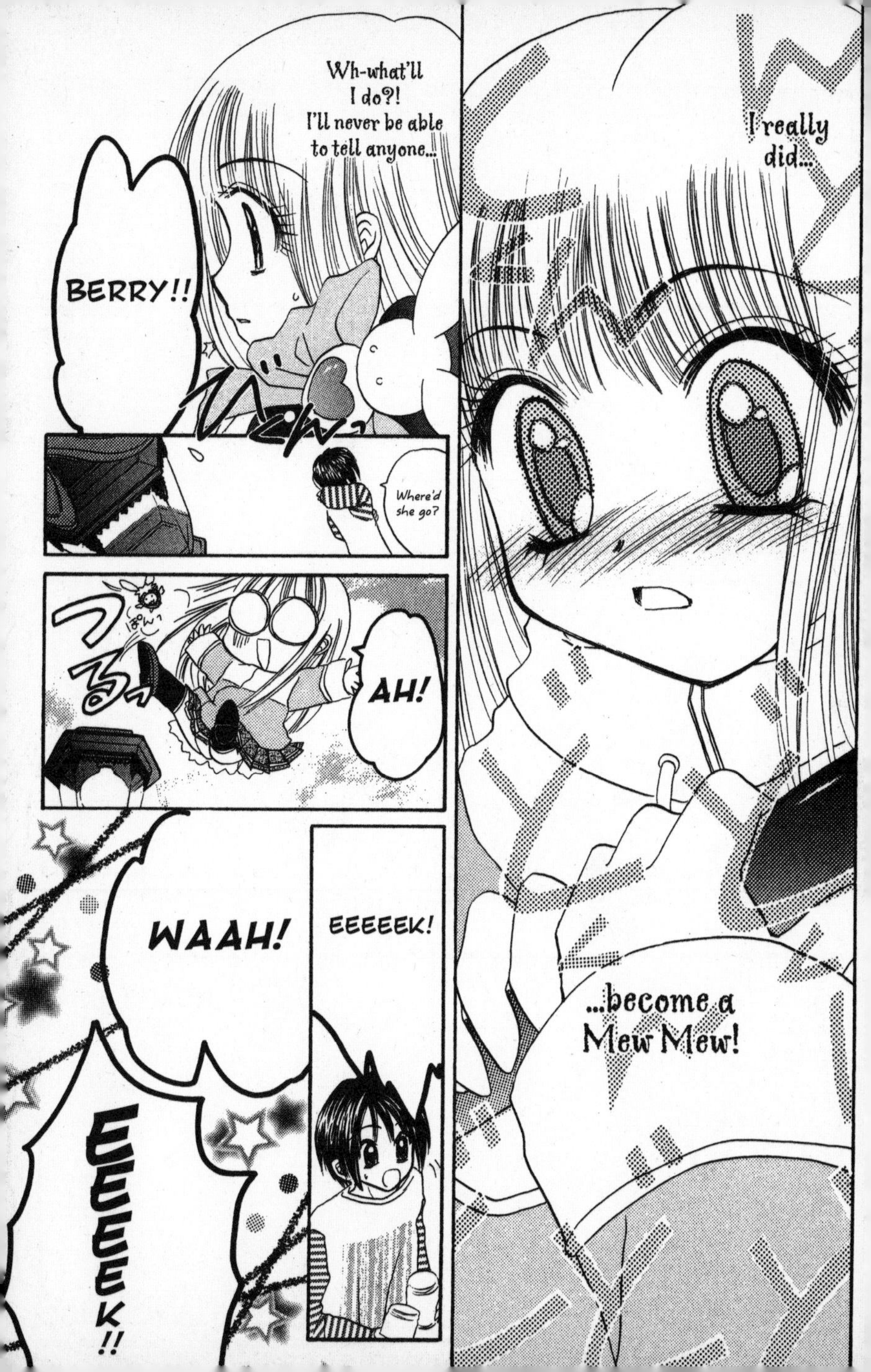
I really did...
...become a Mew Mew!
Wh-what'll I do?! I'll never be able to tell anyone...
BERRY!!
Where'd she go?
AH!
EEEEEK!
WAAH!
EEEEEEK!!

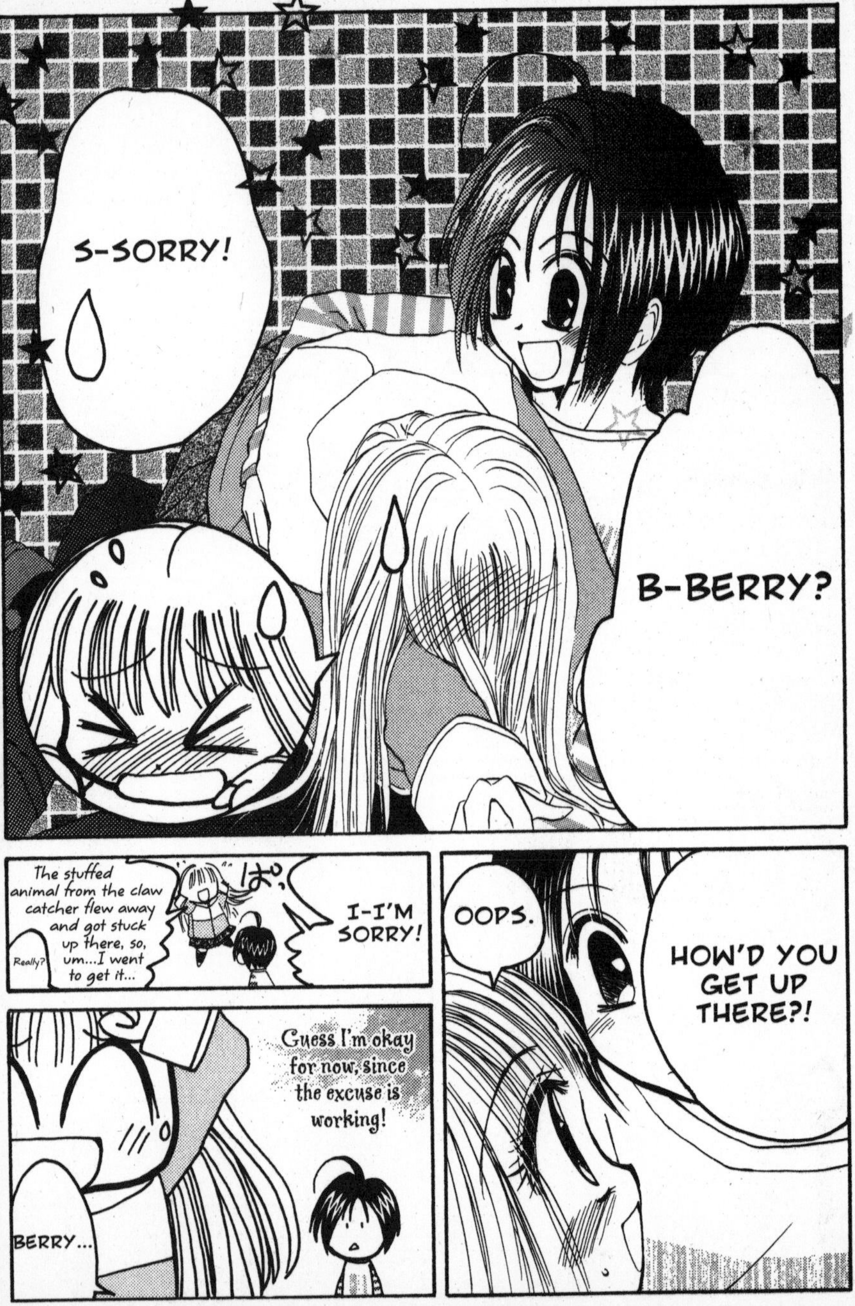
B-BERRY?
S-SORRY!
HOW'D YOU GET UP THERE?!
OOPS.
I-I'M SORRY!
ぱ
The stuffed animal from the claw catcher flew away and got stuck up there, so, um...I went to get it...
Really?
Guess I'm okay for now, since the excuse is working!
BERRY...

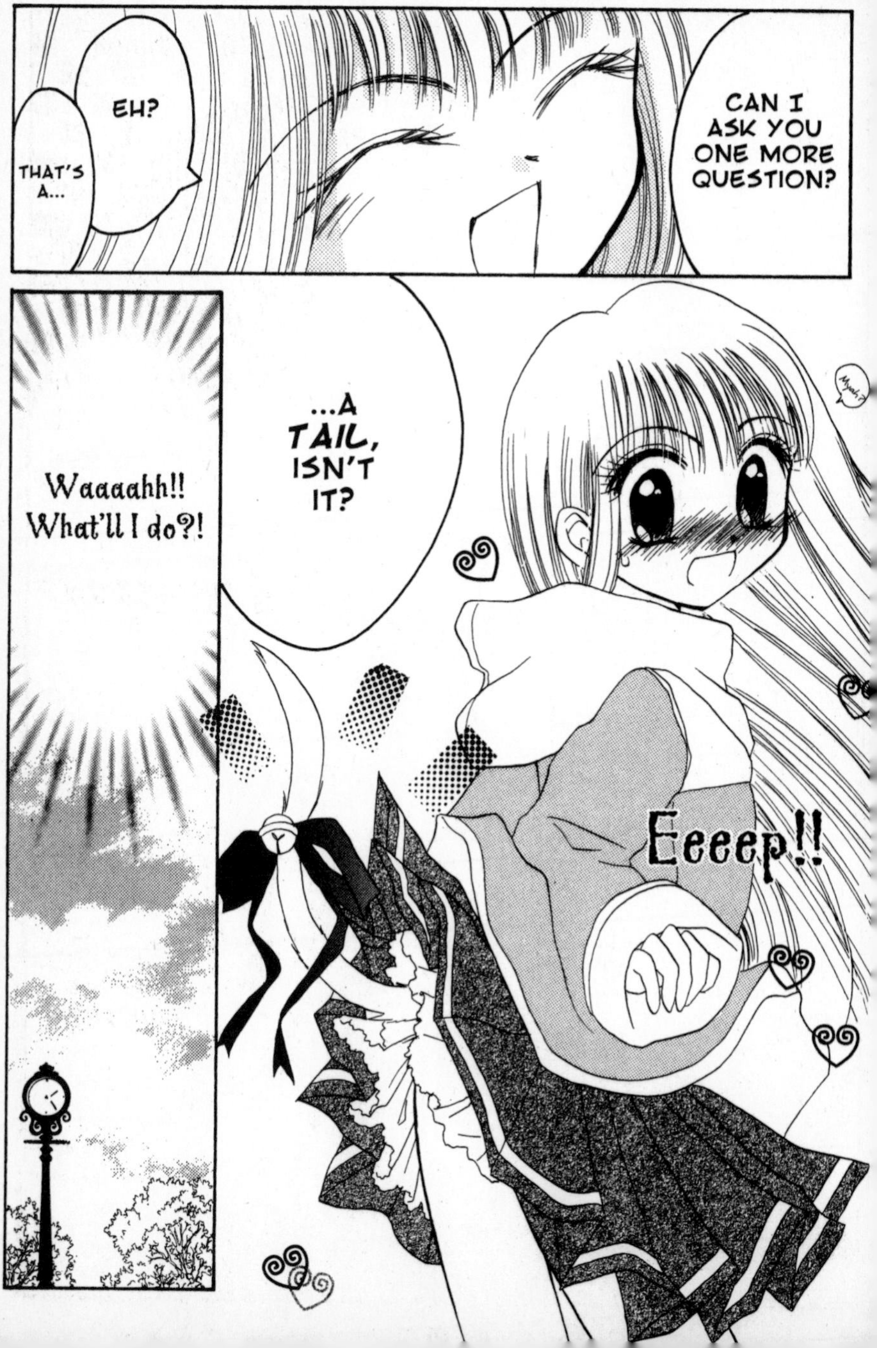

CAN I ASK YOU ONE MORE QUESTION?
EH?
THAT'S A...
...A *TAIL*, ISN'T IT?
Myah?
Eeeep!!
Waaaahh!! What'll I do?!

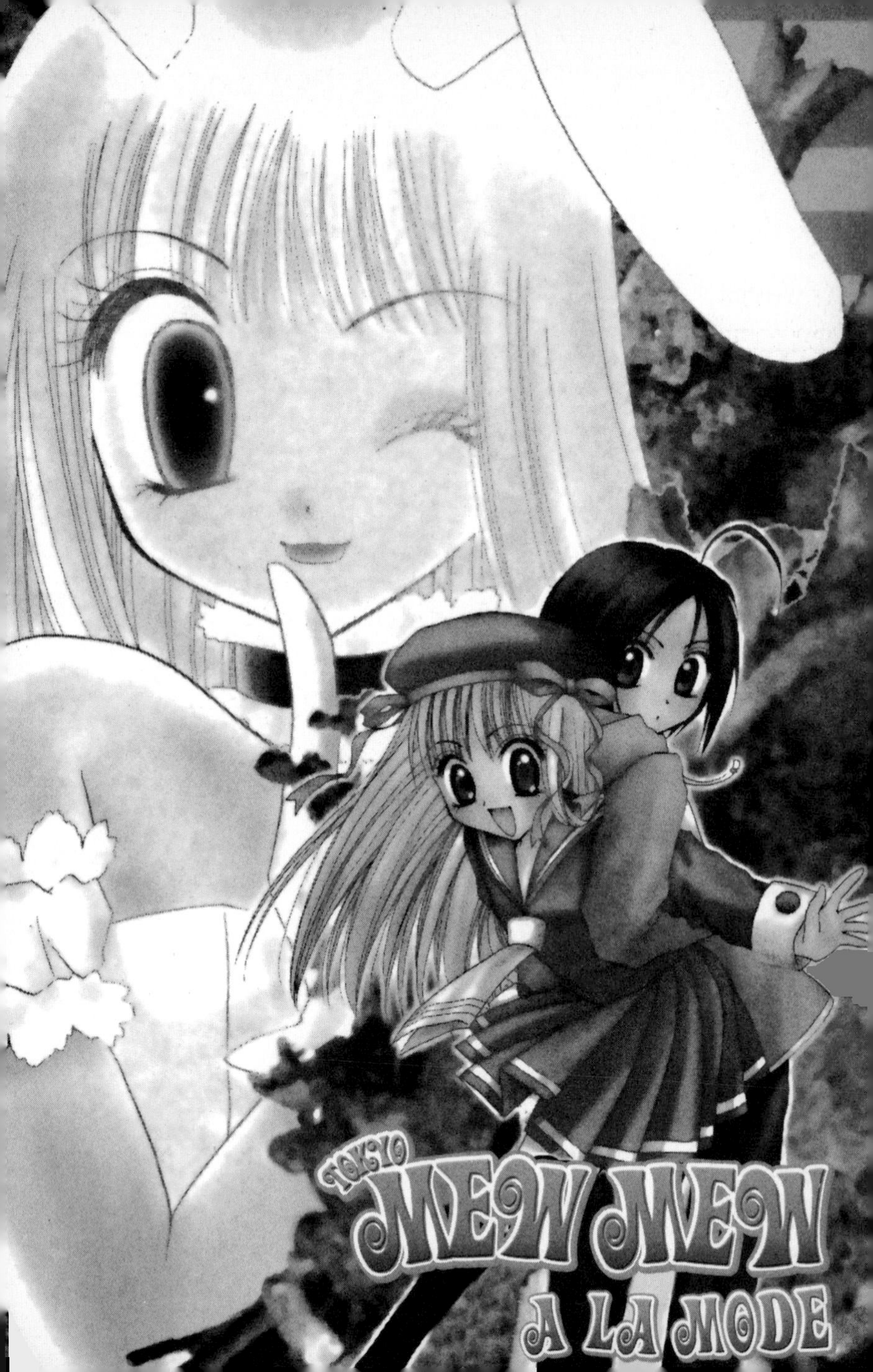
TOKYO
MEW MEW
A LA MODE

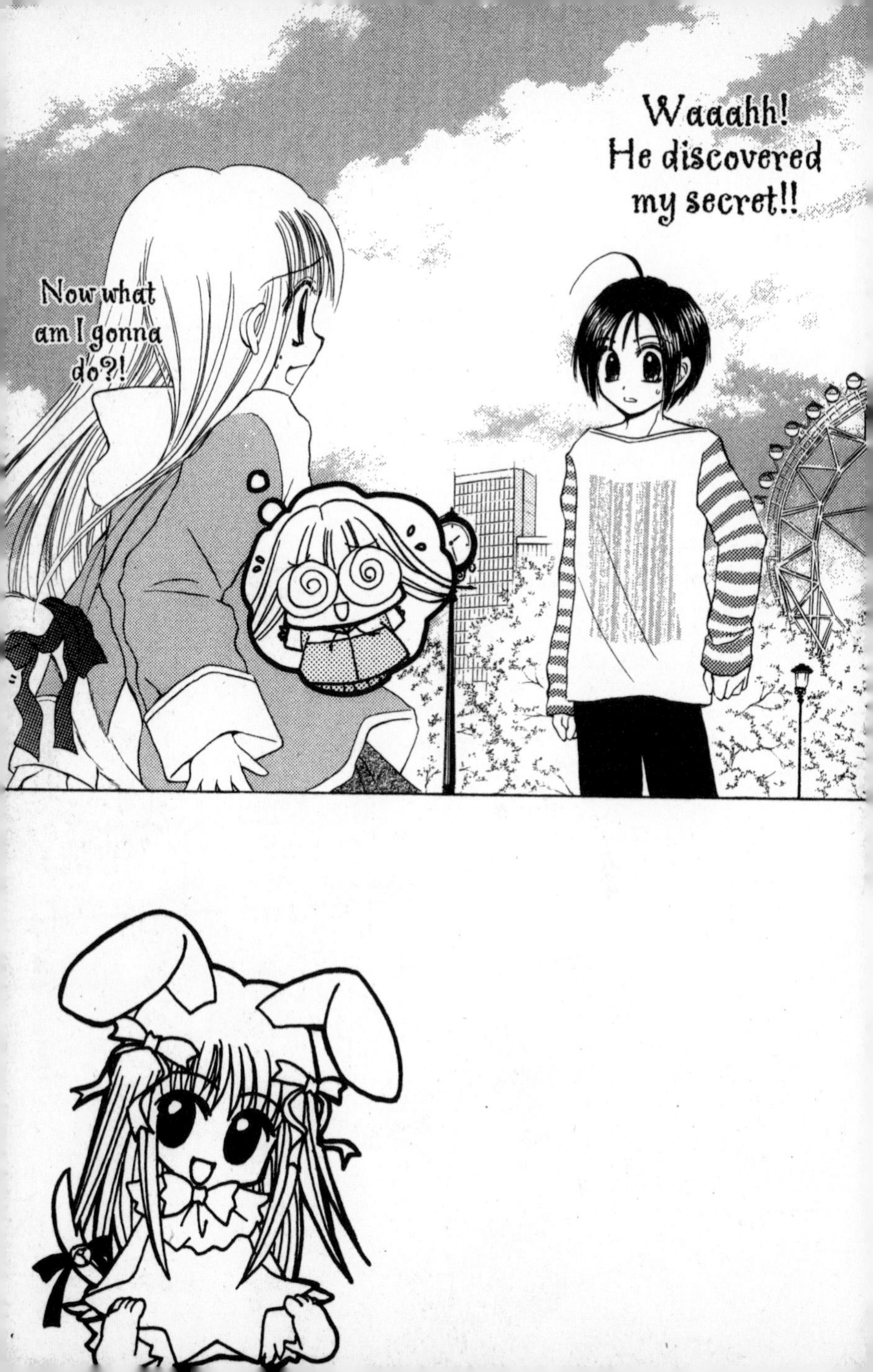
Waaahh!
He discovered
my secret!!
Now what
am I gonna
do?!

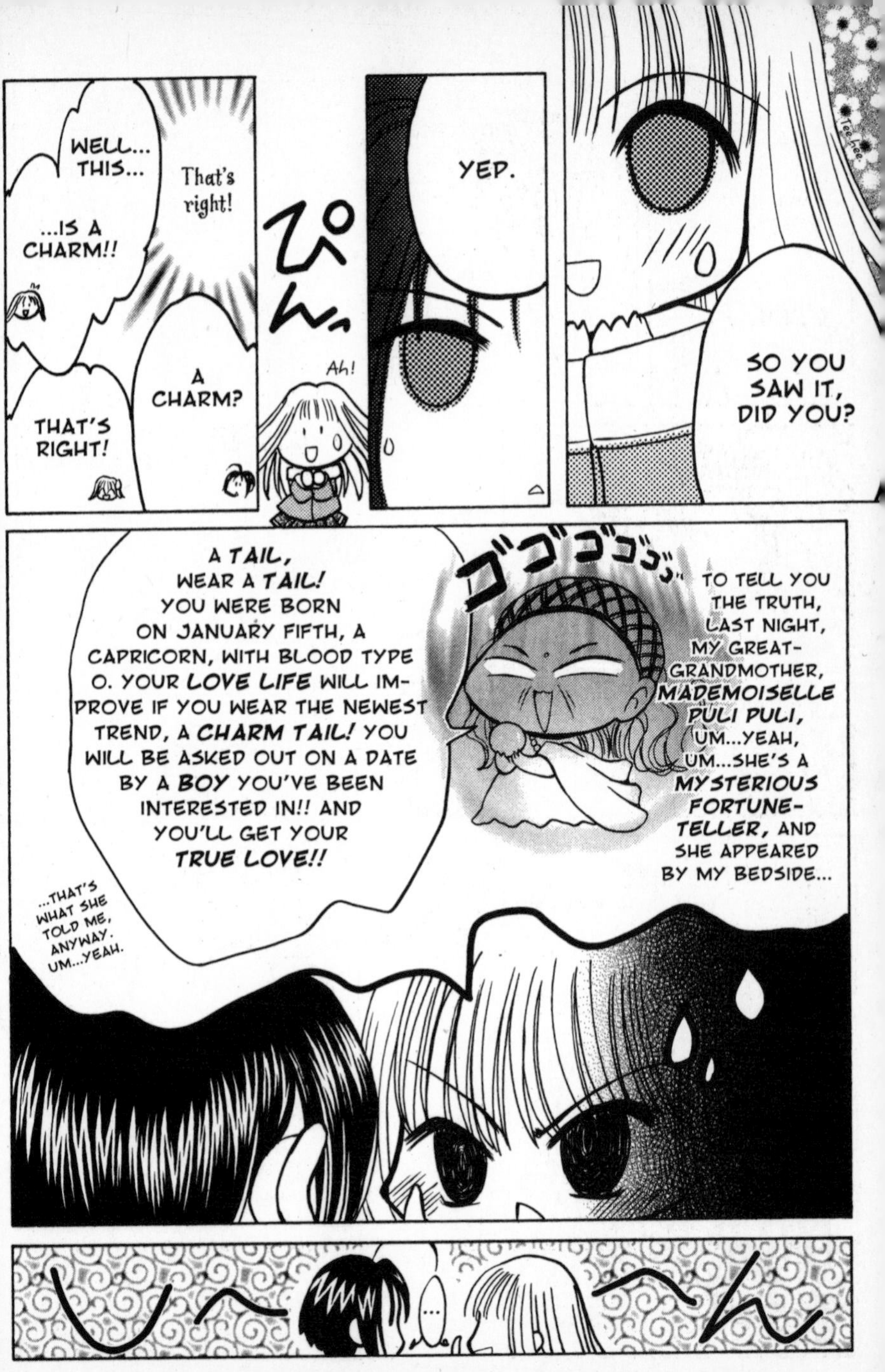
Tee hee.
SO YOU SAW IT, DID YOU?
YEP.
ぴん
Ah!
WELL... THIS...
...IS A CHARM!!
That's right!
A CHARM?
THAT'S RIGHT!
TO TELL YOU THE TRUTH, LAST NIGHT, MY GREAT-GRANDMOTHER, MADEMOISELLE PULI PULI, UM...YEAH, UM...SHE'S A MYSTERIOUS FORTUNE-TELLER, AND SHE APPEARED BY MY BEDSIDE...
A TAIL, WEAR A TAIL! YOU WERE BORN ON JANUARY FIFTH, A CAPRICORN, WITH BLOOD TYPE O. YOUR LOVE LIFE WILL IMPROVE IF YOU WEAR THE NEWEST TREND, A CHARM TAIL! YOU WILL BE ASKED OUT ON A DATE BY A BOY YOU'VE BEEN INTERESTED IN!! AND YOU'LL GET YOUR TRUE LOVE!!
...THAT'S WHAT SHE TOLD ME, ANYWAY. UM...YEAH.
...

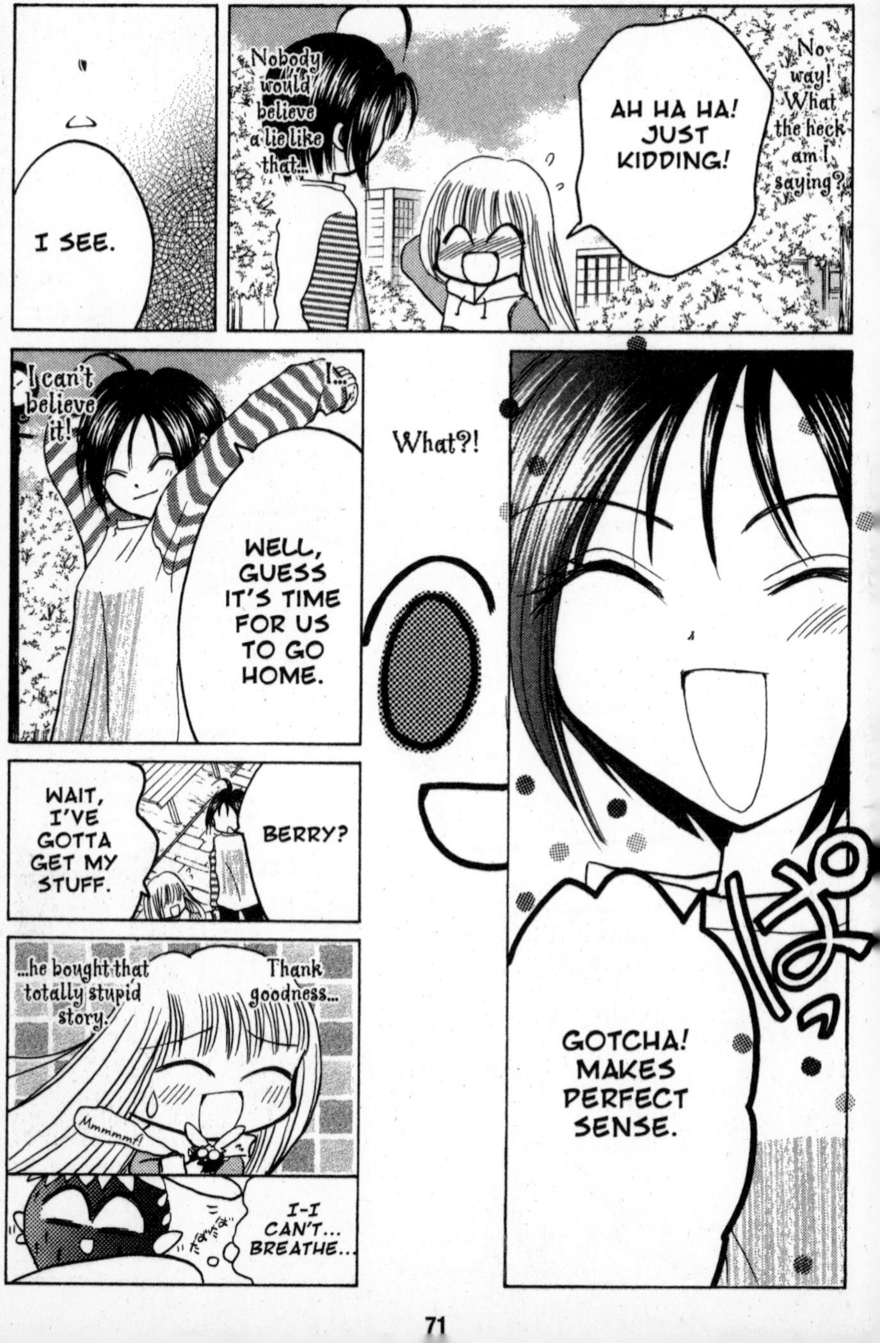

No way! What the heck am I saying?
AH HA HA! JUST KIDDING!
Nobody would believe a lie like that...
I SEE.
GOTCHA! MAKES PERFECT SENSE.
What?!
I...
I can't believe it!
WELL, GUESS IT'S TIME FOR US TO GO HOME.
BERRY?
WAIT, I'VE GOTTA GET MY STUFF.
Thank goodness...
...he bought that totally stupid story.
Mmmmmf!
I-I CAN'T... BREATHE...

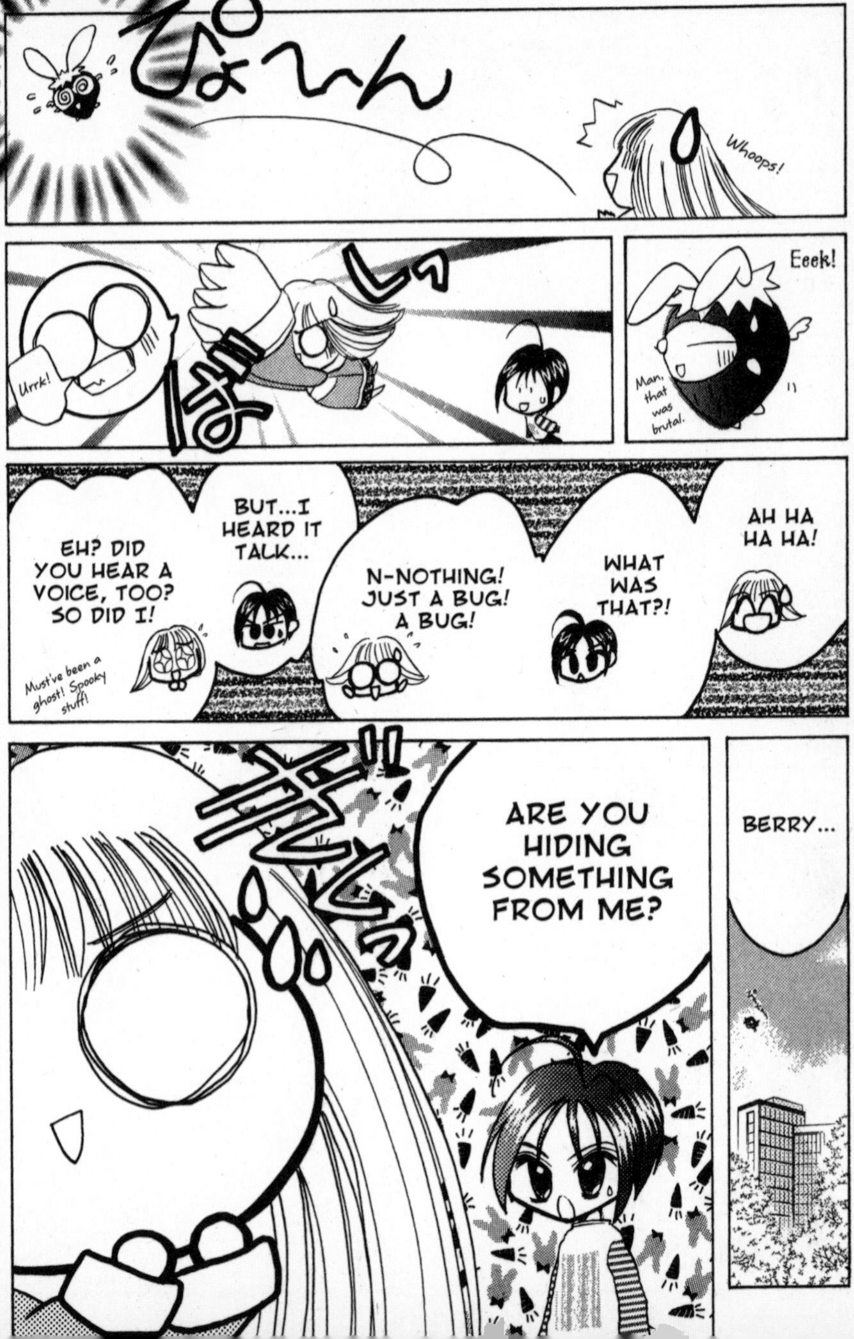
Whoops!
Eeek!
Man, that was brutal.
Urrk!
AH HA HA HA!
WHAT WAS THAT?!
N-NOTHING! JUST A BUG! A BUG!
BUT...I HEARD IT TALK...
EH? DID YOU HEAR A VOICE, TOO? SO DID I!
Must've been a ghost! Spooky stuff!
BERRY...
ARE YOU HIDING SOMETHING FROM ME?

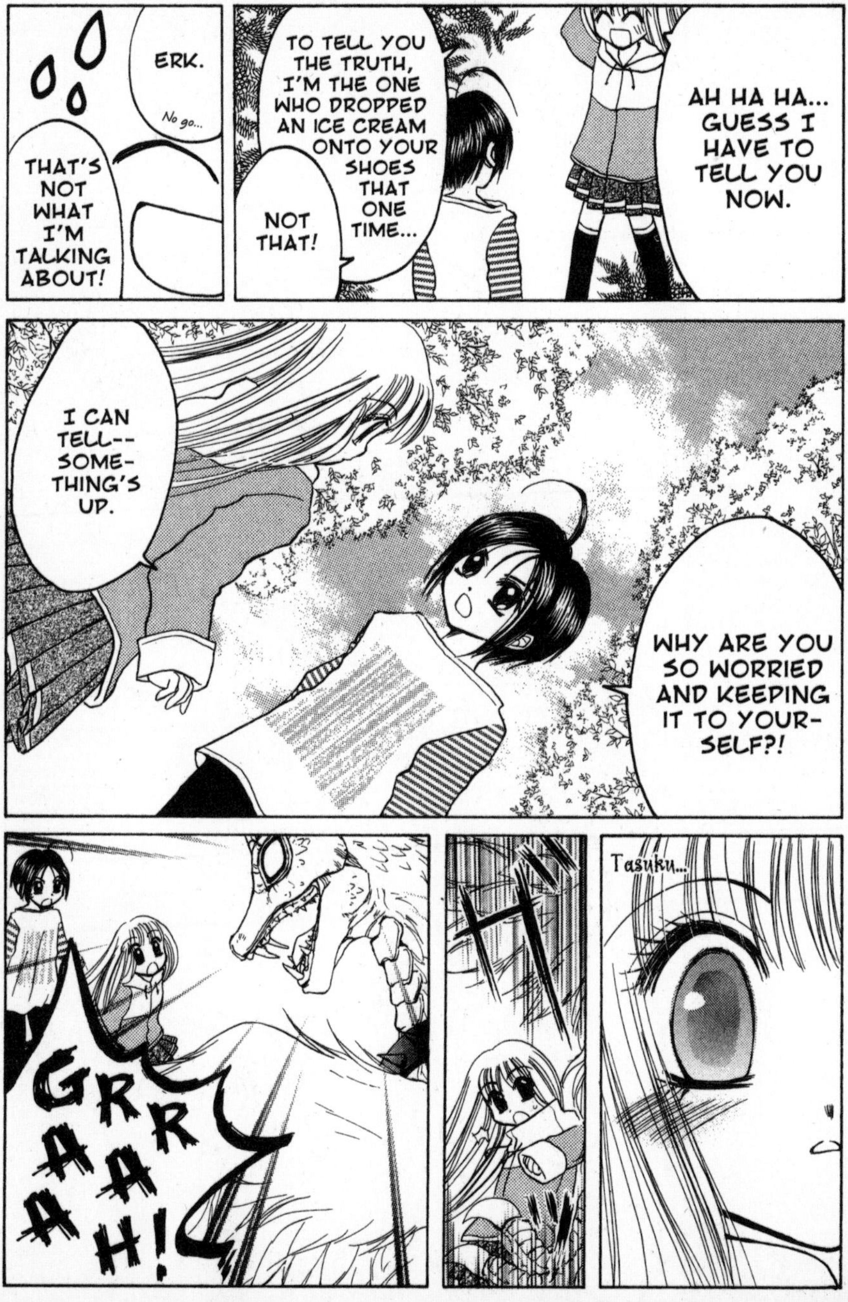
AH HA HA... GUESS I HAVE TO TELL YOU NOW.
TO TELL YOU THE TRUTH, I'M THE ONE WHO DROPPED AN ICE CREAM ONTO YOUR SHOES THAT ONE TIME...
NOT THAT!
ERK.
No go...
THAT'S NOT WHAT I'M TALKING ABOUT!
I CAN TELL--SOMETHING'S UP.
WHY ARE YOU SO WORRIED AND KEEPING IT TO YOUR-SELF?!
Tasuku...
GRRAAAAH!

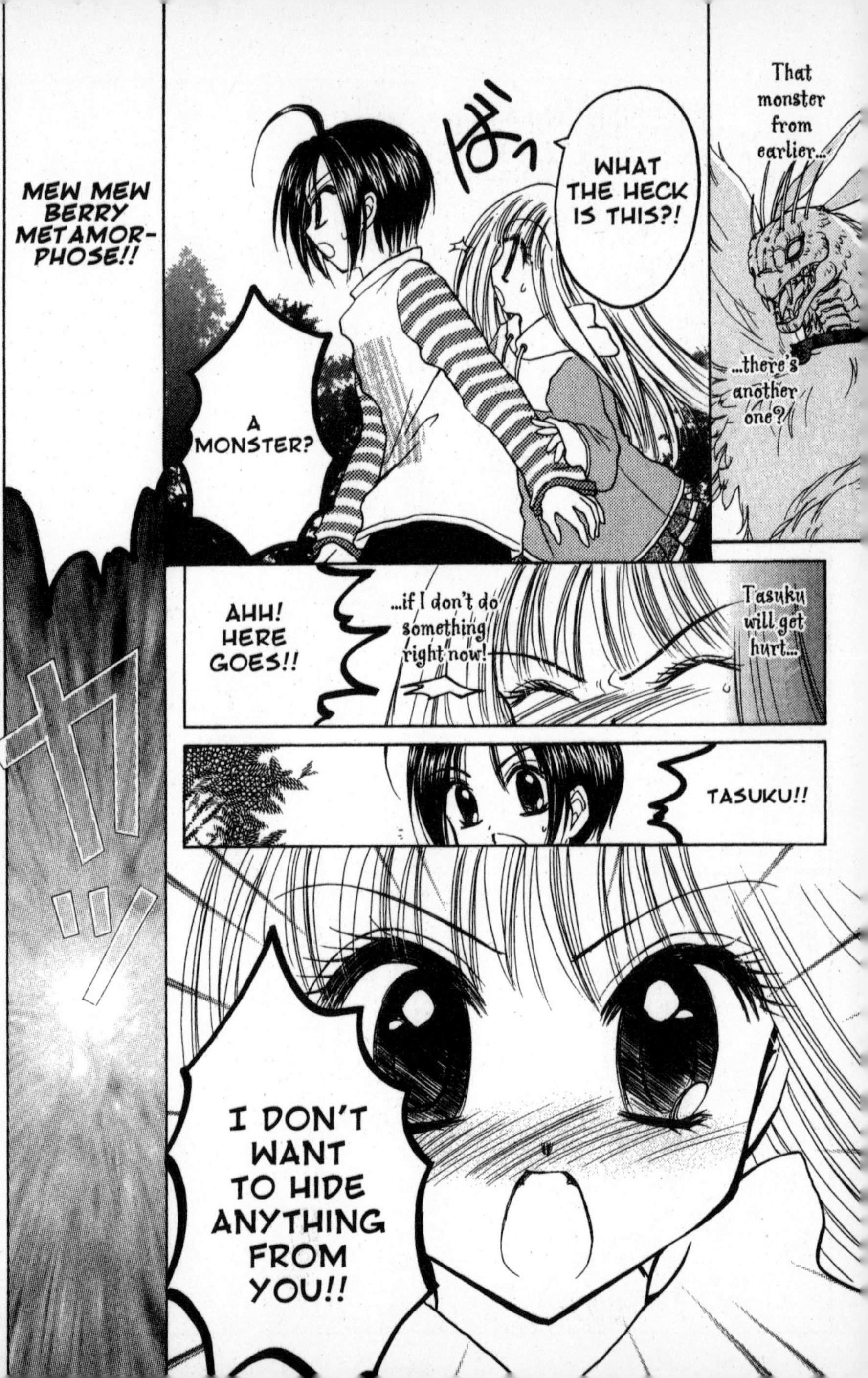
That monster from earlier...
...there's another one?
WHAT THE HECK IS THIS?!
A MONSTER?
Tasuku will get hurt...
...if I don't do something right now!
AHH! HERE GOES!!
TASUKU!!
I DON'T WANT TO HIDE ANYTHING FROM YOU!!
MEW MEW BERRY METAMORPHOSE!!

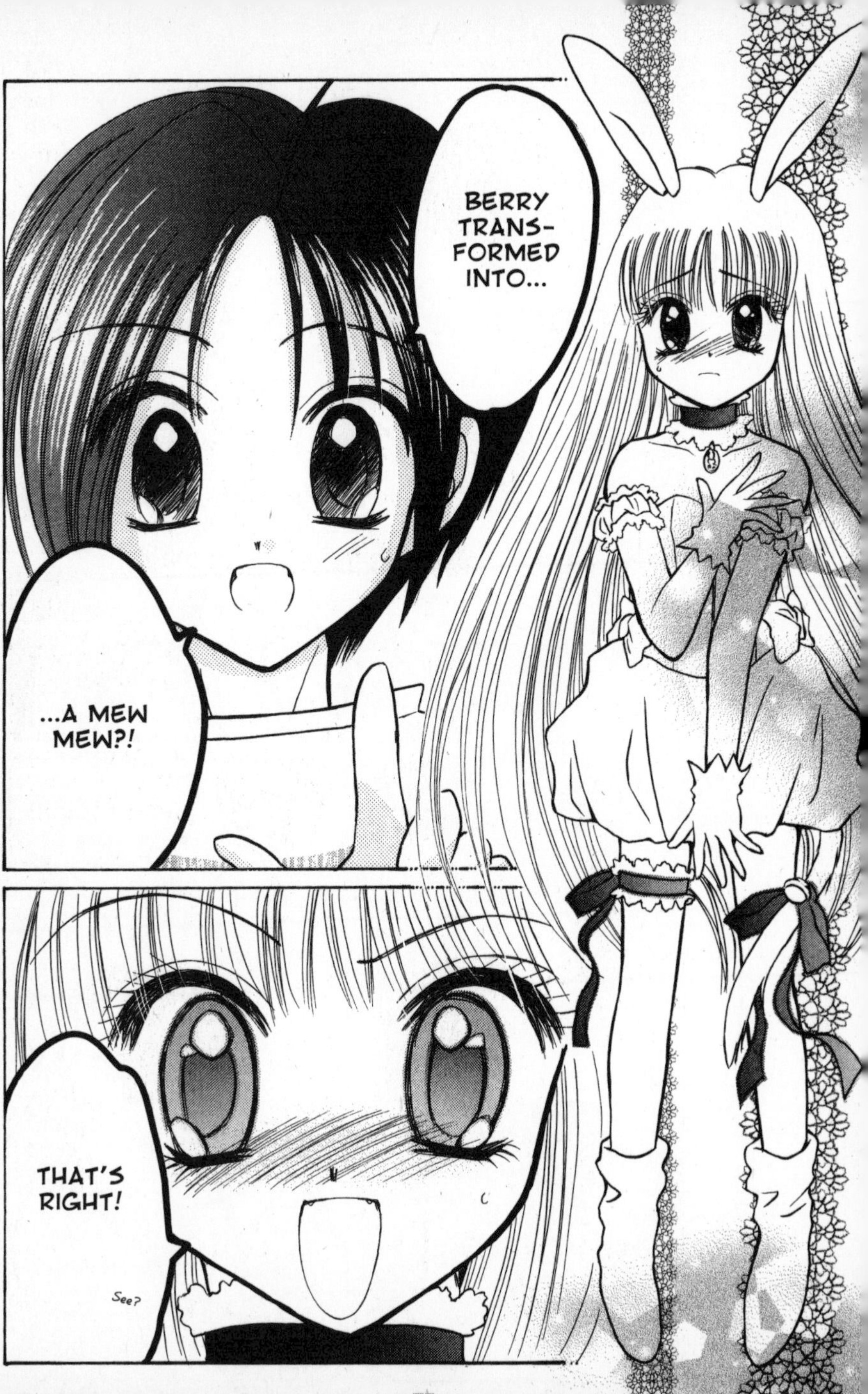
BERRY TRANSFORMED INTO...
...A MEW MEW?!
THAT'S RIGHT!
See?

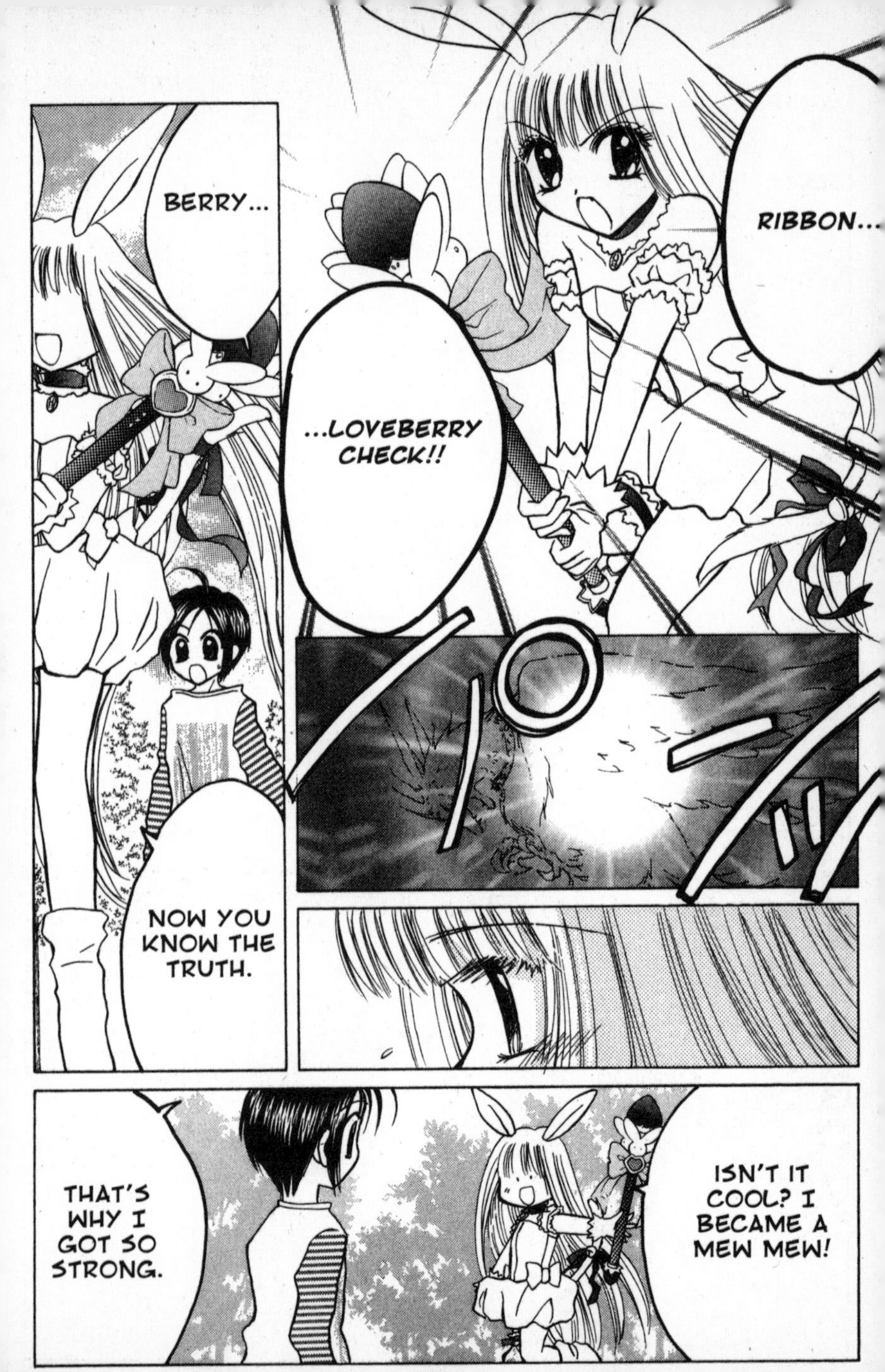
RIBBON...
...LOVEBERRY CHECK!!
BERRY...
NOW YOU KNOW THE TRUTH.
ISN'T IT COOL? I BECAME A MEW MEW!
THAT'S WHY I GOT SO STRONG.

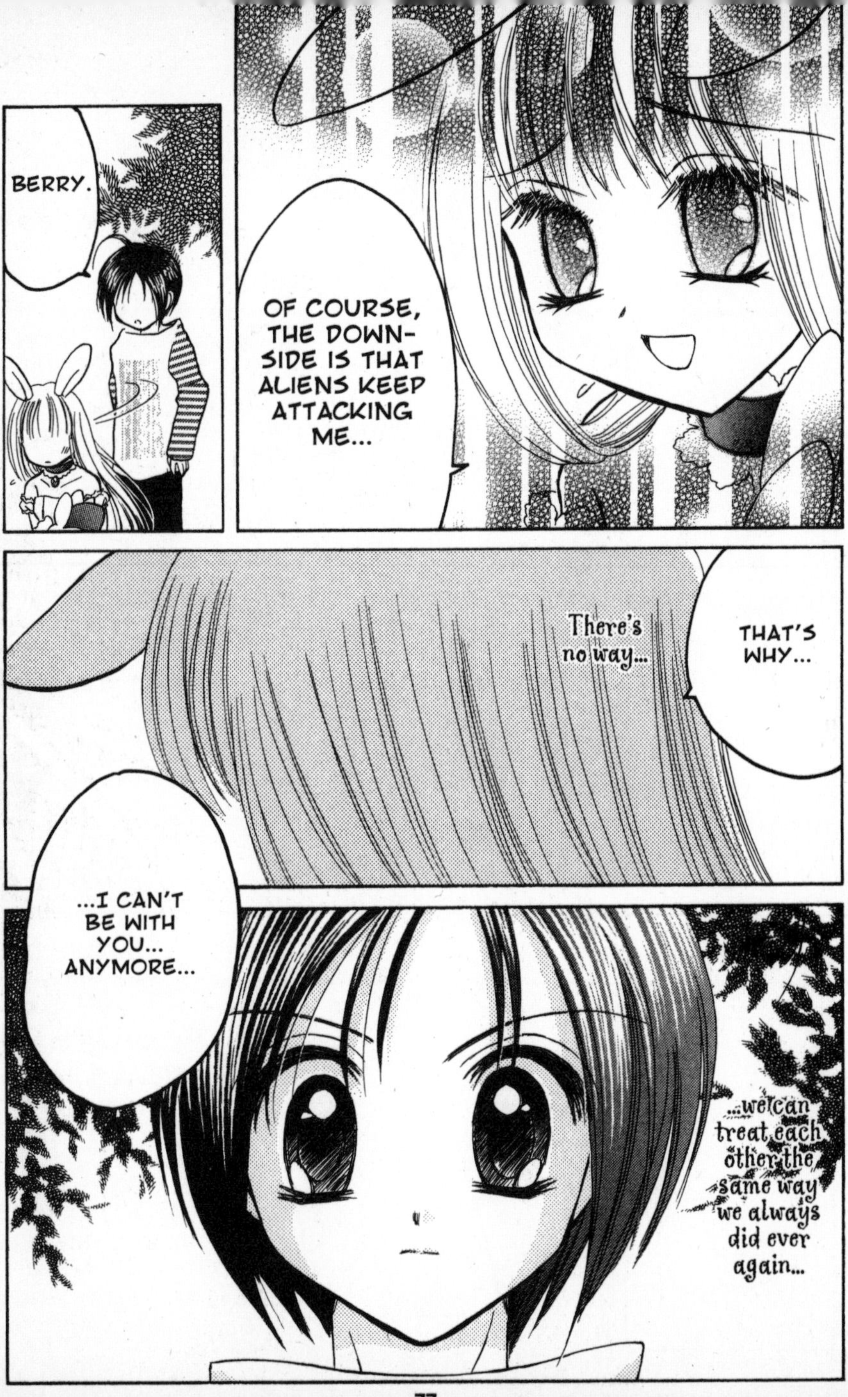
OF COURSE, THE DOWN-SIDE IS THAT ALIENS KEEP ATTACKING ME...
BERRY.
THAT'S WHY...
There's no way...
...I CAN'T BE WITH YOU... ANYMORE...
...we can treat each other the same way we always did ever again...

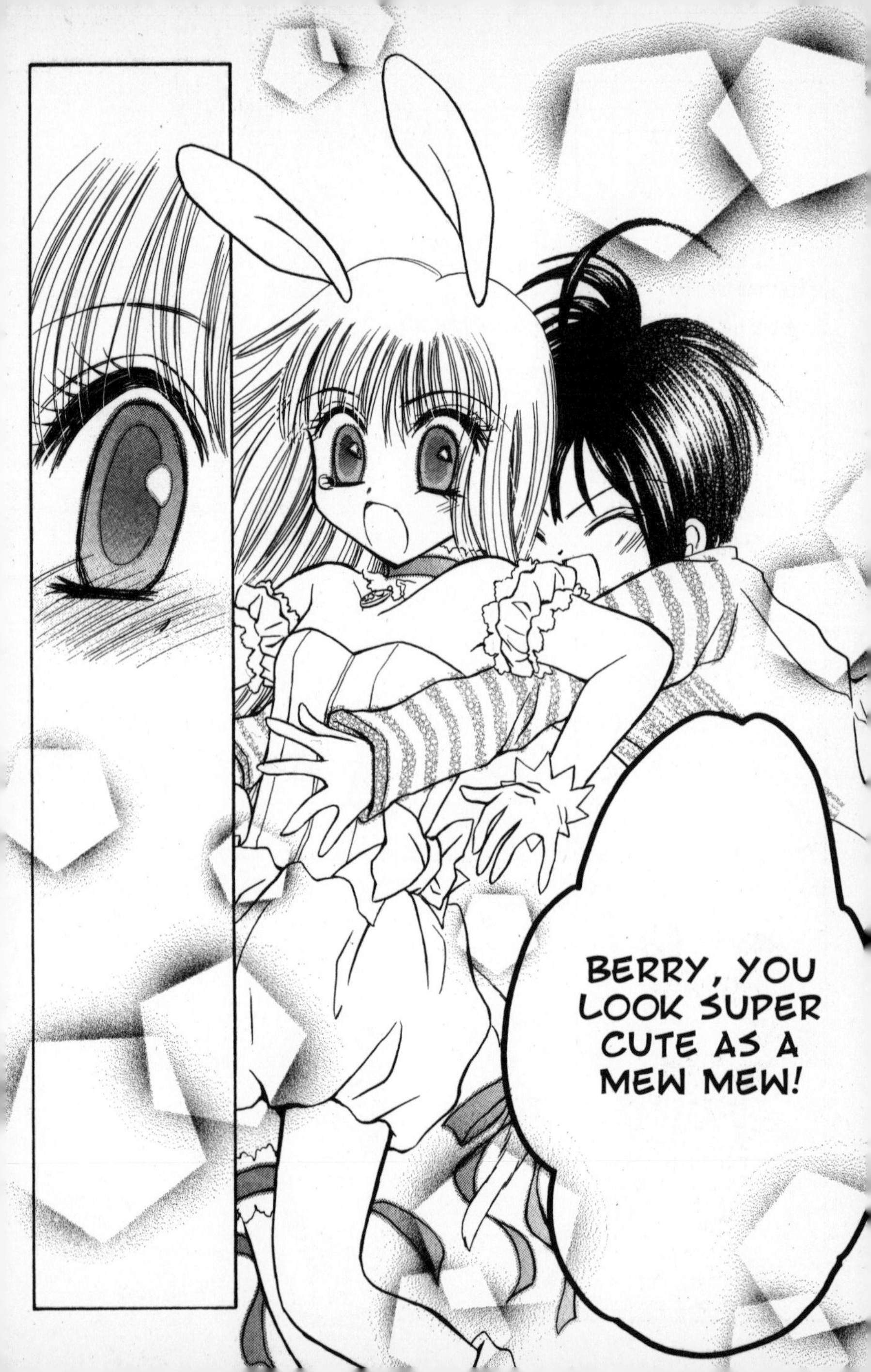
BERRY, YOU LOOK SUPER CUTE AS A MEW MEW!

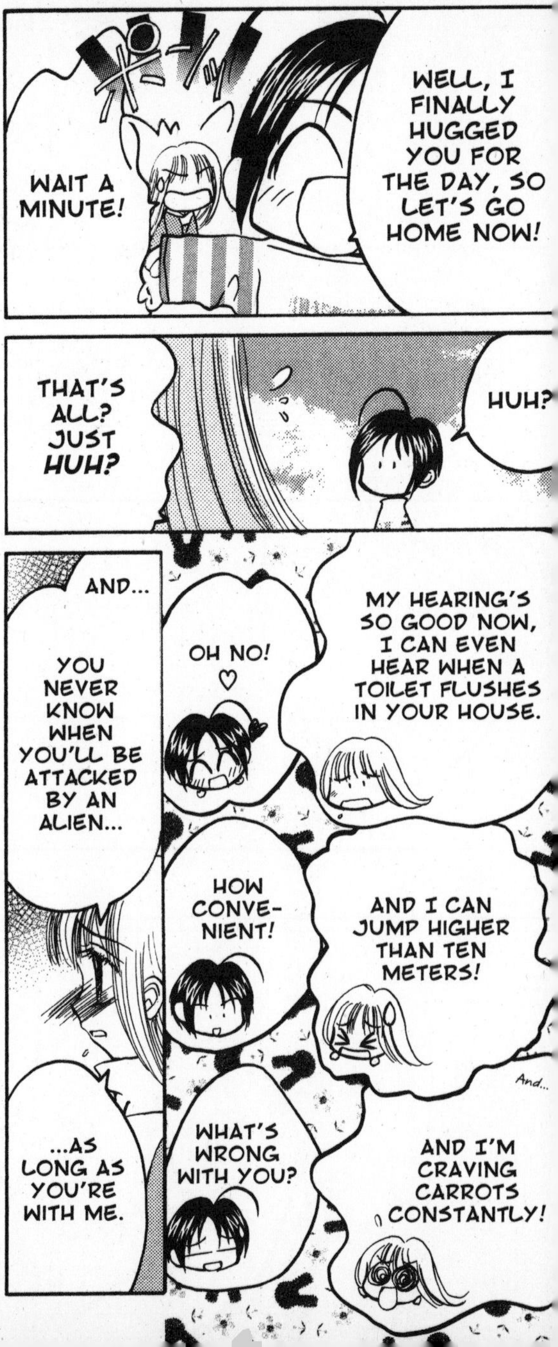
WELL, I FINALLY HUGGED YOU FOR THE DAY, SO LET'S GO HOME NOW!
WAIT A MINUTE!
HUH?
THAT'S ALL? JUST *HUH?*
MY HEARING'S SO GOOD NOW, I CAN EVEN HEAR WHEN A TOILET FLUSHES IN YOUR HOUSE.
OH NO! ♡
AND I CAN JUMP HIGHER THAN TEN METERS!
HOW CONVENIENT!
And...
AND I'M CRAVING CARROTS CONSTANTLY!
WHAT'S WRONG WITH YOU?
AND...
YOU NEVER KNOW WHEN YOU'LL BE ATTACKED BY AN ALIEN...
...AS LONG AS YOU'RE WITH ME.

3

It was one of my friends who originally gave me the idea for the casting in these illustrations. I got so psyched by the idea that I decided to draw them. Do you like them? Each character fits their role well, don't you think?

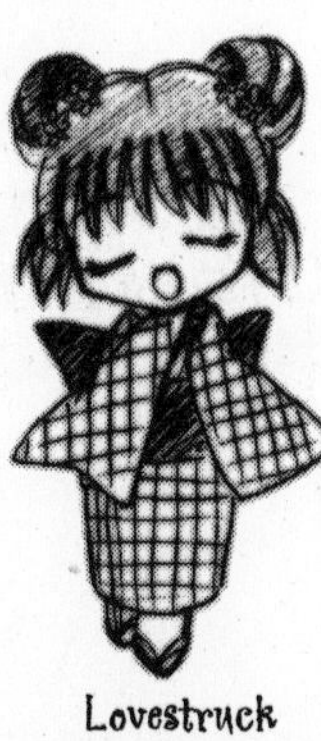

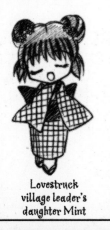

Lovestruck village leader's daughter Mint

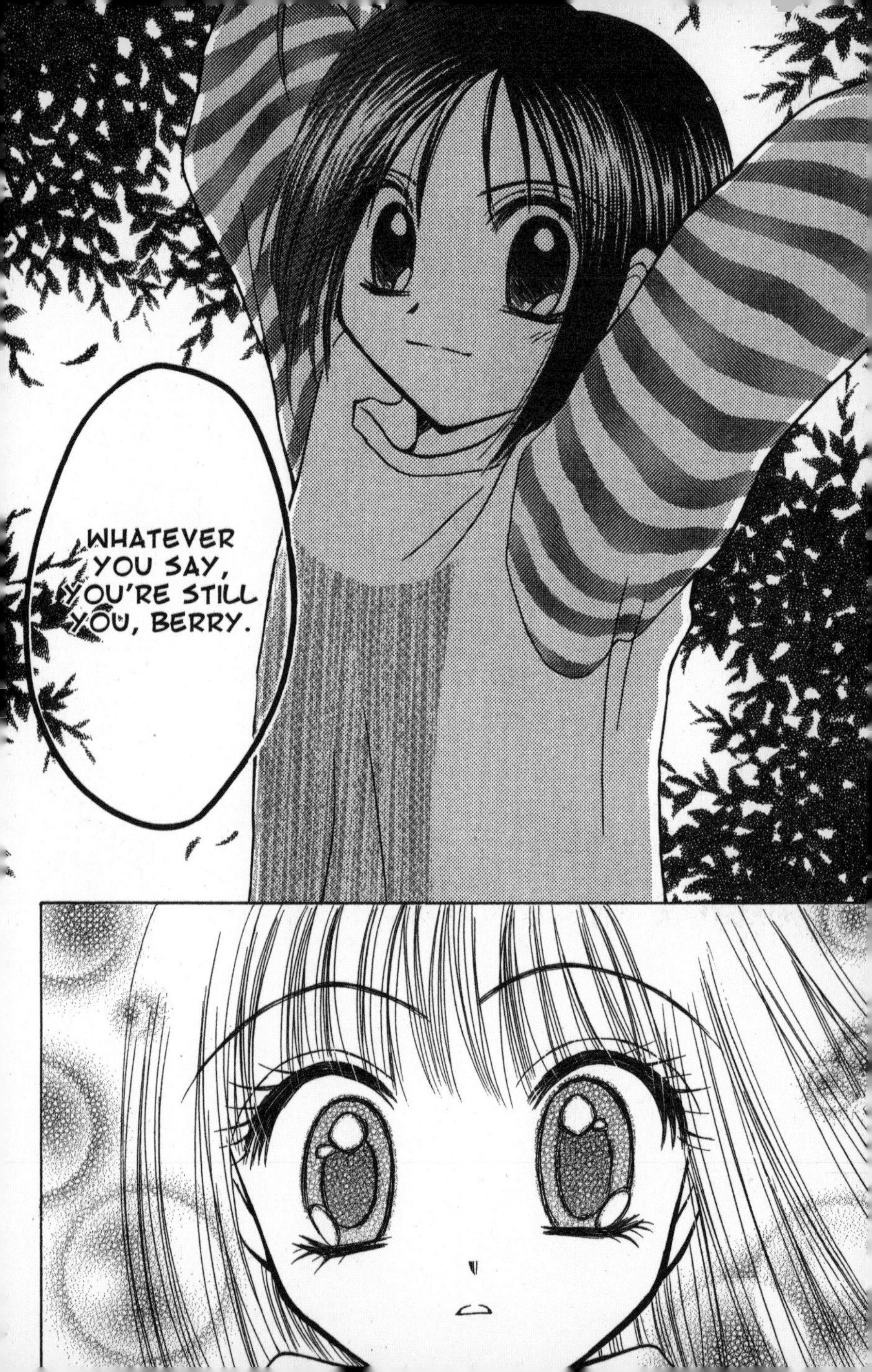
WHATEVER YOU SAY, YOU'RE STILL YOU, BERRY.

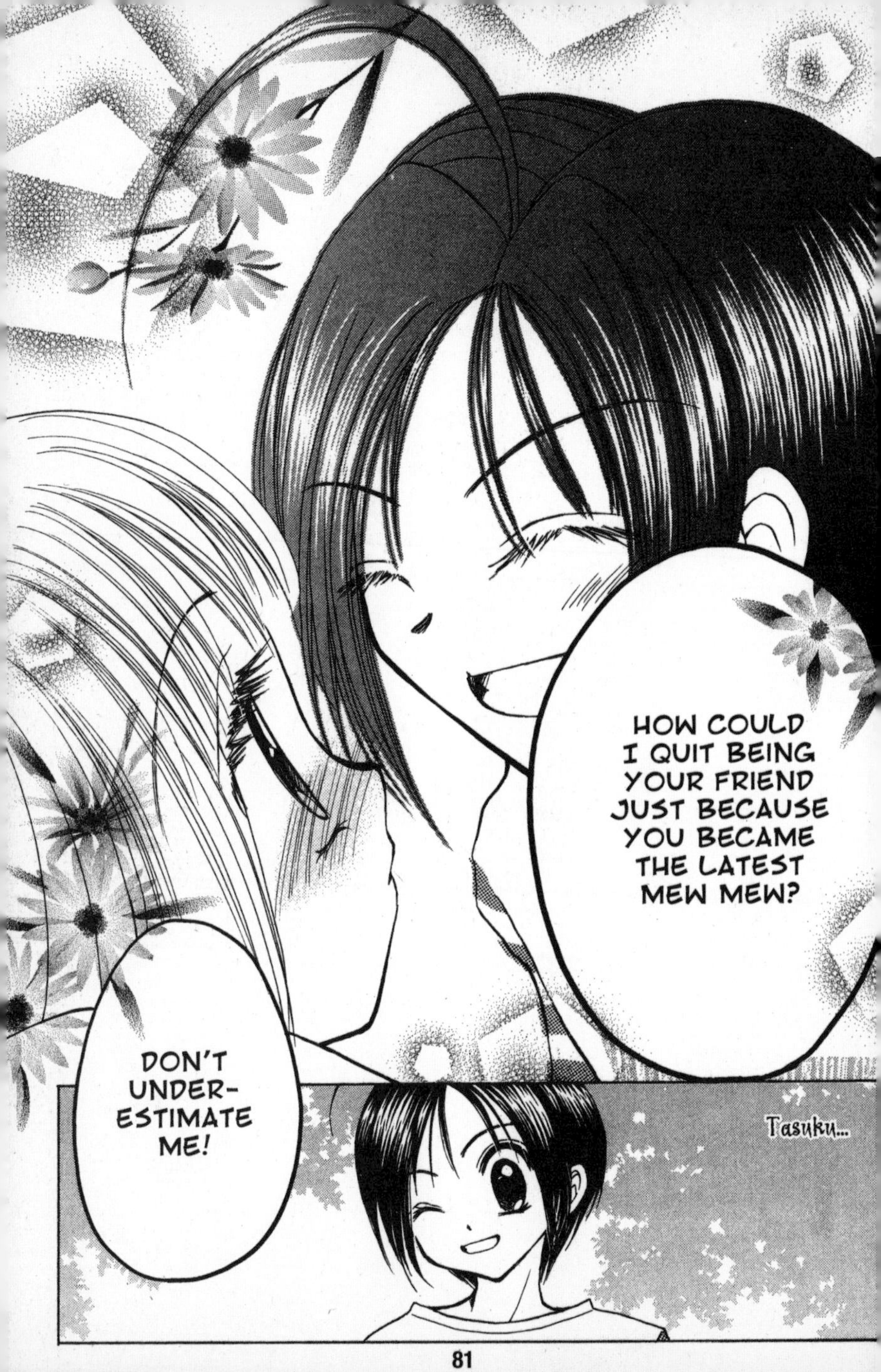
HOW COULD I QUIT BEING YOUR FRIEND JUST BECAUSE YOU BECAME THE LATEST MEW MEW?
DON'T UNDER-ESTIMATE ME!
Tasuku...

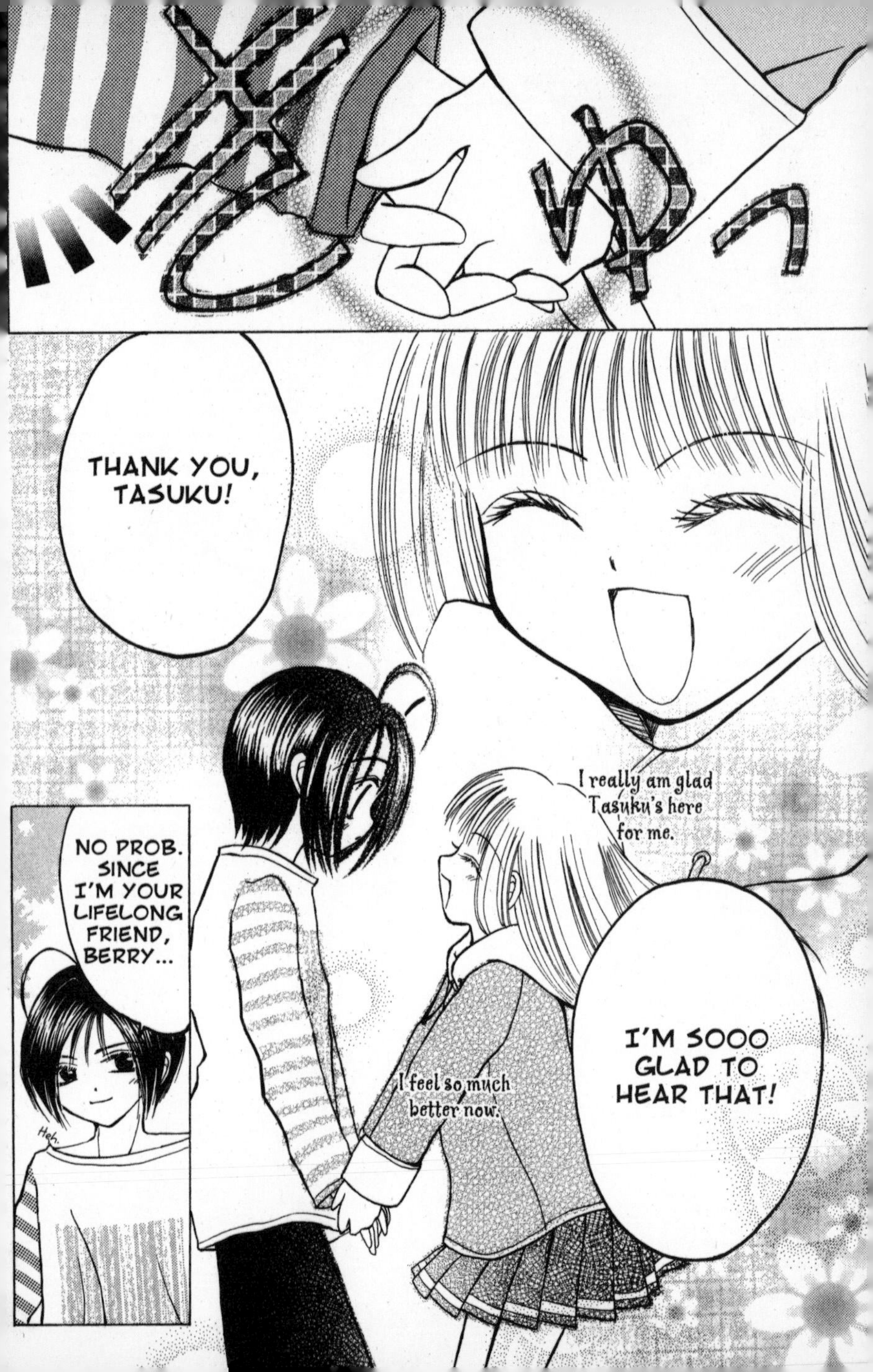
THANK YOU, TASUKU!
I really am glad Tasuku's here for me.
I'M SOOO GLAD TO HEAR THAT!
I feel so much better now.
NO PROB. SINCE I'M YOUR LIFELONG FRIEND, BERRY...
Heh.

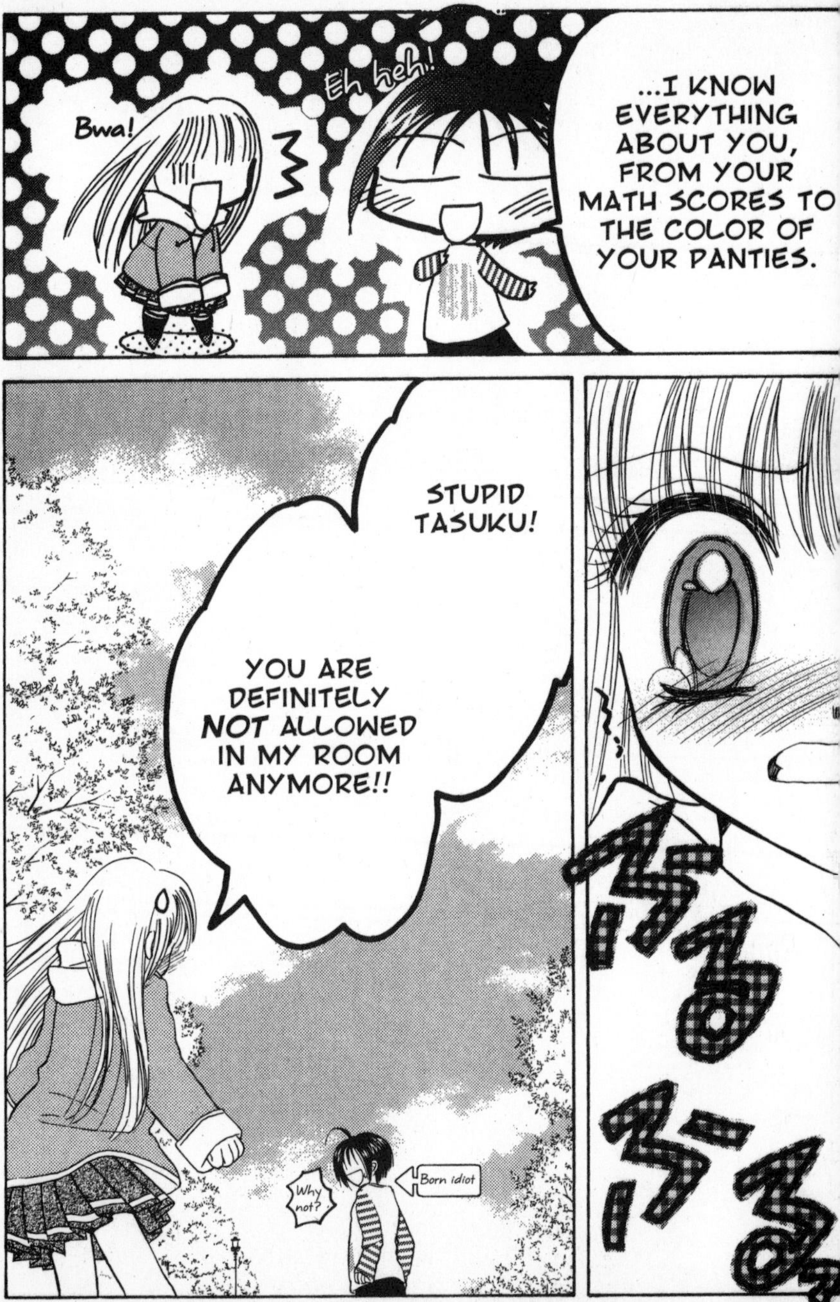
...I KNOW EVERYTHING ABOUT YOU, FROM YOUR MATH SCORES TO THE COLOR OF YOUR PANTIES.
Eh heh!
Bwa!
STUPID TASUKU!
YOU ARE DEFINITELY *NOT* ALLOWED IN MY ROOM ANYMORE!!
Born idiot
Why not?

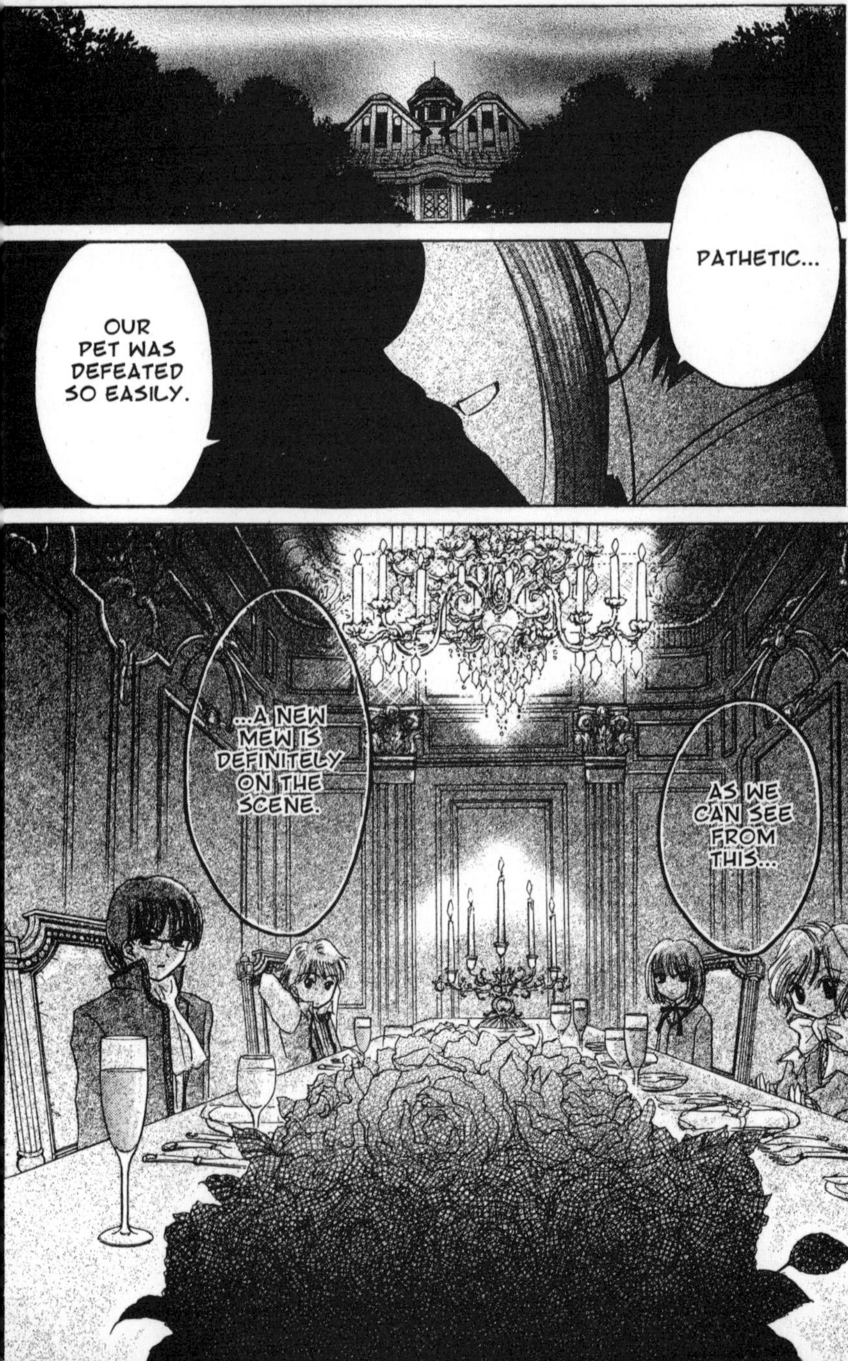
PATHETIC...
OUR PET WAS DEFEATED SO EASILY.
AS WE CAN SEE FROM THIS...
...A NEW MEW IS DEFINITELY ON THE SCENE.

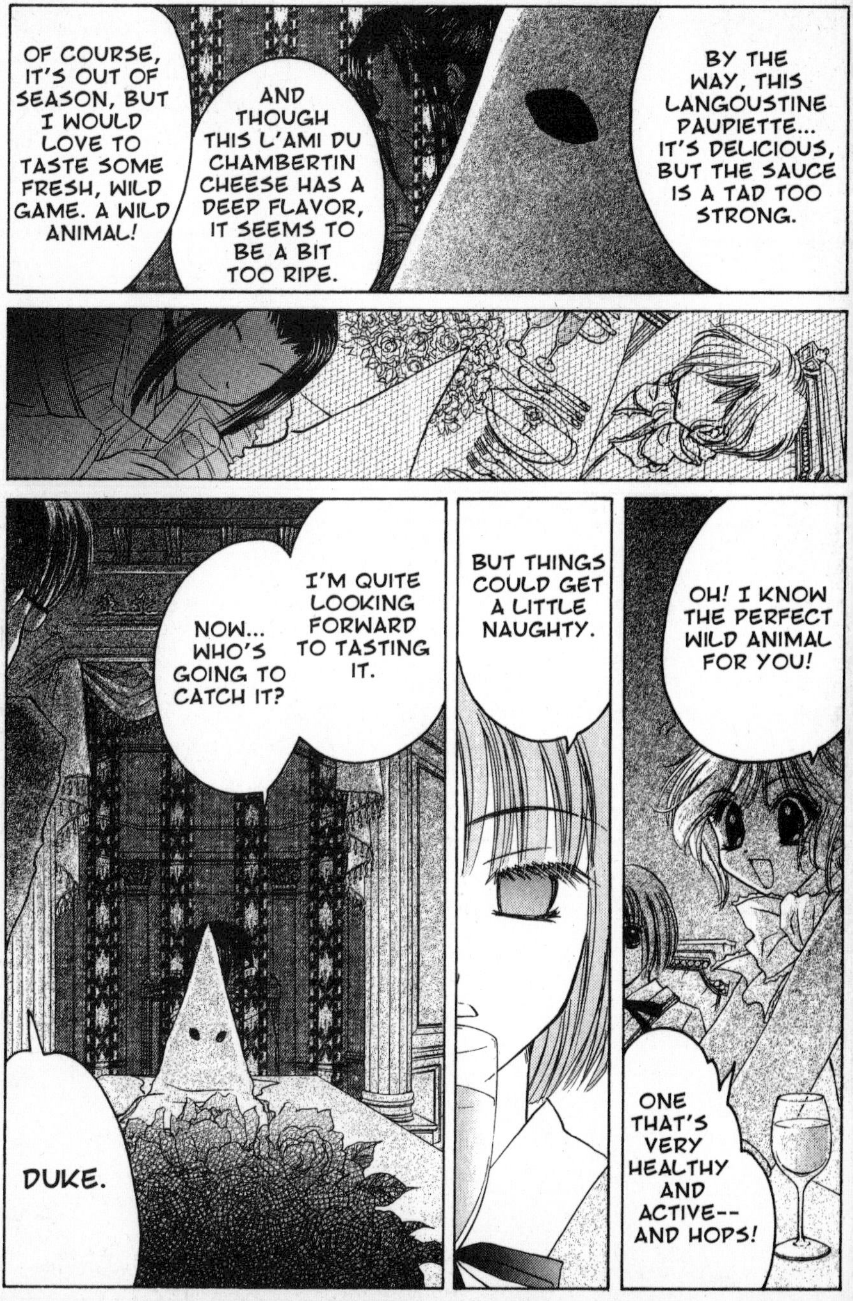
BY THE WAY, THIS LANGOUSTINE PAUPIETTE... IT'S DELICIOUS, BUT THE SAUCE IS A TAD TOO STRONG.
AND THOUGH THIS L'AMI DU CHAMBERTIN CHEESE HAS A DEEP FLAVOR, IT SEEMS TO BE A BIT TOO RIPE.
OF COURSE, IT'S OUT OF SEASON, BUT I WOULD LOVE TO TASTE SOME FRESH, WILD GAME. A WILD ANIMAL!
OH! I KNOW THE PERFECT WILD ANIMAL FOR YOU!
ONE THAT'S VERY HEALTHY AND ACTIVE-- AND HOPS!
BUT THINGS COULD GET A LITTLE NAUGHTY.
I'M QUITE LOOKING FORWARD TO TASTING IT.
NOW... WHO'S GOING TO CATCH IT?
DUKE.

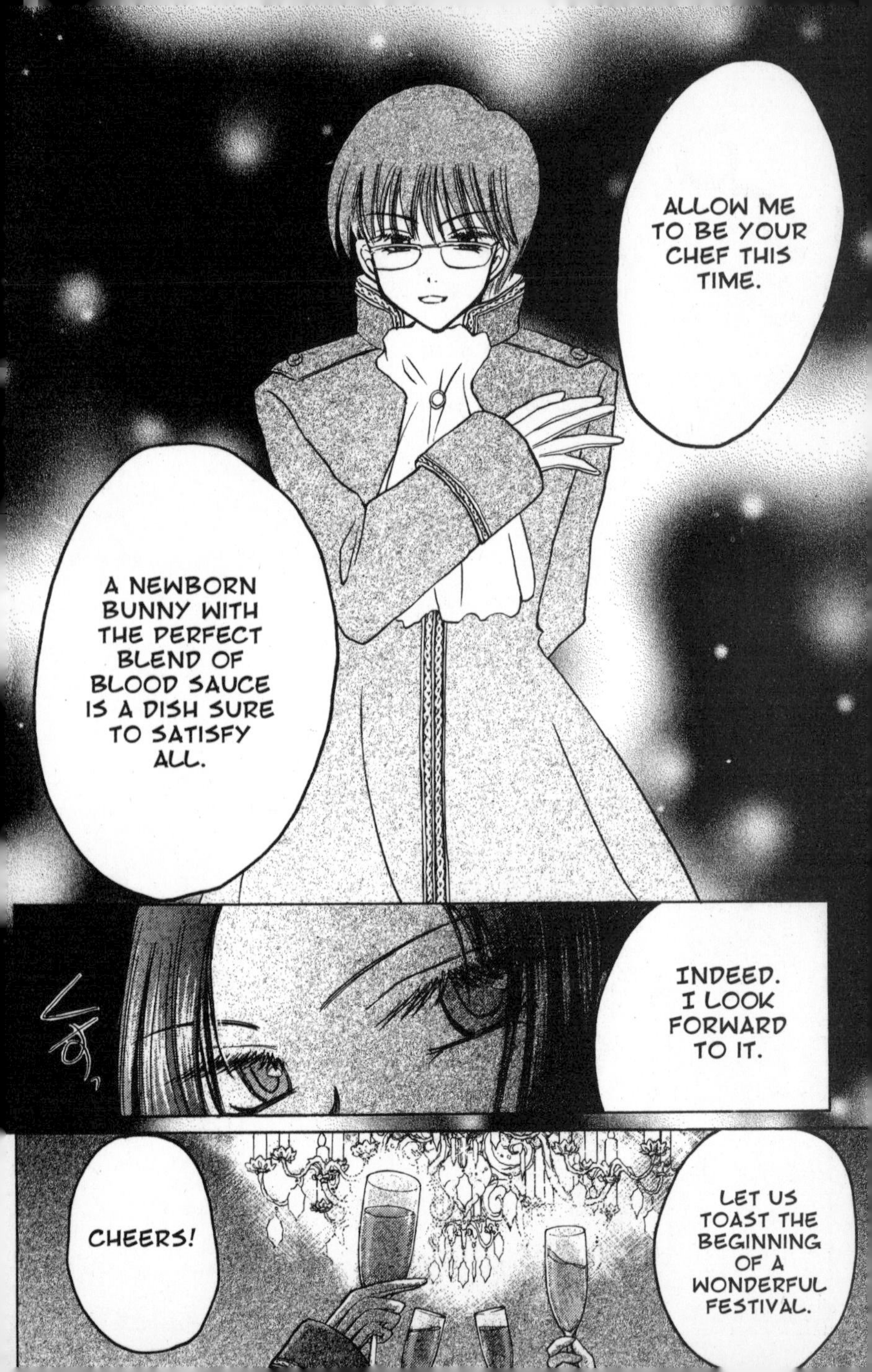
ALLOW ME TO BE YOUR CHEF THIS TIME.
A NEWBORN BUNNY WITH THE PERFECT BLEND OF BLOOD SAUCE IS A DISH SURE TO SATISFY ALL.
INDEED. I LOOK FORWARD TO IT.
LET US TOAST THE BEGINNING OF A WONDERFUL FESTIVAL.
CHEERS!

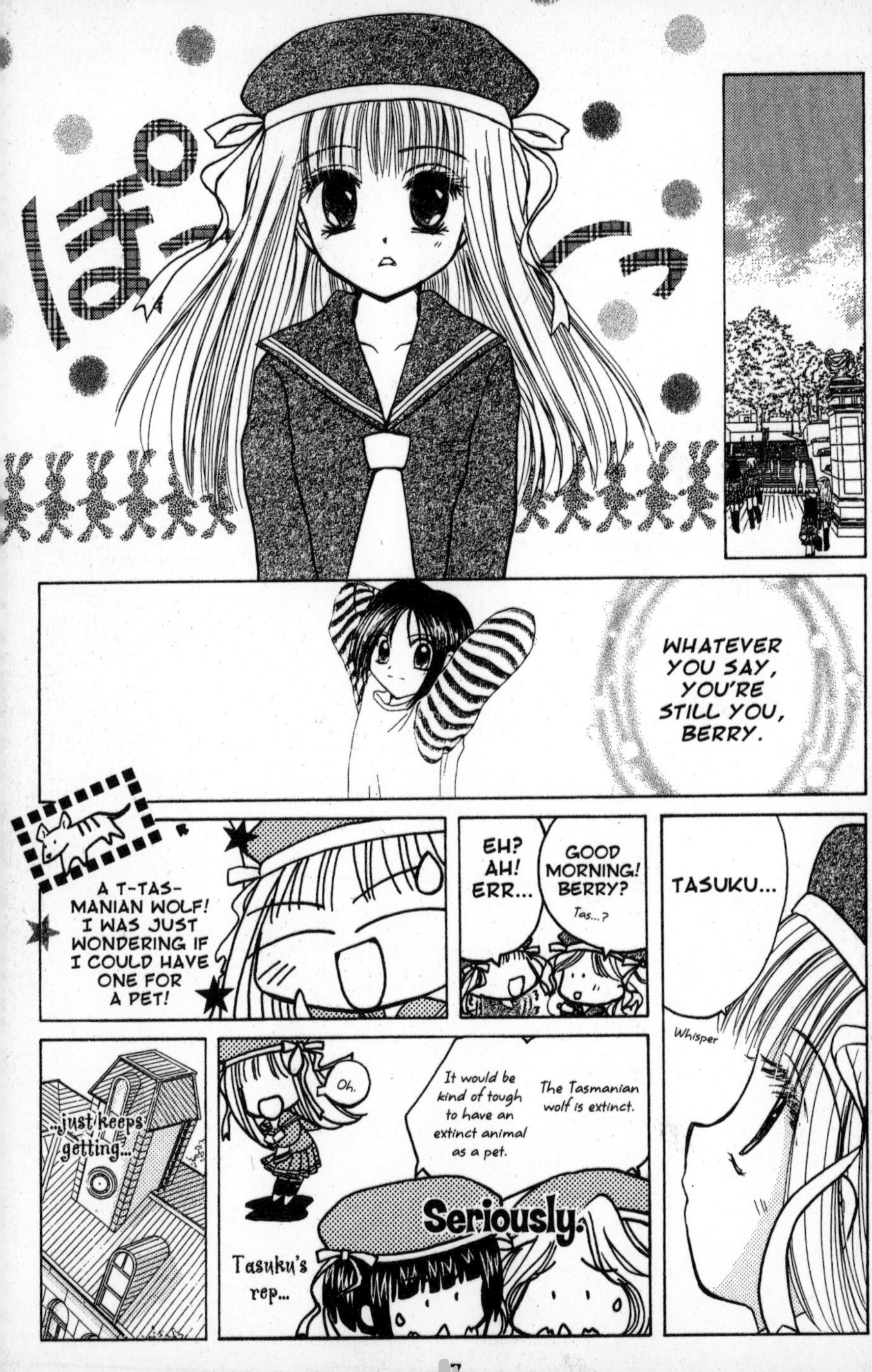

ぽ〜っ
WHATEVER YOU SAY, YOU'RE STILL YOU, BERRY.
TASUKU...
Whisper
GOOD MORNING! BERRY?
Tas...?
EH? AH! ERR...
A T-TAS-MANIAN WOLF! I WAS JUST WONDERING IF I COULD HAVE ONE FOR A PET!
The Tasmanian wolf is extinct.
It would be kind of tough to have an extinct animal as a pet.
Oh.
Seriously.
Tasuku's rep...
...just keeps getting...

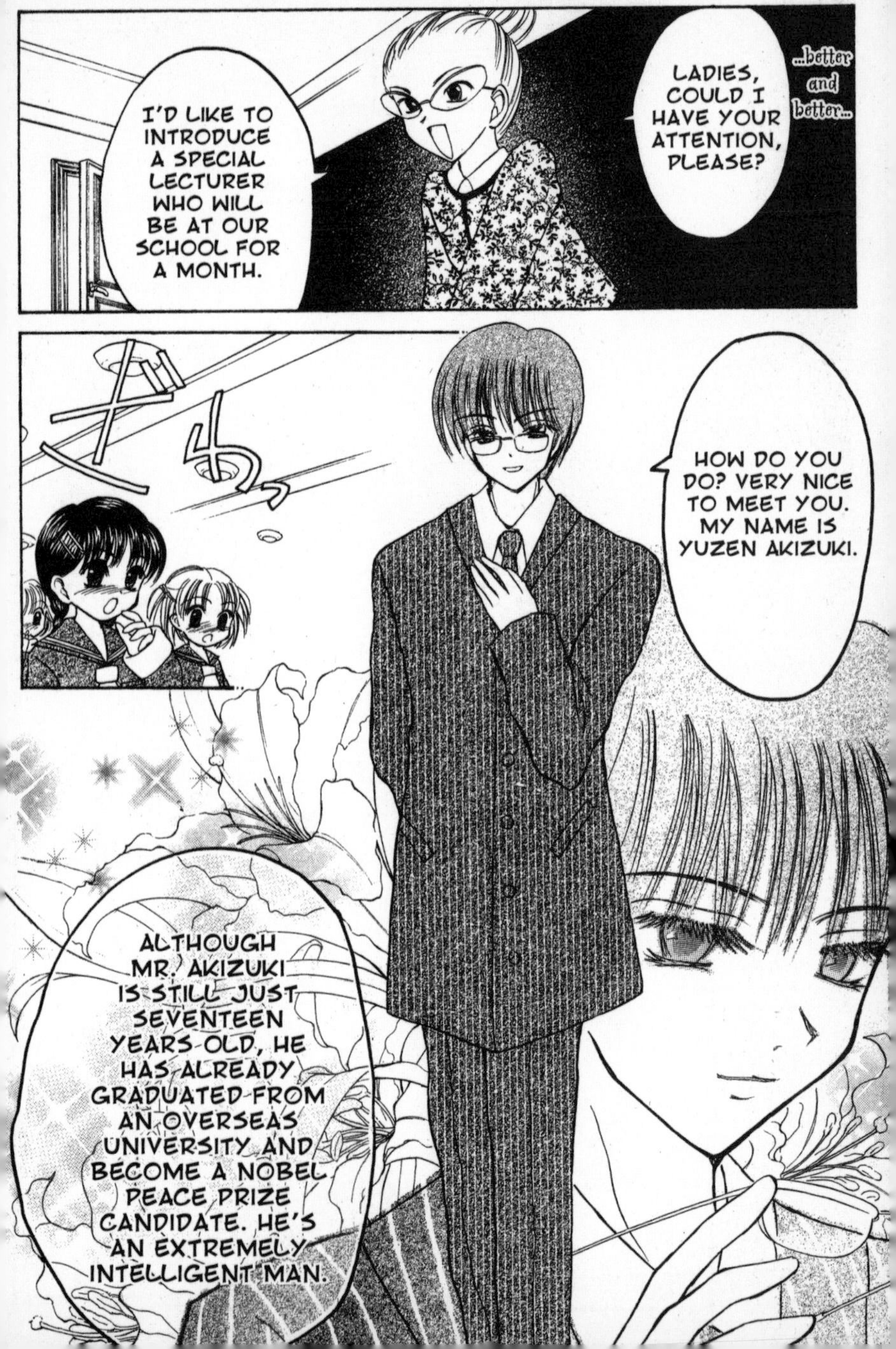
...better and better...
LADIES, COULD I HAVE YOUR ATTENTION, PLEASE?
I'D LIKE TO INTRODUCE A SPECIAL LECTURER WHO WILL BE AT OUR SCHOOL FOR A MONTH.
HOW DO YOU DO? VERY NICE TO MEET YOU. MY NAME IS YUZEN AKIZUKI.
ALTHOUGH MR. AKIZUKI IS STILL JUST SEVENTEEN YEARS OLD, HE HAS ALREADY GRADUATED FROM AN OVERSEAS UNIVERSITY AND BECOME A NOBEL PEACE PRIZE CANDIDATE. HE'S AN EXTREMELY INTELLIGENT MAN.

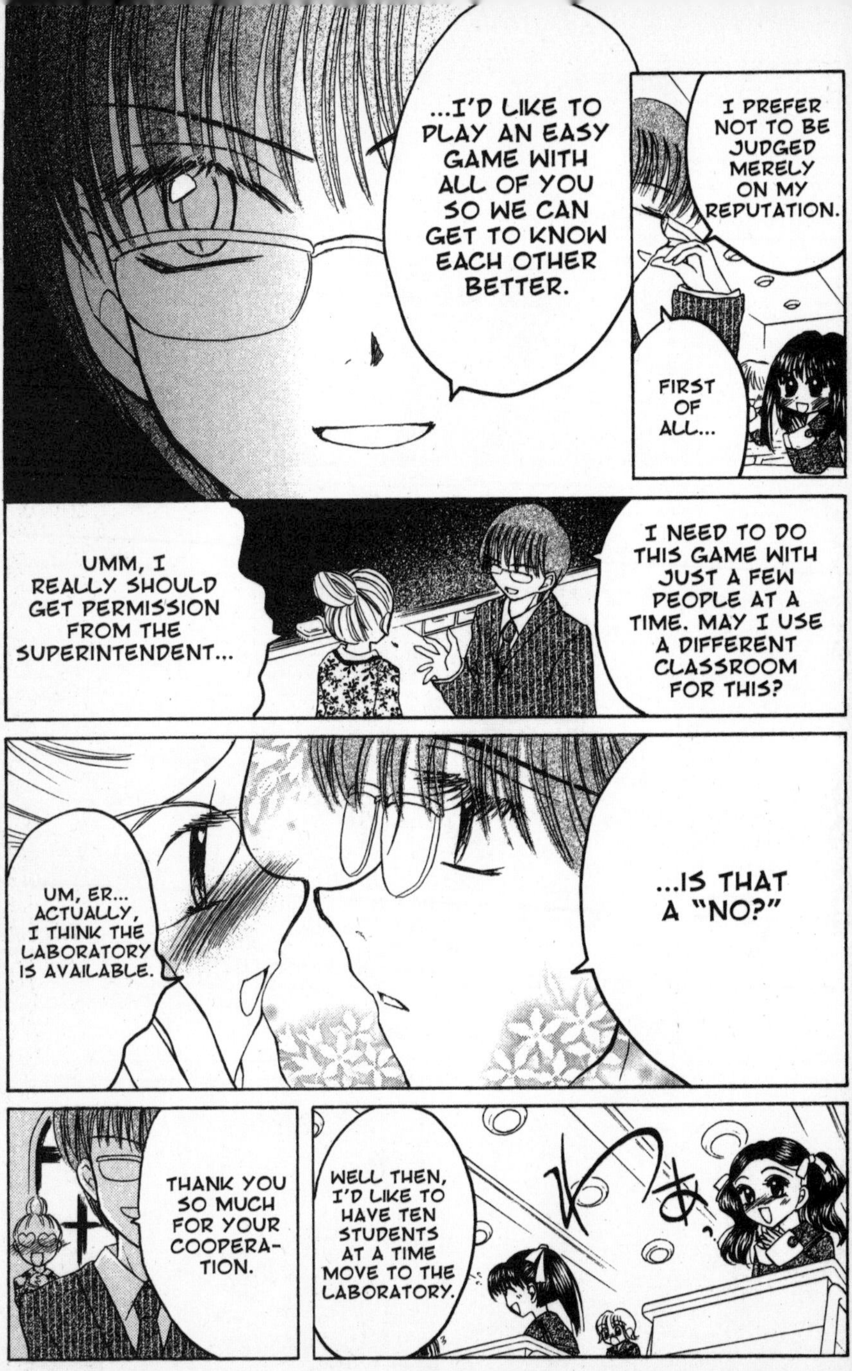
I PREFER NOT TO BE JUDGED MERELY ON MY REPUTATION.
FIRST OF ALL...
...I'D LIKE TO PLAY AN EASY GAME WITH ALL OF YOU SO WE CAN GET TO KNOW EACH OTHER BETTER.
I NEED TO DO THIS GAME WITH JUST A FEW PEOPLE AT A TIME. MAY I USE A DIFFERENT CLASSROOM FOR THIS?
UMM, I REALLY SHOULD GET PERMISSION FROM THE SUPERINTENDENT...
...IS THAT A "NO?"
UM, ER... ACTUALLY, I THINK THE LABORATORY IS AVAILABLE.
わあ
WELL THEN, I'D LIKE TO HAVE TEN STUDENTS AT A TIME MOVE TO THE LABORATORY.
THANK YOU SO MUCH FOR YOUR COOPERA-TION.

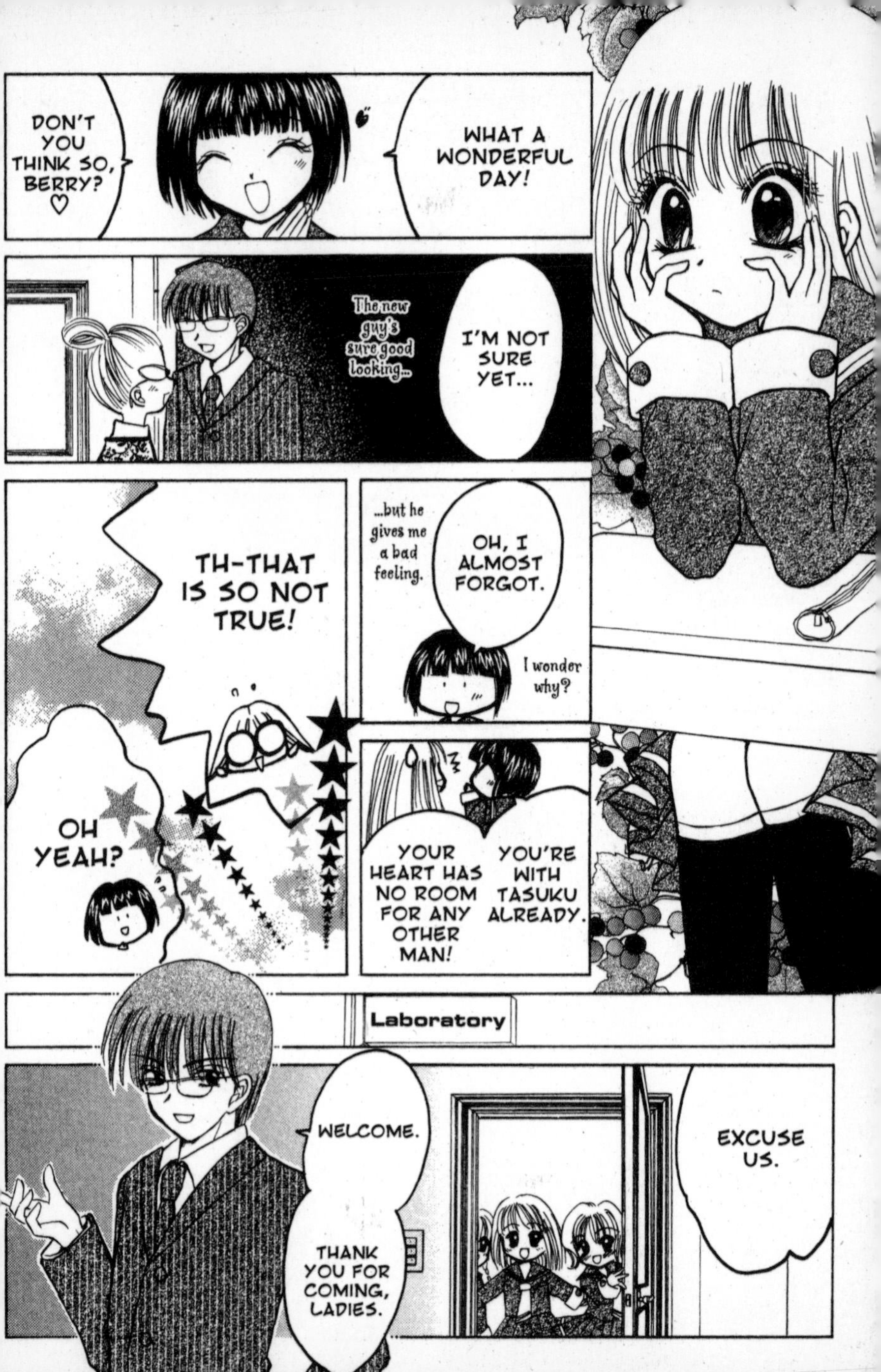
WHAT A WONDERFUL DAY!
DON'T YOU THINK SO, BERRY? ♡
I'M NOT SURE YET...
The new guy's sure good looking...
OH, I ALMOST FORGOT.
...but he gives me a bad feeling.
I wonder why?
YOU'RE WITH TASUKU ALREADY.
YOUR HEART HAS NO ROOM FOR ANY OTHER MAN!
TH-THAT IS SO NOT TRUE!
OH YEAH?
Laboratory
EXCUSE US.
WELCOME.
THANK YOU FOR COMING, LADIES.

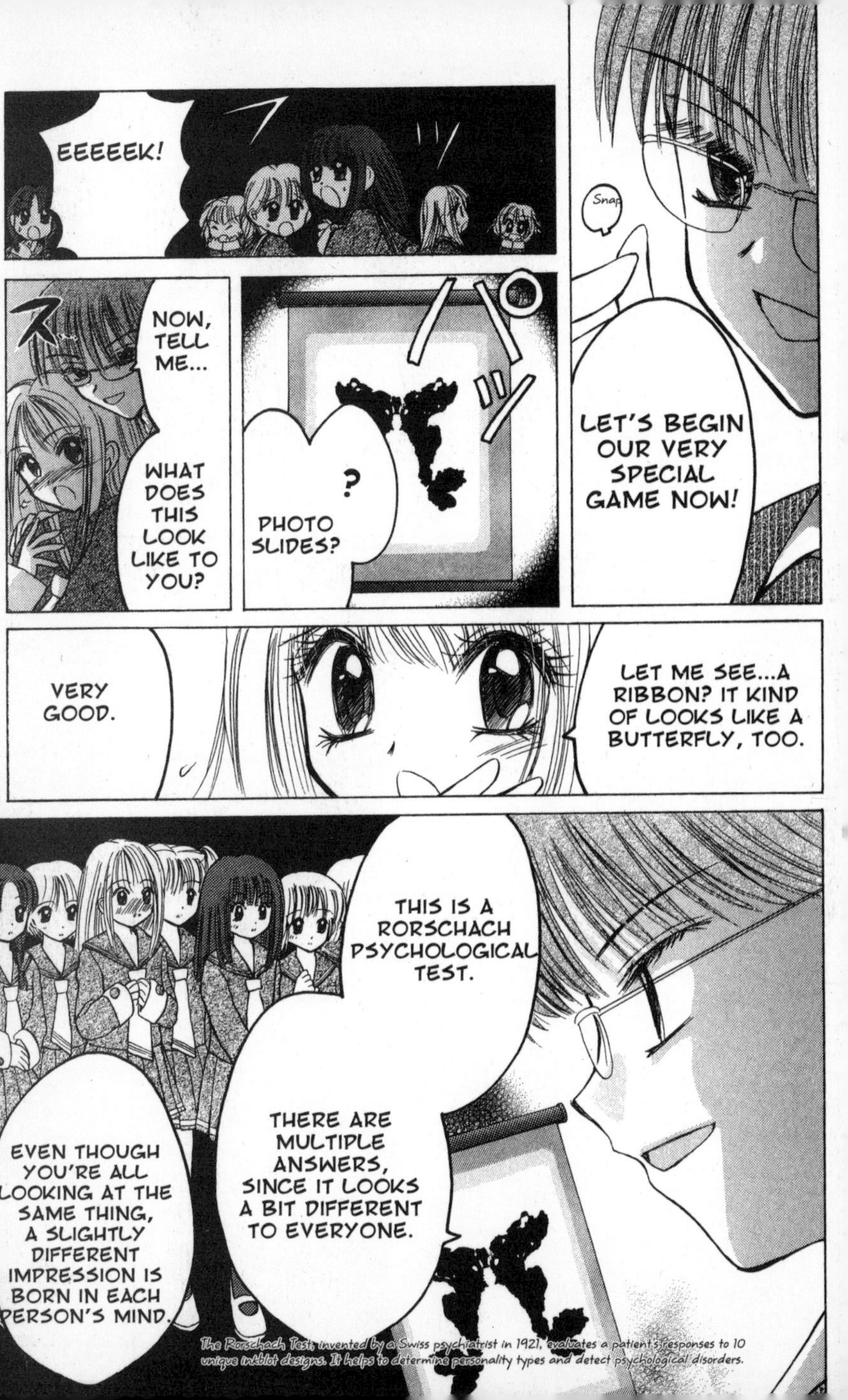
Snap
LET'S BEGIN OUR VERY SPECIAL GAME NOW!
EEEEEK!
?
PHOTO SLIDES?
NOW, TELL ME...
WHAT DOES THIS LOOK LIKE TO YOU?
LET ME SEE...A RIBBON? IT KIND OF LOOKS LIKE A BUTTERFLY, TOO.
VERY GOOD.
THIS IS A RORSCHACH PSYCHOLOGICAL TEST.
THERE ARE MULTIPLE ANSWERS, SINCE IT LOOKS A BIT DIFFERENT TO EVERYONE.
EVEN THOUGH YOU'RE ALL LOOKING AT THE SAME THING, A SLIGHTLY DIFFERENT IMPRESSION IS BORN IN EACH PERSON'S MIND.
The Rorschach Test, invented by a Swiss psychiatrist in 1921, evaluates a patient's responses to 10 unique inkblot designs. It helps to determine personality types and detect psychological disorders.

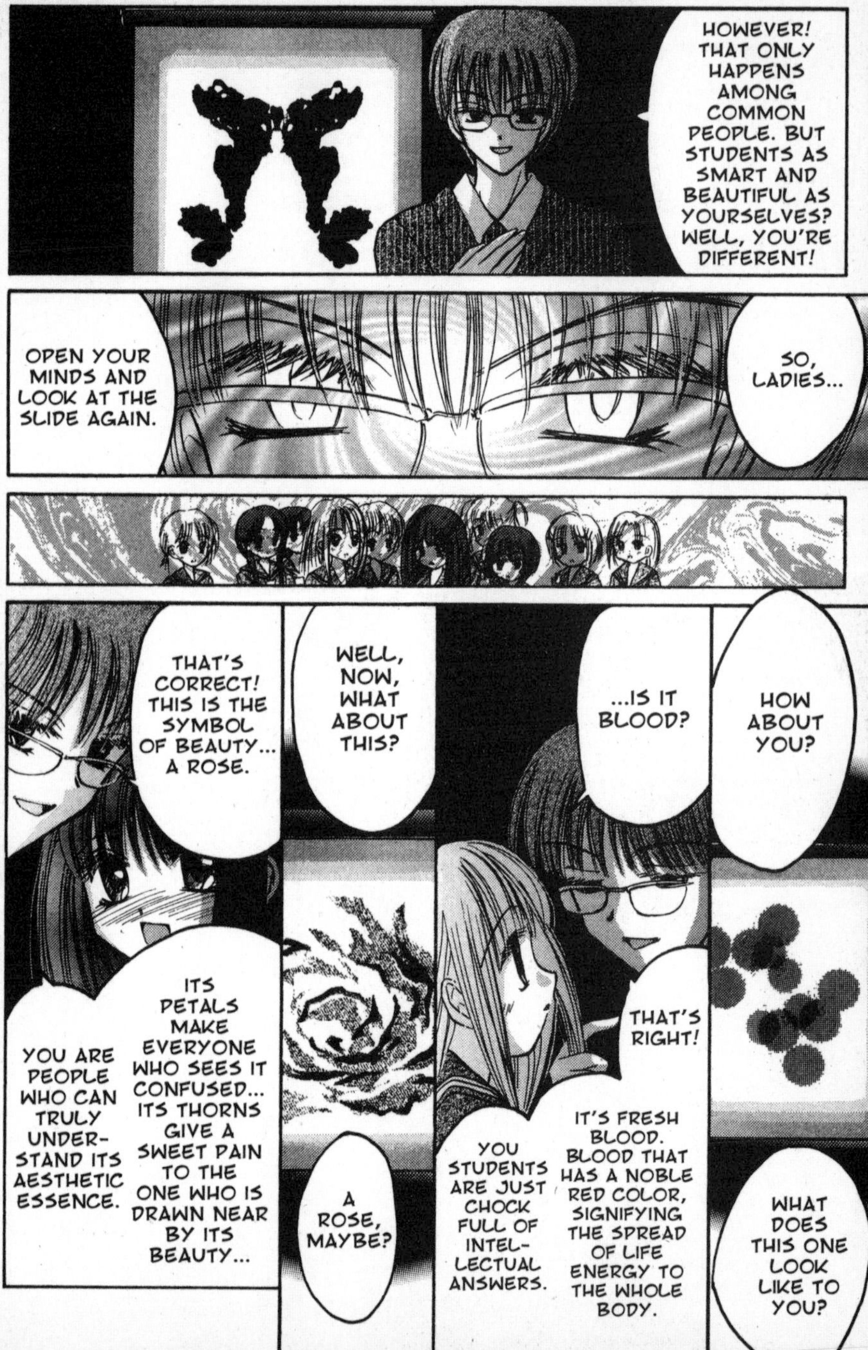
HOWEVER! THAT ONLY HAPPENS AMONG COMMON PEOPLE. BUT STUDENTS AS SMART AND BEAUTIFUL AS YOURSELVES? WELL, YOU'RE DIFFERENT!
SO, LADIES...
OPEN YOUR MINDS AND LOOK AT THE SLIDE AGAIN.
WHAT DOES THIS ONE LOOK LIKE TO YOU?
HOW ABOUT YOU?
...IS IT BLOOD?
THAT'S RIGHT!
IT'S FRESH BLOOD. BLOOD THAT HAS A NOBLE RED COLOR, SIGNIFYING THE SPREAD OF LIFE ENERGY TO THE WHOLE BODY.
YOU STUDENTS ARE JUST CHOCK FULL OF INTEL-LECTUAL ANSWERS.
WELL, NOW, WHAT ABOUT THIS?
A ROSE, MAYBE?
THAT'S CORRECT! THIS IS THE SYMBOL OF BEAUTY... A ROSE.
ITS PETALS MAKE EVERYONE WHO SEES IT CONFUSED... ITS THORNS GIVE A SWEET PAIN TO THE ONE WHO IS DRAWN NEAR BY ITS BEAUTY...
YOU ARE PEOPLE WHO CAN TRULY UNDER-STAND ITS AESTHETIC ESSENCE.

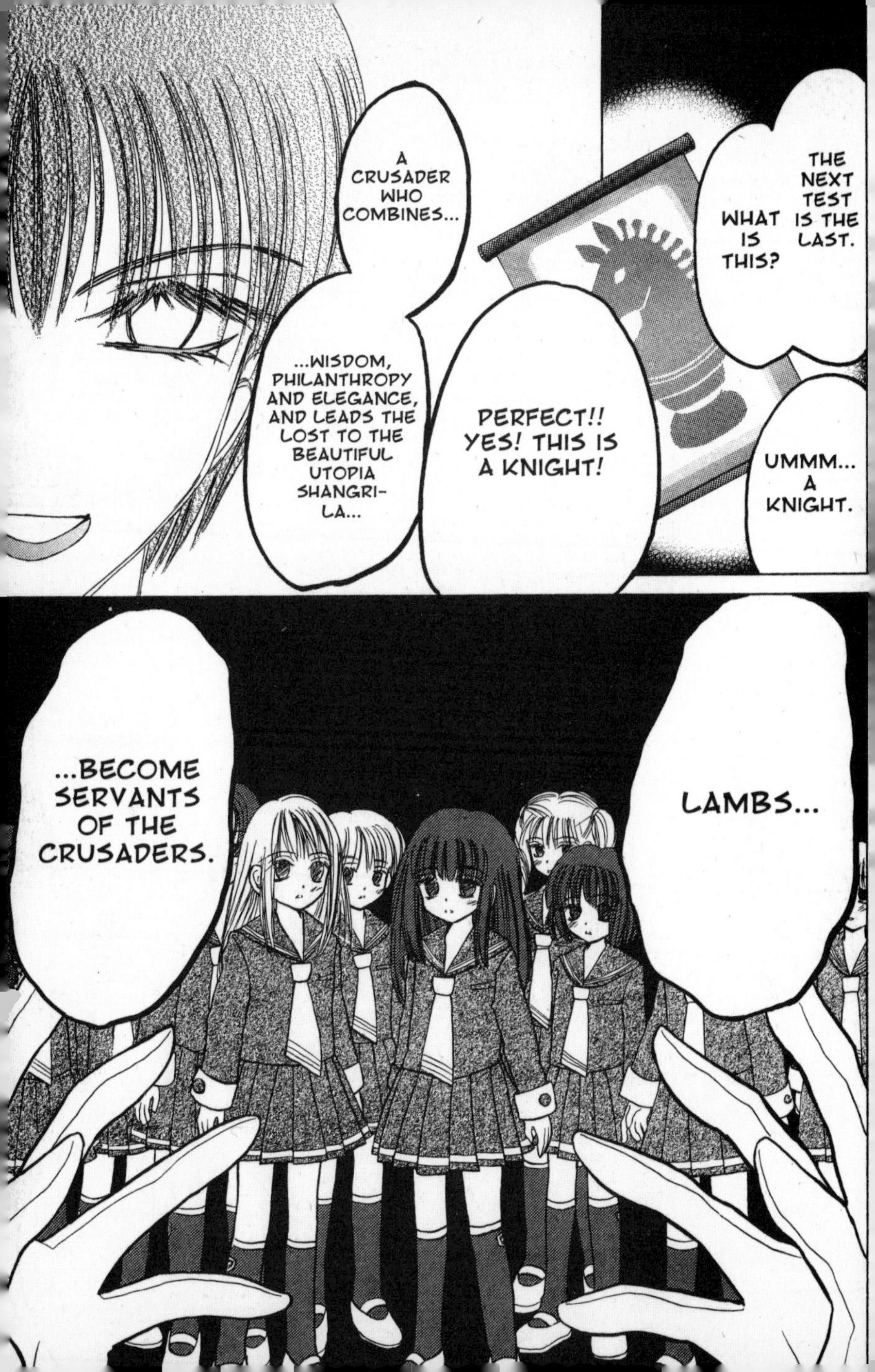
THE NEXT TEST IS THE LAST.
WHAT IS THIS?
UMMM... A KNIGHT.
PERFECT!! YES! THIS IS A KNIGHT!
A CRUSADER WHO COMBINES...
...WISDOM, PHILANTHROPY AND ELEGANCE, AND LEADS THE LOST TO THE BEAUTIFUL UTOPIA SHANGRI-LA...
LAMBS...
...BECOME SERVANTS OF THE CRUSADERS.

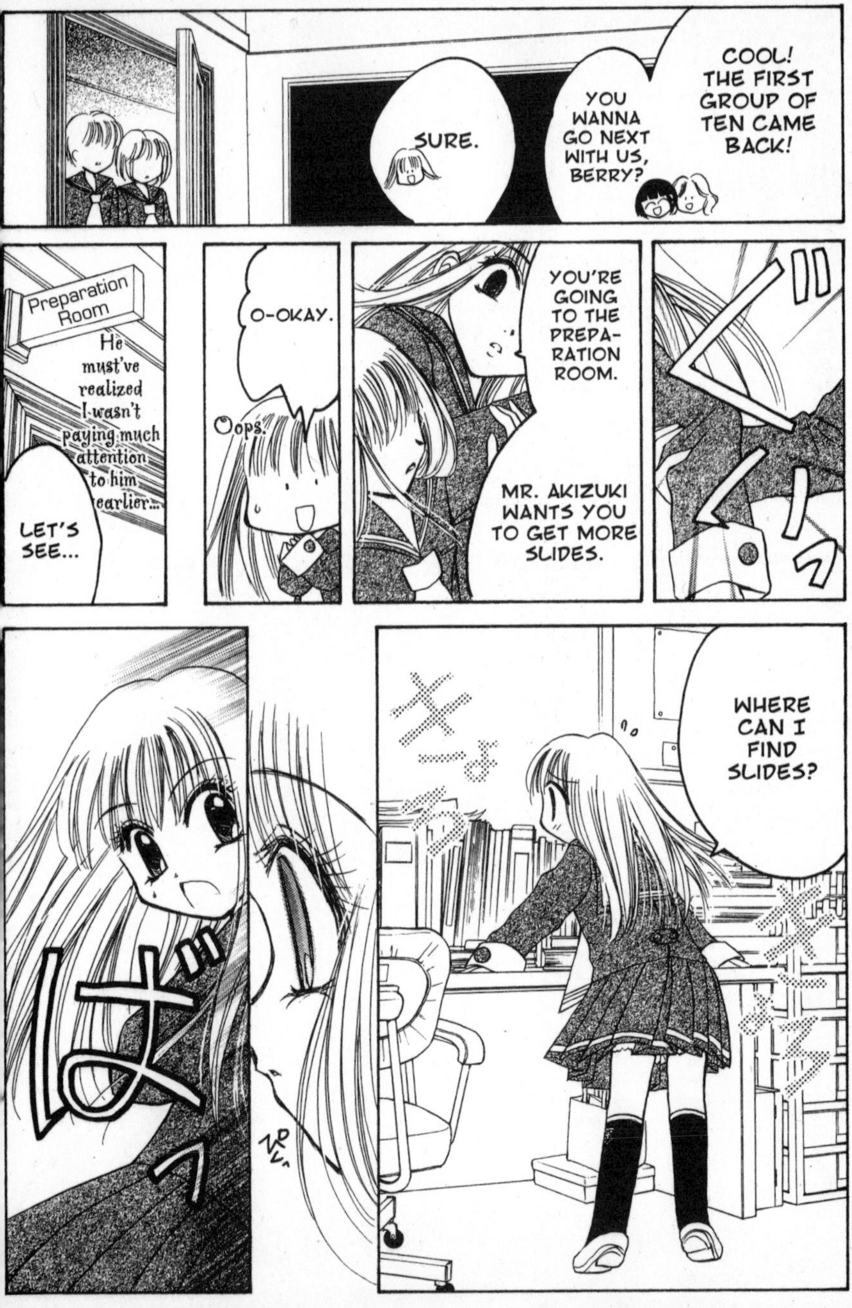
COOL! THE FIRST GROUP OF TEN CAME BACK!
YOU WANNA GO NEXT WITH US, BERRY?
SURE.
YOU'RE GOING TO THE PREPARATION ROOM.
MR. AKIZUKI WANTS YOU TO GET MORE SLIDES.
O-OKAY.
Oops.
Preparation Room
He must've realized I wasn't paying much attention to him earlier...
LET'S SEE...
WHERE CAN I FIND SLIDES?
は

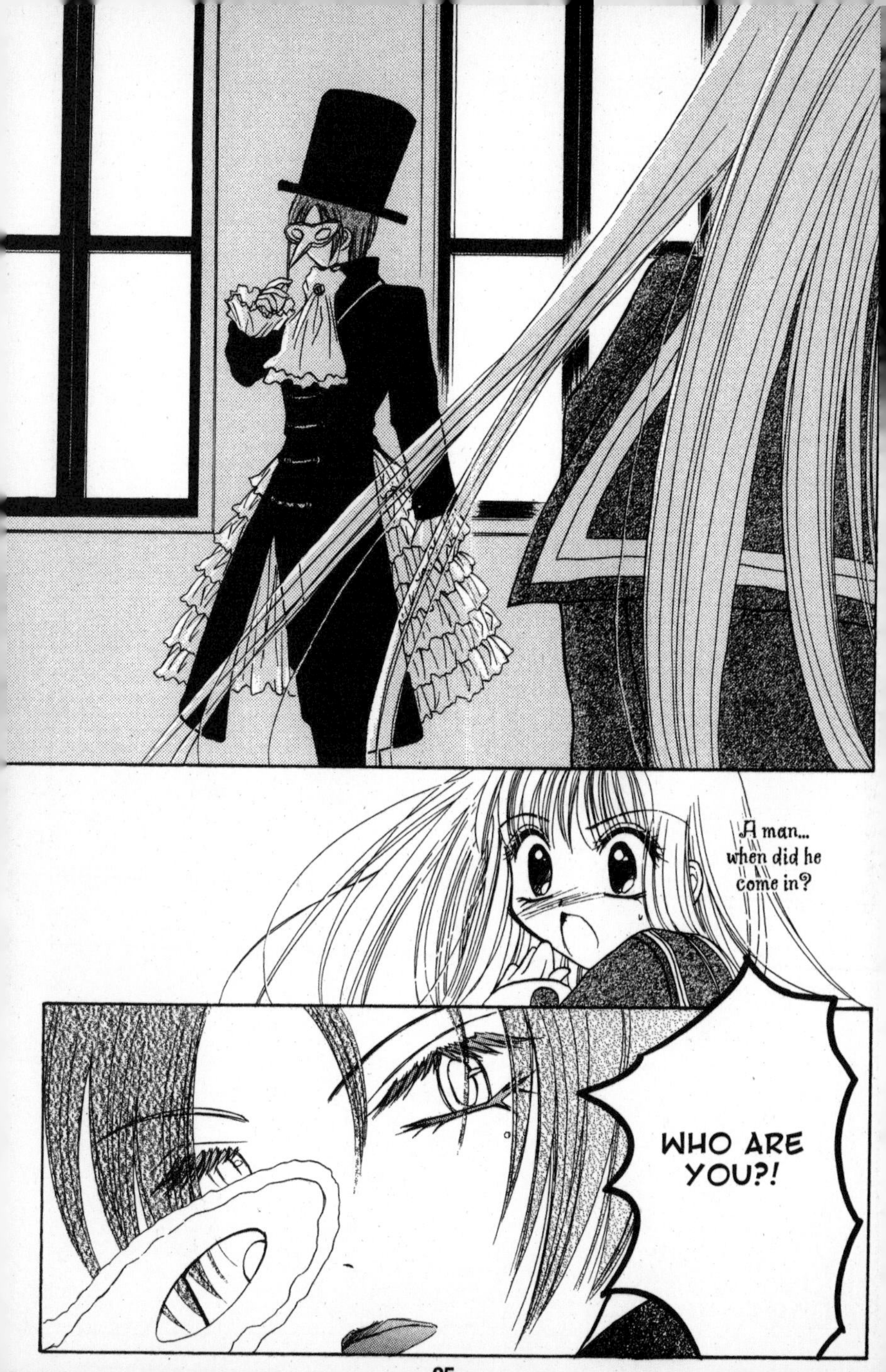
A man...
when did he
come in?
WHO ARE
YOU?!

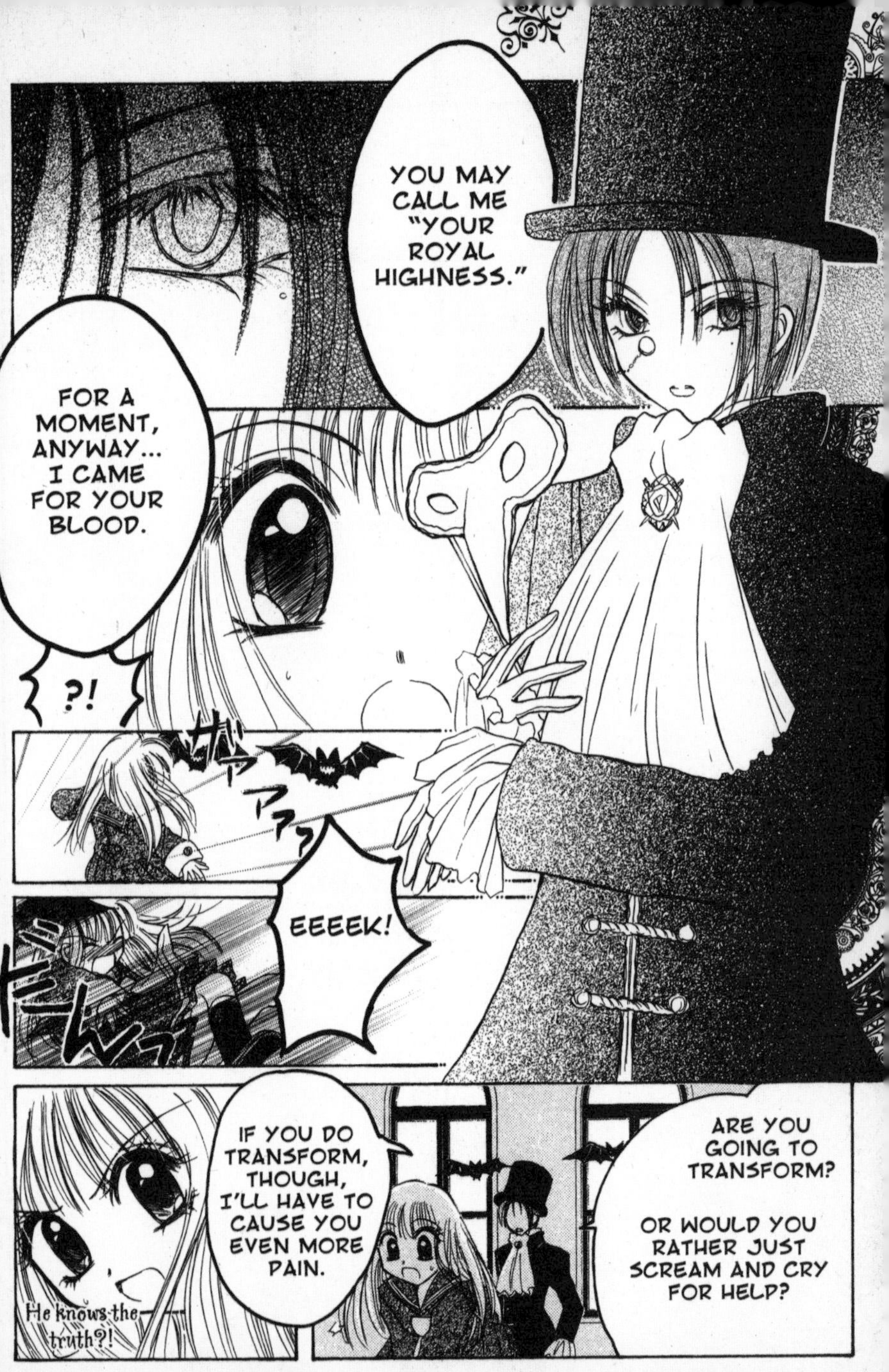
YOU MAY CALL ME "YOUR ROYAL HIGHNESS."
FOR A MOMENT, ANYWAY... I CAME FOR YOUR BLOOD.
?!
EEEEK!
ARE YOU GOING TO TRANSFORM?
OR WOULD YOU RATHER JUST SCREAM AND CRY FOR HELP?
IF YOU DO TRANSFORM, THOUGH, I'LL HAVE TO CAUSE YOU EVEN MORE PAIN.
He knows the truth?!

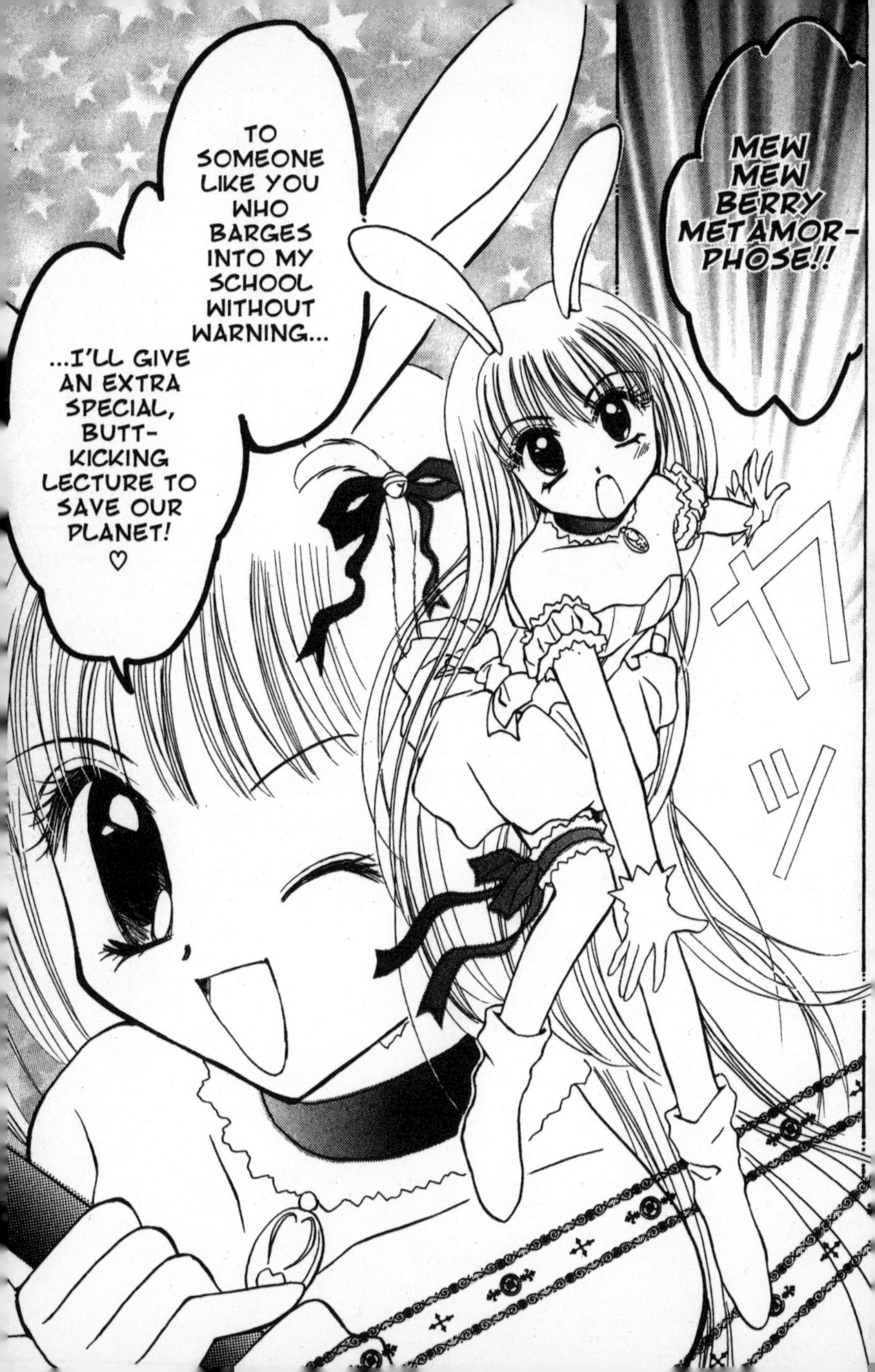
MEW MEW BERRY METAMORPHOSE!!
TO SOMEONE LIKE YOU WHO BARGES INTO MY SCHOOL WITHOUT WARNING...
...I'LL GIVE AN EXTRA SPECIAL, BUTT-KICKING LECTURE TO SAVE OUR PLANET! ♡

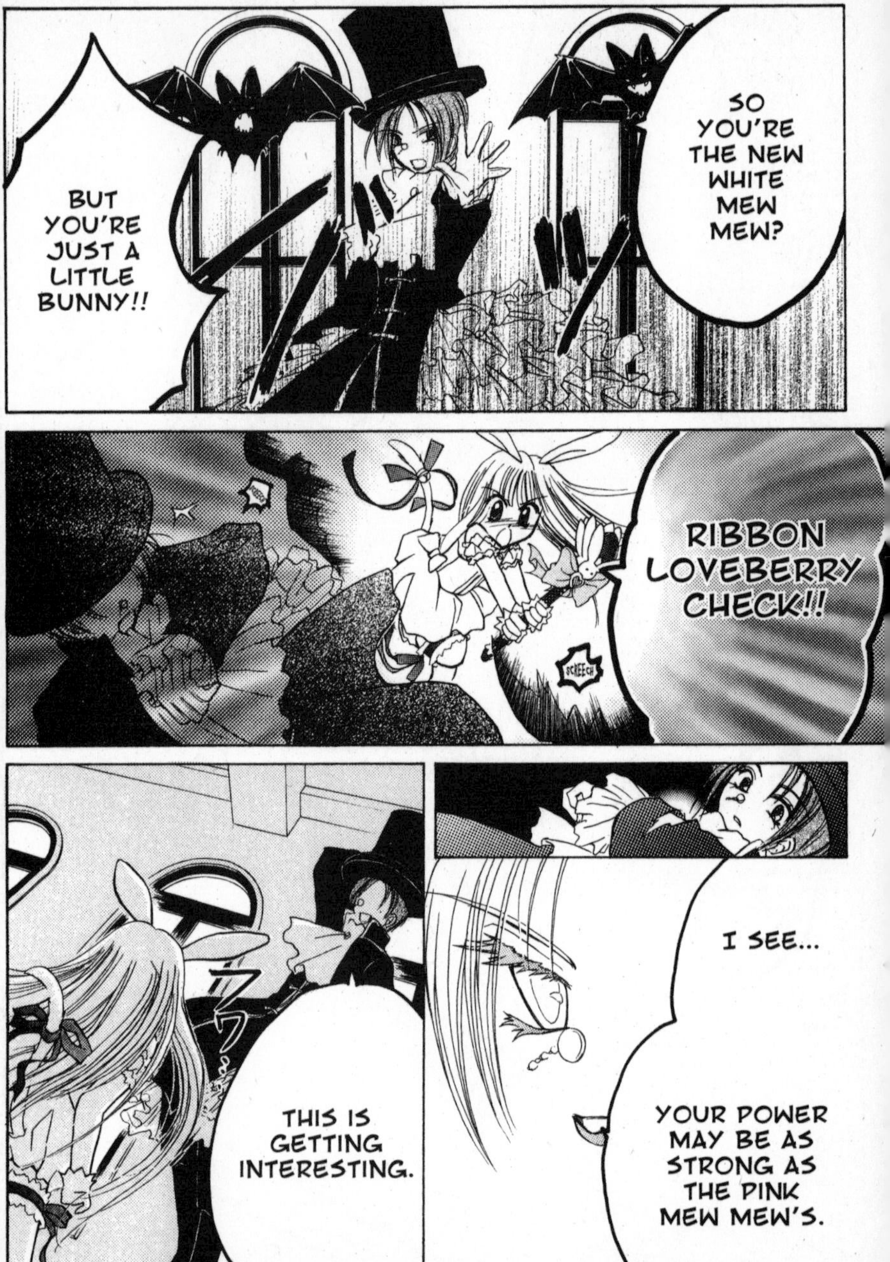
SO YOU'RE THE NEW WHITE MEW MEW?
BUT YOU'RE JUST A LITTLE BUNNY!!
RIBBON LOVEBERRY CHECK!!
SCREECH
I SEE...
YOUR POWER MAY BE AS STRONG AS THE PINK MEW MEW'S.
THIS IS GETTING INTERESTING.

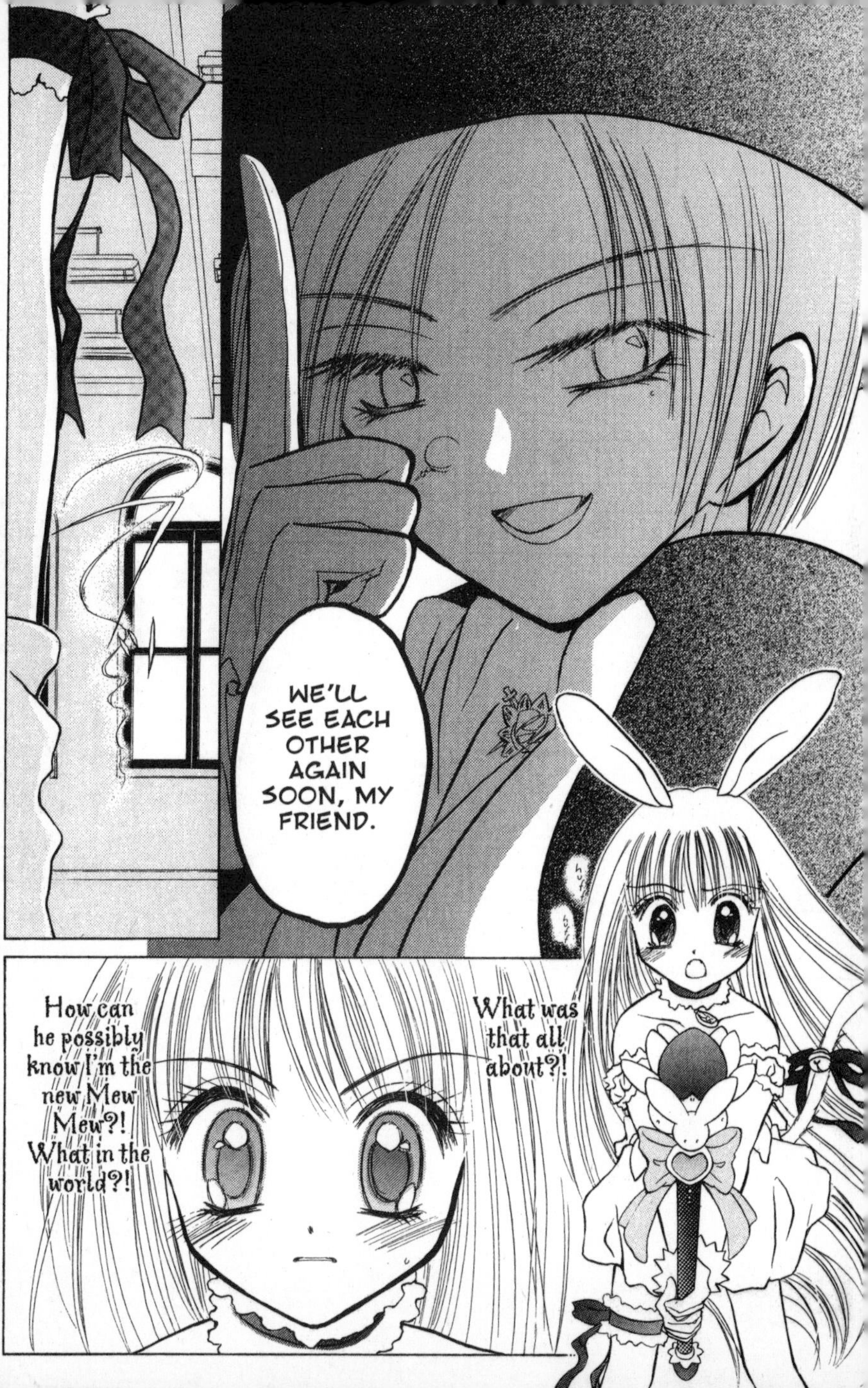
WE'LL SEE EACH OTHER AGAIN SOON, MY FRIEND.
What was that all about?!
How can he possibly know I'm the new Mew Mew?! What in the world?!

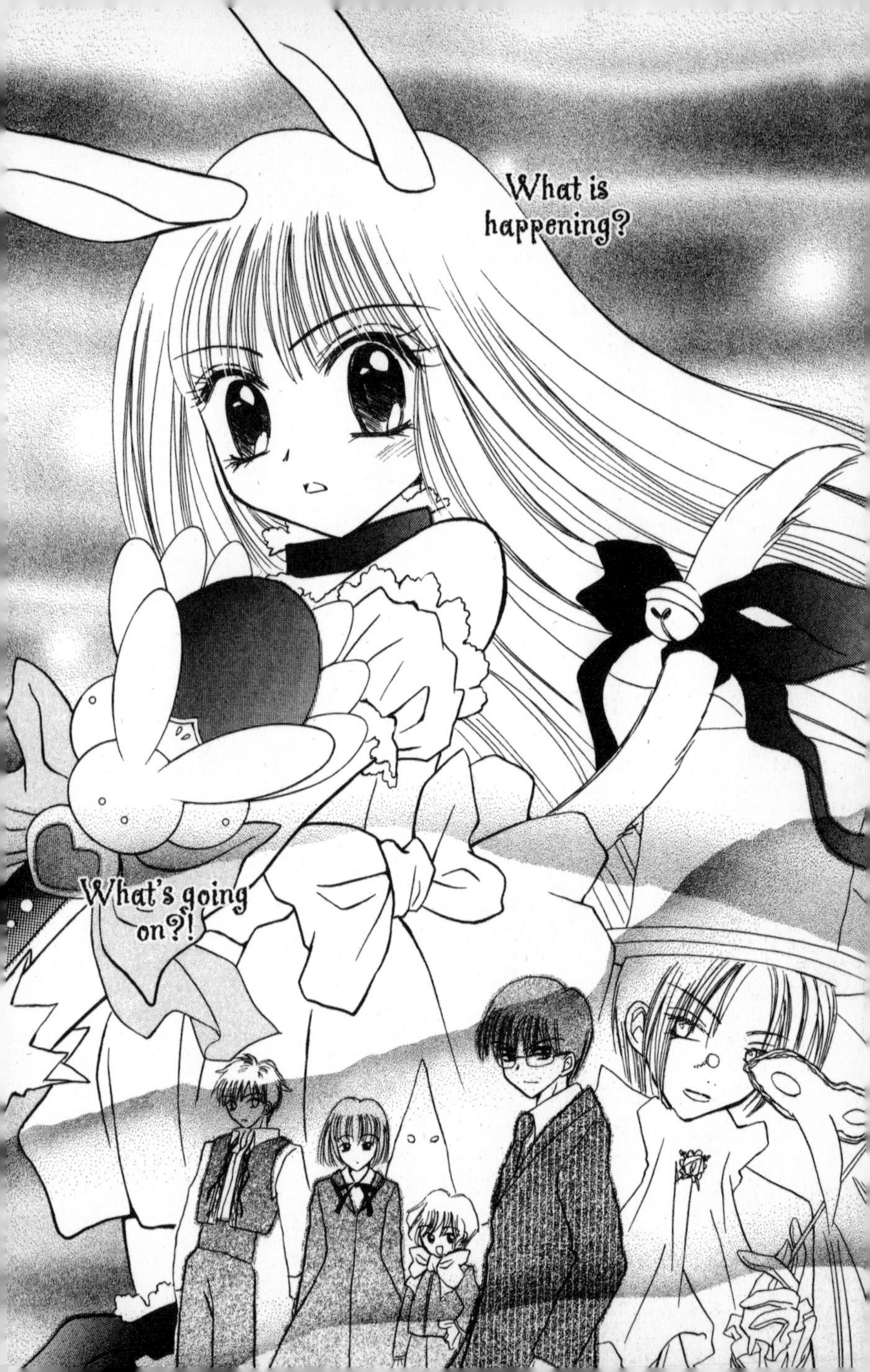
What is happening?
What's going on?!

Hello! It's me, Ikumi!

Long time no see! How do you do? Nice to meet you--Ikumi here! Welcome to Volume One of *Tokyo Mew Mew a la Mode.* Even though this is volume one of the story, it seems like Volume Eight for me, since I've produced a total of seven volumes of *Tokyo Mew Mew* before this.

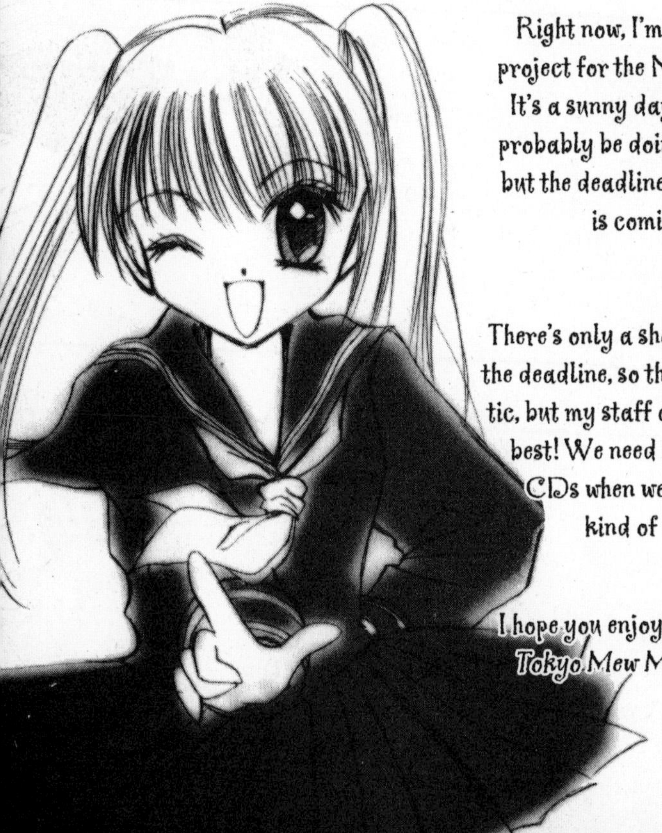

Right now, I'm working on a project for the November issue. It's a sunny day and I should probably be doing my laundry, but the deadline for the manga is coming up! ☆

There's only a short time left before the deadline, so things have been hectic, but my staff and I are doing our best! We need some good music CDs when we're stuck in this kind of situation.

I hope you enjoy Volume One of *Tokyo Mew Mew a la Mode!* ♡♡

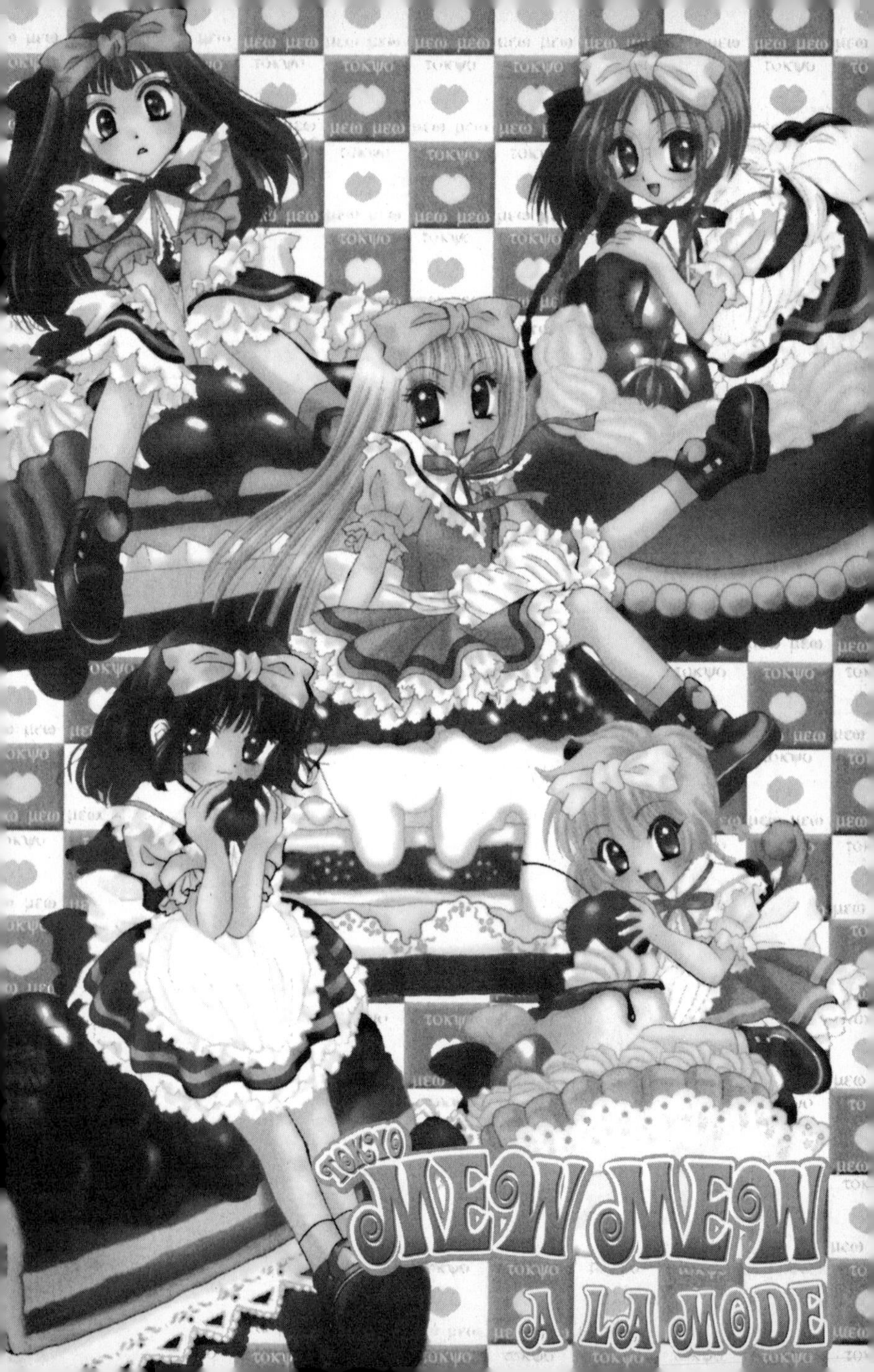
TOKYO
MEW MEW
A LA MODE

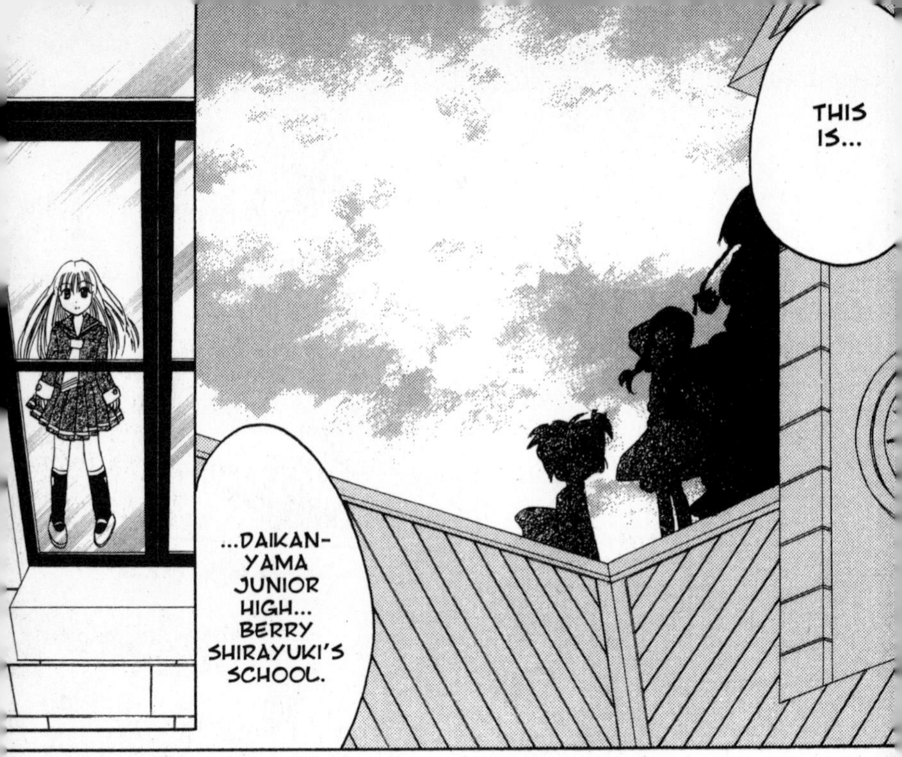
THIS IS...
...DAIKAN-YAMA JUNIOR HIGH... BERRY SHIRAYUKI'S SCHOOL.
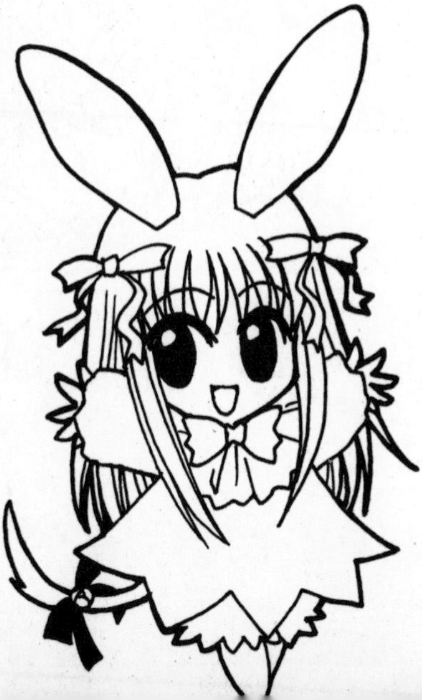

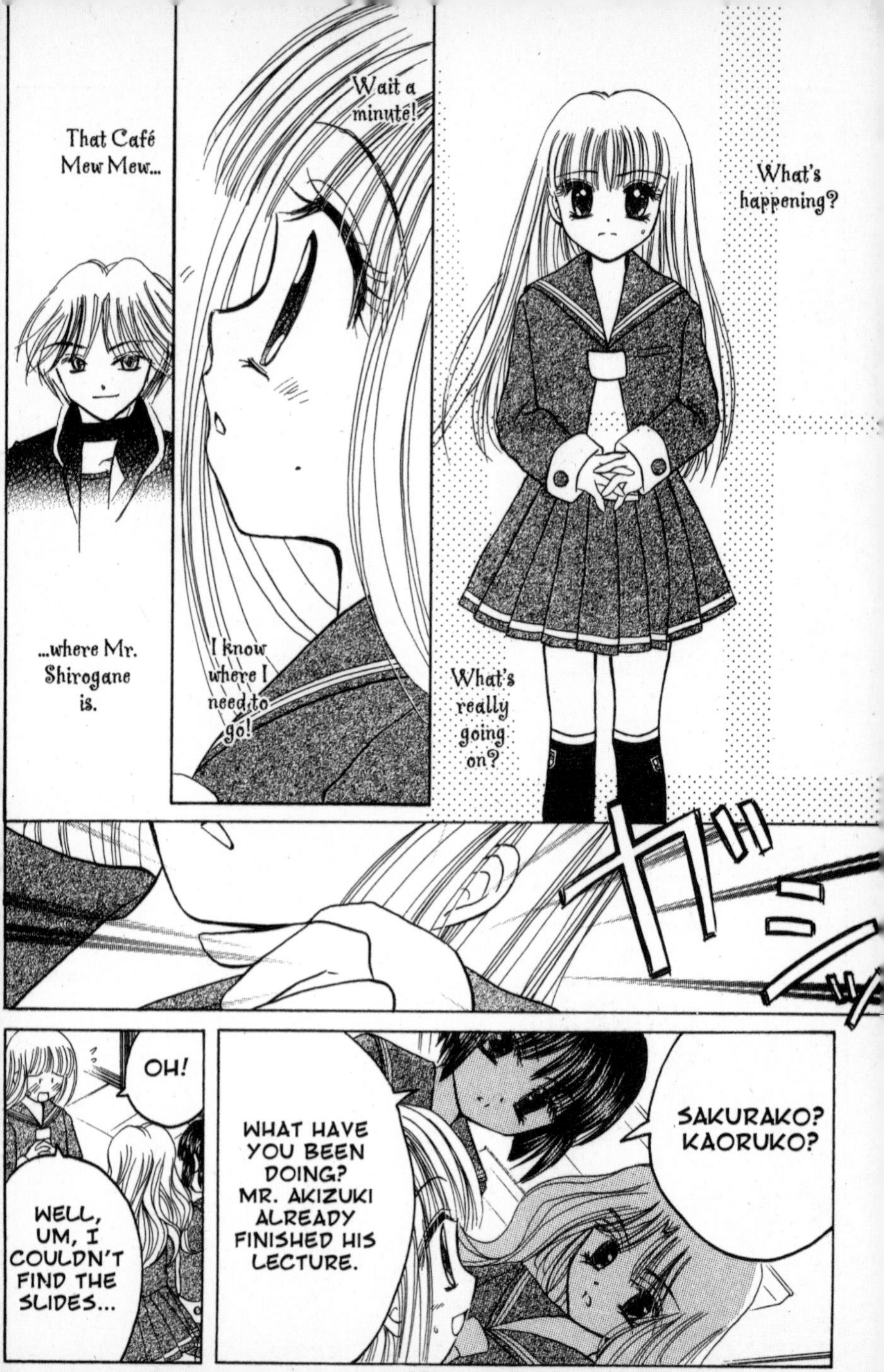
What's happening?
What's really going on?
Wait a minute!
I know where I need to go!
That Café Mew Mew...
...where Mr. Shirogane is.
SAKURAKO? KAORUKO?
WHAT HAVE YOU BEEN DOING? MR. AKIZUKI ALREADY FINISHED HIS LECTURE.
OH!
WELL, UM, I COULDN'T FIND THE SLIDES...

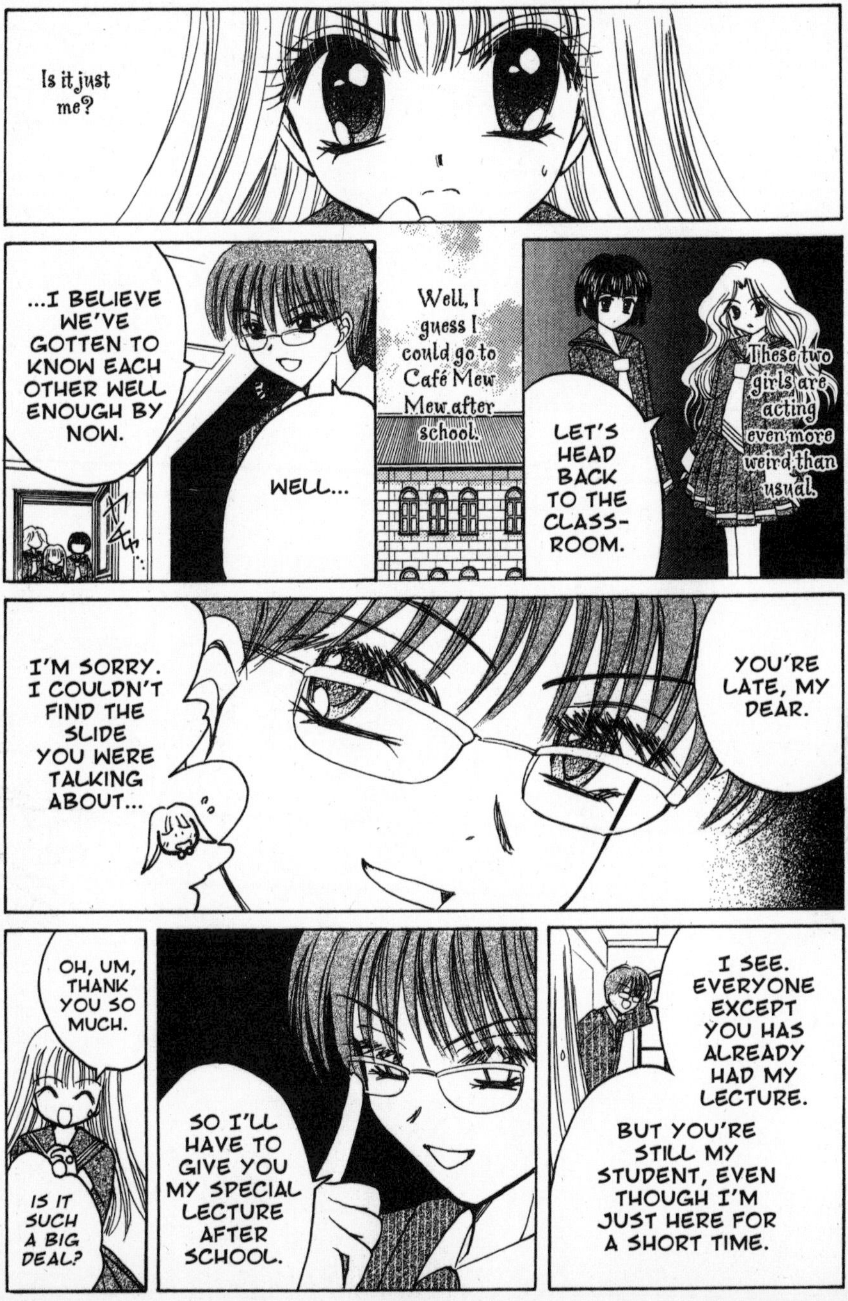
Is it just me?
These two girls are acting even more weird than usual.
LET'S HEAD BACK TO THE CLASSROOM.
Well, I guess I could go to Café Mew Mew after school.
...I BELIEVE WE'VE GOTTEN TO KNOW EACH OTHER WELL ENOUGH BY NOW.
WELL...
YOU'RE LATE, MY DEAR.
I'M SORRY. I COULDN'T FIND THE SLIDE YOU WERE TALKING ABOUT...
I SEE. EVERYONE EXCEPT YOU HAS ALREADY HAD MY LECTURE.
BUT YOU'RE STILL MY STUDENT, EVEN THOUGH I'M JUST HERE FOR A SHORT TIME.
SO I'LL HAVE TO GIVE YOU MY SPECIAL LECTURE AFTER SCHOOL.
OH, UM, THANK YOU SO MUCH.
IS IT SUCH A BIG DEAL?

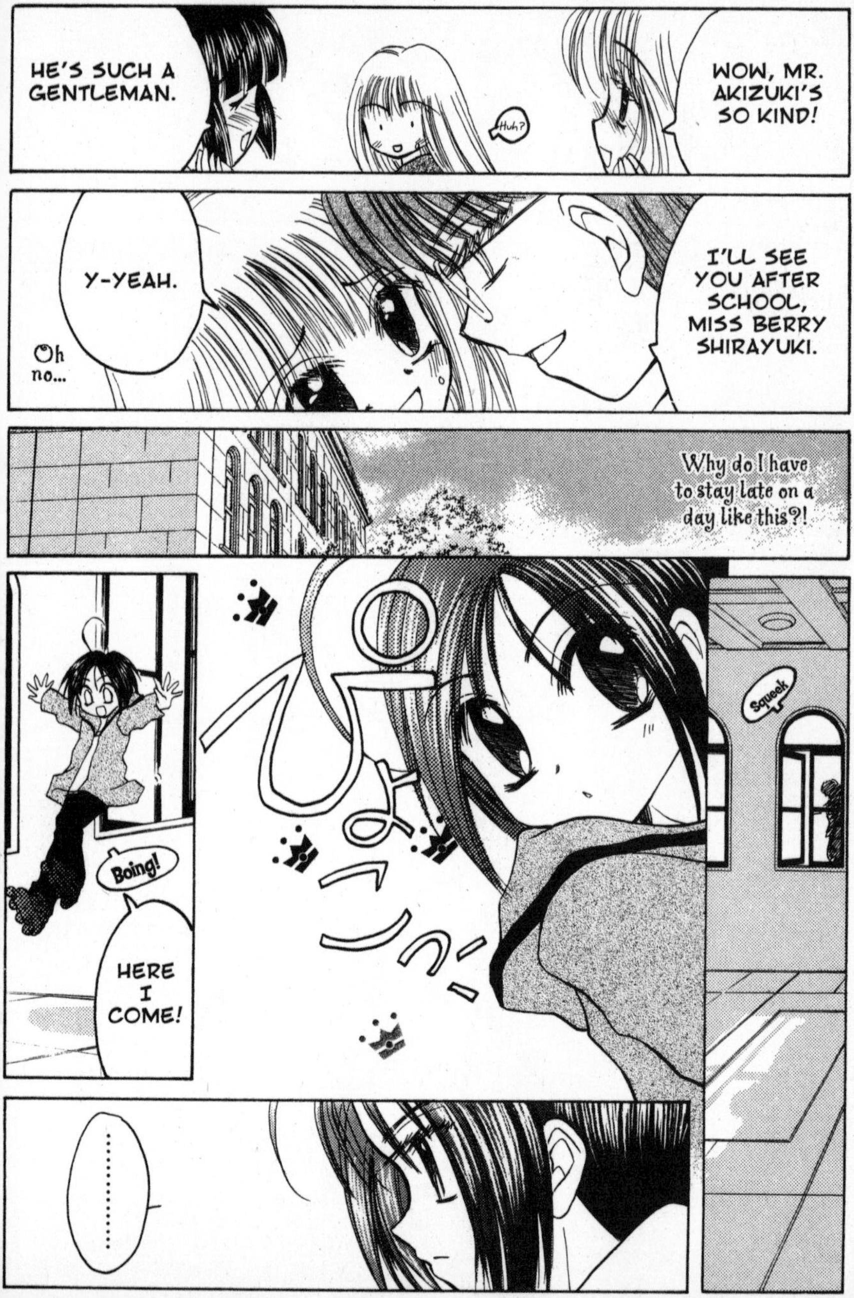
WOW, MR. AKIZUKI'S SO KIND!
Huh?
HE'S SUCH A GENTLEMAN.
I'LL SEE YOU AFTER SCHOOL, MISS BERRY SHIRAYUKI.
Y-YEAH.
Oh no...
Why do I have to stay late on a day like this?!
Squeek
Boing!
HERE I COME!
......

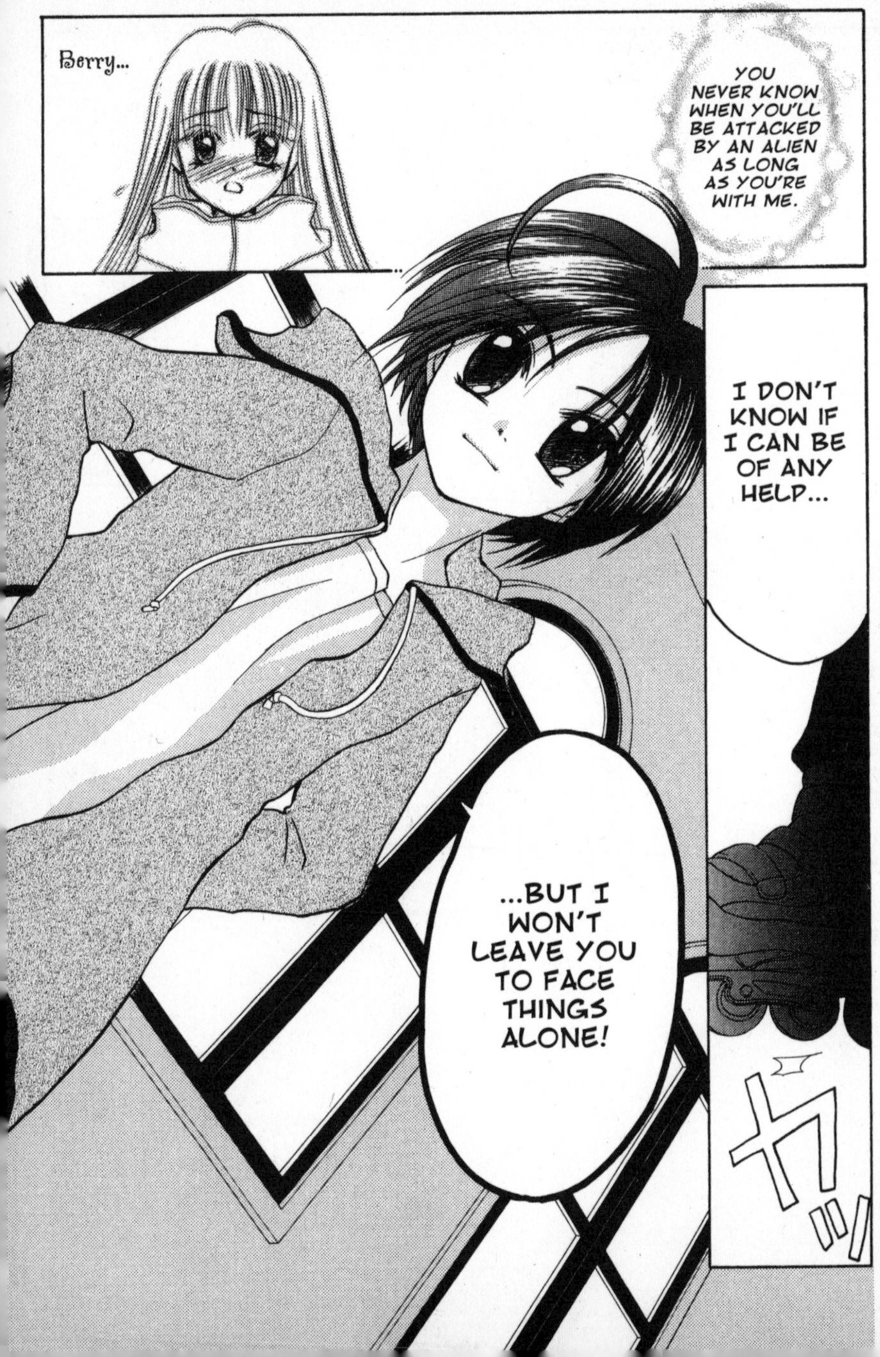
YOU NEVER KNOW WHEN YOU'LL BE ATTACKED BY AN ALIEN AS LONG AS YOU'RE WITH ME.
Berry...
I DON'T KNOW IF I CAN BE OF ANY HELP...
...BUT I WON'T LEAVE YOU TO FACE THINGS ALONE!

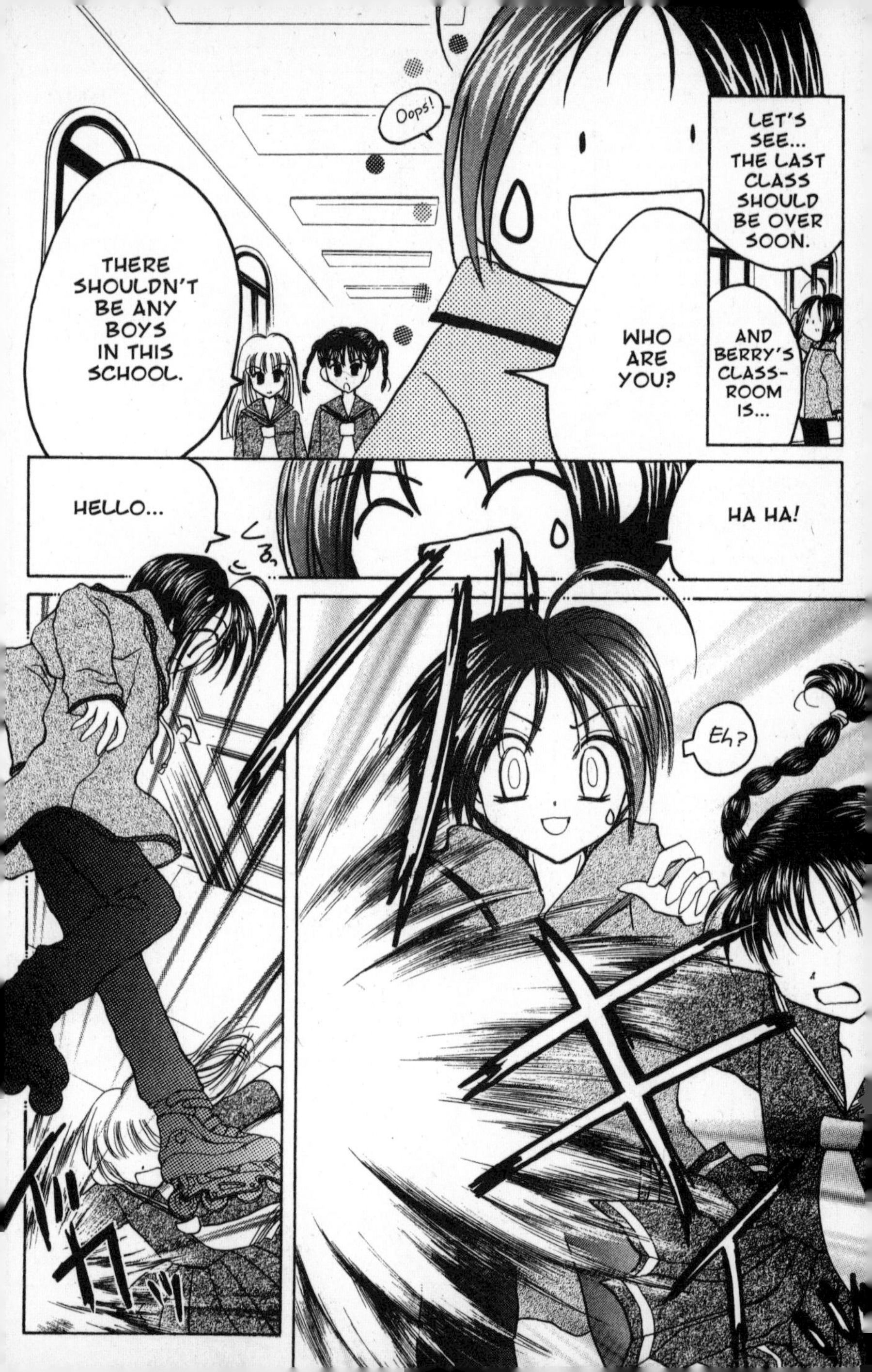
LET'S SEE... THE LAST CLASS SHOULD BE OVER SOON.
AND BERRY'S CLASSROOM IS...
Oops!
WHO ARE YOU?
THERE SHOULDN'T BE ANY BOYS IN THIS SCHOOL.
HA HA!
HELLO...
Eh?

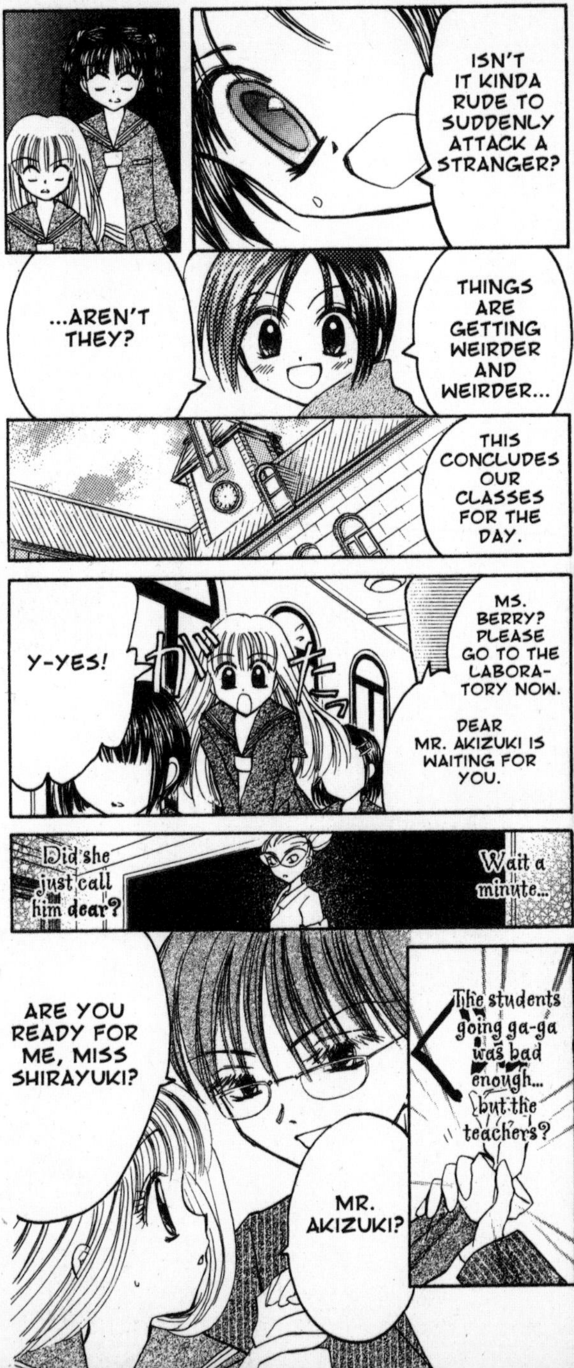
ISN'T IT KINDA RUDE TO SUDDENLY ATTACK A STRANGER?
THINGS ARE GETTING WEIRDER AND WEIRDER...
...AREN'T THEY?
THIS CONCLUDES OUR CLASSES FOR THE DAY.
MS. BERRY? PLEASE GO TO THE LABORATORY NOW.
DEAR MR. AKIZUKI IS WAITING FOR YOU.
Y-YES!
Wait a minute...
Did she just call him dear?
The students going ga-ga was bad enough... but the teachers?
ARE YOU READY FOR ME, MISS SHIRAYUKI?
MR. AKIZUKI?

4

Actually, the Mew Mew calendar project existed before I was assigned *Tokyo Mew Mew a la Mode*. At first I had no clue what I was even going to write about in *a la Mode*. On that note, I'd have to say my favorite project has been the calendar. I wanted to make new stories for both projects, though! The story I was going to write for the calendar is totally different from the casting in these illustrations. I hope I can create a new manga from it.

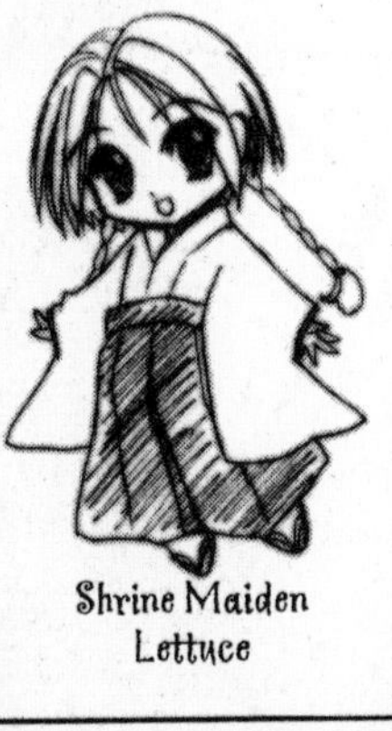

Shrine Maiden Lettuce

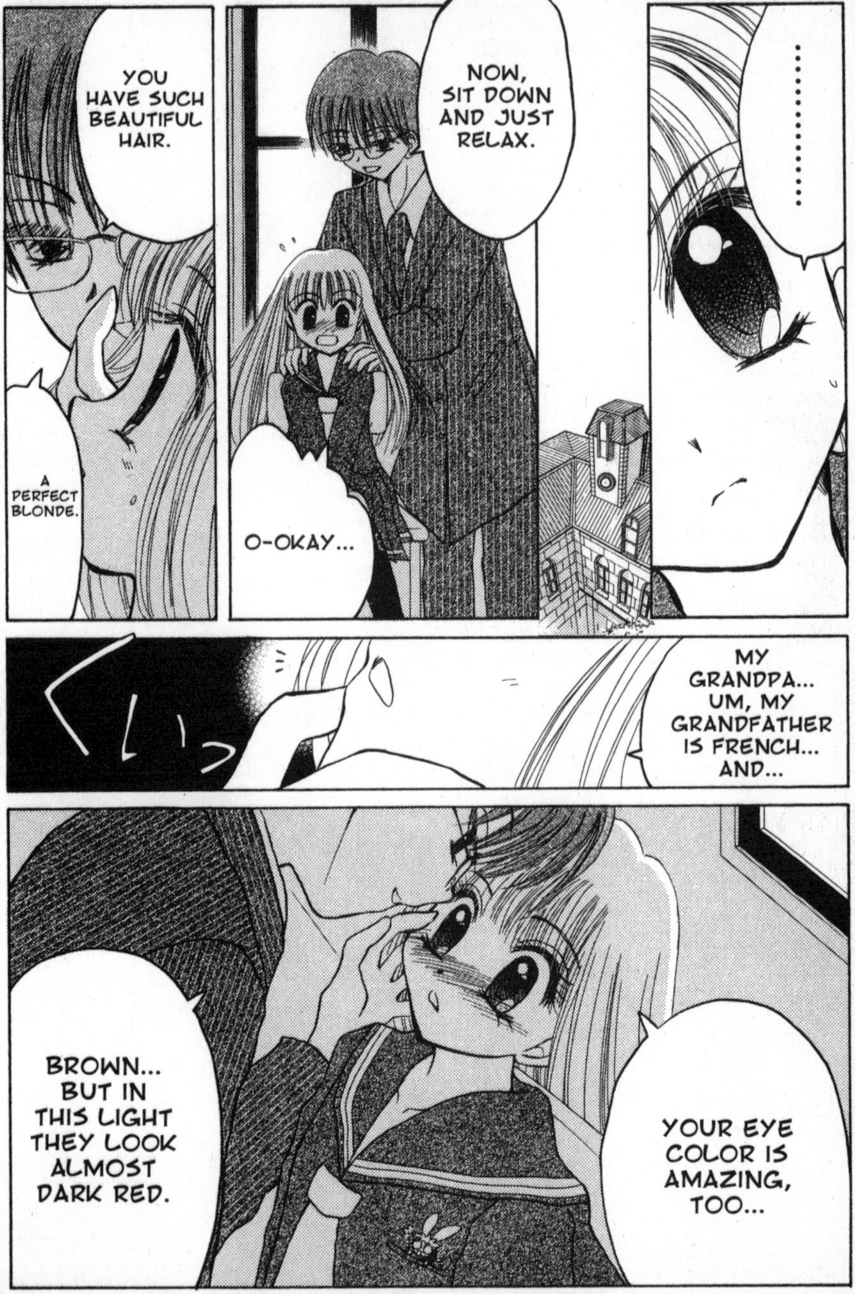
......
NOW, SIT DOWN AND JUST RELAX.
O-OKAY...
YOU HAVE SUCH BEAUTIFUL HAIR.
A PERFECT BLONDE.
MY GRANDPA... UM, MY GRANDFATHER IS FRENCH... AND...
YOUR EYE COLOR IS AMAZING, TOO...
BROWN... BUT IN THIS LIGHT THEY LOOK ALMOST DARK RED.

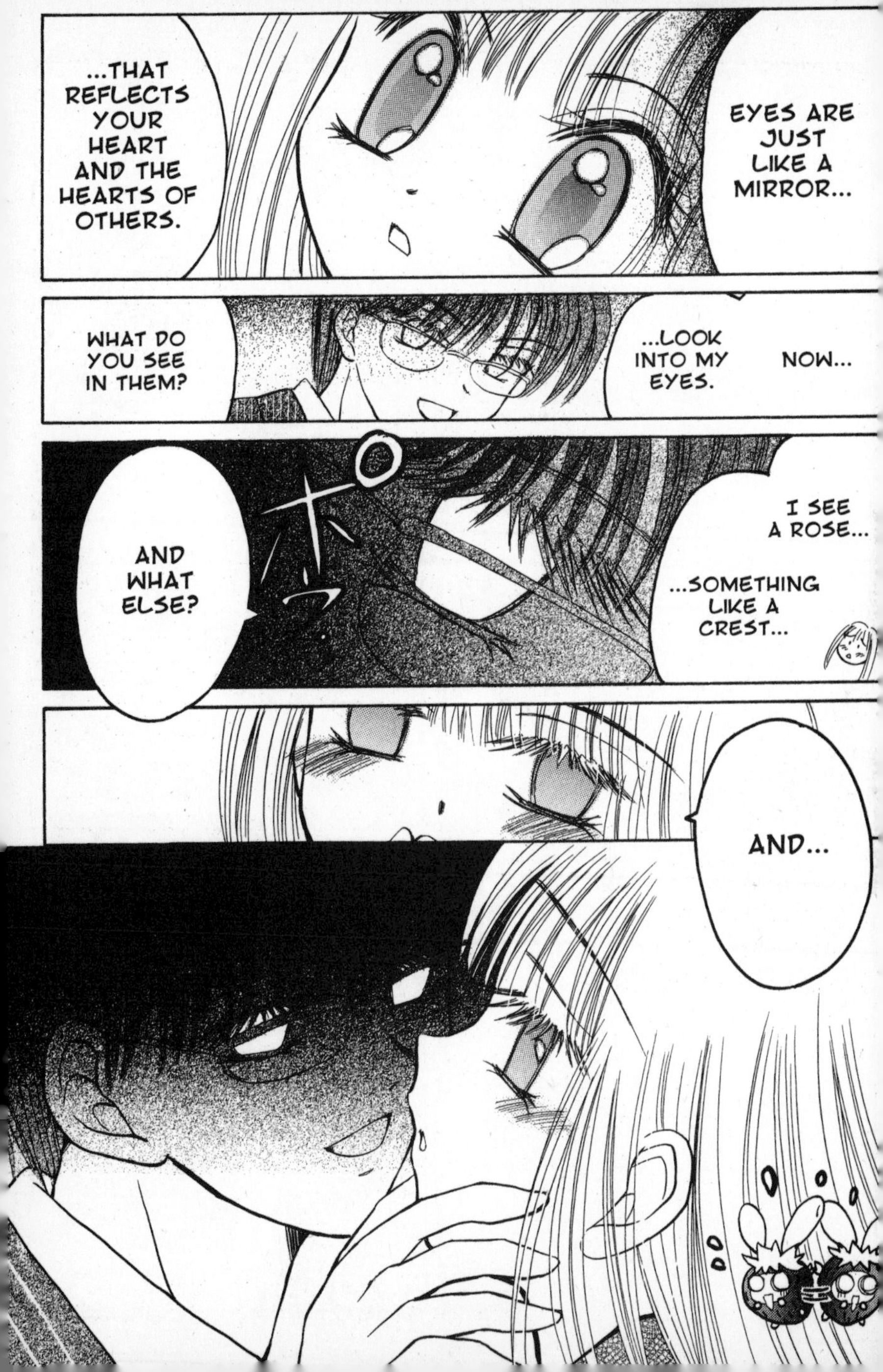
EYES ARE JUST LIKE A MIRROR...
...THAT REFLECTS YOUR HEART AND THE HEARTS OF OTHERS.
NOW...
...LOOK INTO MY EYES.
WHAT DO YOU SEE IN THEM?
I SEE A ROSE...
...SOMETHING LIKE A CREST...
AND WHAT ELSE?
AND...

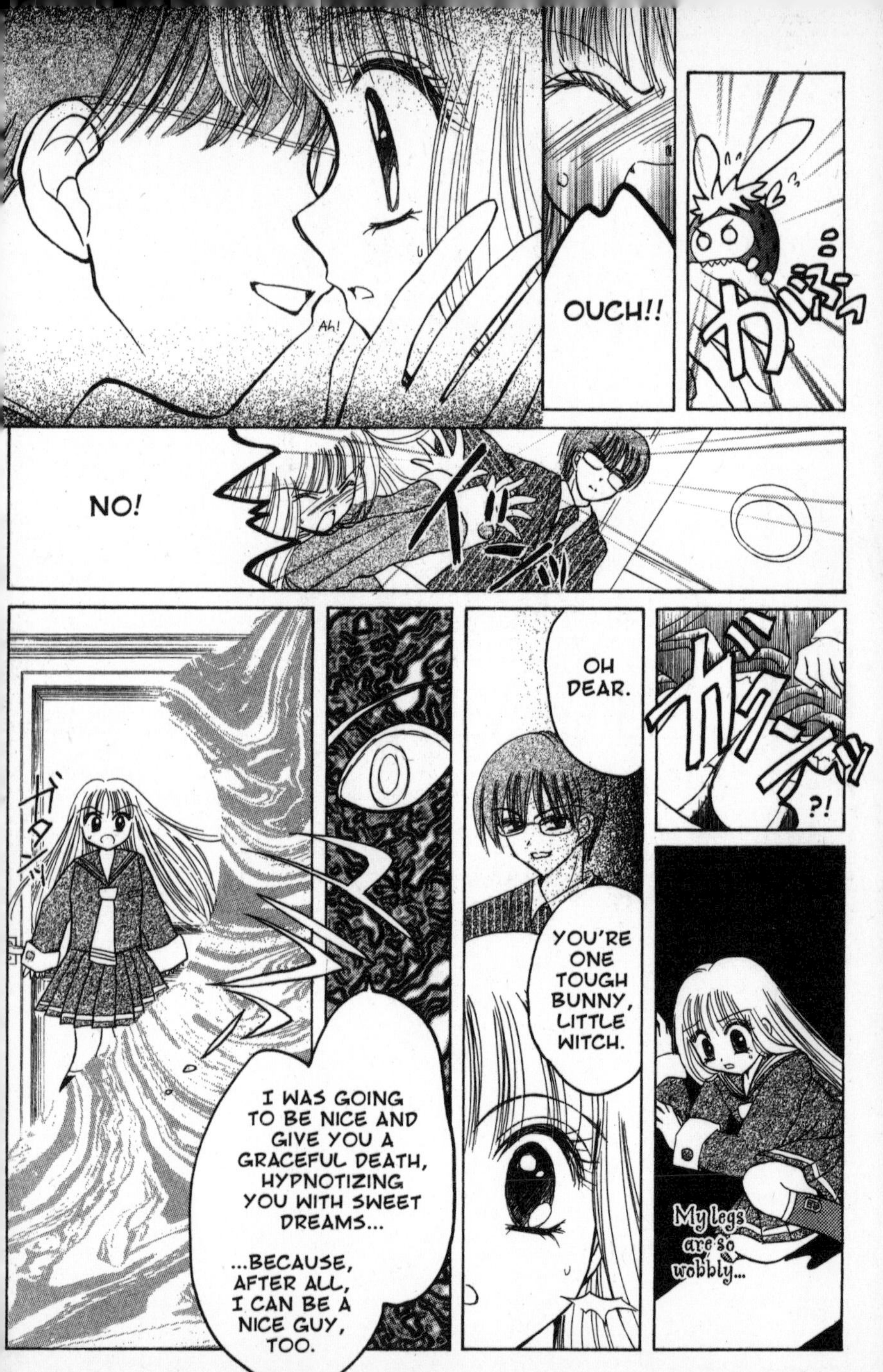
OUCH!!
Ah!
NO!
?!
My legs are so wobbly...
OH DEAR.
YOU'RE ONE TOUGH BUNNY, LITTLE WITCH.
I WAS GOING TO BE NICE AND GIVE YOU A GRACEFUL DEATH, HYPNOTIZING YOU WITH SWEET DREAMS...
...BECAUSE, AFTER ALL, I CAN BE A NICE GUY, TOO.

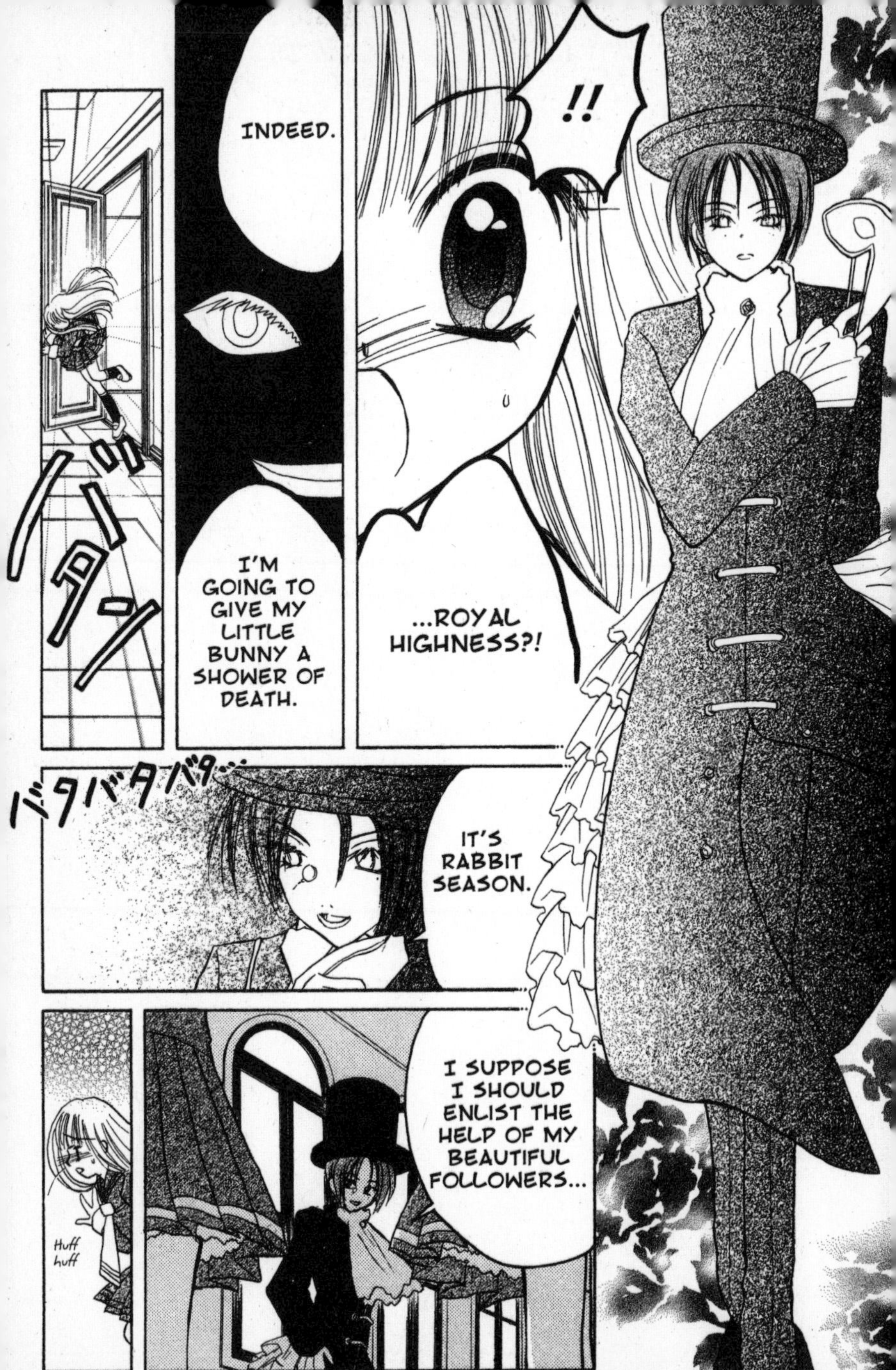

!!
...ROYAL HIGHNESS?!
INDEED.
I'M GOING TO GIVE MY LITTLE BUNNY A SHOWER OF DEATH.
IT'S RABBIT SEASON.
バタバタバタ…
I SUPPOSE I SHOULD ENLIST THE HELP OF MY BEAUTIFUL FOLLOWERS...
Huff huff

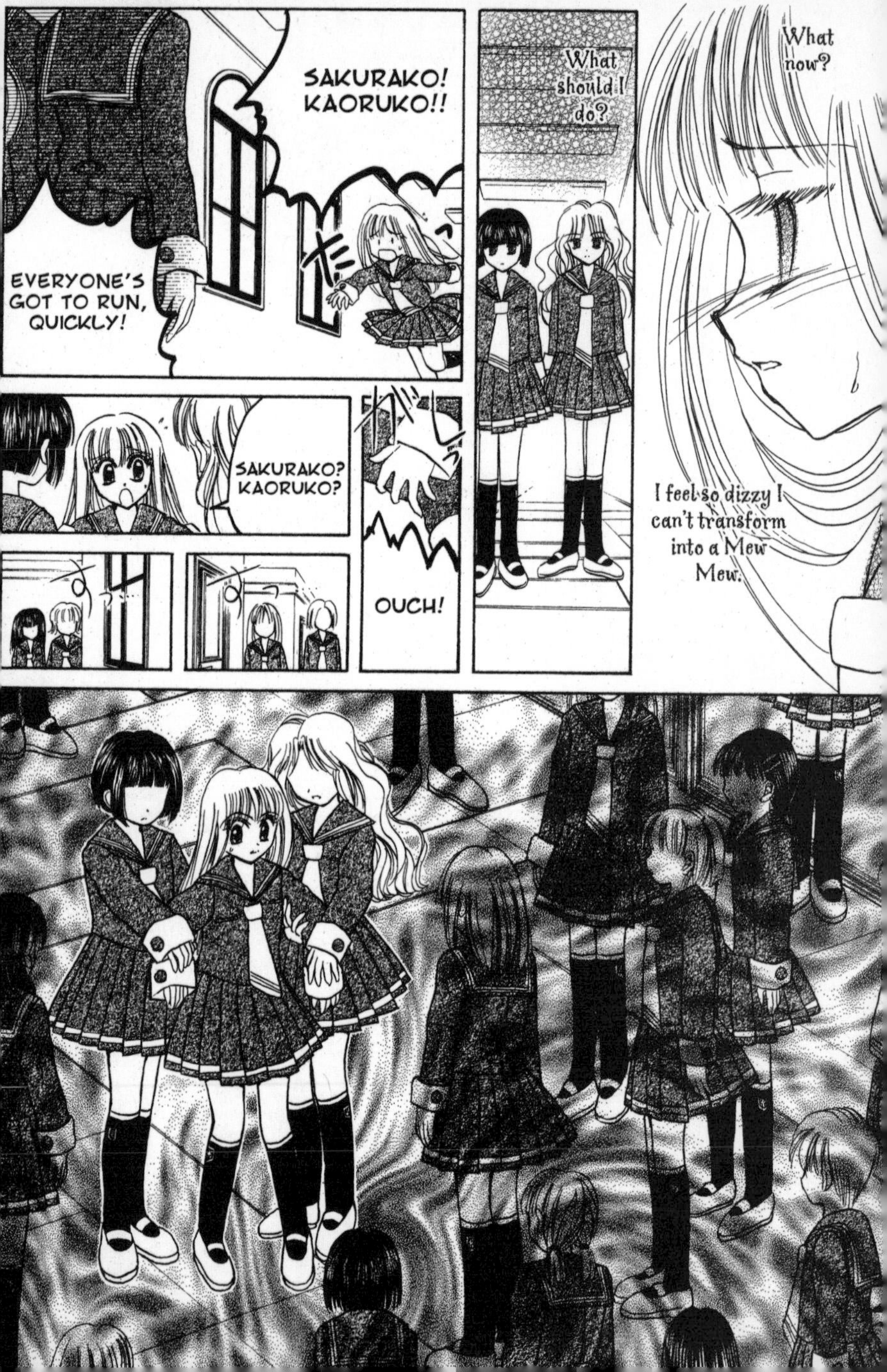
What now?
I feel so dizzy I can't transform into a Mew Mew.
What should I do?
SAKURAKO! KAORUKO!!
EVERYONE'S GOT TO RUN, QUICKLY!
OUCH!
SAKURAKO? KAORUKO?

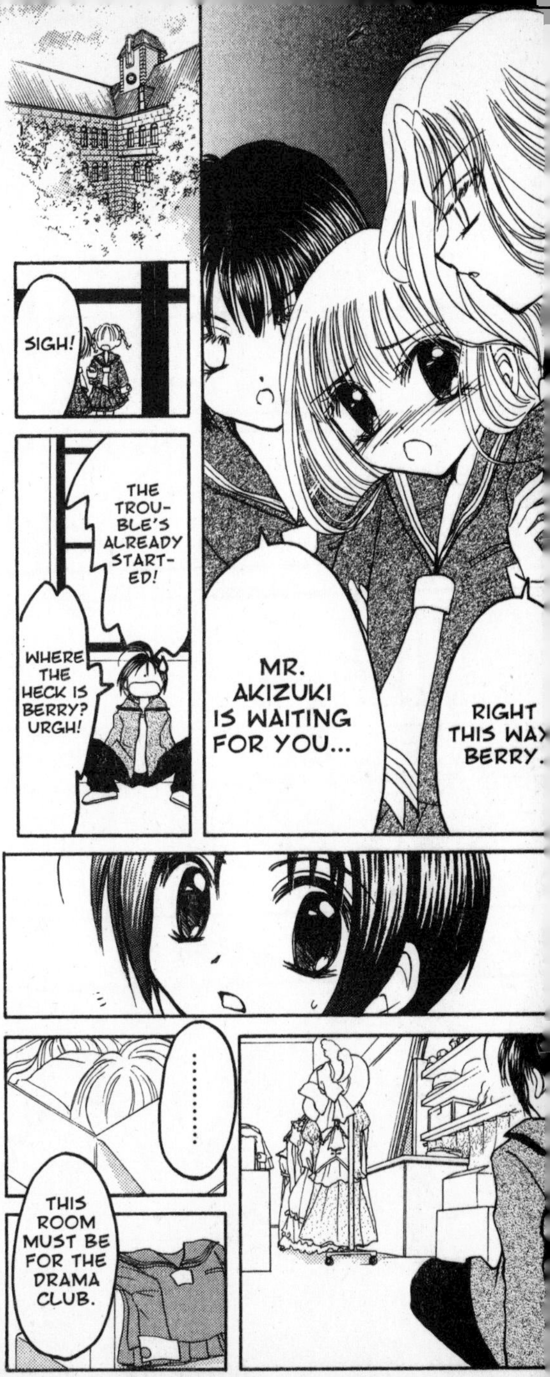
RIGHT THIS WAY BERRY.
MR. AKIZUKI IS WAITING FOR YOU...
SIGH!
THE TROUBLE'S ALREADY STARTED!
WHERE THE HECK IS BERRY? URGH!
......
THIS ROOM MUST BE FOR THE DRAMA CLUB.

5

I know I keep talking about the calendar, but I drew some other illustrations I wanted to chat about. I worked three times harder on this one compared to the first two calendars. Because of this, I feel like I definitely made the illustrations better. I love improving my work—it makes me feel great!

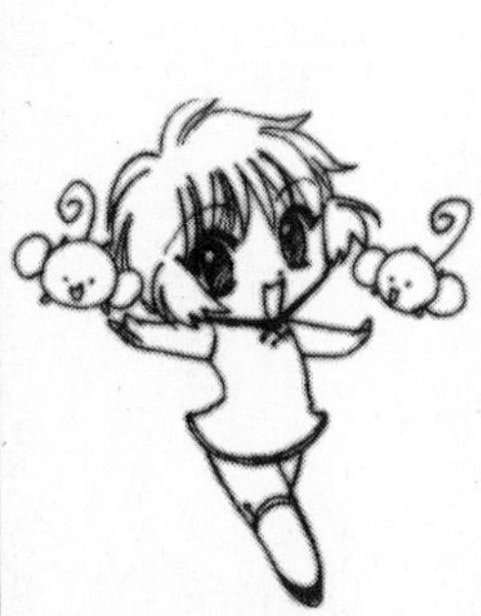

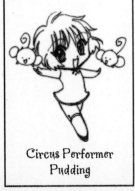

Circus Performer Pudding

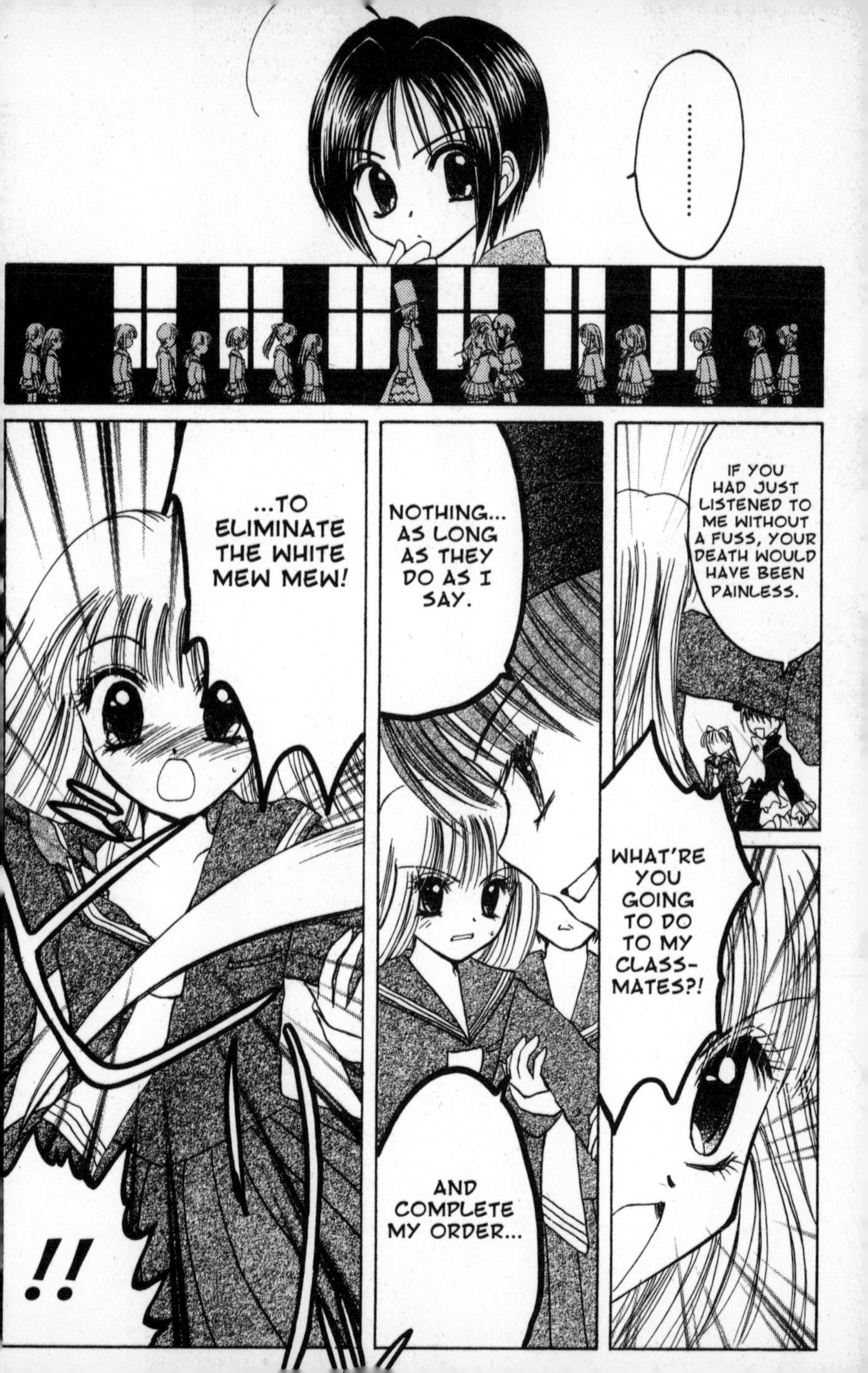
......
IF YOU HAD JUST LISTENED TO ME WITHOUT A FUSS, YOUR DEATH WOULD HAVE BEEN PAINLESS.
WHAT'RE YOU GOING TO DO TO MY CLASS-MATES?!
NOTHING... AS LONG AS THEY DO AS I SAY.
AND COMPLETE MY ORDER...
...TO ELIMINATE THE WHITE MEW MEW!
!!

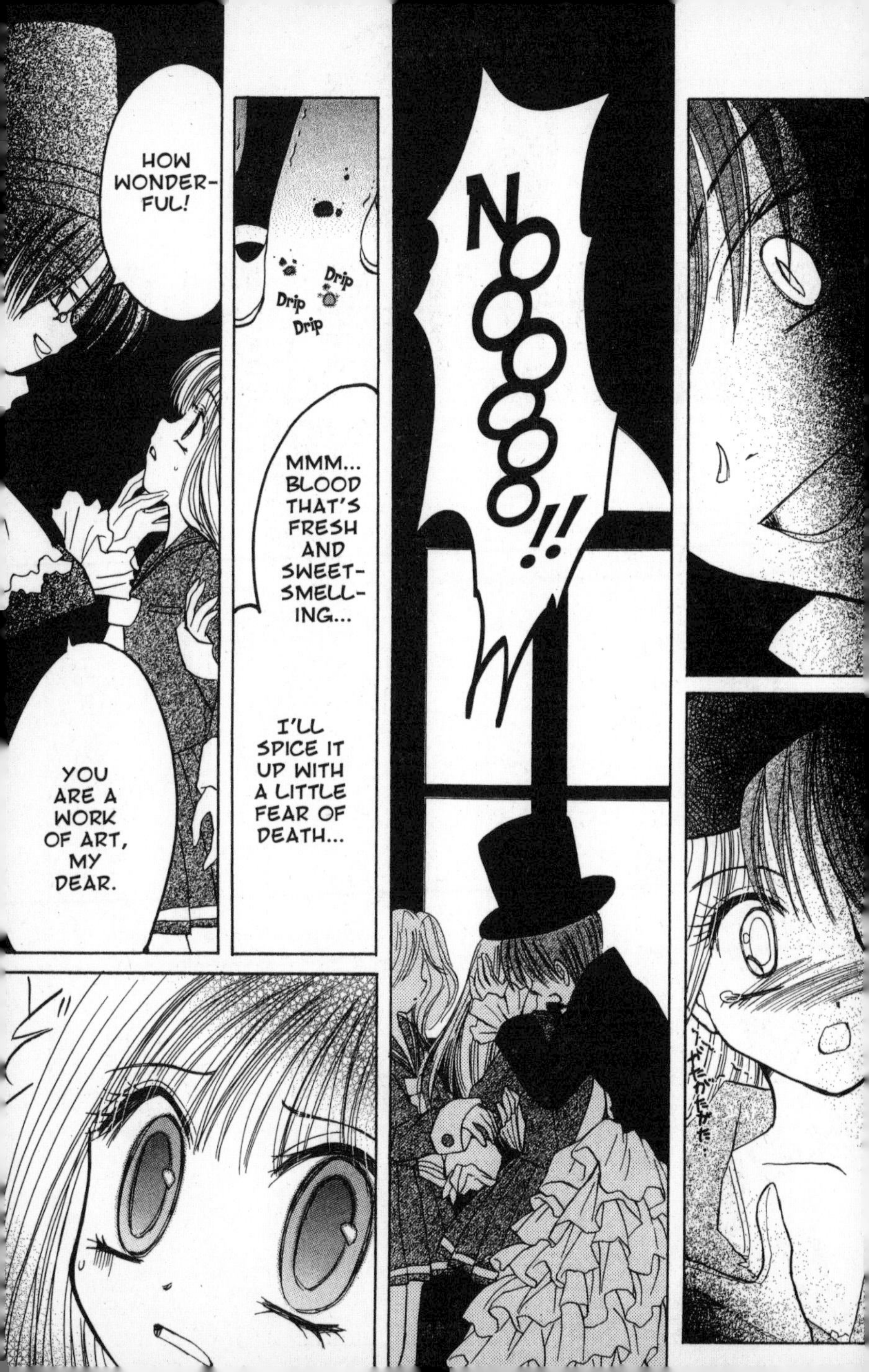
NOOOOOO!!
Drip
Drip
Drip
MMM... BLOOD THAT'S FRESH AND SWEET-SMELLING...
I'LL SPICE IT UP WITH A LITTLE FEAR OF DEATH...
HOW WONDER-FUL!
YOU ARE A WORK OF ART, MY DEAR.

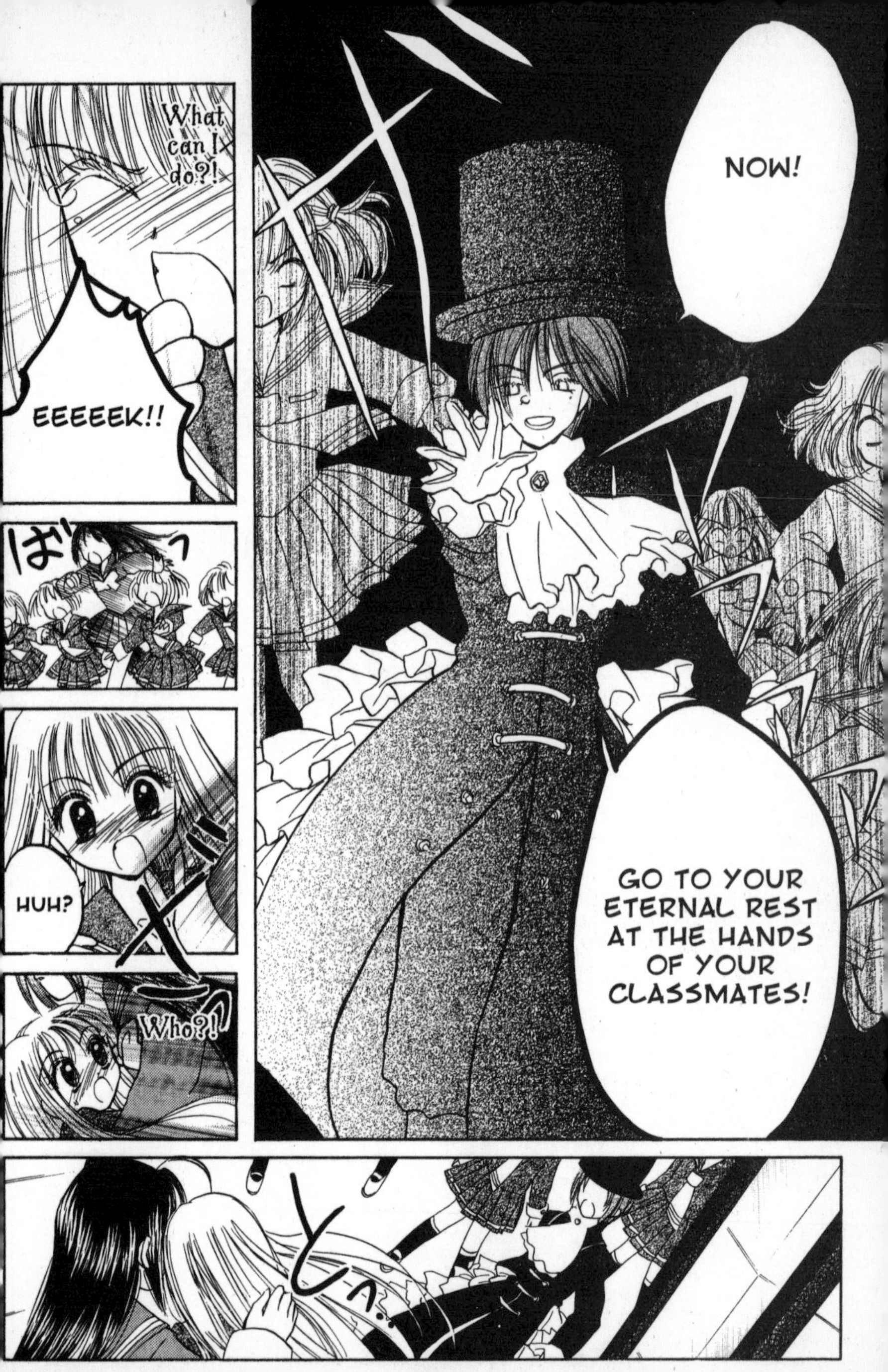
NOW!
GO TO YOUR ETERNAL REST AT THE HANDS OF YOUR CLASSMATES!
What can I do?!
EEEEEK!!
ばっ
HUH?
Who?!

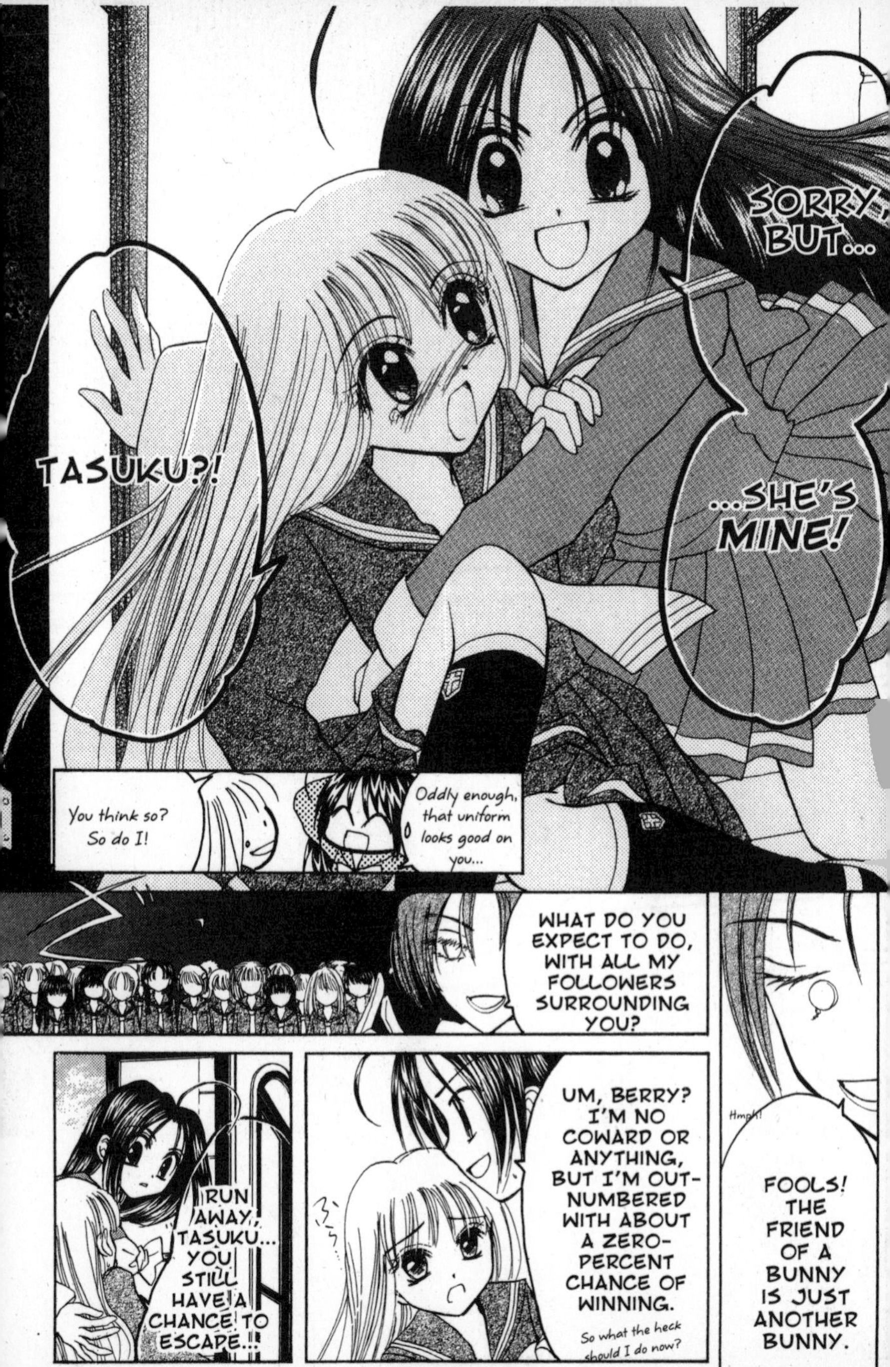
SORRY, BUT...
...SHE'S MINE!
TASUKU?!
Oddly enough, that uniform looks good on you...
You think so? So do I!
Hmph!
FOOLS! THE FRIEND OF A BUNNY IS JUST ANOTHER BUNNY.
WHAT DO YOU EXPECT TO DO, WITH ALL MY FOLLOWERS SURROUNDING YOU?
UM, BERRY? I'M NO COWARD OR ANYTHING, BUT I'M OUT-NUMBERED WITH ABOUT A ZERO-PERCENT CHANCE OF WINNING.
So what the heck should I do now?
RUN AWAY, TASUKU... YOU STILL HAVE A CHANCE TO ESCAPE...!

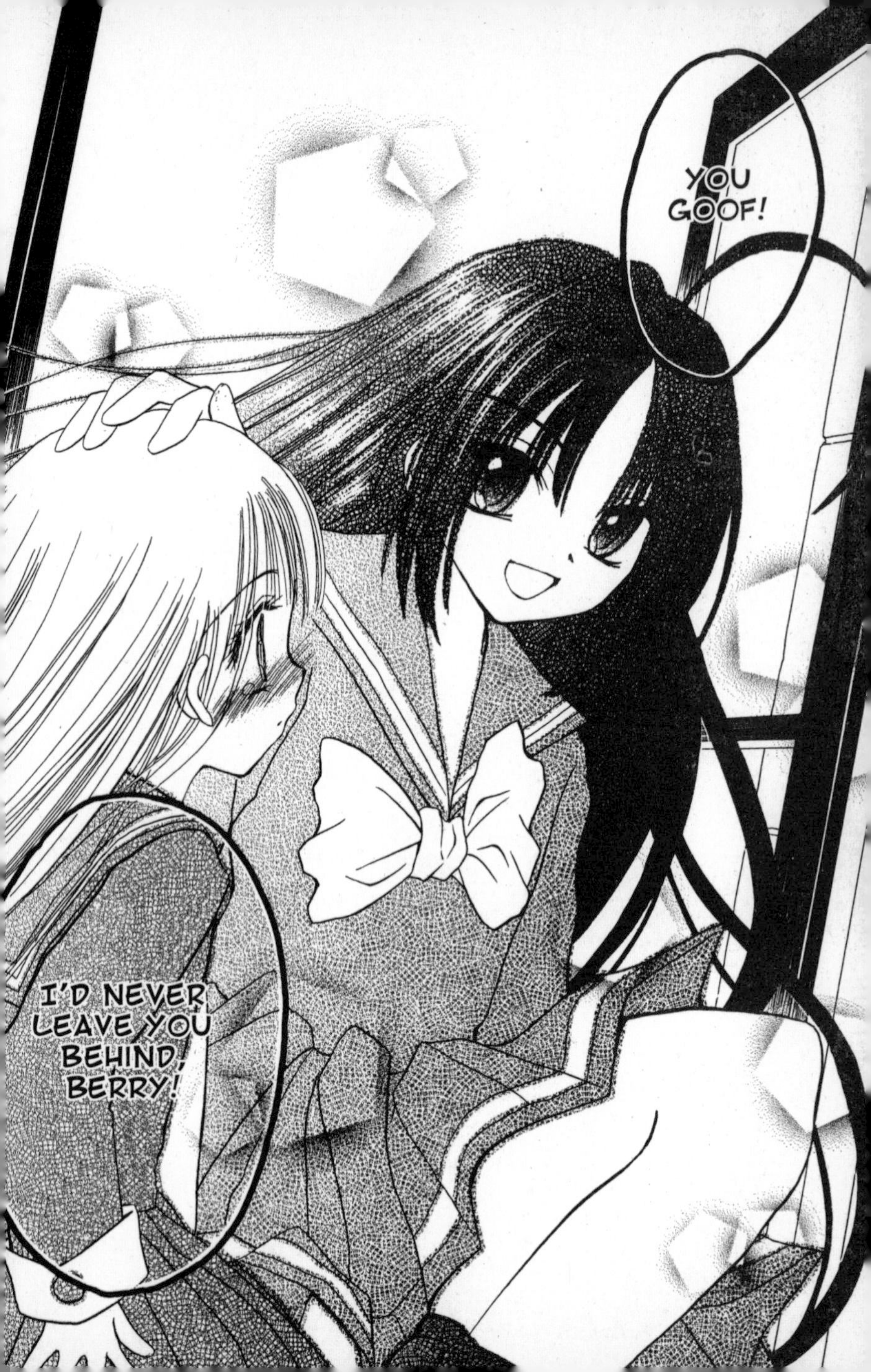
YOU GOOF!
I'D NEVER LEAVE YOU BEHIND, BERRY!

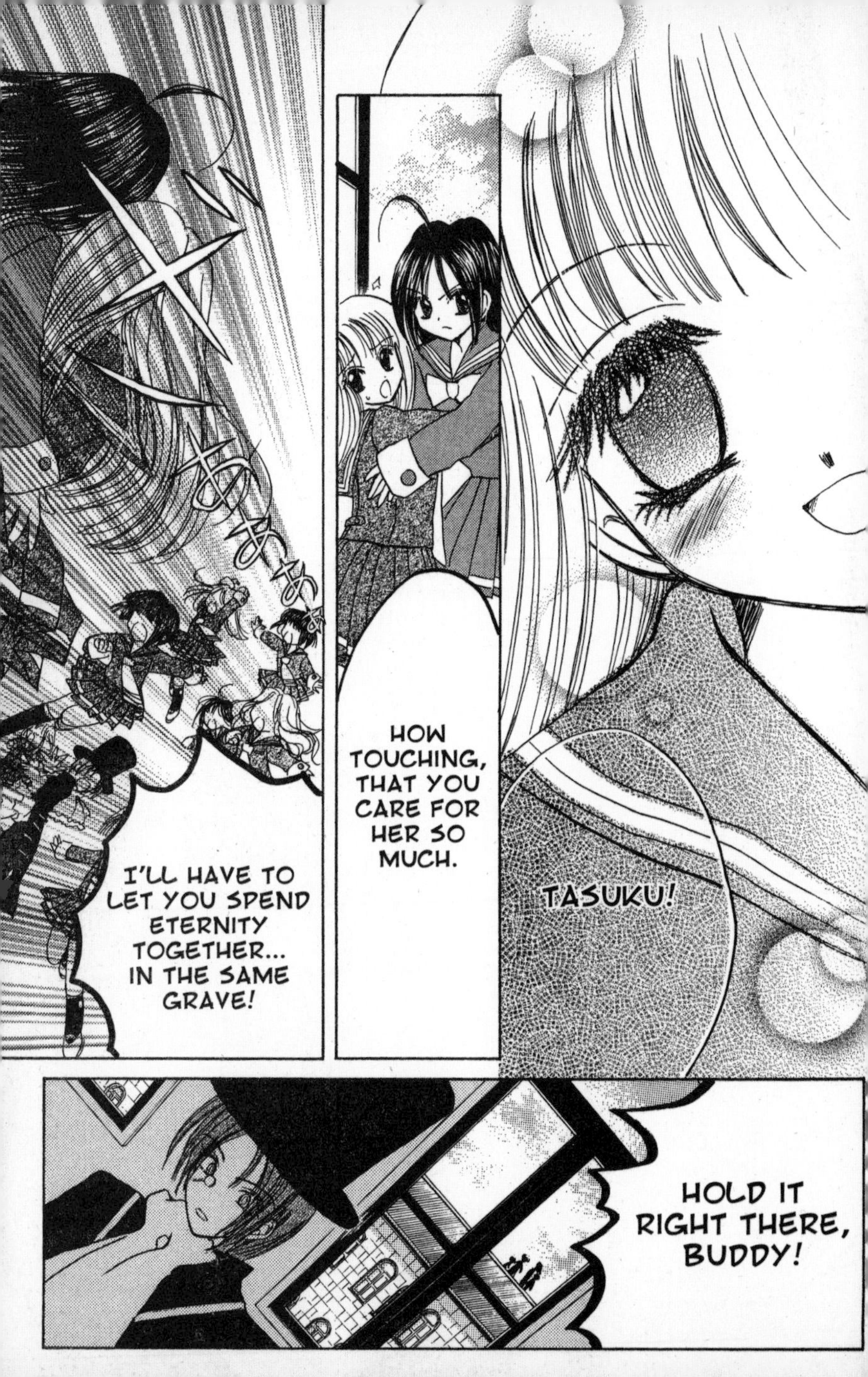
TASUKU!
HOW TOUCHING, THAT YOU CARE FOR HER SO MUCH.
I'LL HAVE TO LET YOU SPEND ETERNITY TOGETHER... IN THE SAME GRAVE!
HOLD IT RIGHT THERE, BUDDY!

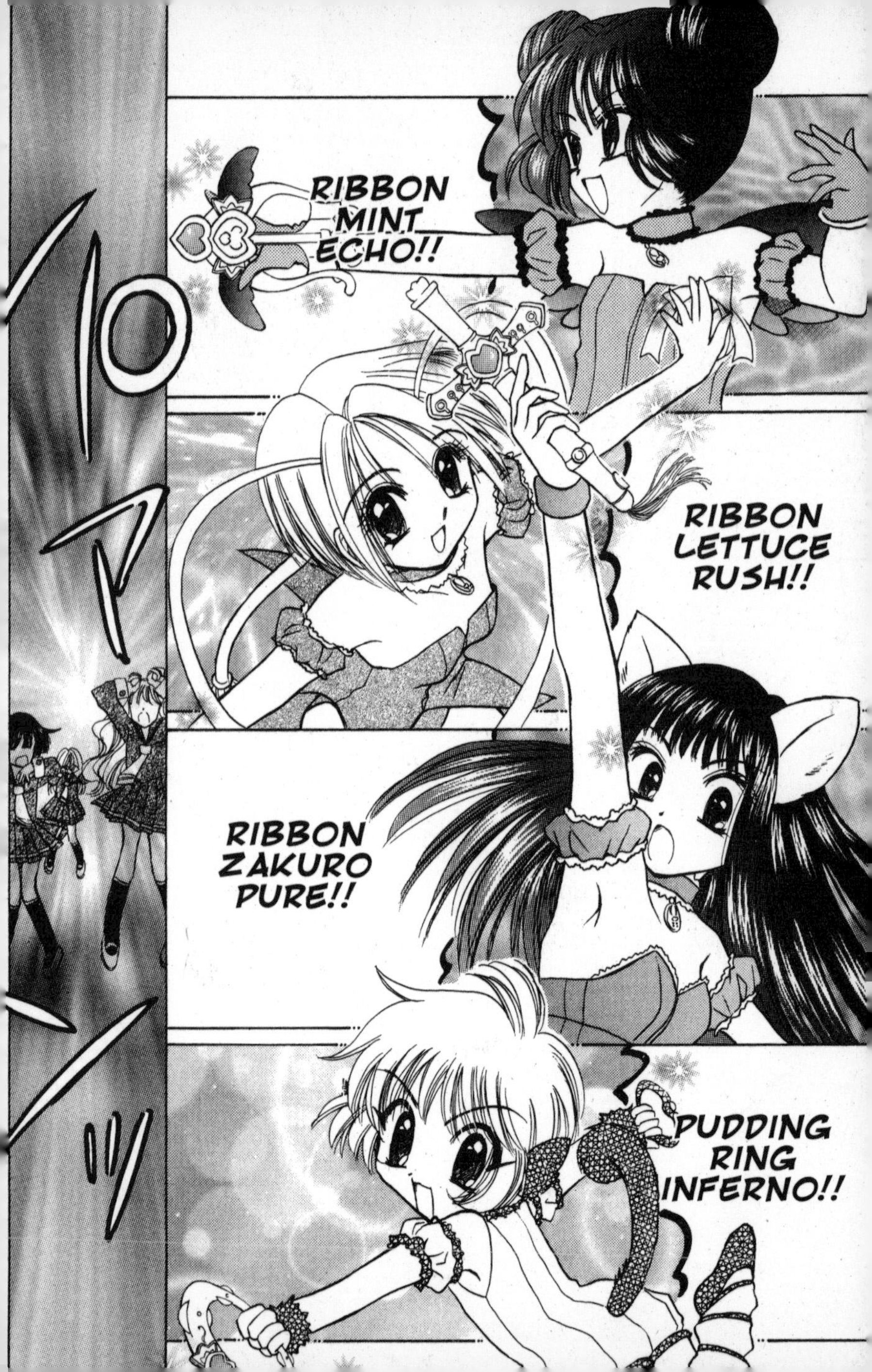
RIBBON MINT ECHO!!
RIBBON LETTUCE RUSH!!
RIBBON ZAKURO PURE!!
PUDDING RING INFERNO!!

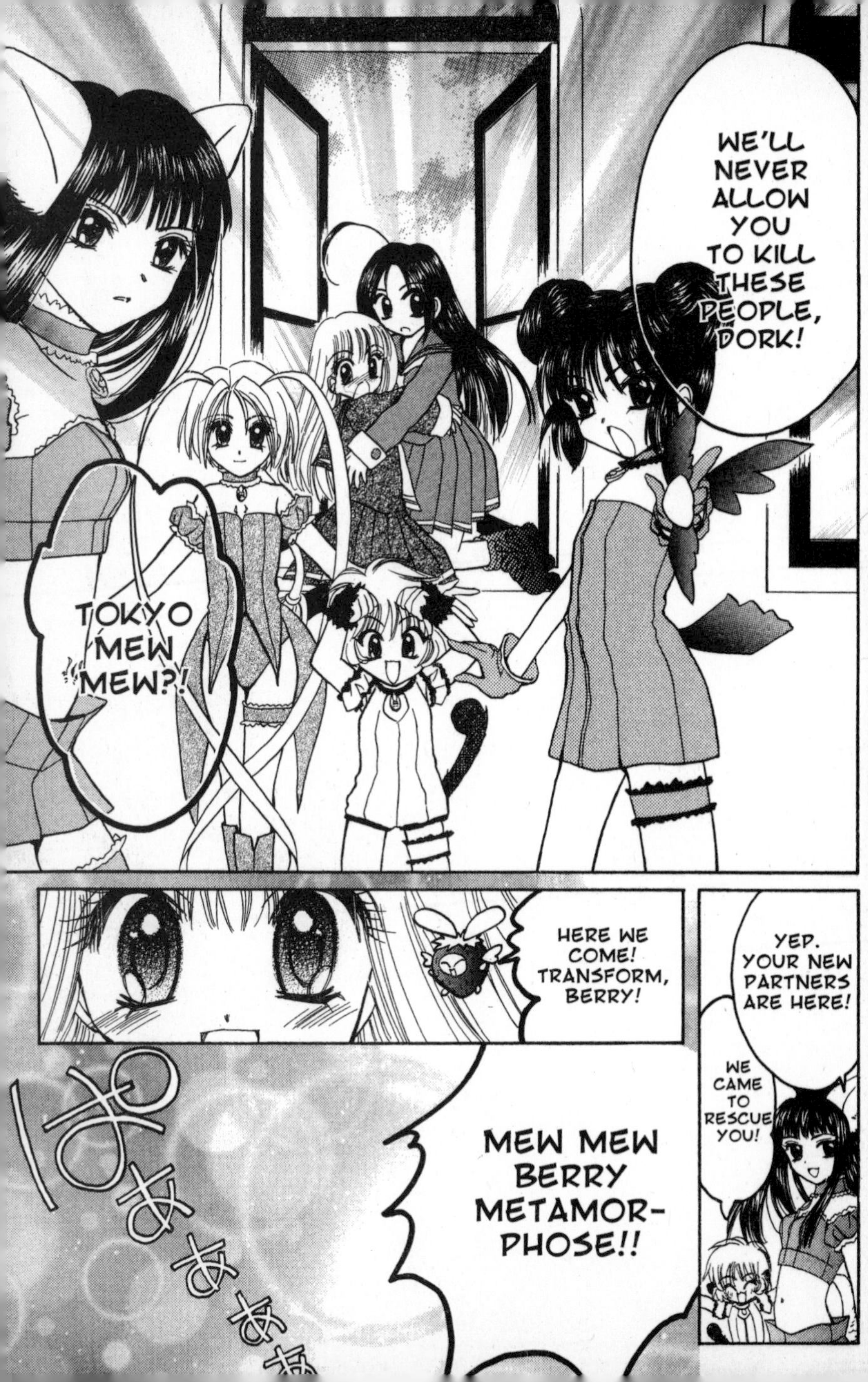
WE'LL NEVER ALLOW YOU TO KILL THESE PEOPLE, DORK!
TOKYO MEW MEW?!
YEP. YOUR NEW PARTNERS ARE HERE!
WE CAME TO RESCUE YOU!
HERE WE COME! TRANSFORM, BERRY!
MEW MEW BERRY METAMOR-PHOSE!!

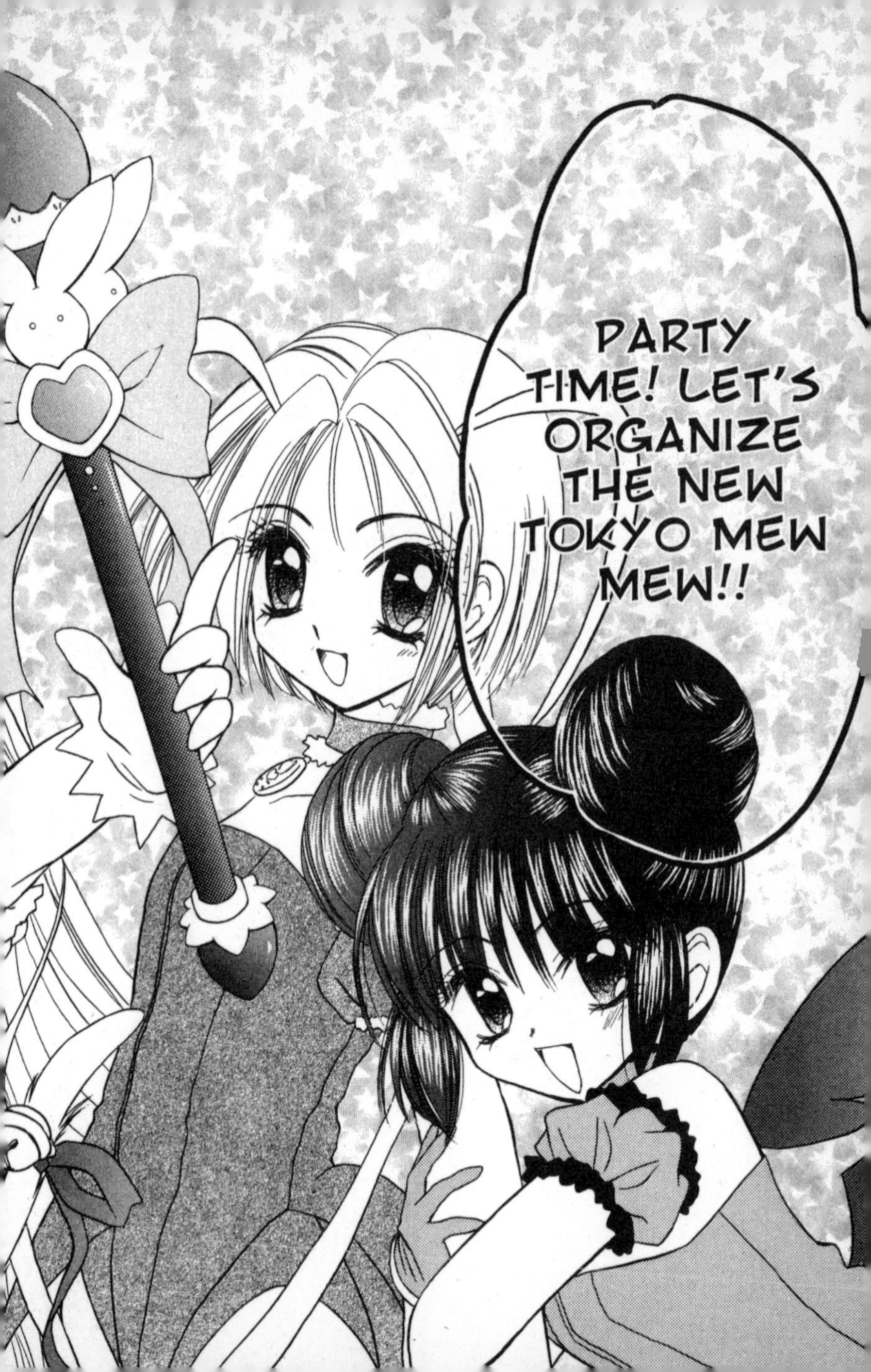
PARTY TIME! LET'S ORGANIZE THE NEW TOKYO MEW MEW!!

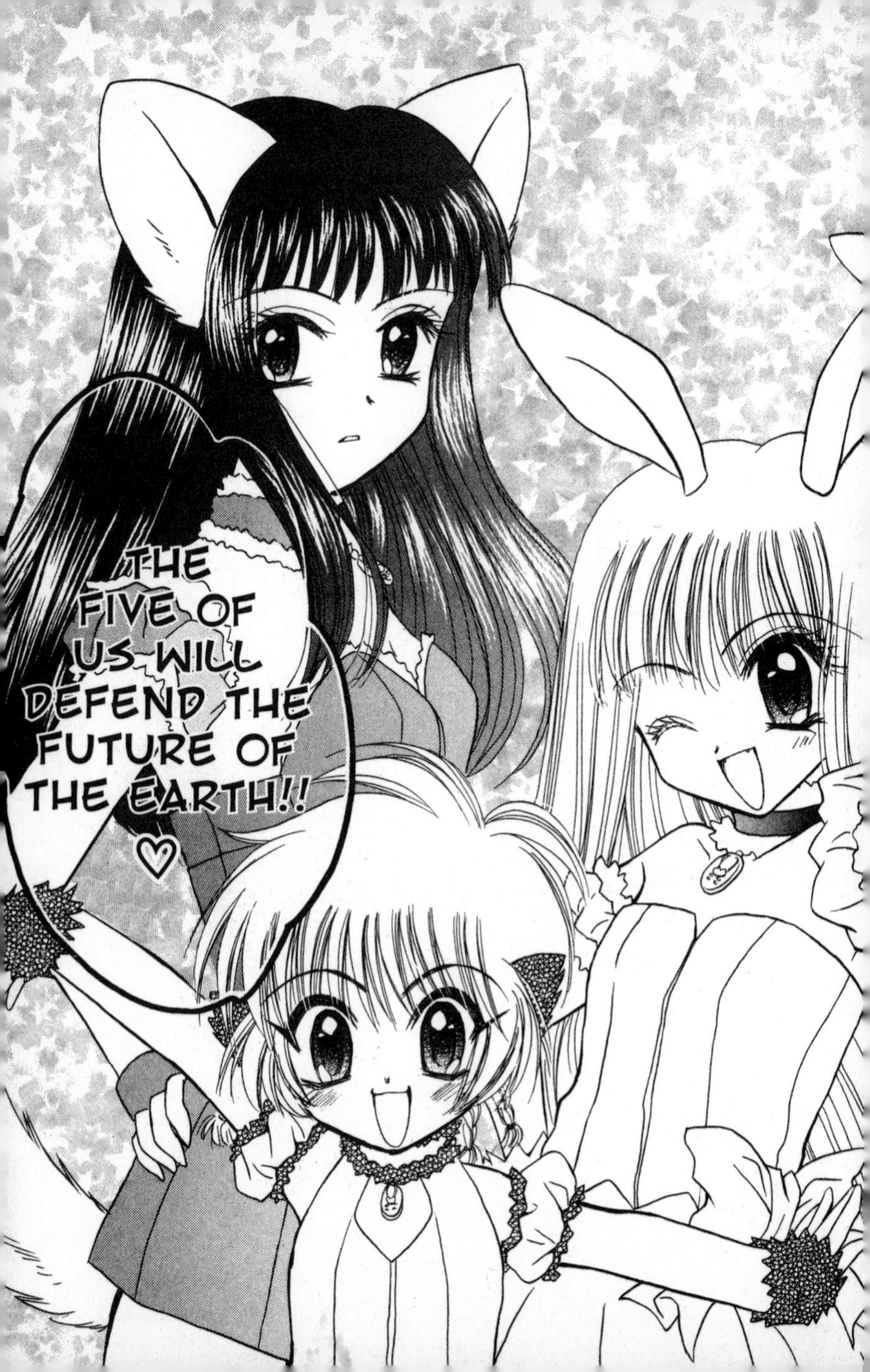
THE FIVE OF US WILL DEFEND THE FUTURE OF THE EARTH!! ♡

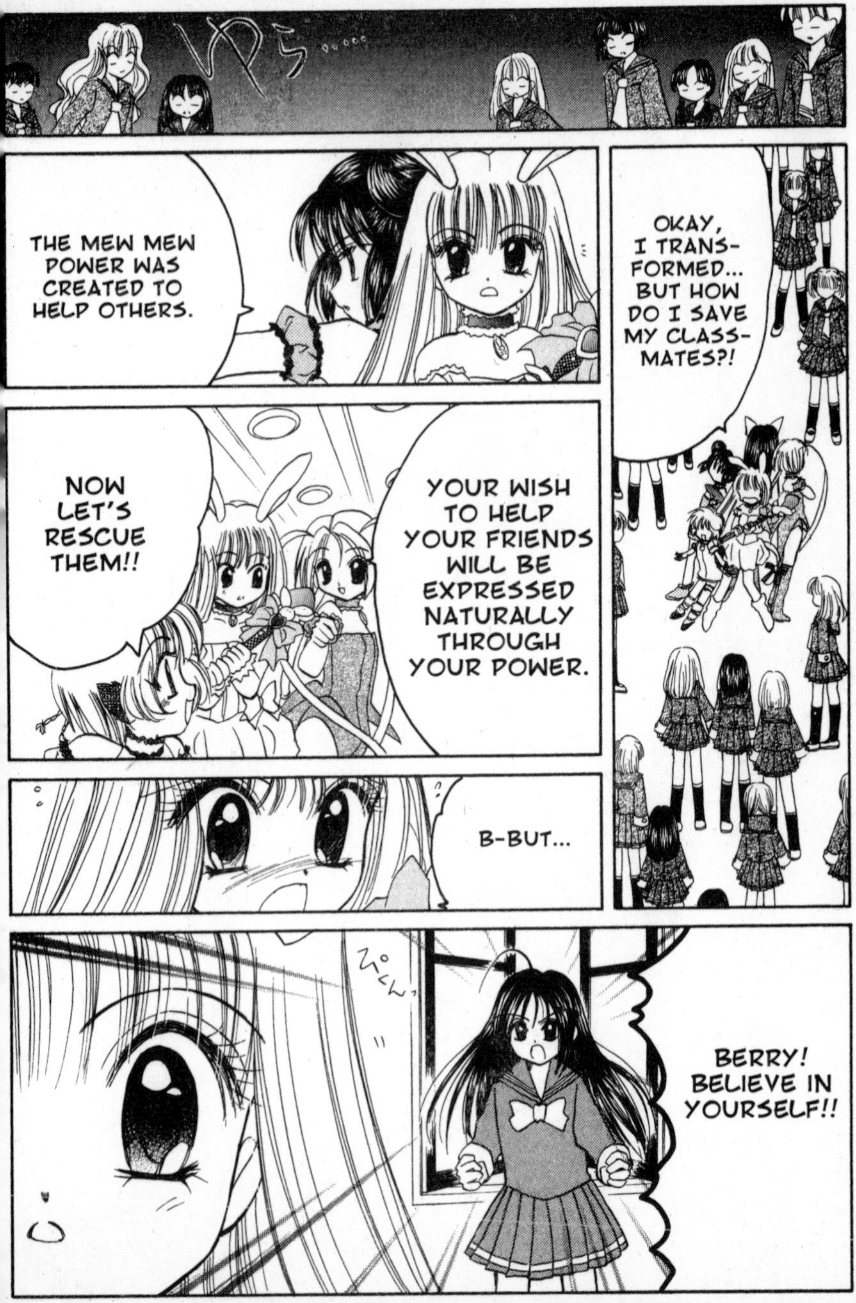
OKAY, I TRANS-FORMED... BUT HOW DO I SAVE MY CLASS-MATES?!
THE MEW MEW POWER WAS CREATED TO HELP OTHERS.
YOUR WISH TO HELP YOUR FRIENDS WILL BE EXPRESSED NATURALLY THROUGH YOUR POWER.
NOW LET'S RESCUE THEM!!
B-BUT...
ぴくん
BERRY! BELIEVE IN YOURSELF!!

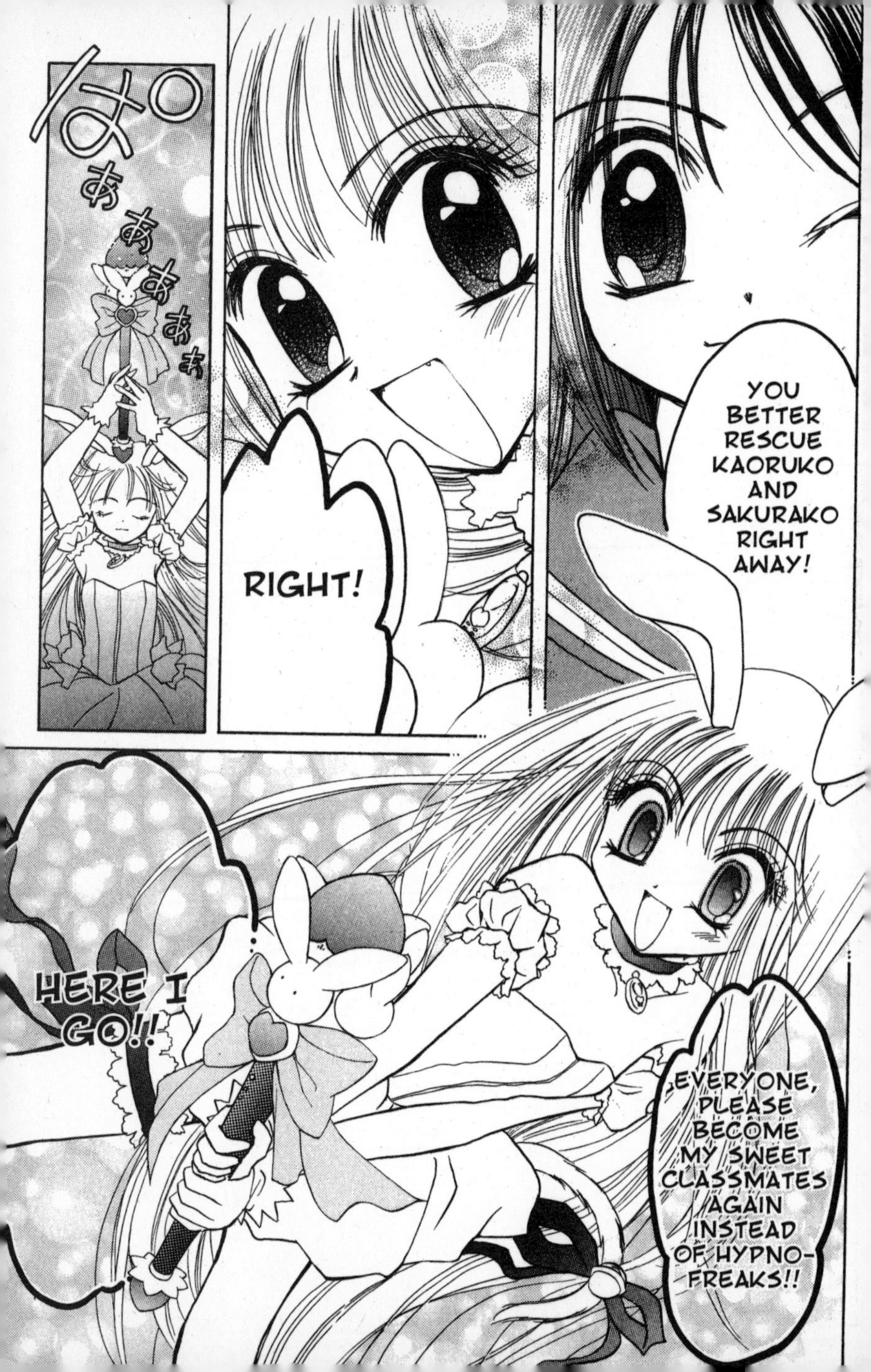
YOU BETTER RESCUE KAORUKO AND SAKURAKO RIGHT AWAY!
RIGHT!
はぁぁぁぁぁ
EVERYONE, PLEASE BECOME MY SWEET CLASSMATES AGAIN INSTEAD OF HYPNO-FREAKS!!
HERE I GO!!

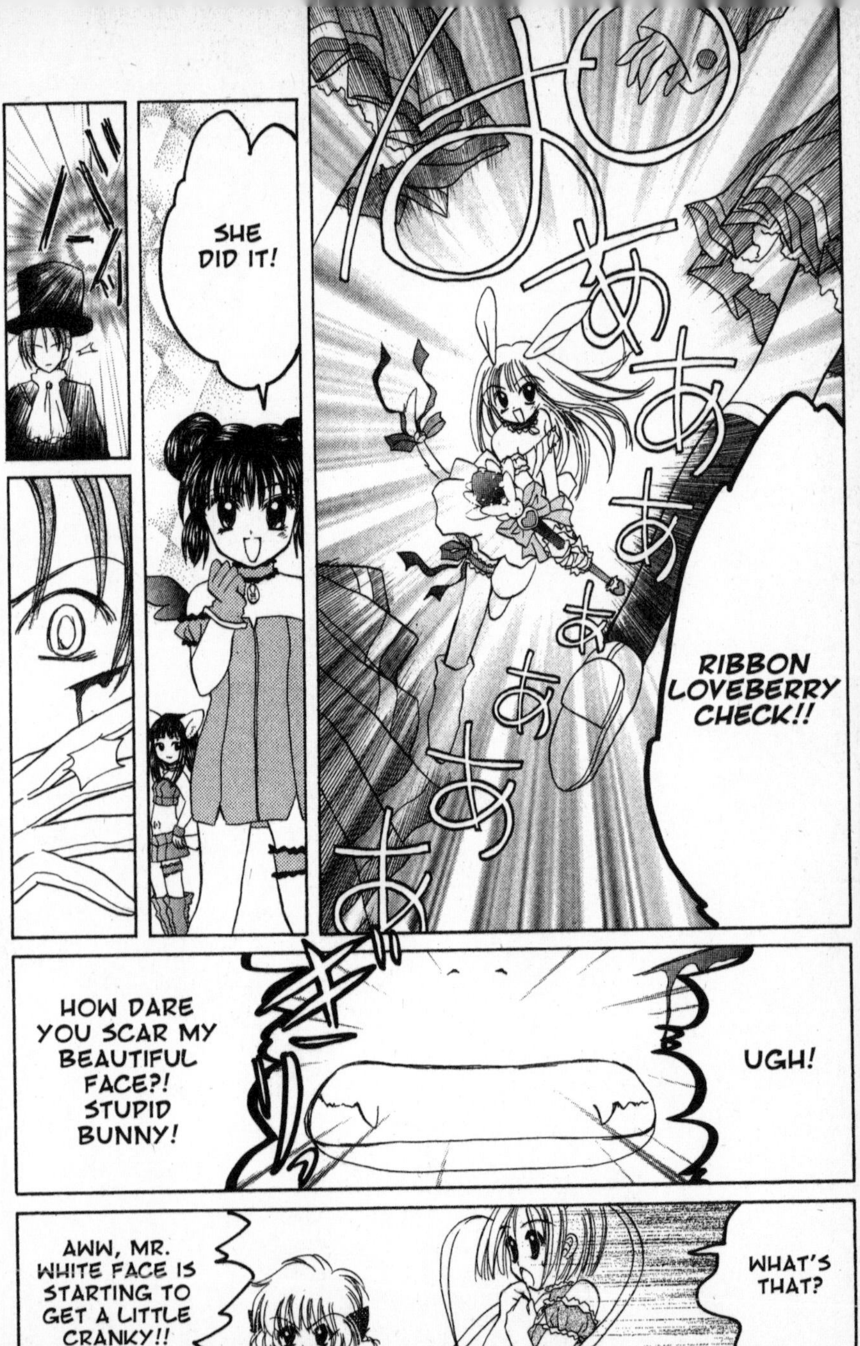
RIBBON LOVEBERRY CHECK!!
SHE DID IT!
UGH!
HOW DARE YOU SCAR MY BEAUTIFUL FACE?! STUPID BUNNY!
WHAT'S THAT?
AWW, MR. WHITE FACE IS STARTING TO GET A LITTLE CRANKY!!

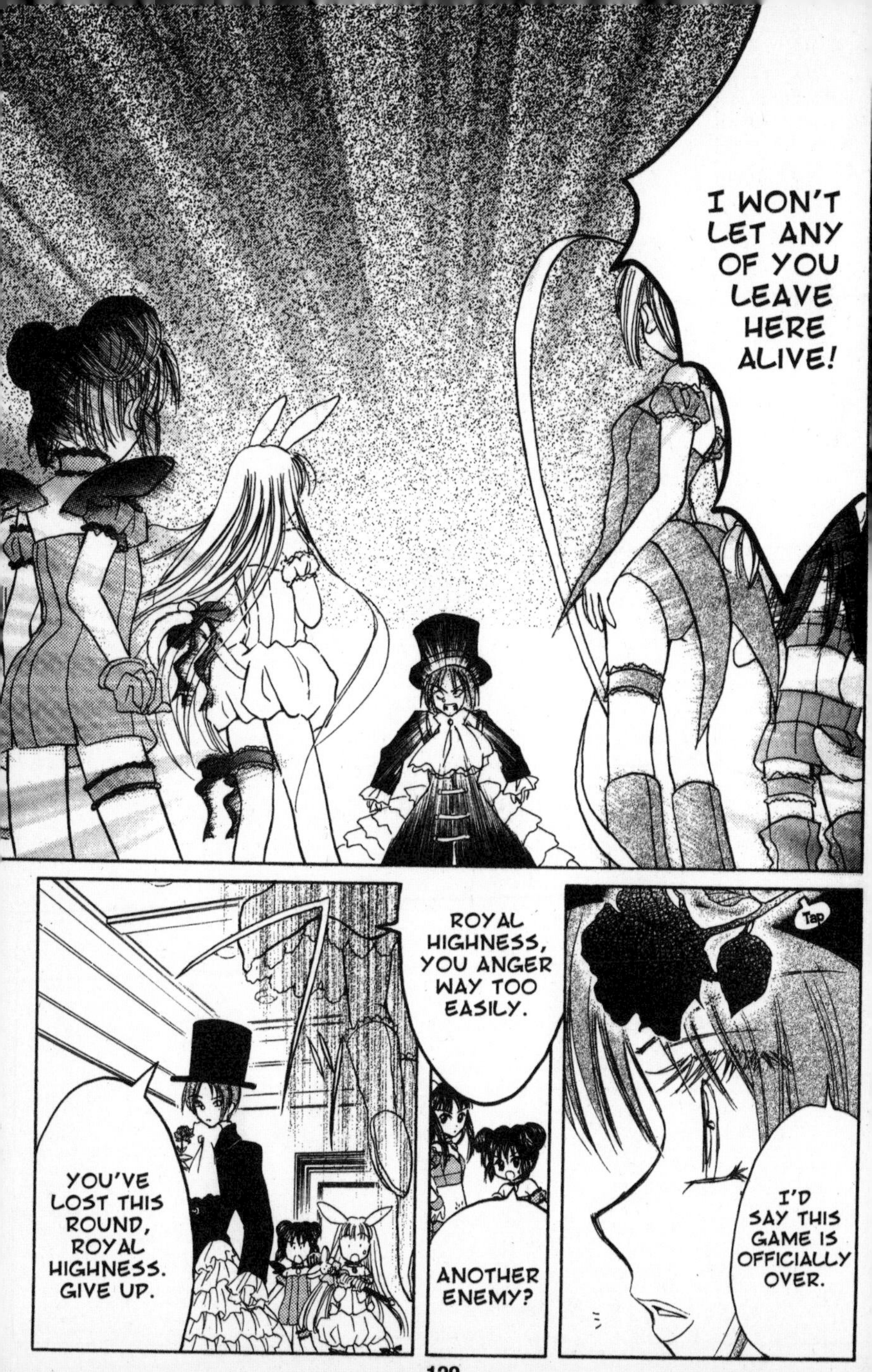
I WON'T LET ANY OF YOU LEAVE HERE ALIVE!
Tap
I'D SAY THIS GAME IS OFFICIALLY OVER.
ROYAL HIGHNESS, YOU ANGER WAY TOO EASILY.
ANOTHER ENEMY?
YOU'VE LOST THIS ROUND, ROYAL HIGHNESS. GIVE UP.

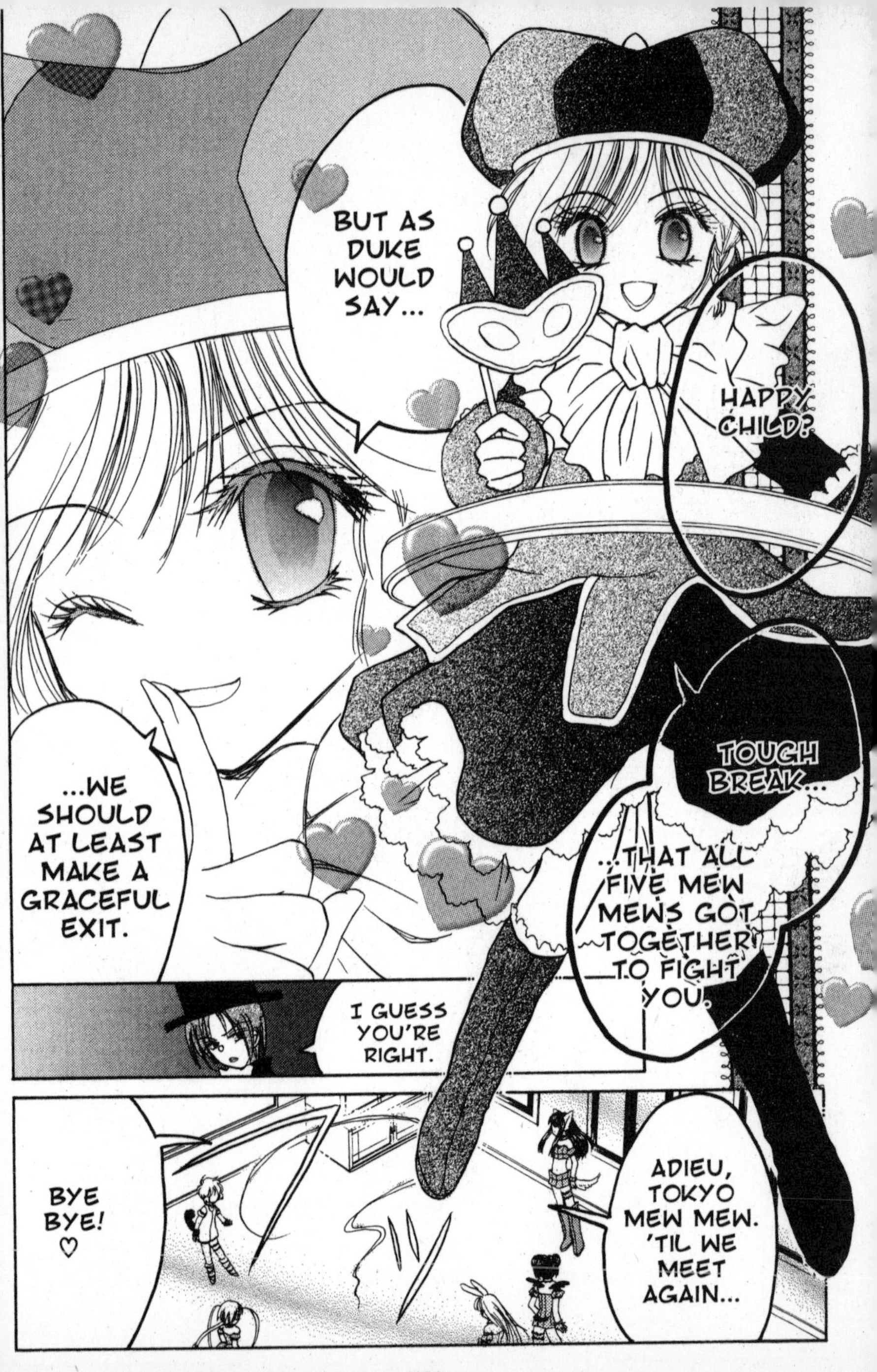
HAPPY CHILD?
TOUGH BREAK...
...THAT ALL FIVE MEW MEWS GOT TOGETHER TO FIGHT YOU.
BUT AS DUKE WOULD SAY...
...WE SHOULD AT LEAST MAKE A GRACEFUL EXIT.
I GUESS YOU'RE RIGHT.
ADIEU, TOKYO MEW MEW. 'TIL WE MEET AGAIN...
BYE BYE! ♡

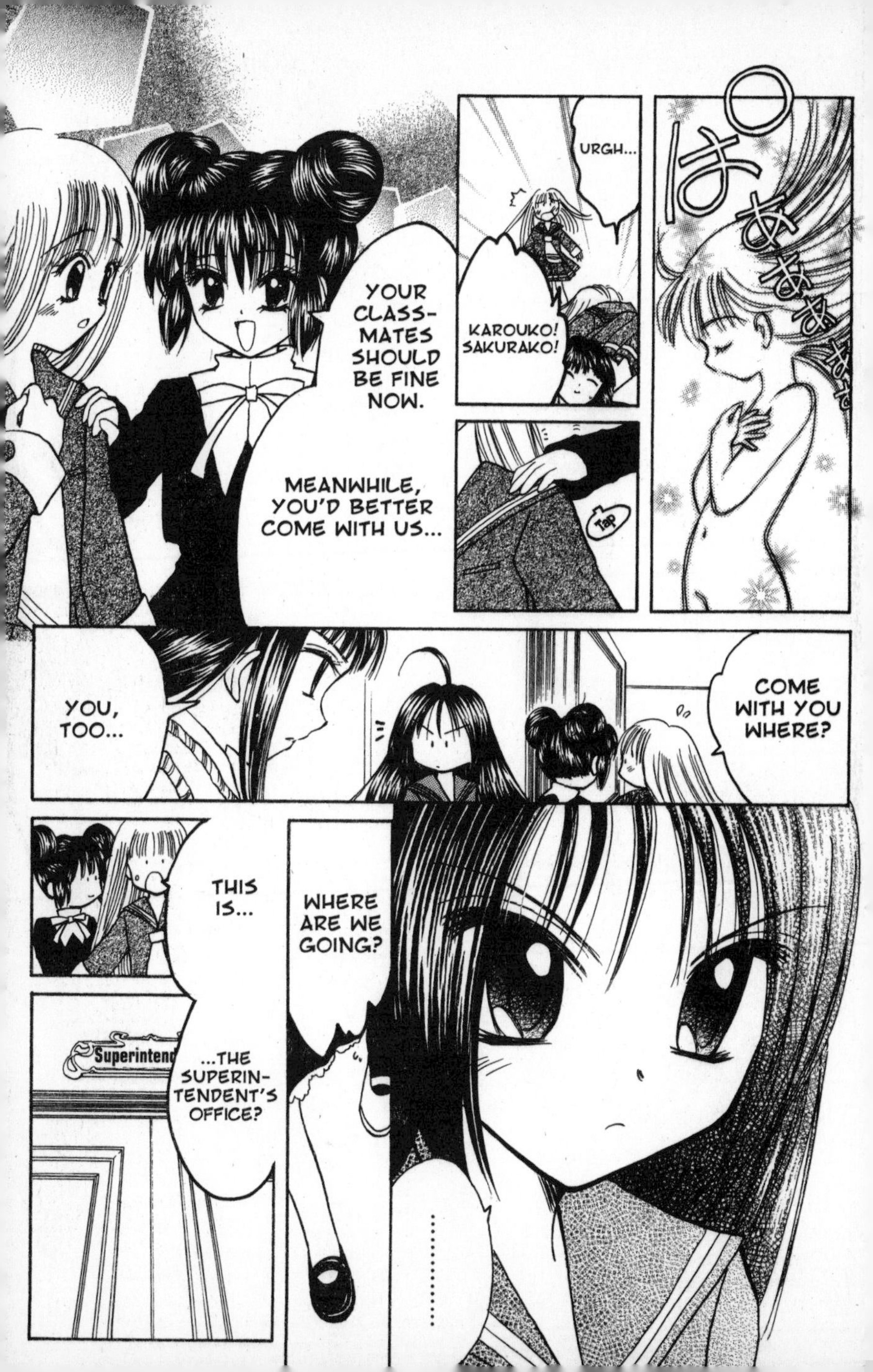
URGH...
KAROUKO! SAKURAKO!
TAP
YOUR CLASS-MATES SHOULD BE FINE NOW.
MEANWHILE, YOU'D BETTER COME WITH US...
COME WITH YOU WHERE?
YOU, TOO...
......
WHERE ARE WE GOING?
THIS IS...
Superintend
...THE SUPERIN-TENDENT'S OFFICE?

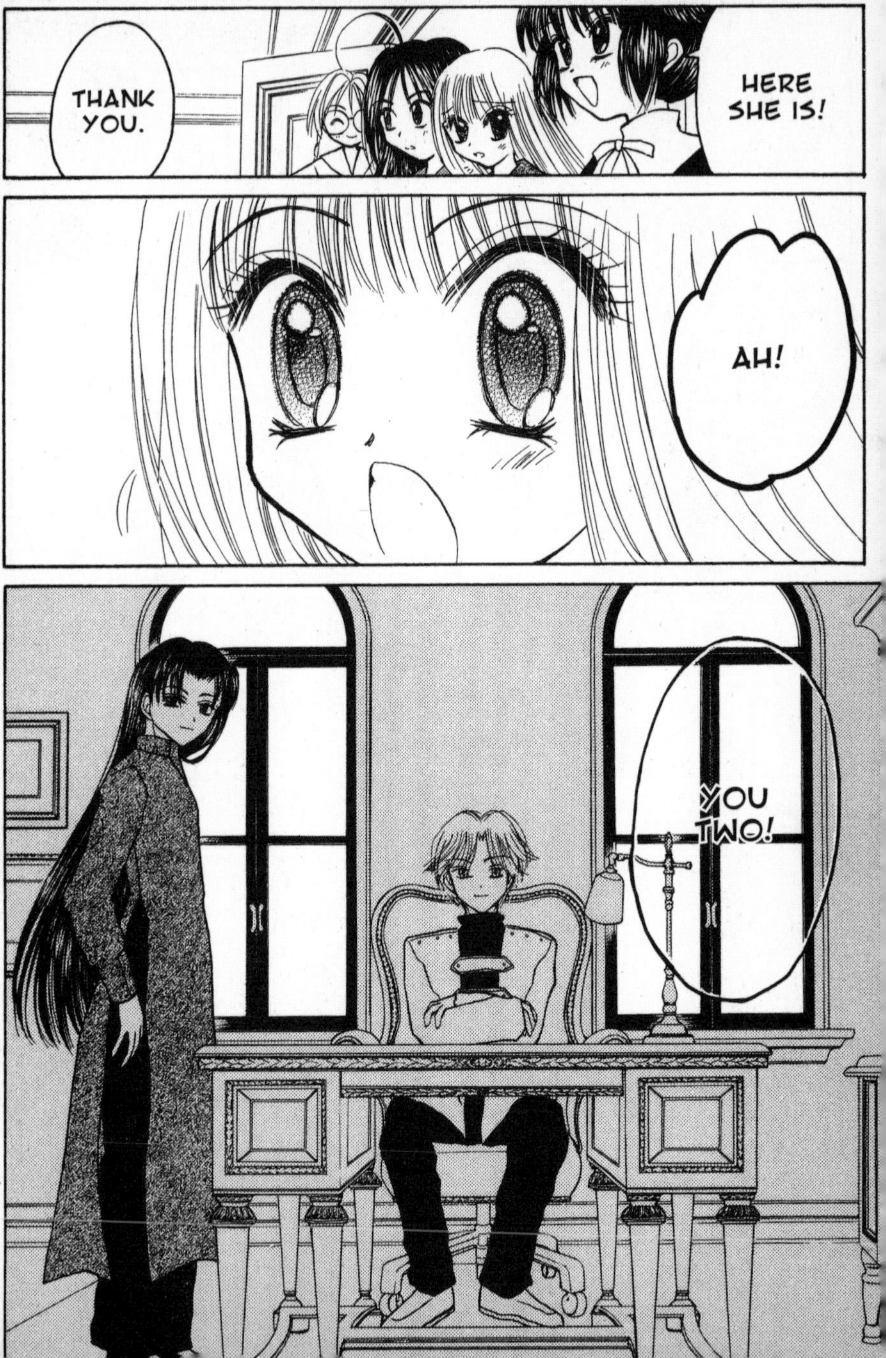
HERE SHE IS!
THANK YOU.
AH!
YOU TWO!

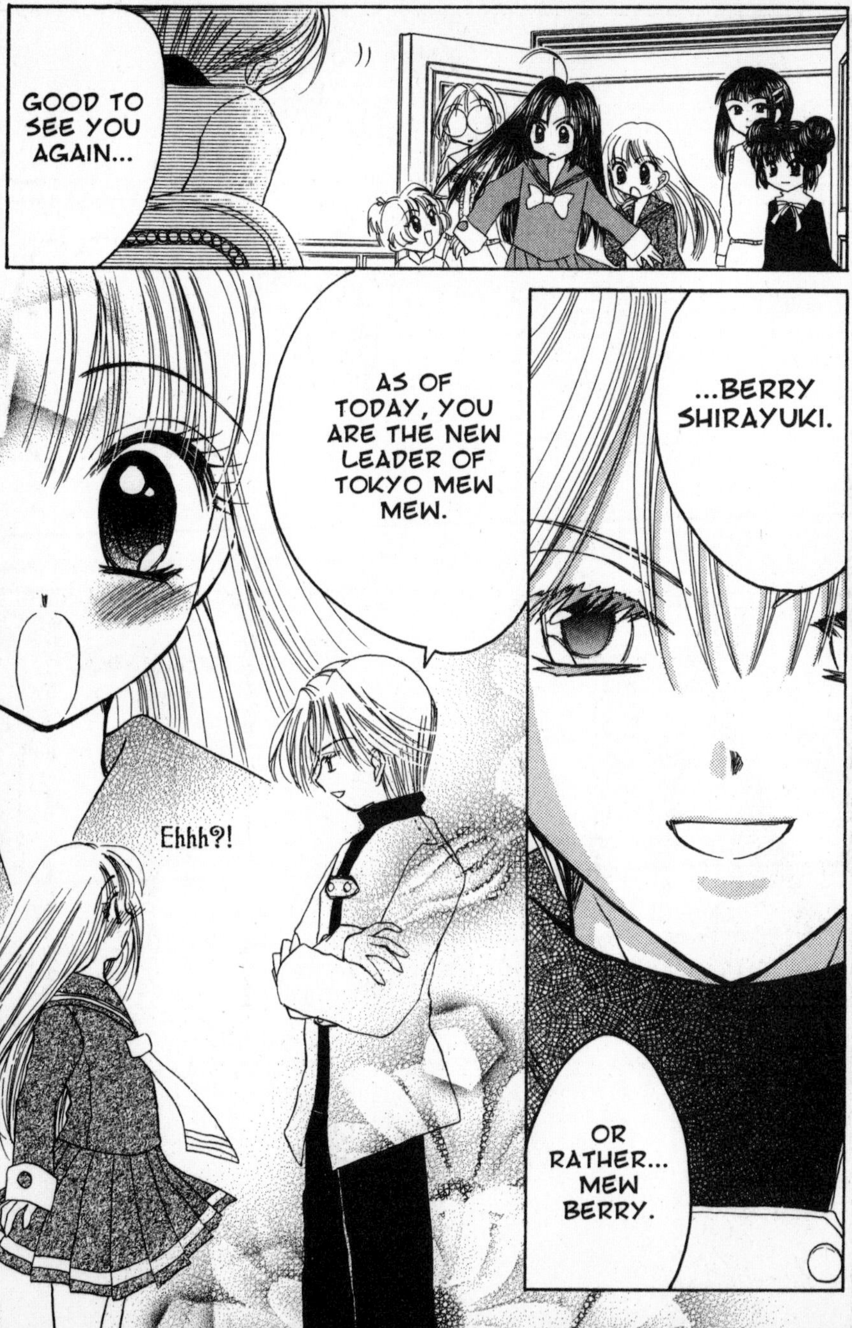
GOOD TO SEE YOU AGAIN...
...BERRY SHIRAYUKI.
OR RATHER... MEW BERRY.
AS OF TODAY, YOU ARE THE NEW LEADER OF TOKYO MEW MEW.
Ehhh?!

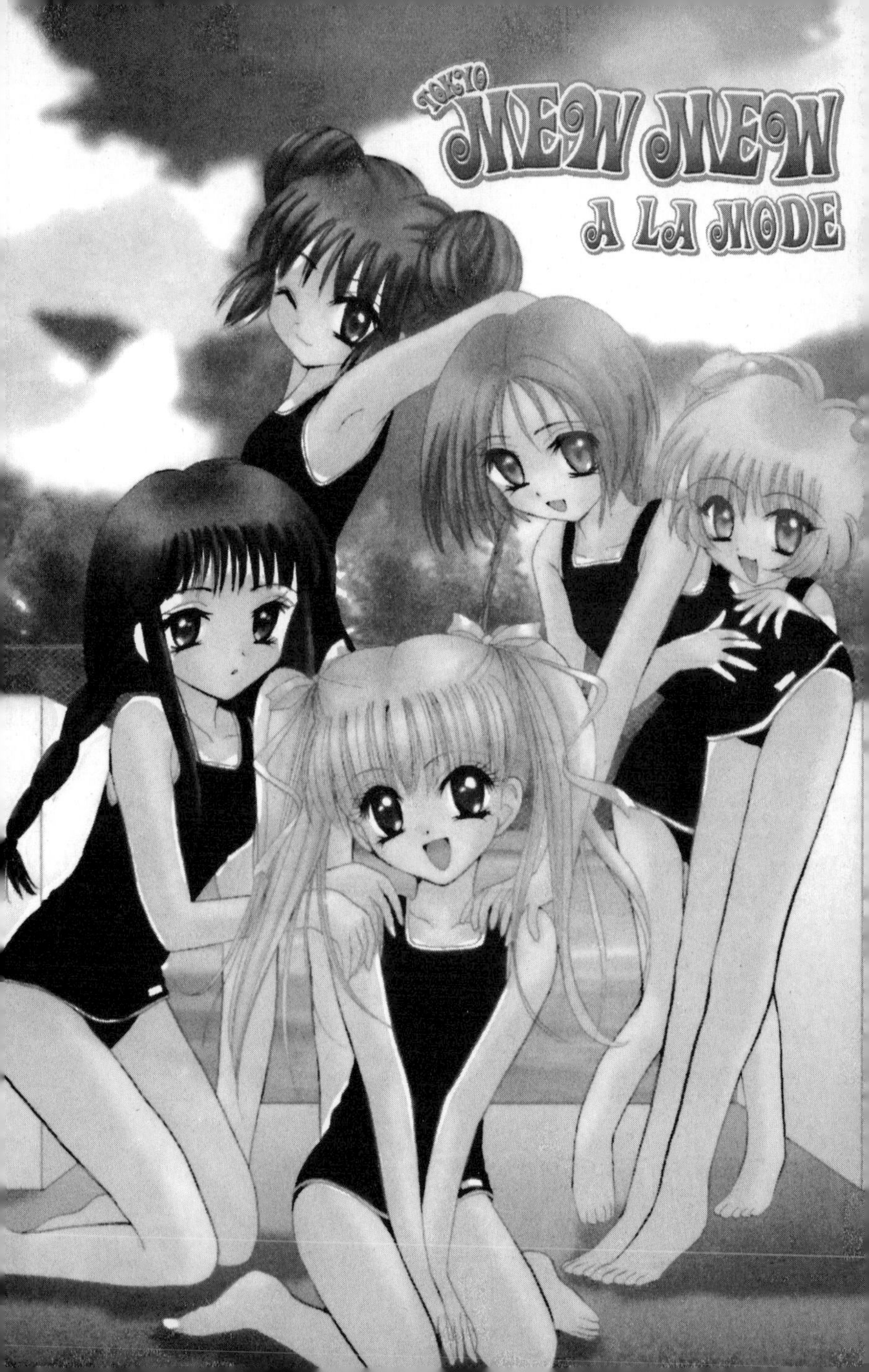
TOKYO
MEW MEW
A LA MODE

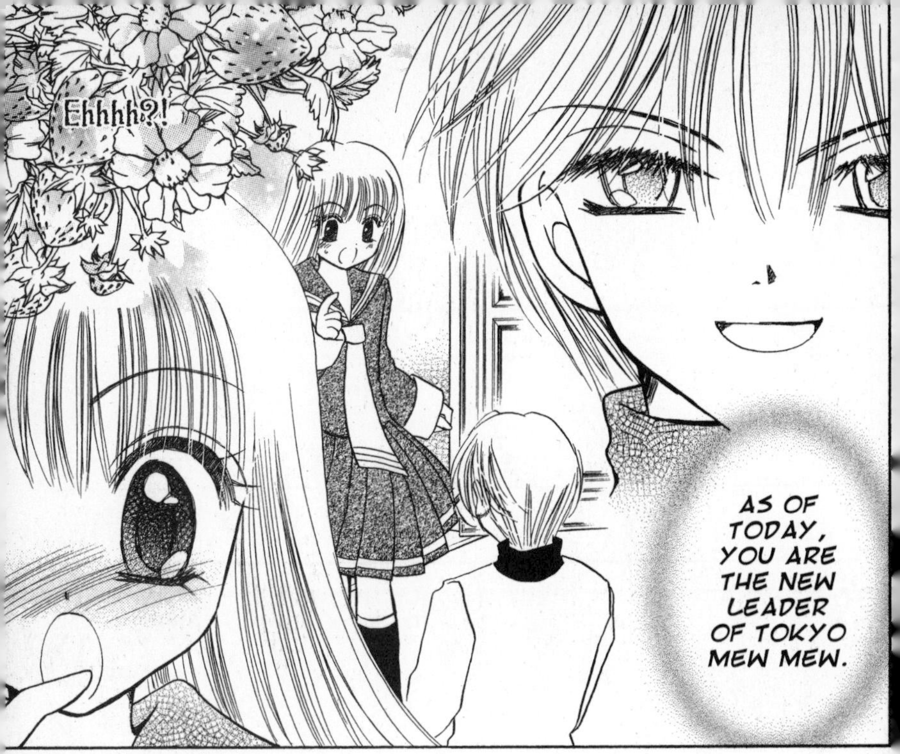
AS OF TODAY, YOU ARE THE NEW LEADER OF TOKYO MEW MEW.
Ehhhh?!

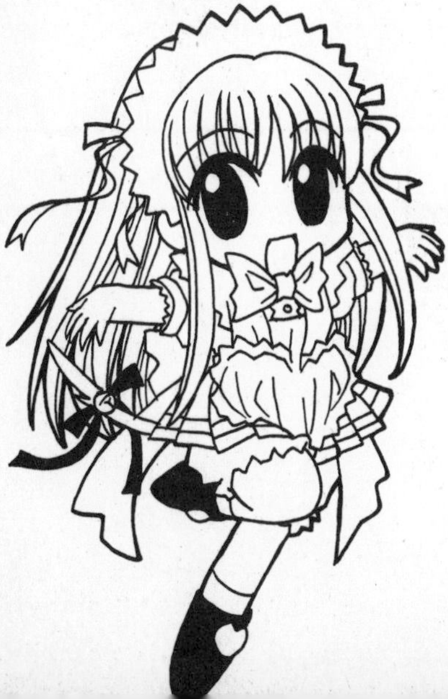

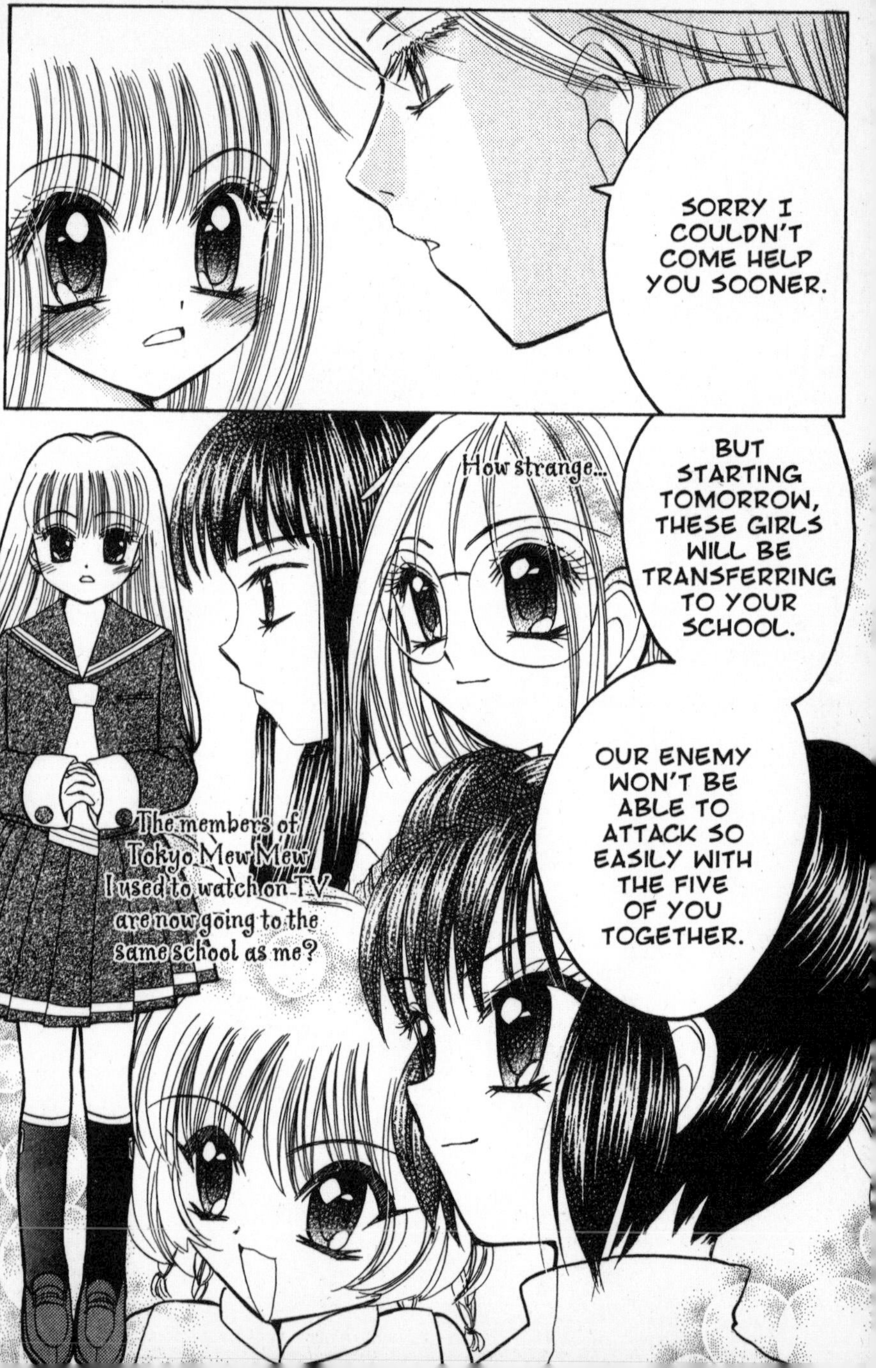
SORRY I COULDN'T COME HELP YOU SOONER.
BUT STARTING TOMORROW, THESE GIRLS WILL BE TRANSFERRING TO YOUR SCHOOL.
How strange...
OUR ENEMY WON'T BE ABLE TO ATTACK SO EASILY WITH THE FIVE OF YOU TOGETHER.
The members of Tokyo Mew Mew I used to watch on TV are now going to the same school as me?

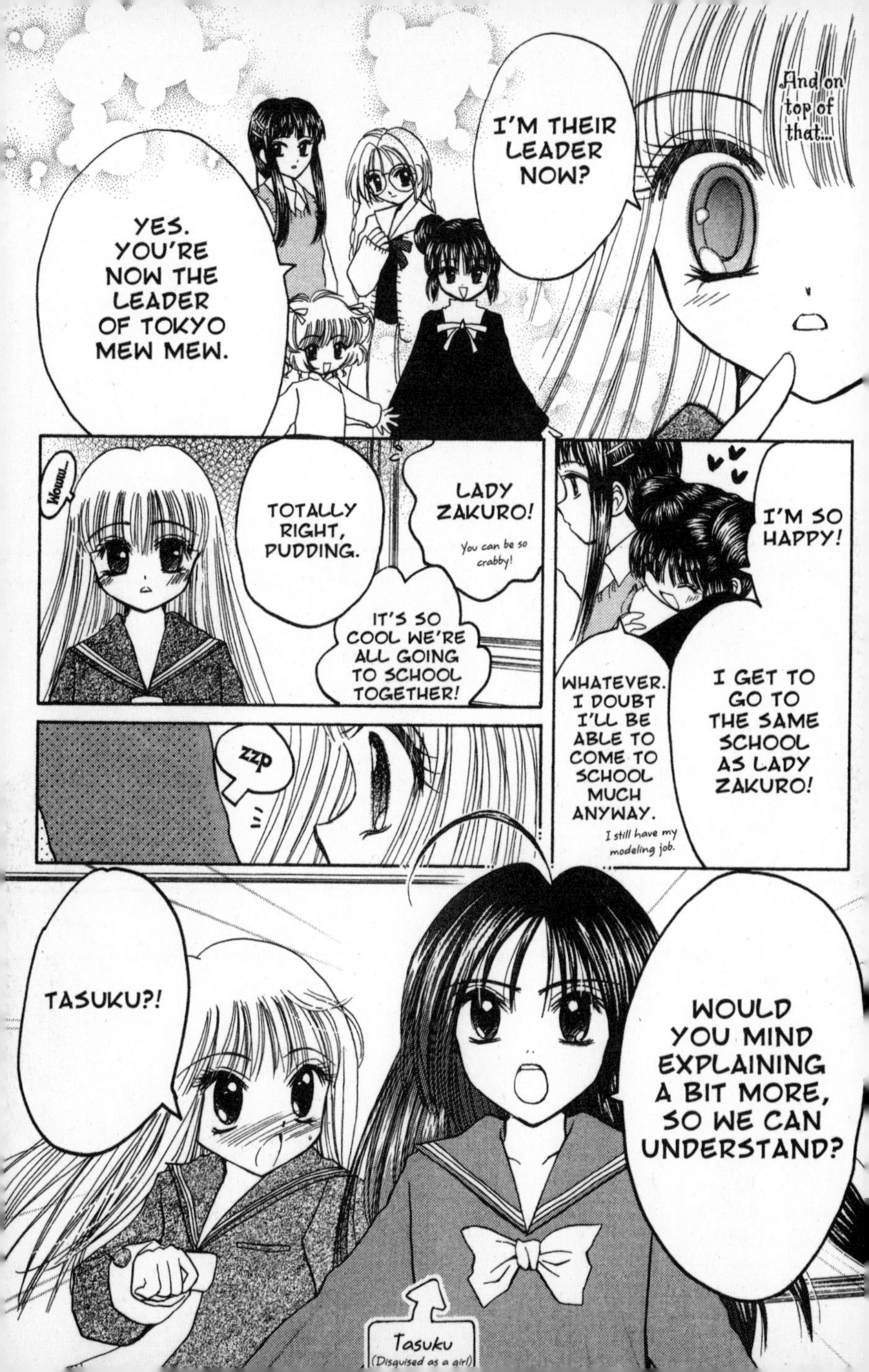
And on top of that...
I'M THEIR LEADER NOW?
YES. YOU'RE NOW THE LEADER OF TOKYO MEW MEW.
I'M SO HAPPY!
I GET TO GO TO THE SAME SCHOOL AS LADY ZAKURO!
WHATEVER. I DOUBT I'LL BE ABLE TO COME TO SCHOOL MUCH ANYWAY.
I still have my modeling job.
LADY ZAKURO!
You can be so crabby!
TOTALLY RIGHT, PUDDING.
IT'S SO COOL WE'RE ALL GOING TO SCHOOL TOGETHER!
Wowww...
ZZP
WOULD YOU MIND EXPLAINING A BIT MORE, SO WE CAN UNDERSTAND?
TASUKU?!
Tasuku
(Disguised as a girl)

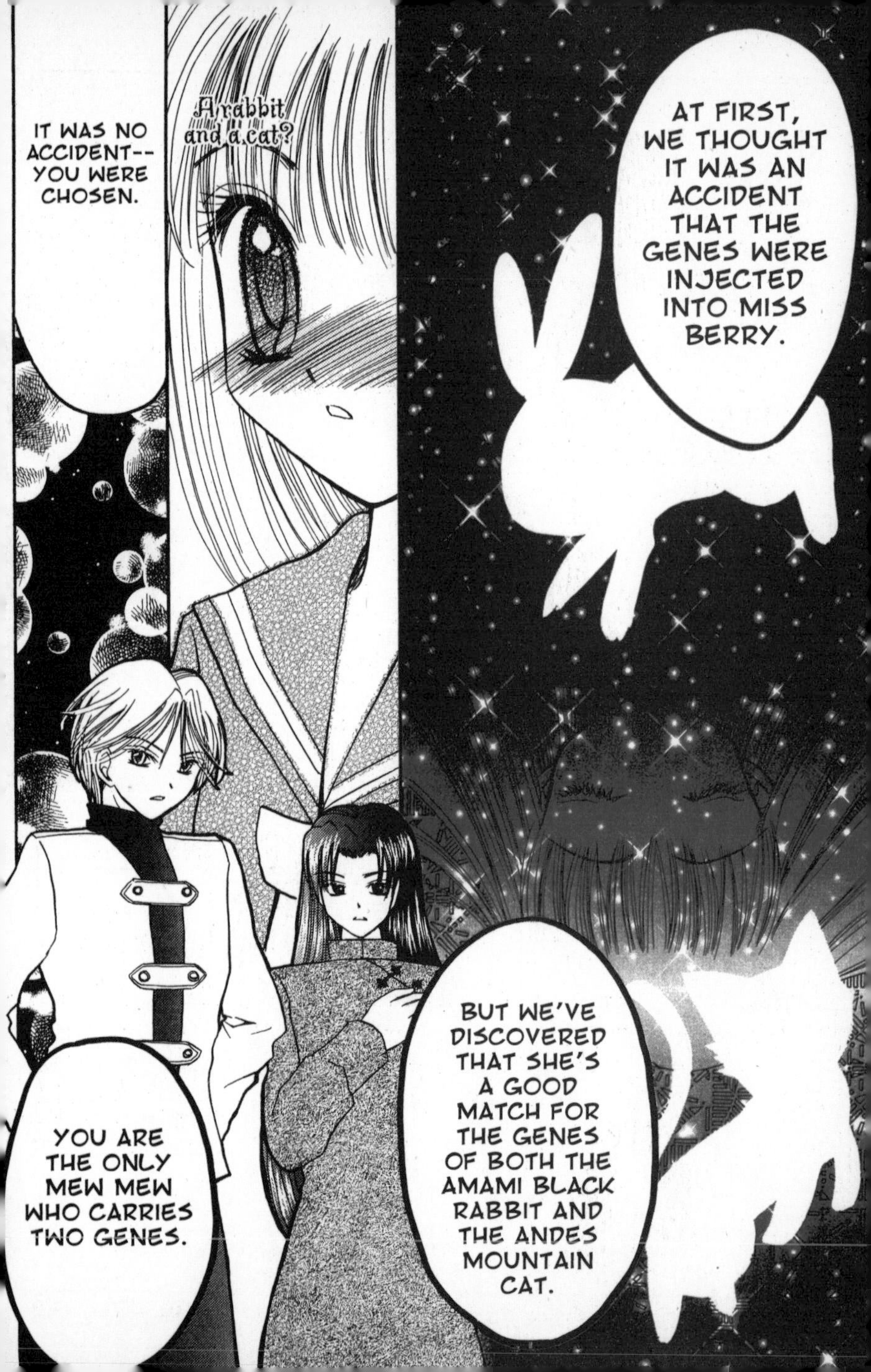
AT FIRST, WE THOUGHT IT WAS AN ACCIDENT THAT THE GENES WERE INJECTED INTO MISS BERRY.
BUT WE'VE DISCOVERED THAT SHE'S A GOOD MATCH FOR THE GENES OF BOTH THE AMAMI BLACK RABBIT AND THE ANDES MOUNTAIN CAT.
A rabbit and a cat?
IT WAS NO ACCIDENT--YOU WERE CHOSEN.
YOU ARE THE ONLY MEW MEW WHO CARRIES TWO GENES.

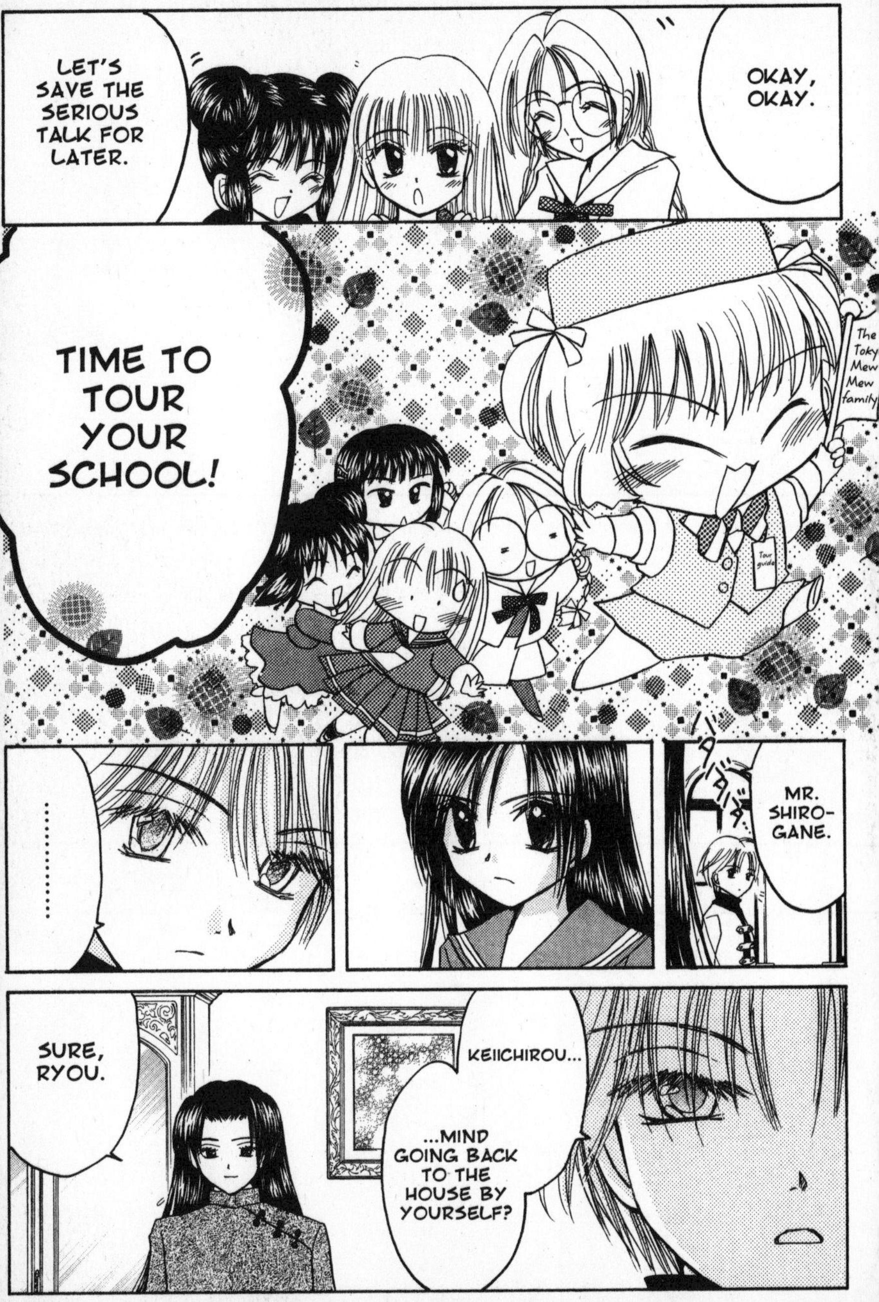
OKAY, OKAY.
LET'S SAVE THE SERIOUS TALK FOR LATER.
The Toky Mew Mew family
Tour guide
TIME TO TOUR YOUR SCHOOL!
MR. SHIRO-GANE.
......
KEIICHIROU...
...MIND GOING BACK TO THE HOUSE BY YOURSELF?
SURE, RYOU.

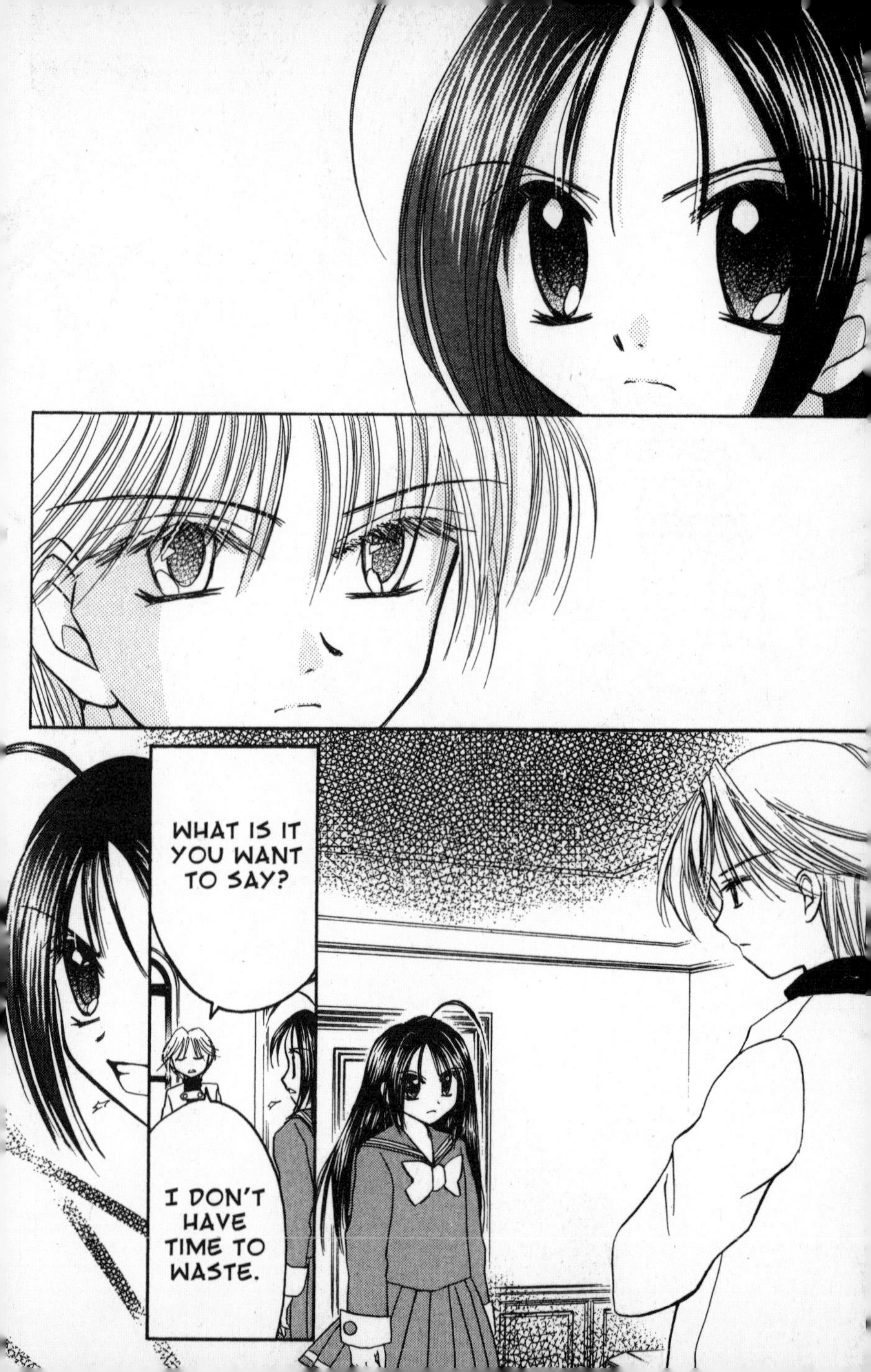
WHAT IS IT YOU WANT TO SAY?
I DON'T HAVE TIME TO WASTE.

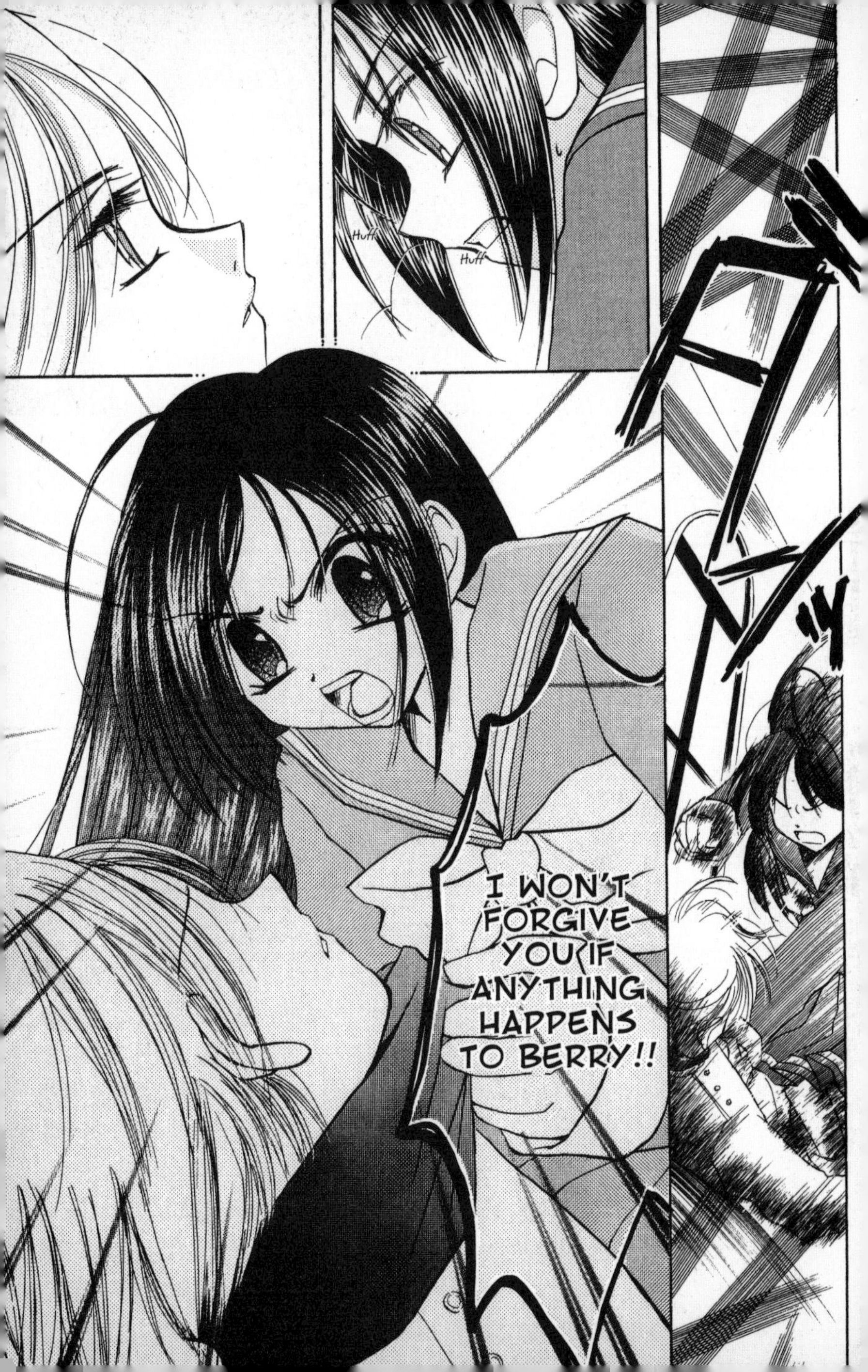
Huff
Huff
I WON'T FORGIVE YOU IF ANYTHING HAPPENS TO BERRY!!

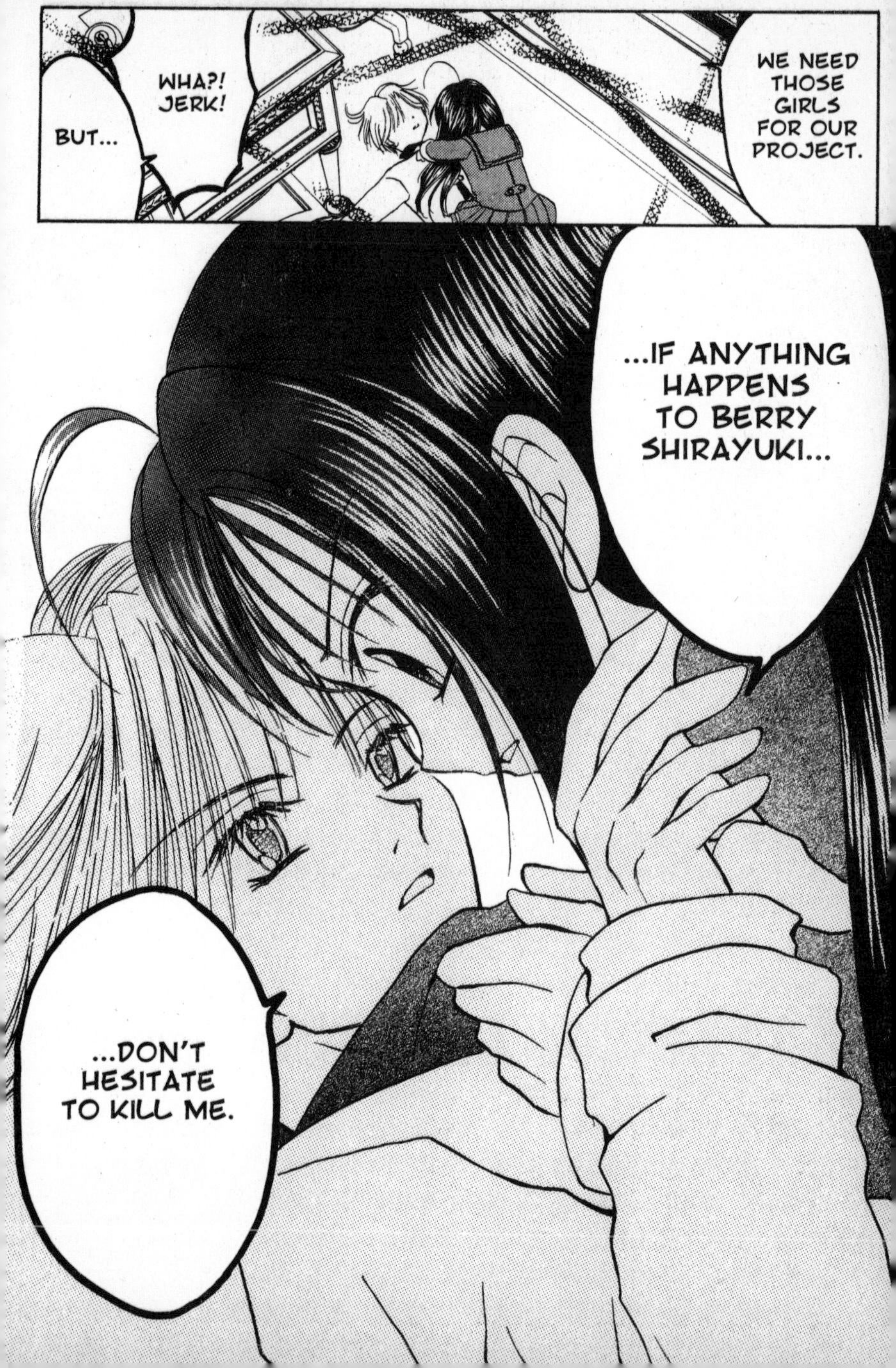
WE NEED THOSE GIRLS FOR OUR PROJECT.
WHA?! JERK!
BUT...
...IF ANYTHING HAPPENS TO BERRY SHIRAYUKI...
...DON'T HESITATE TO KILL ME.

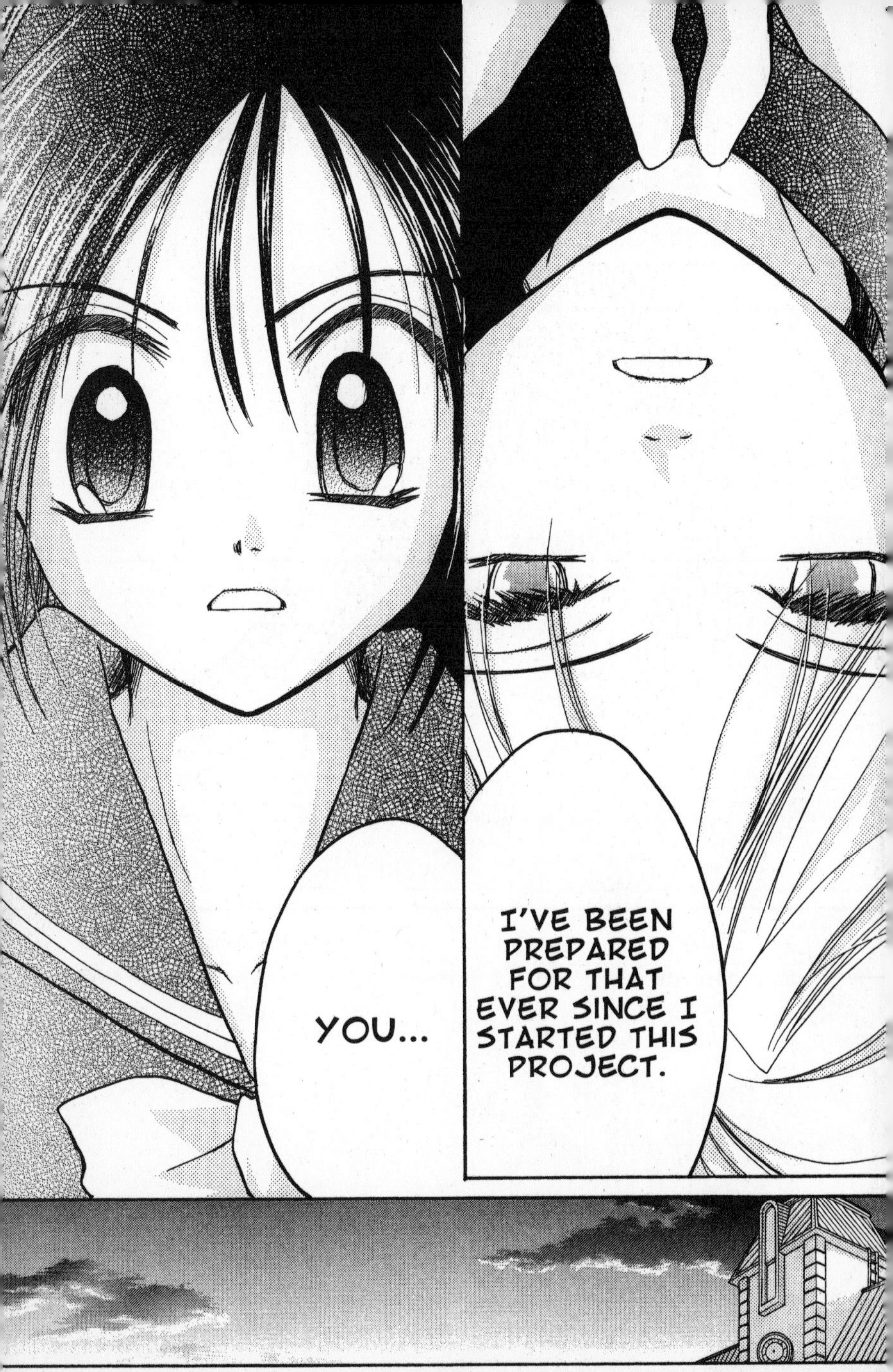
I'VE BEEN PREPARED FOR THAT EVER SINCE I STARTED THIS PROJECT.
YOU...

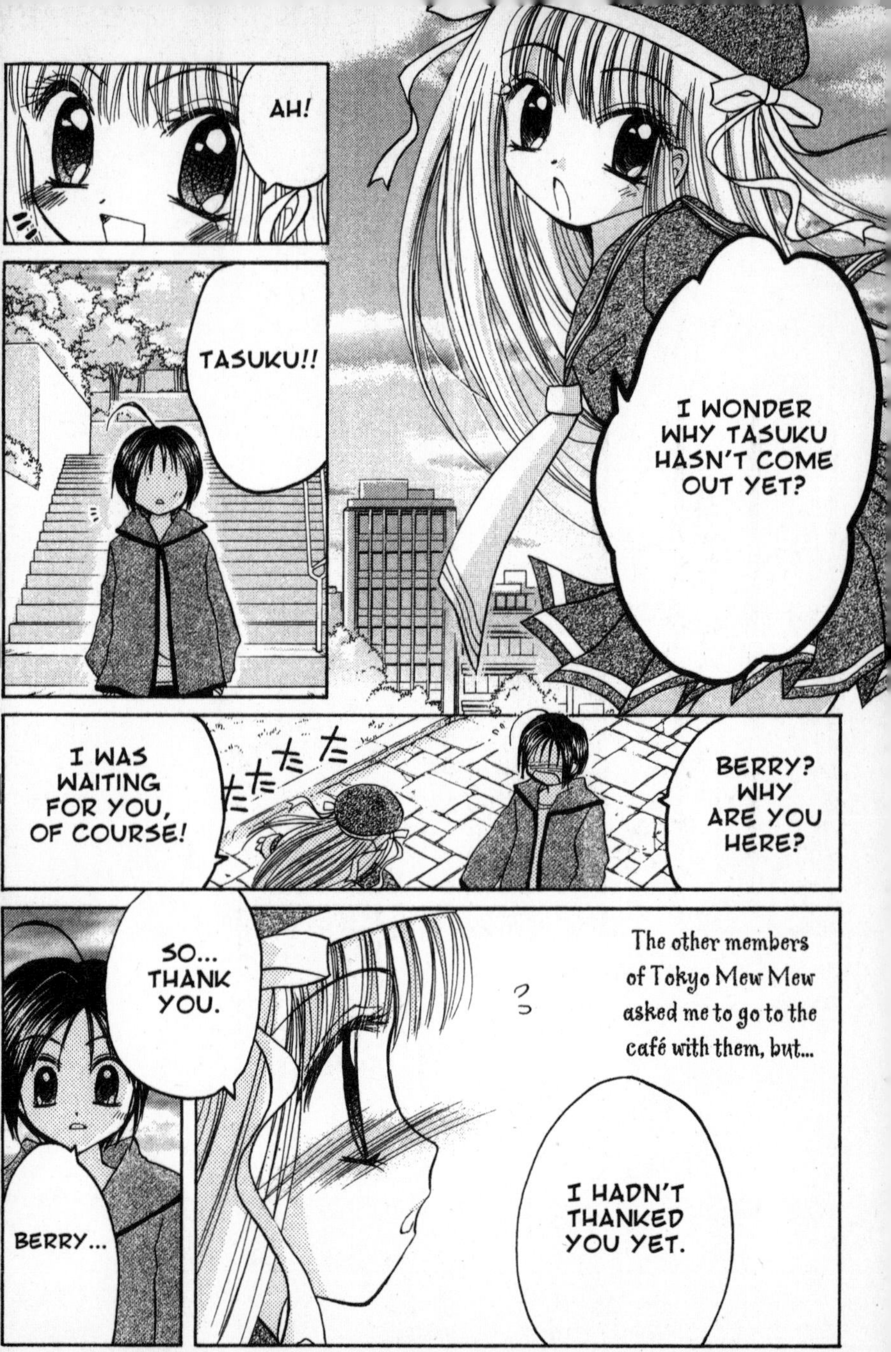
I WONDER WHY TASUKU HASN'T COME OUT YET?
AH!
TASUKU!!
BERRY? WHY ARE YOU HERE?
I WAS WAITING FOR YOU, OF COURSE!
The other members of Tokyo Mew Mew asked me to go to the café with them, but...
I HADN'T THANKED YOU YET.
SO... THANK YOU.
BERRY...

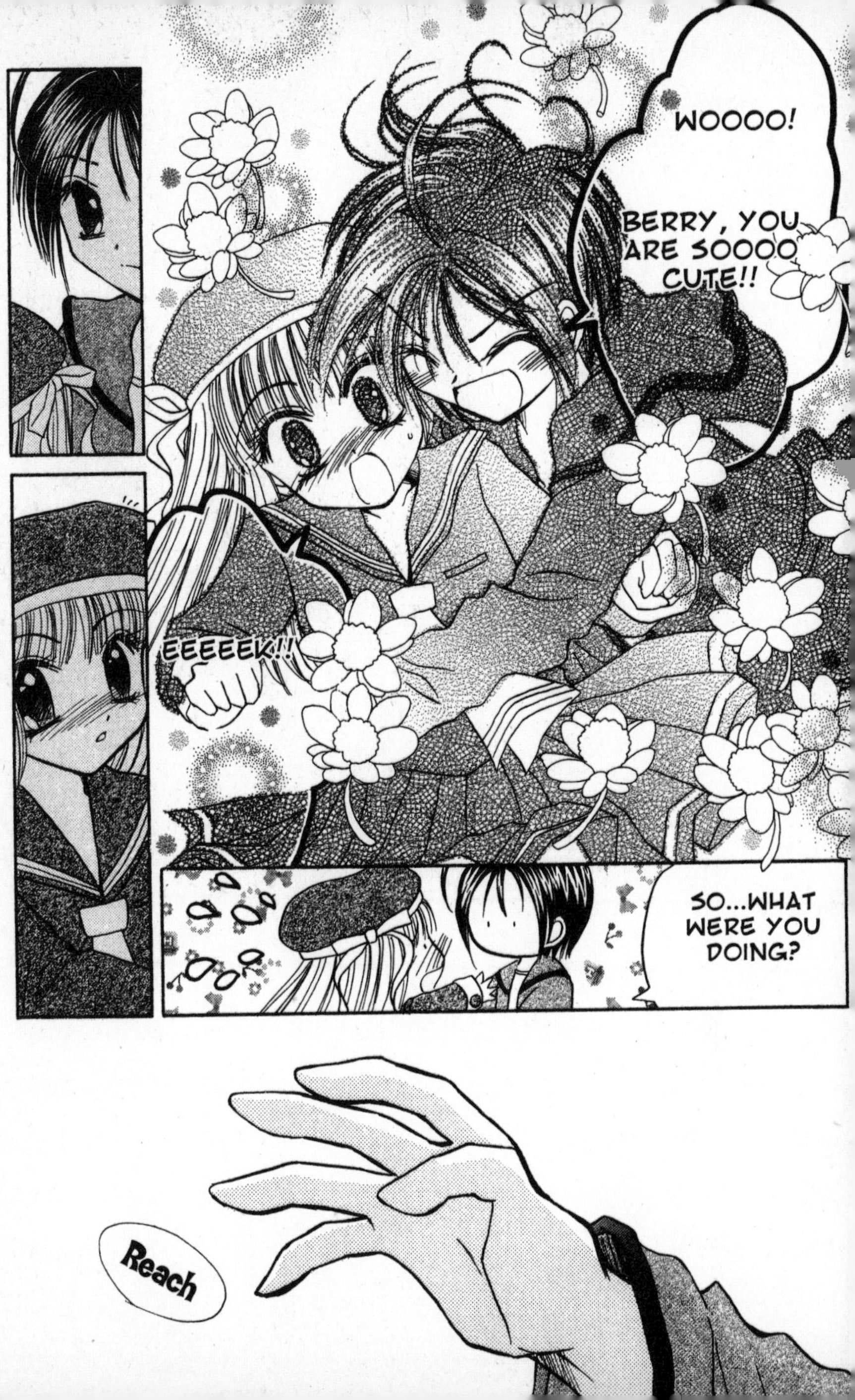
WOOOO!
BERRY, YOU ARE SOOOO CUTE!!
EEEEEK!!
SO...WHAT WERE YOU DOING?
Reach

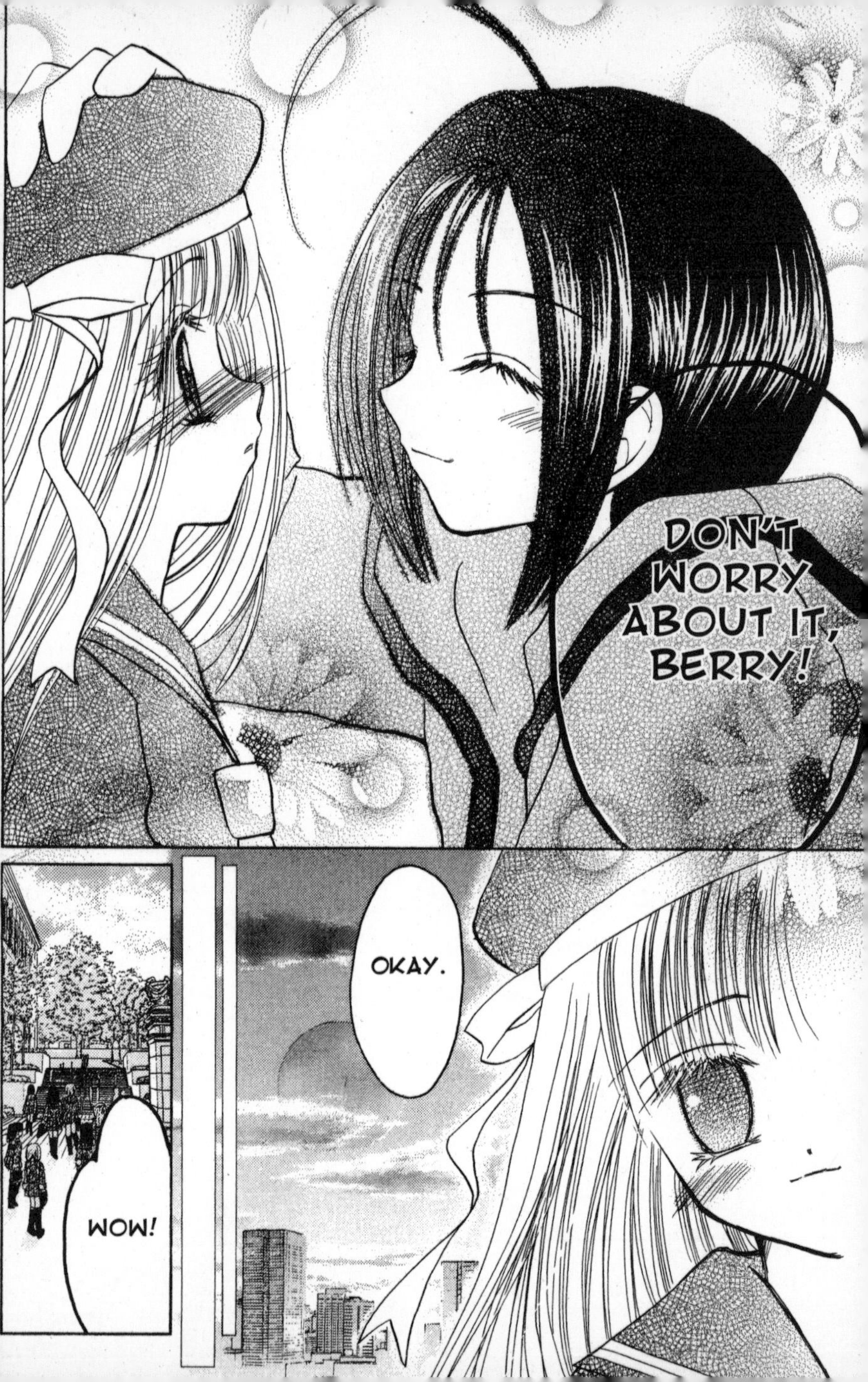
DON'T WORRY ABOUT IT, BERRY!
OKAY.
WOW!

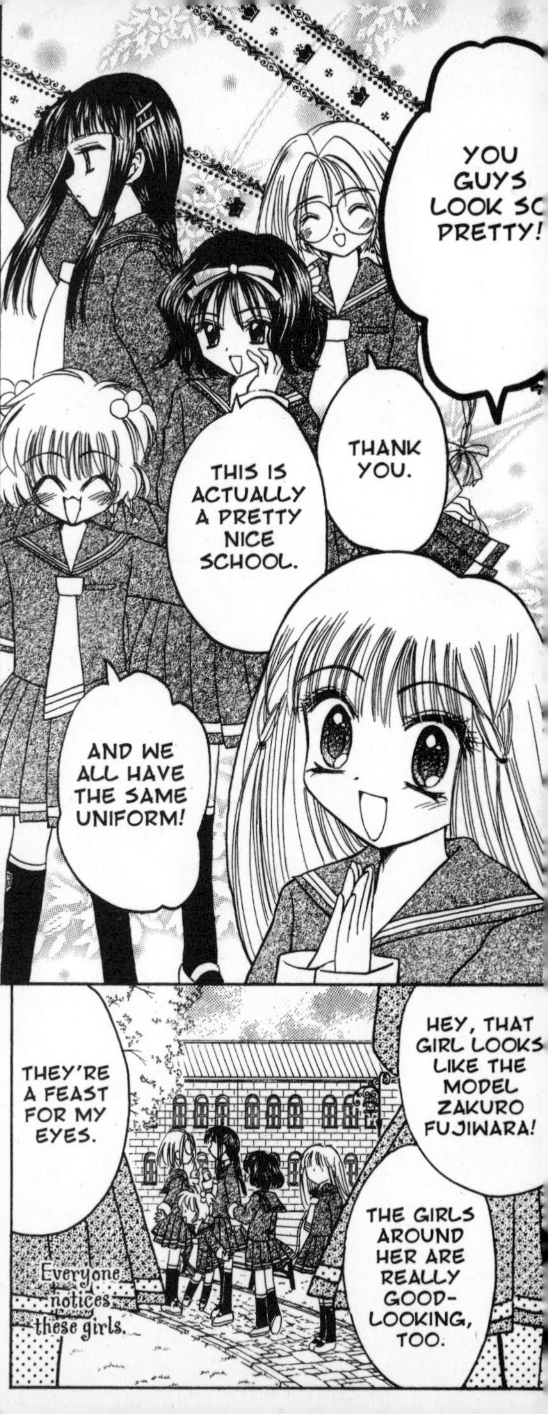
YOU GUYS LOOK SO PRETTY!
THANK YOU.
THIS IS ACTUALLY A PRETTY NICE SCHOOL.
AND WE ALL HAVE THE SAME UNIFORM!
HEY, THAT GIRL LOOKS LIKE THE MODEL ZAKURO FUJIWARA!
THE GIRLS AROUND HER ARE REALLY GOOD-LOOKING, TOO.
THEY'RE A FEAST FOR MY EYES.
Everyone notices these girls.

6

I am so looking forward to seeing the completed calendar! The publisher will put it out for three years. I can't wait to collect all of them. Ouch... and today is the deadline! I've got to get it done! (Sweat) I'll do my best!

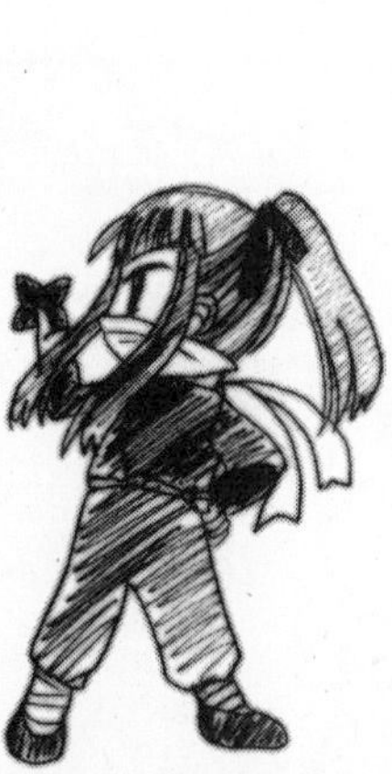

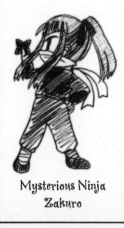

Mysterious Ninja Zakuro

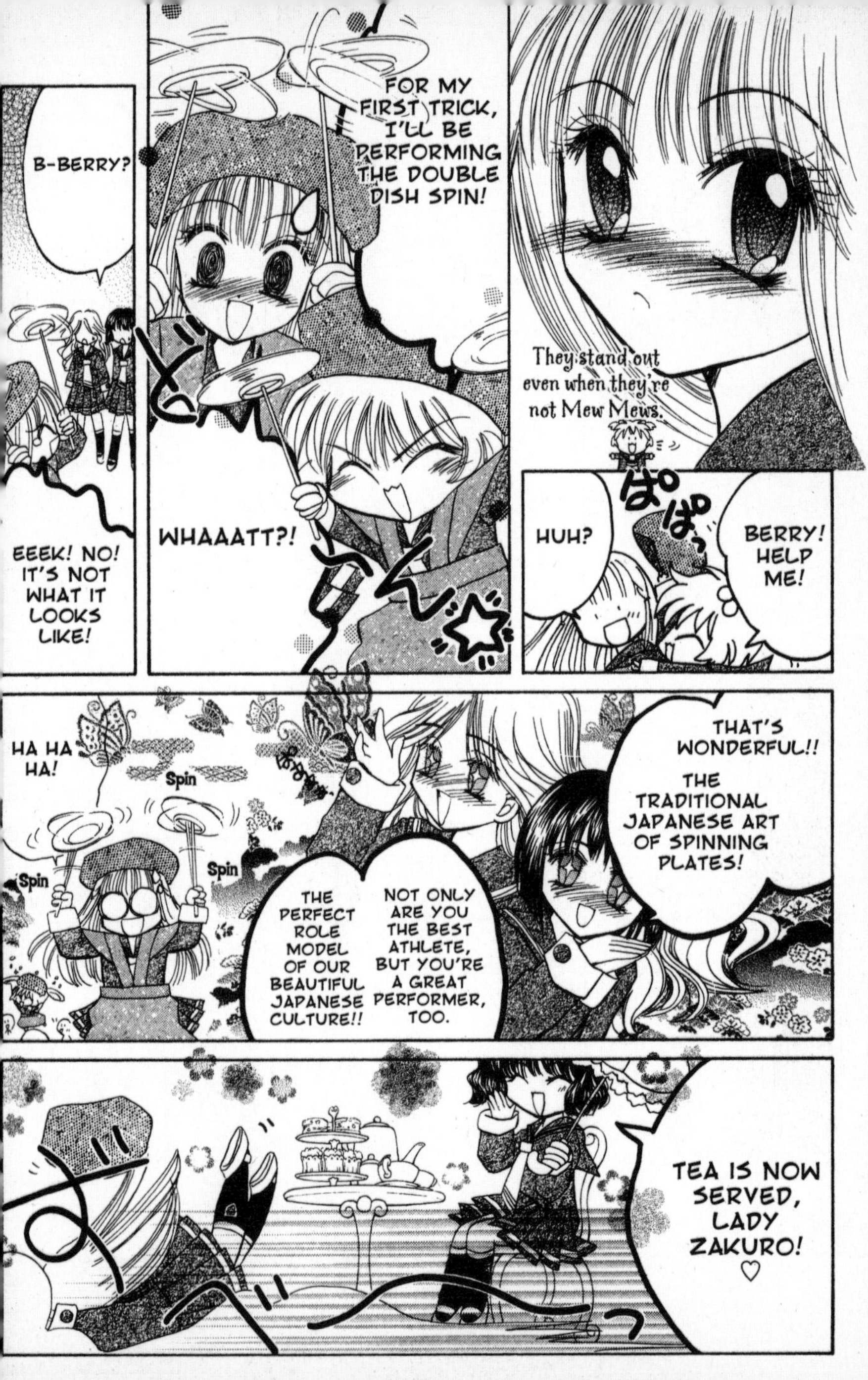
They stand out even when they're not Mew Mews.
BERRY! HELP ME!
ぱぱっ
HUH?
FOR MY FIRST TRICK, I'LL BE PERFORMING THE DOUBLE DISH SPIN!
WHAAATT?!
B-BERRY?
EEEK! NO! IT'S NOT WHAT IT LOOKS LIKE!
THAT'S WONDERFUL!! THE TRADITIONAL JAPANESE ART OF SPINNING PLATES!
NOT ONLY ARE YOU THE BEST ATHLETE, BUT YOU'RE A GREAT PERFORMER, TOO.
THE PERFECT ROLE MODEL OF OUR BEAUTIFUL JAPANESE CULTURE!!
Spin
Spin
Spin
HA HA HA!
TEA IS NOW SERVED, LADY ZAKURO! ♡

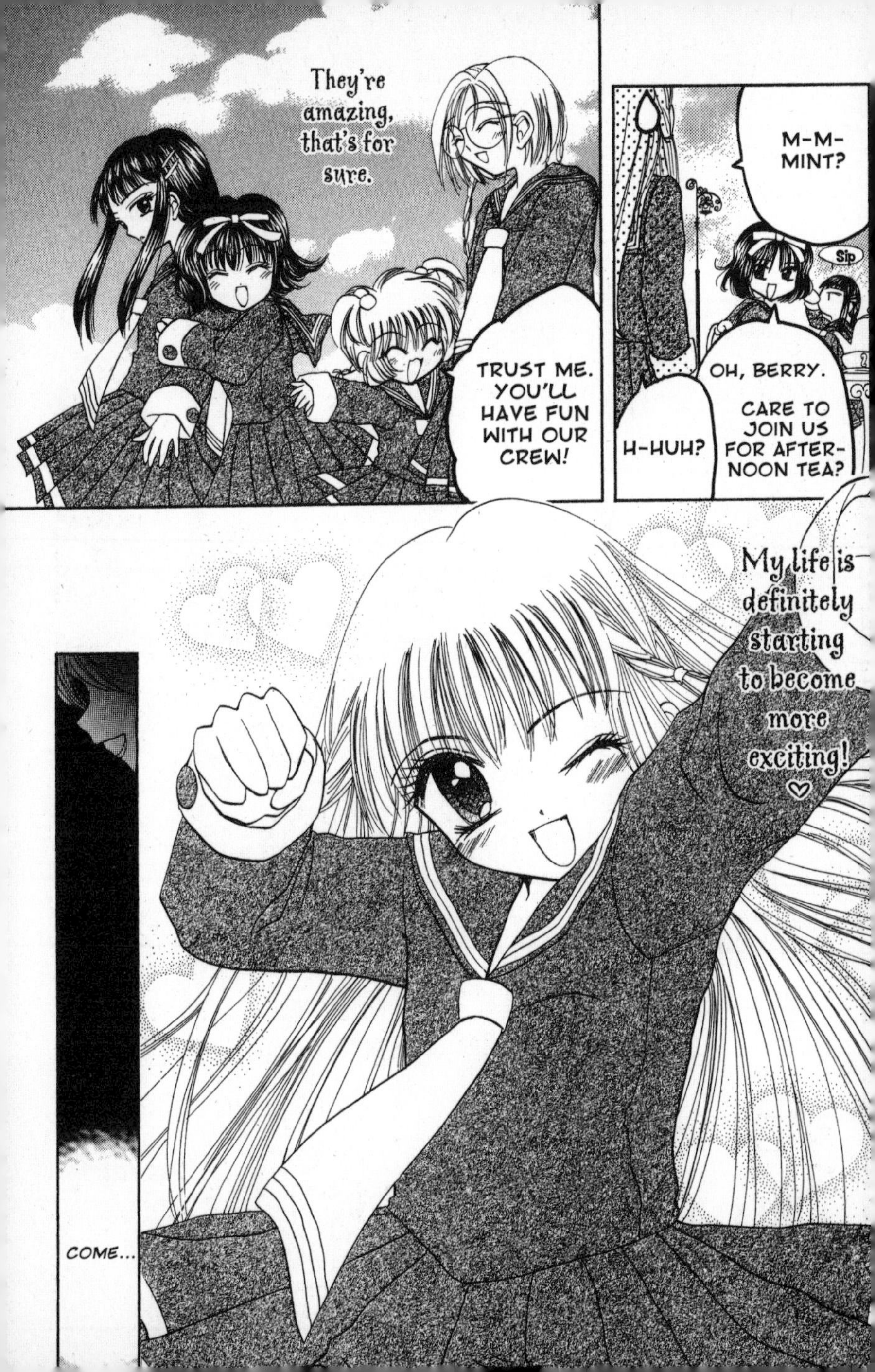
M-M-MINT?
Sip
OH, BERRY. CARE TO JOIN US FOR AFTERNOON TEA?
H-HUH?
They're amazing, that's for sure.
TRUST ME. YOU'LL HAVE FUN WITH OUR CREW!
My life is definitely starting to become more exciting! ♡
COME...

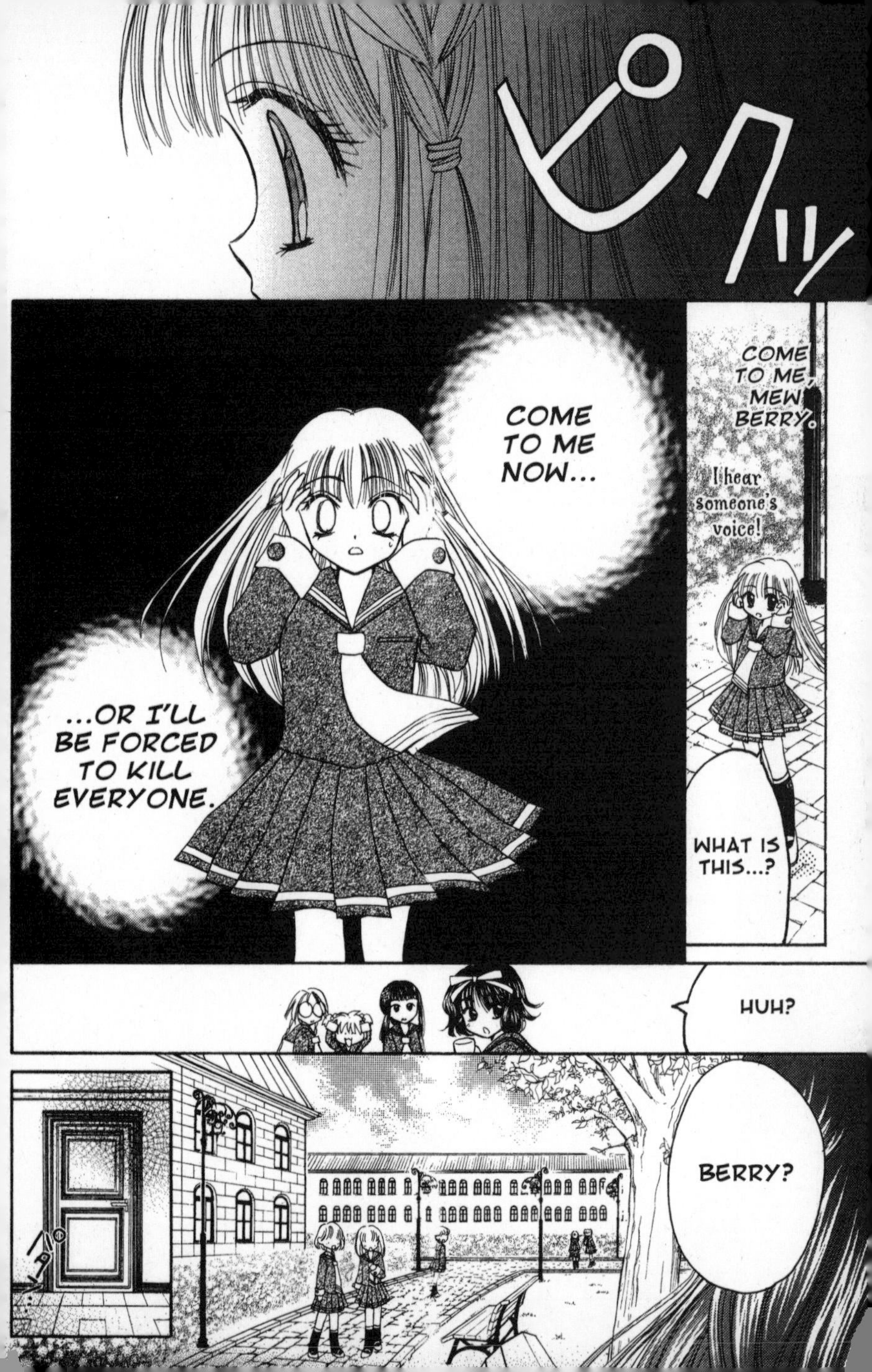
ピクッ
COME TO ME, MEW BERRY.
I hear someone's voice!
WHAT IS THIS...?
COME TO ME NOW...
...OR I'LL BE FORCED TO KILL EVERYONE.
HUH?
BERRY?

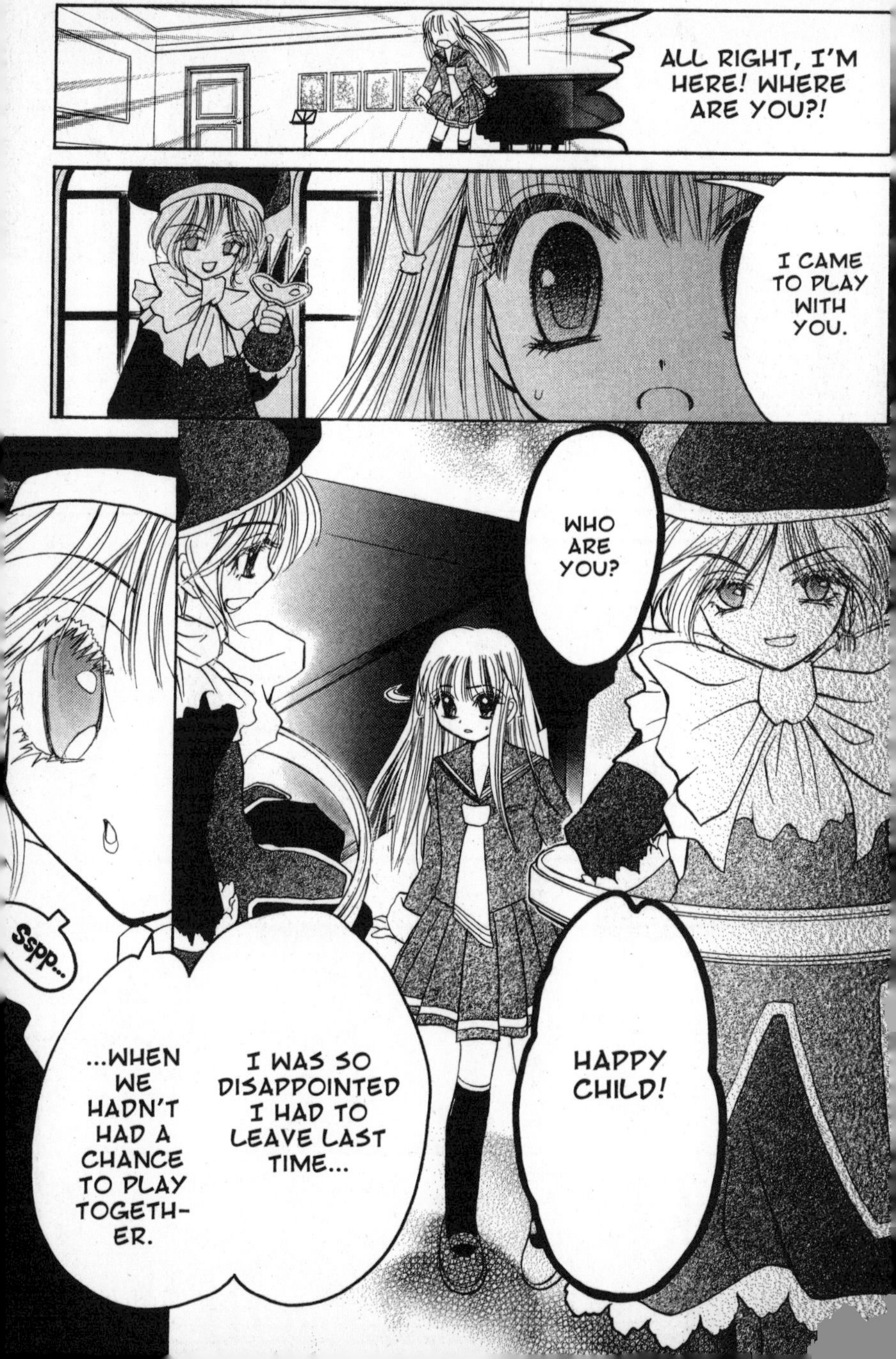
ALL RIGHT, I'M HERE! WHERE ARE YOU?!
I CAME TO PLAY WITH YOU.
WHO ARE YOU?
HAPPY CHILD!
I WAS SO DISAPPOINTED I HAD TO LEAVE LAST TIME...
...WHEN WE HADN'T HAD A CHANCE TO PLAY TOGETH-ER.
Sspp...

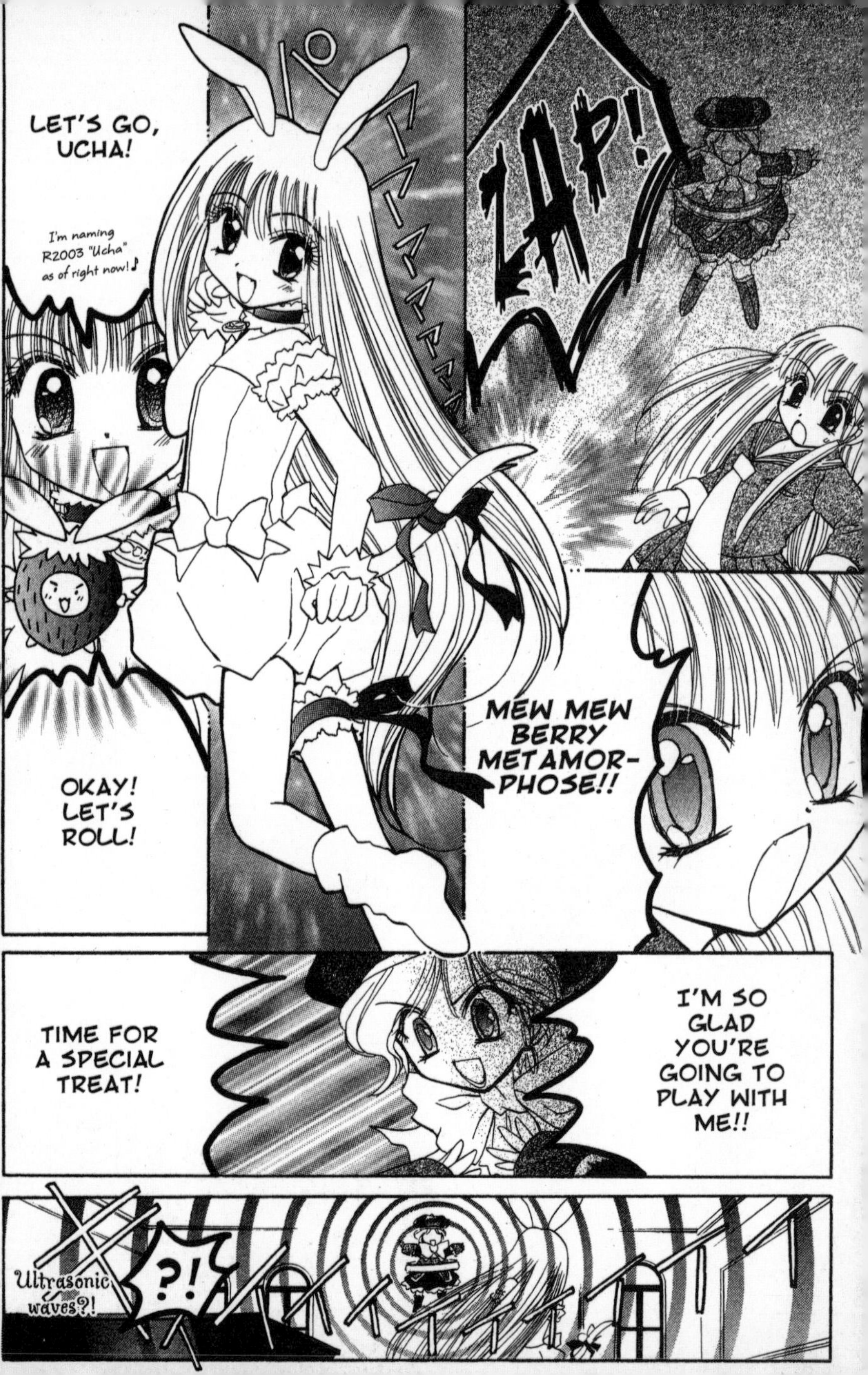
ZAP!
MEW MEW BERRY METAMORPHOSE!!
LET'S GO, UCHA!
I'm naming R2003 "Ucha" as of right now!♪
OKAY! LET'S ROLL!
I'M SO GLAD YOU'RE GOING TO PLAY WITH ME!!
TIME FOR A SPECIAL TREAT!
?!
Ultrasonic waves?!

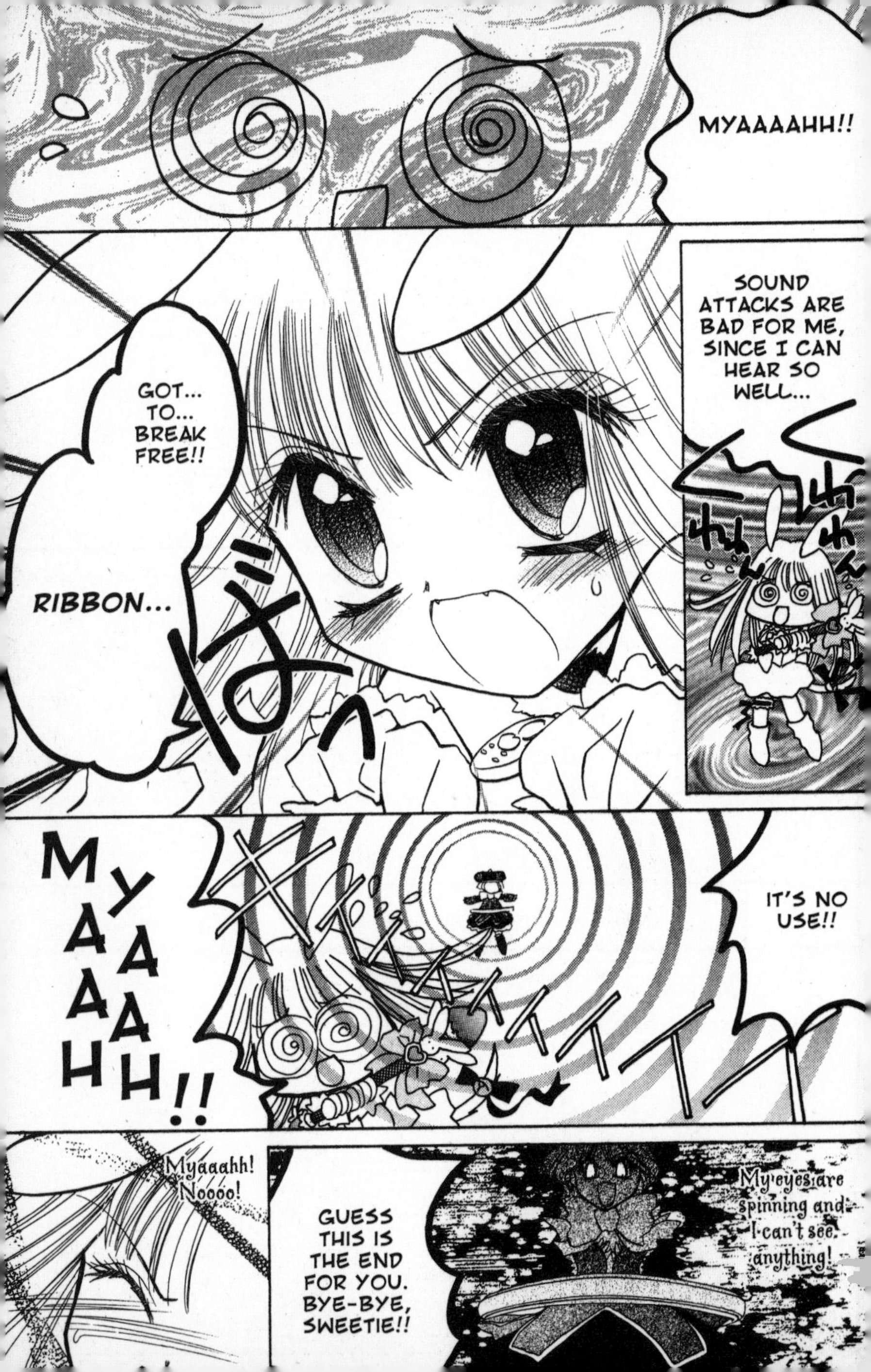
MYAAAAHH!!
SOUND ATTACKS ARE BAD FOR ME, SINCE I CAN HEAR SO WELL...
GOT... TO... BREAK FREE!!
RIBBON...
IT'S NO USE!!
MYAAAAHH!!
My eyes are spinning and I can't see anything!
GUESS THIS IS THE END FOR YOU. BYE-BYE, SWEETIE!!
Myaaahh! Noooo!

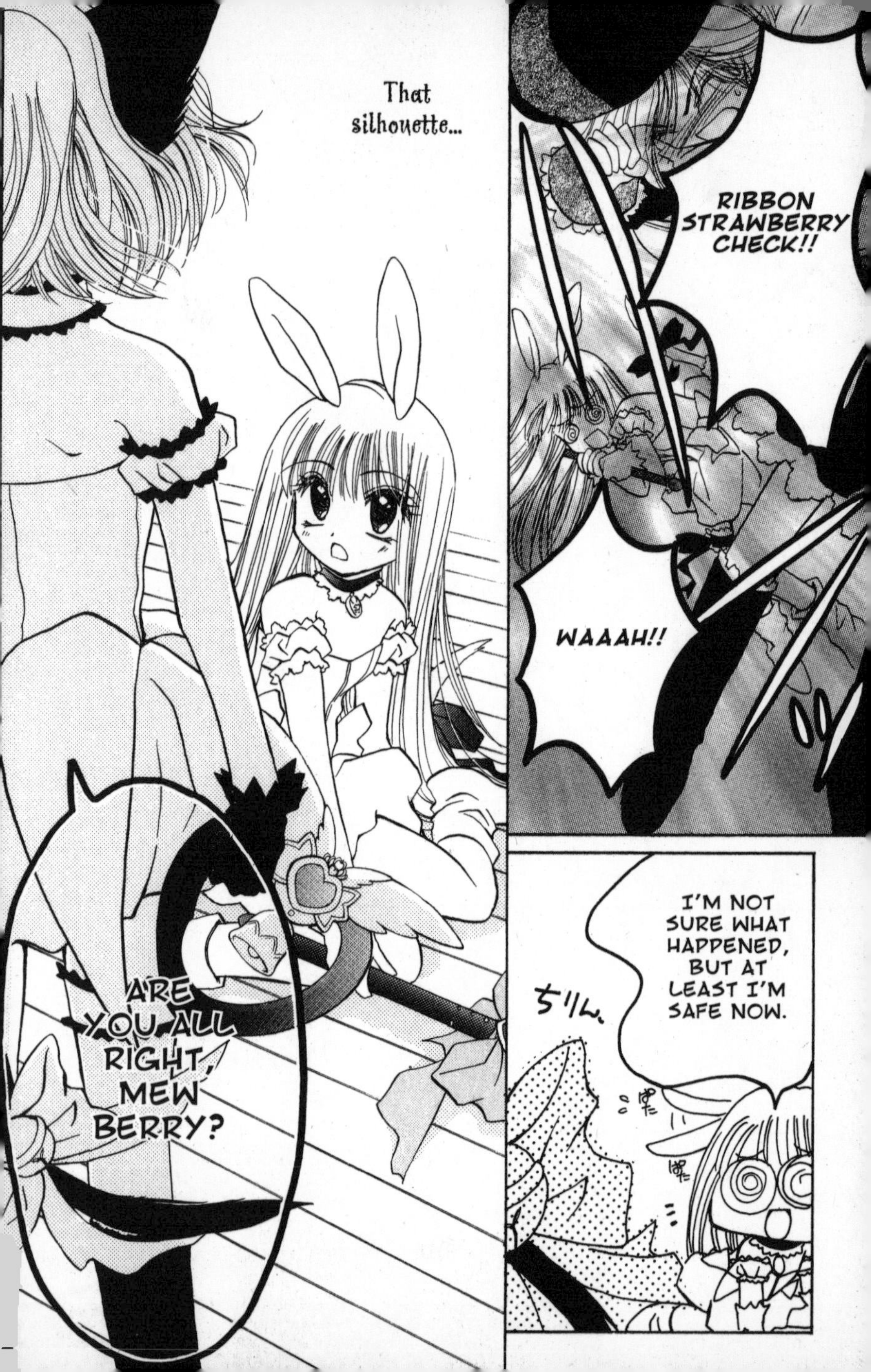
RIBBON STRAWBERRY CHECK!!
WAAAH!!
I'M NOT SURE WHAT HAPPENED, BUT AT LEAST I'M SAFE NOW.
ちりん.
ぱた
ぱた
That silhouette...
ARE YOU ALL RIGHT, MEW BERRY?

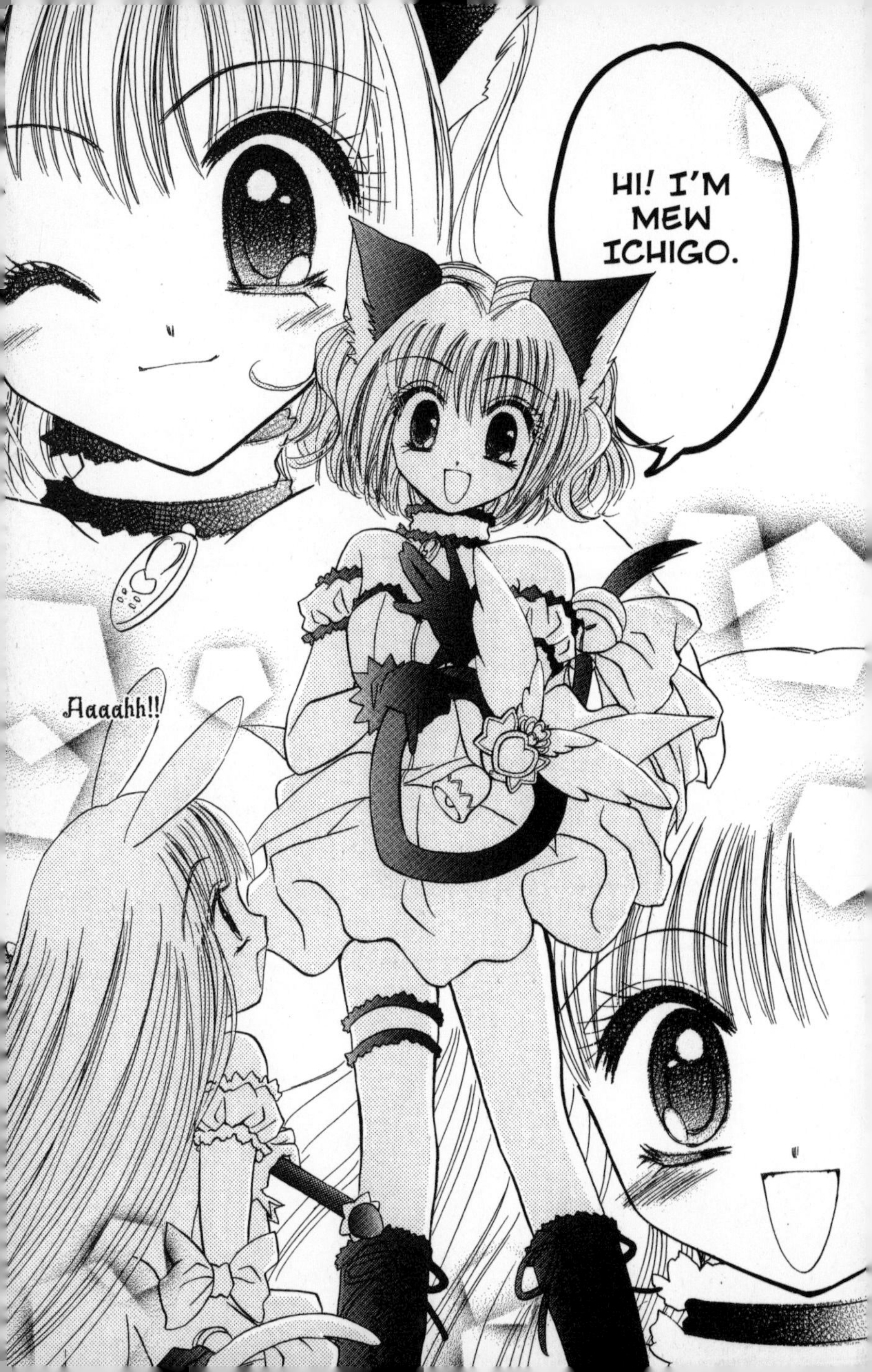
HI! I'M MEW ICHIGO.
Aaaahh!!

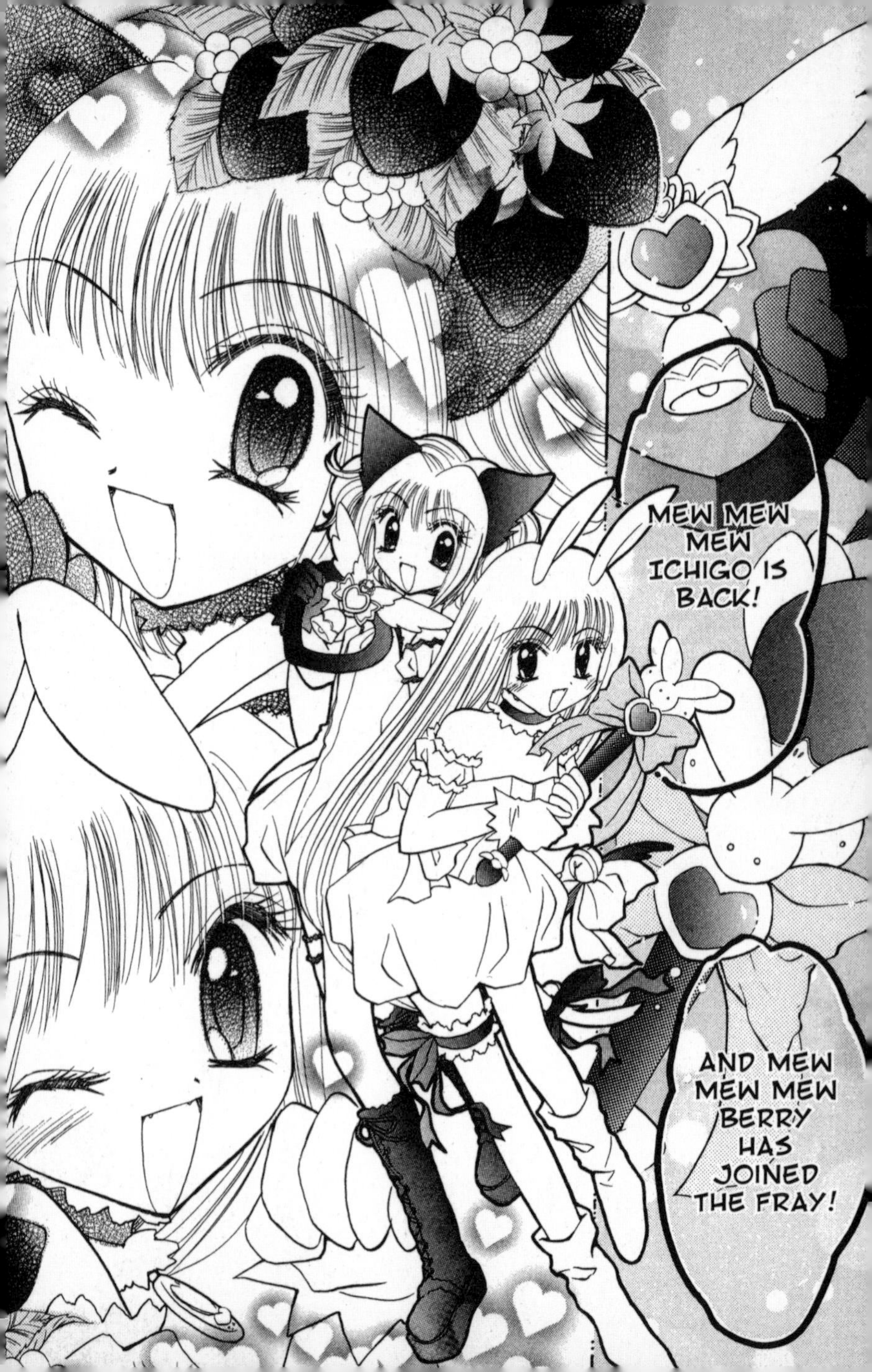
MEW MEW MEW ICHIGO IS BACK!
AND MEW MEW MEW BERRY HAS JOINED THE FRAY!

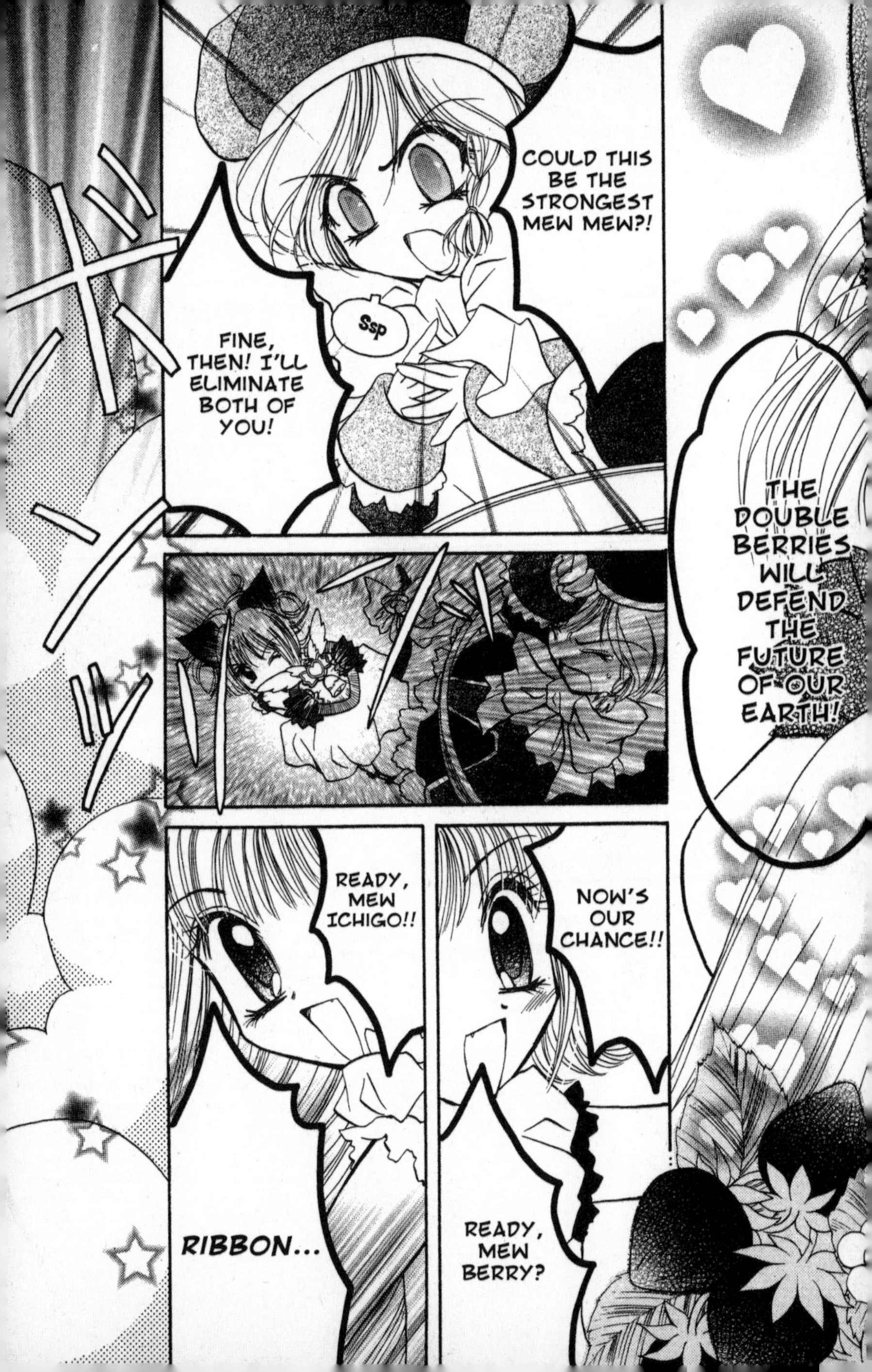
THE DOUBLE BERRIES WILL DEFEND THE FUTURE OF OUR EARTH!
COULD THIS BE THE STRONGEST MEW MEW?!
Ssp
FINE, THEN! I'LL ELIMINATE BOTH OF YOU!
NOW'S OUR CHANCE!!
READY, MEW BERRY?
READY, MEW ICHIGO!!
RIBBON...

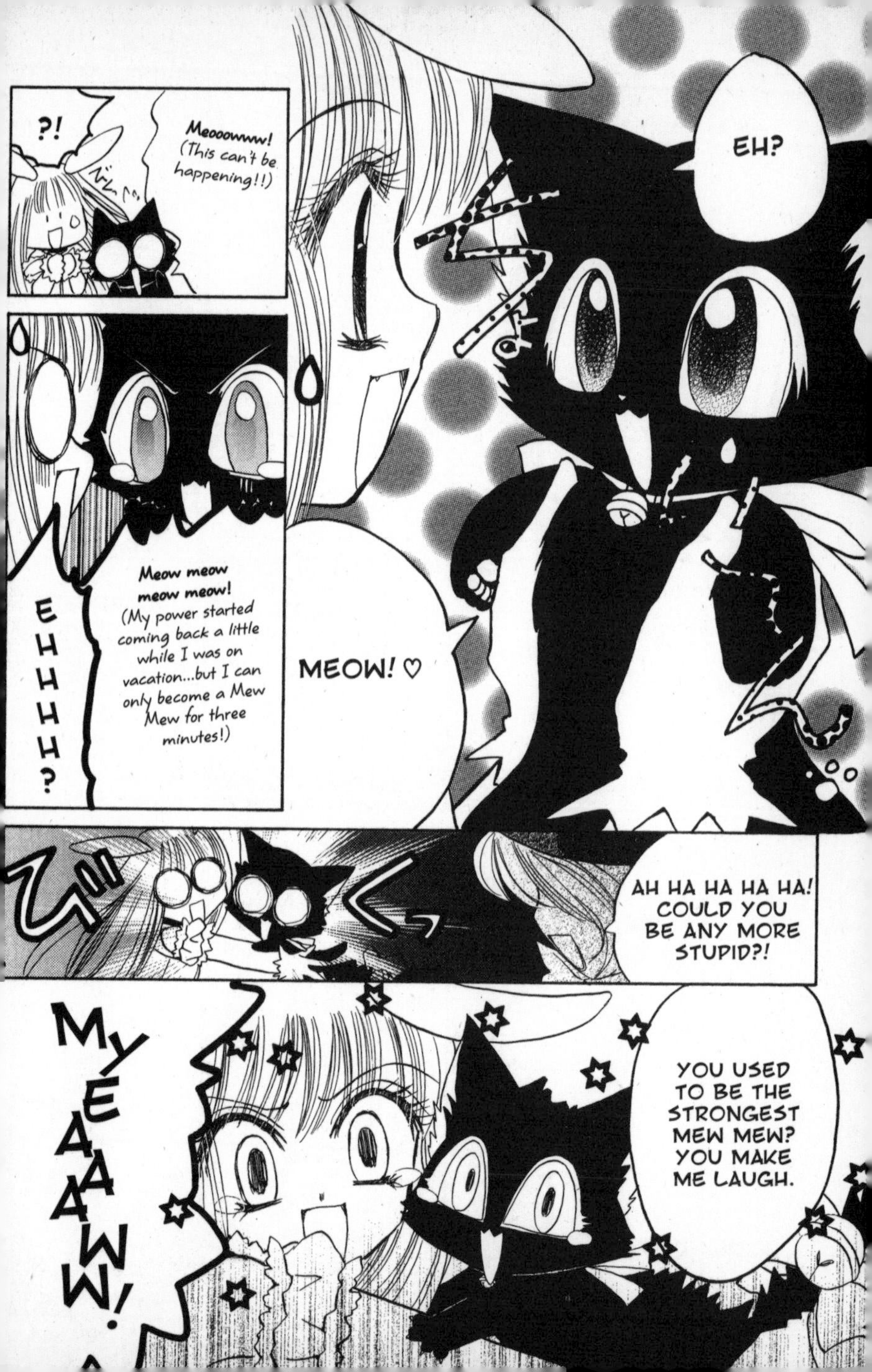
EH?
MEOW! ♡
?!
Meooowww! (This can't be happening!!)
Meow meow meow meow! (My power started coming back a little while I was on vacation...but I can only become a Mew Mew for three minutes!)
EHHHHH?
AH HA HA HA HA! COULD YOU BE ANY MORE STUPID?!
YOU USED TO BE THE STRONGEST MEW MEW? YOU MAKE ME LAUGH.
MYEAAAAWW!

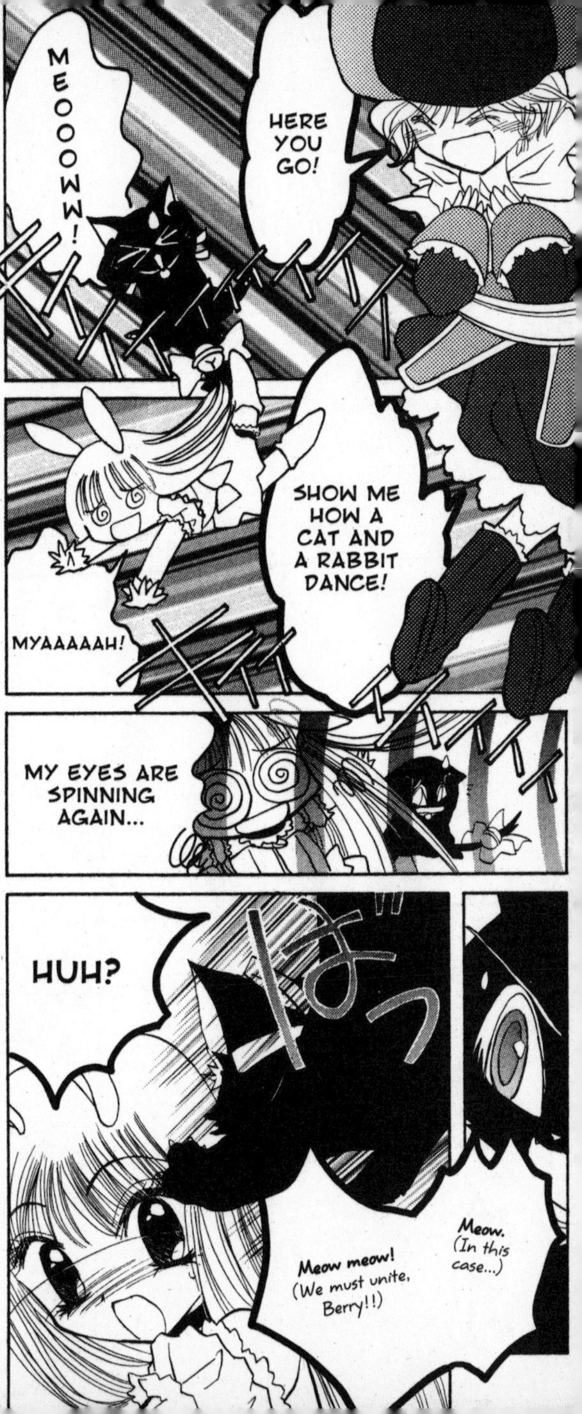
HERE YOU GO!
MEOOOWW!
SHOW ME HOW A CAT AND A RABBIT DANCE!
MYAAAAAH!
MY EYES ARE SPINNING AGAIN...
HUH?
Meow. (In this case...)
Meow meow! (We must unite, Berry!!)

Special Thanks!!

T. Matsumoto
M. Omori

A. Okawa
S. Nakazawa
K. Honda
S. Naohara
A. Horie

H. Oikawa

Hara Asumin
M. Sekiya
K. Nakama

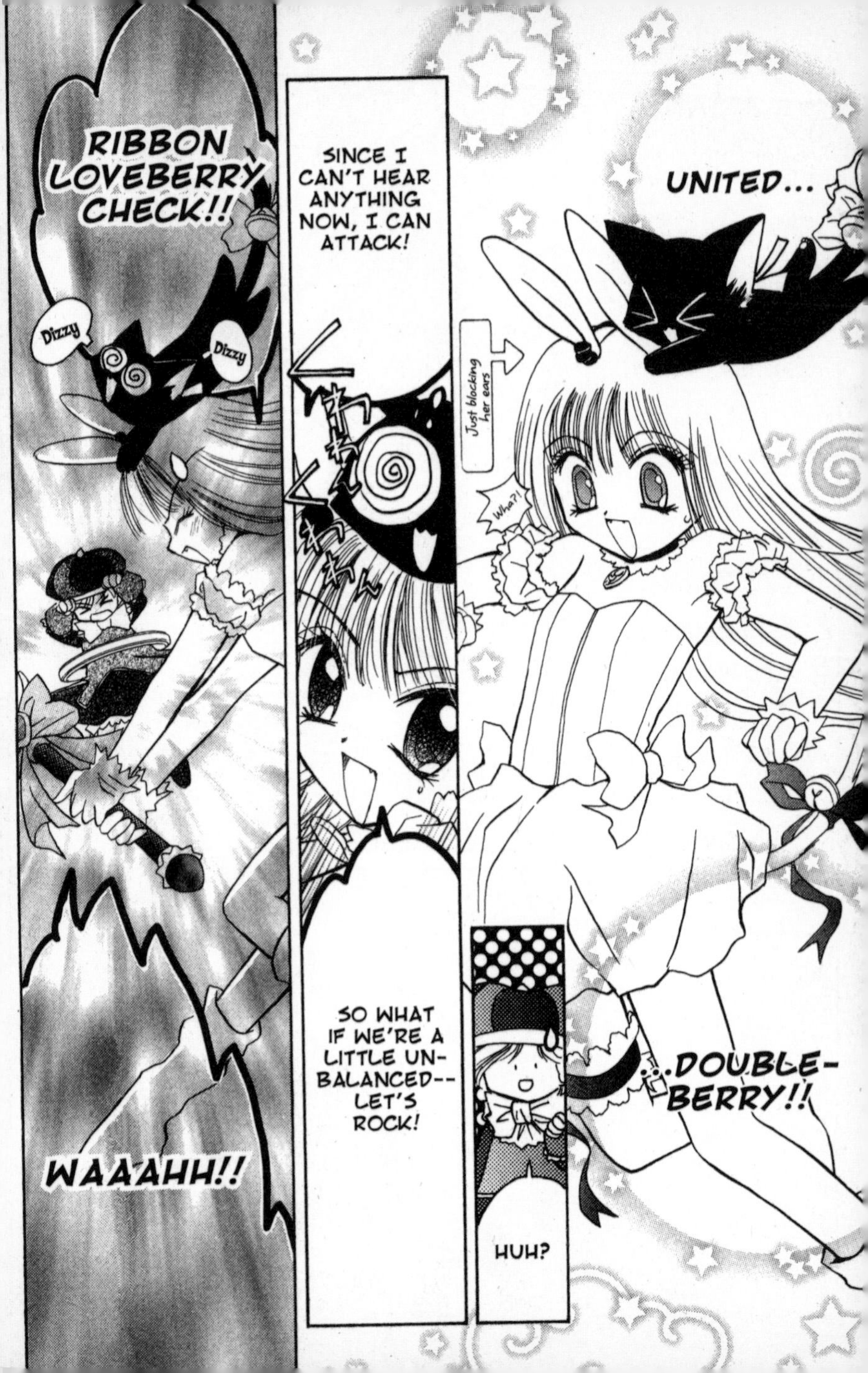
UNITED...
Just blocking her ears
Wha?!
...DOUBLE-BERRY!!
HUH?
SINCE I CAN'T HEAR ANYTHING NOW, I CAN ATTACK!
SO WHAT IF WE'RE A LITTLE UN-BALANCED--LET'S ROCK!
RIBBON LOVEBERRY CHECK!!
Dizzy
Dizzy
WAAAHH!!

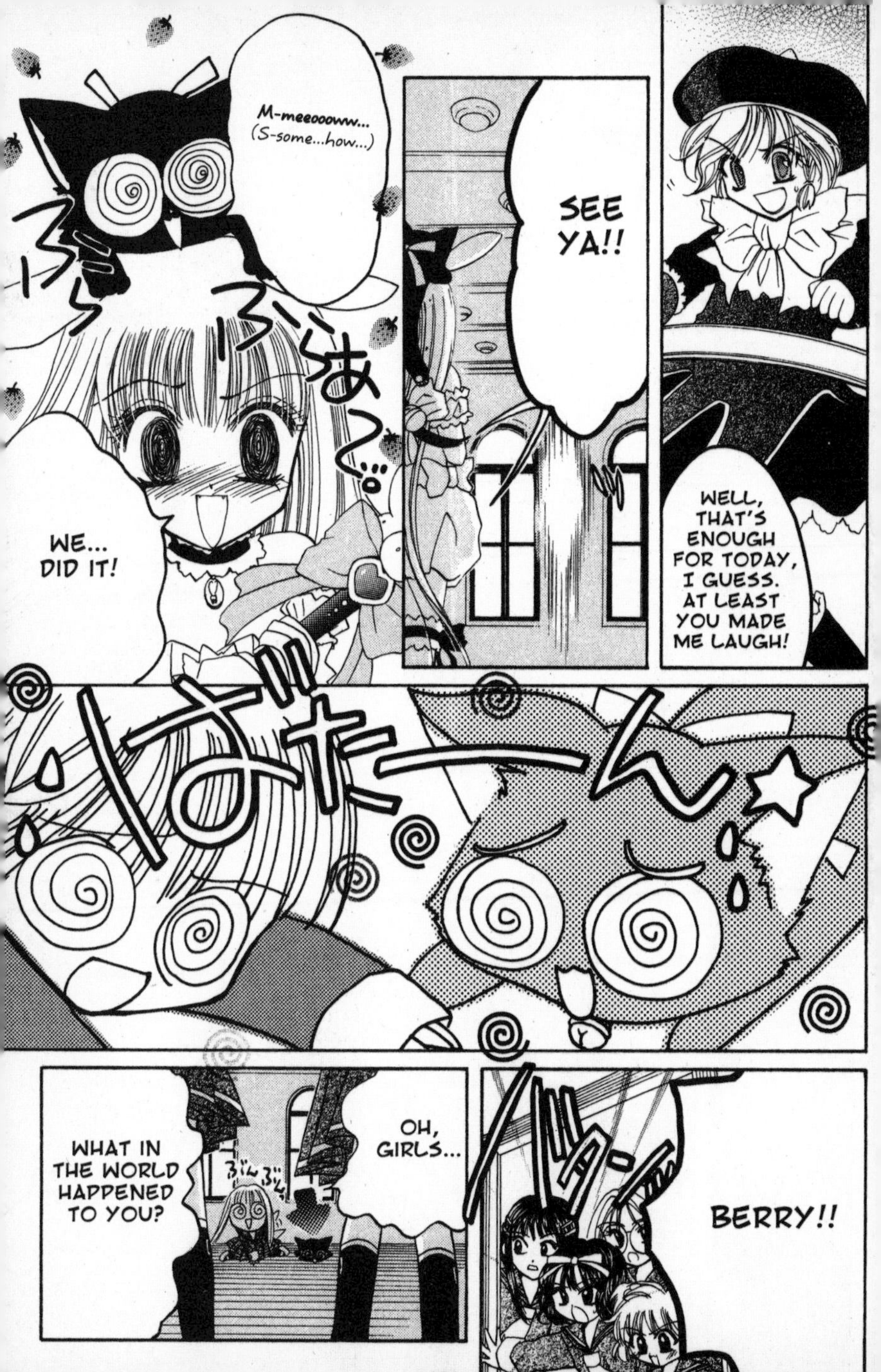
WELL, THAT'S ENOUGH FOR TODAY, I GUESS. AT LEAST YOU MADE ME LAUGH!
SEE YA!!
M-meeooowww... (S-some...how...)
WE... DID IT!
OH, GIRLS...
WHAT IN THE WORLD HAPPENED TO YOU?
BERRY!!

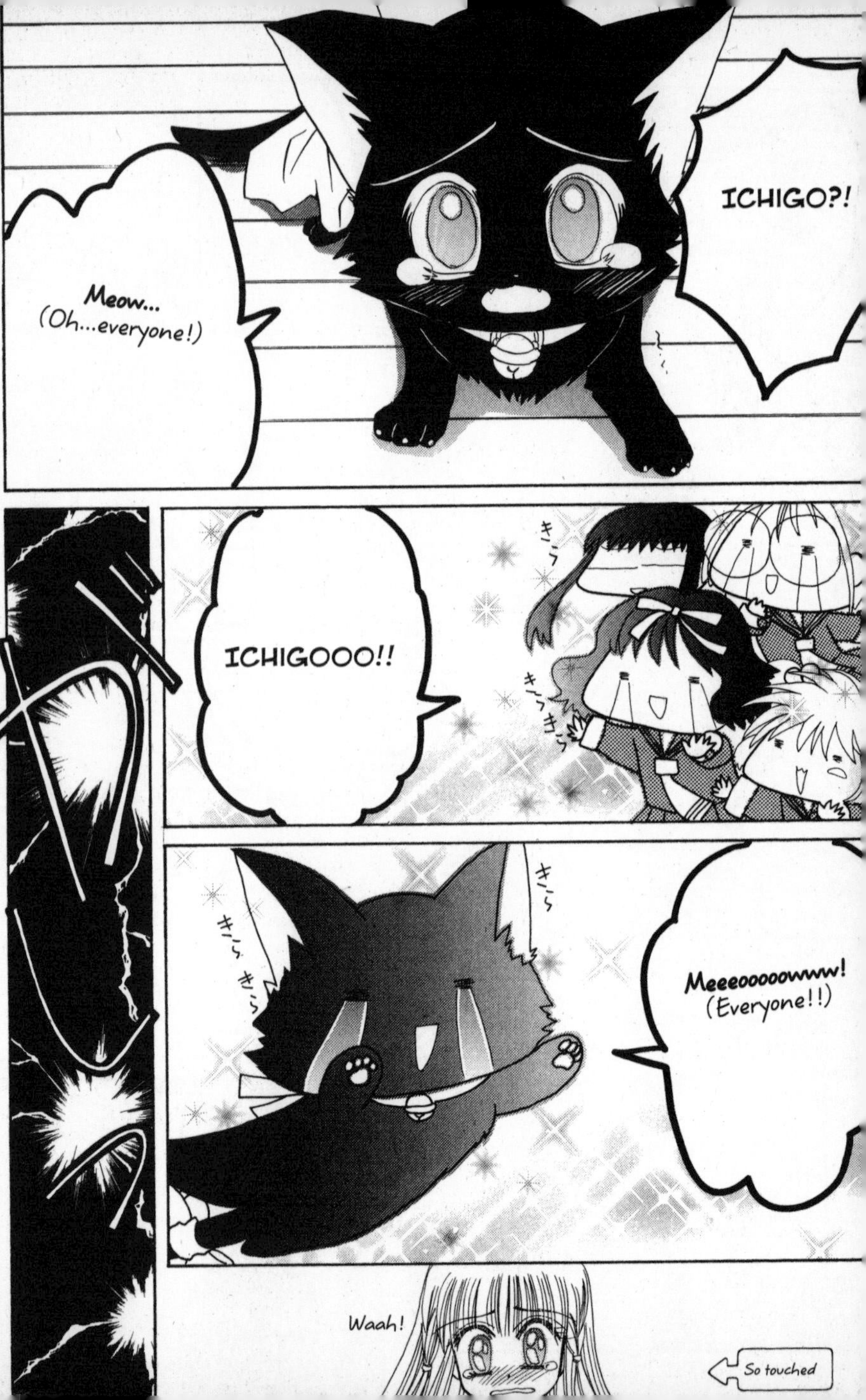
ICHIGO?!
Meow... (Oh...everyone!)
ICHIGOOO!!
きら
きら きら
Meeeooooowww! (Everyone!!)
So touched
Waah!

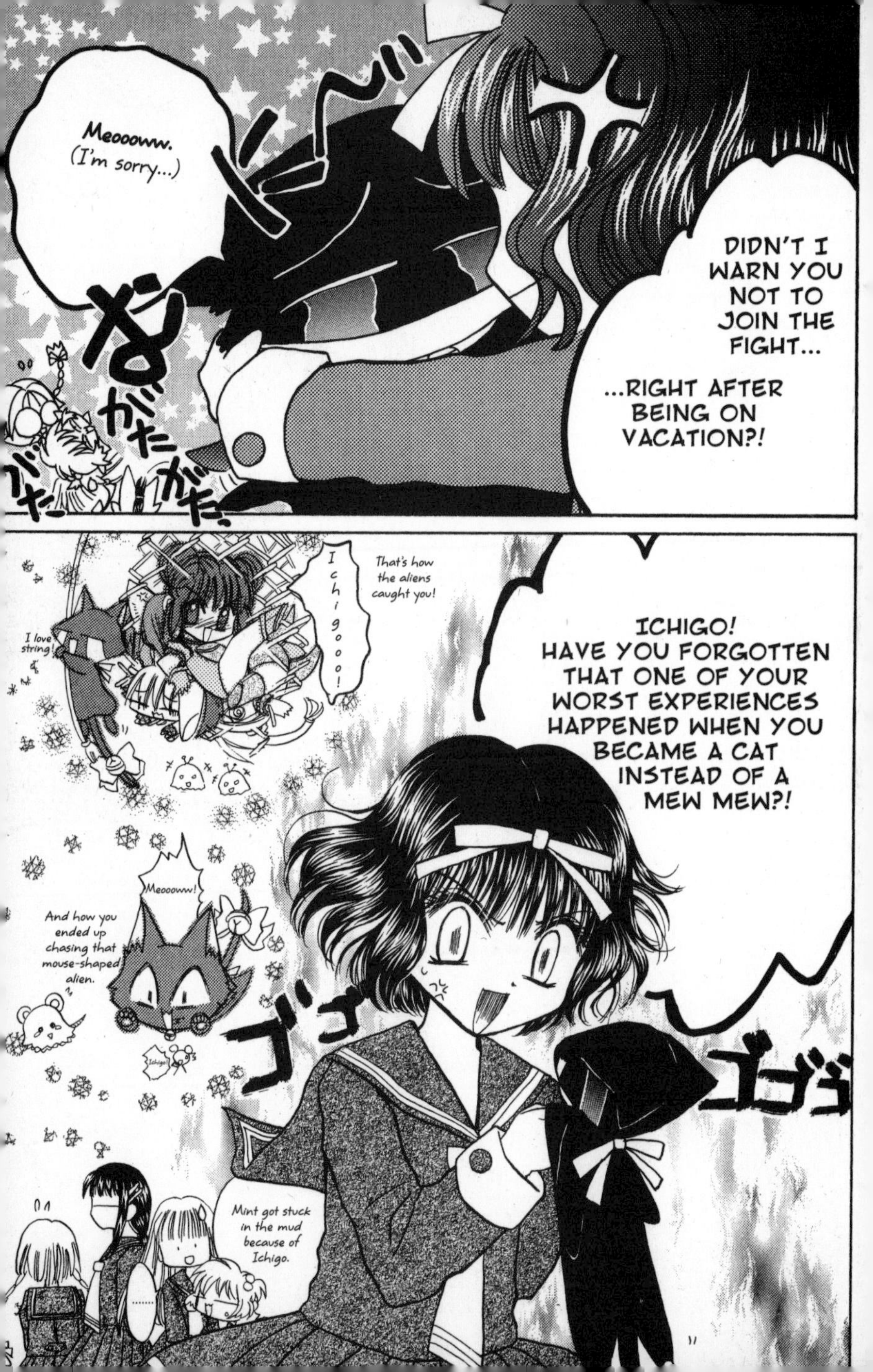
DIDN'T I WARN YOU NOT TO JOIN THE FIGHT...
...RIGHT AFTER BEING ON VACATION?!
Meooww. (I'm sorry...)
ICHIGO! HAVE YOU FORGOTTEN THAT ONE OF YOUR WORST EXPERIENCES HAPPENED WHEN YOU BECAME A CAT INSTEAD OF A MEW MEW?!
That's how the aliens caught you!
Ichigoooo!
I love string!
Meooww!
And how you ended up chasing that mouse-shaped alien.
Ichigo!
Mint got stuck in the mud because of Ichigo.
....

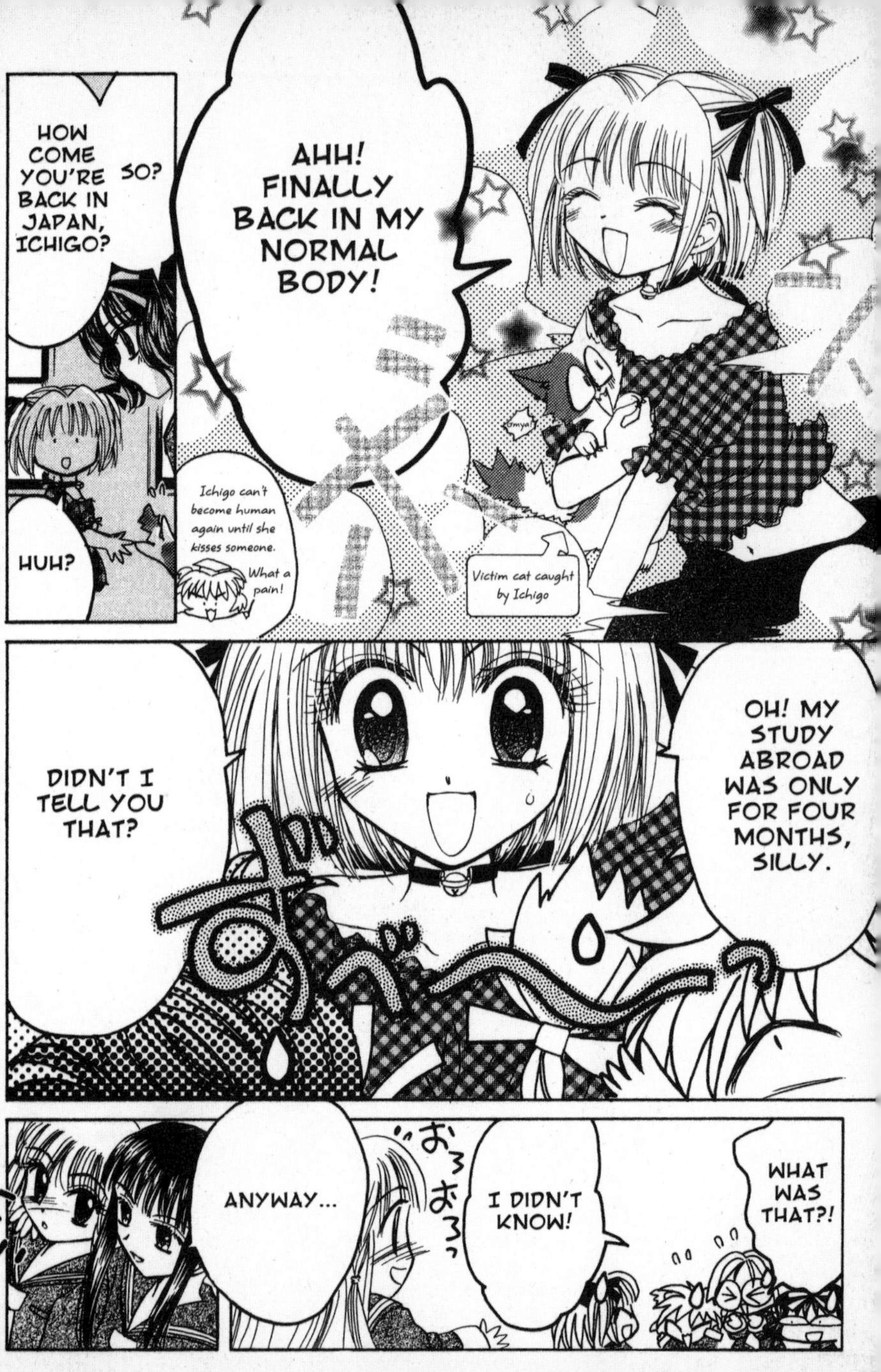
AHH! FINALLY BACK IN MY NORMAL BODY!
Gmya!
Victim cat caught by Ichigo
Ichigo can't become human again until she kisses someone.
What a pain!
SO?
HOW COME YOU'RE BACK IN JAPAN, ICHIGO?
HUH?
OH! MY STUDY ABROAD WAS ONLY FOR FOUR MONTHS, SILLY.
DIDN'T I TELL YOU THAT?
WHAT WAS THAT?!
I DIDN'T KNOW!
ANYWAY...

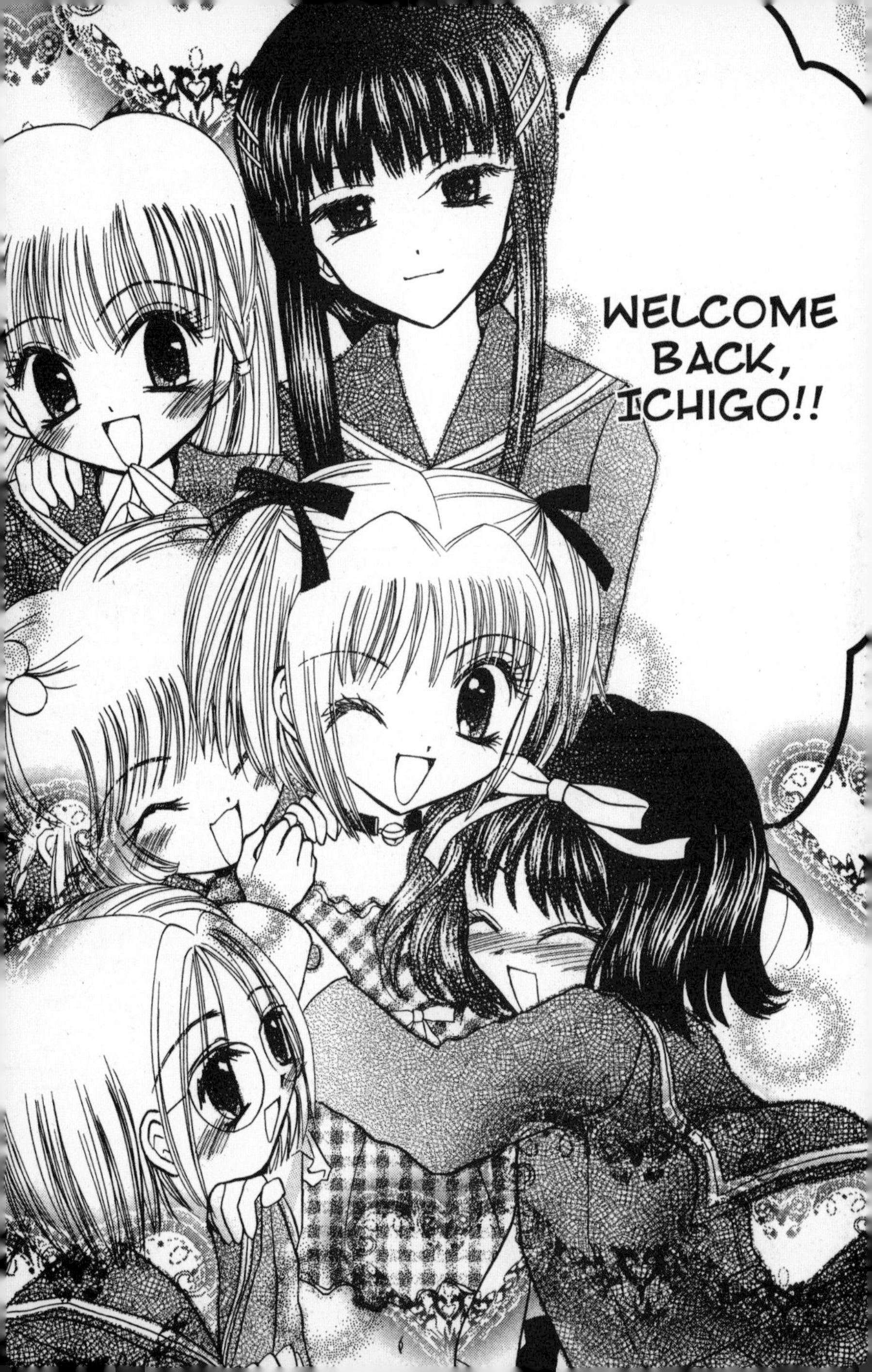
WELCOME BACK, ICHIGO!!

Pointless Bloomers Drawing

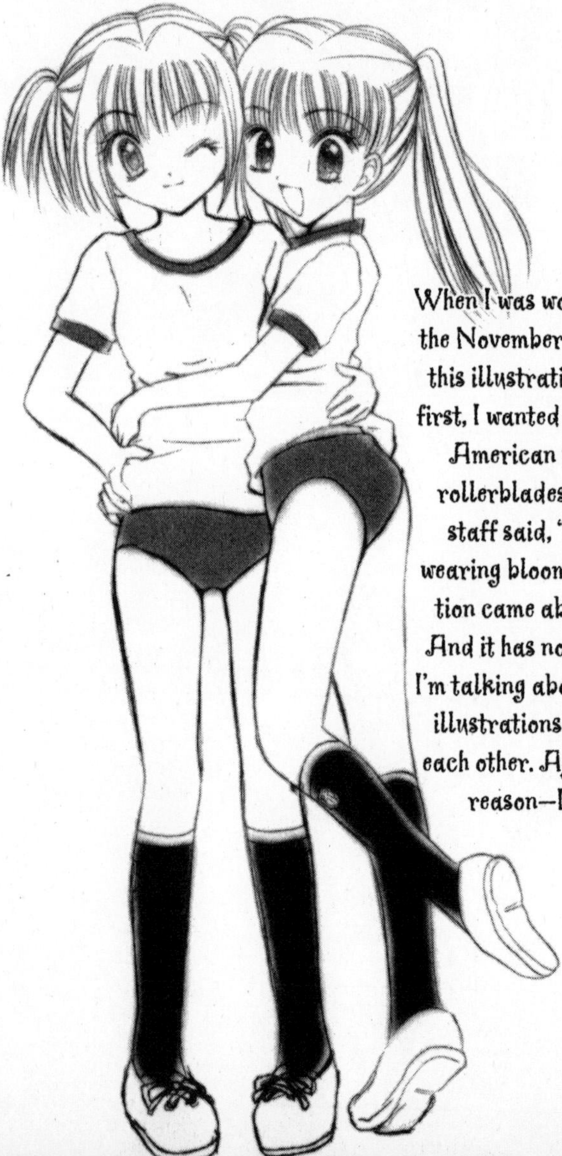

When I was working on the story for the November 2003 issue, I drew this illustration for no reason. At first, I wanted to draw a girl with an American waitress dress and rollerblades, but then one of my staff said, "I want to see a girl wearing bloomers." So this illustration came about because of that. And it has nothing to do with what I'm talking about, but I love drawing illustrations of two girls hugging each other. Again, for no apparent reason—I don't know why!

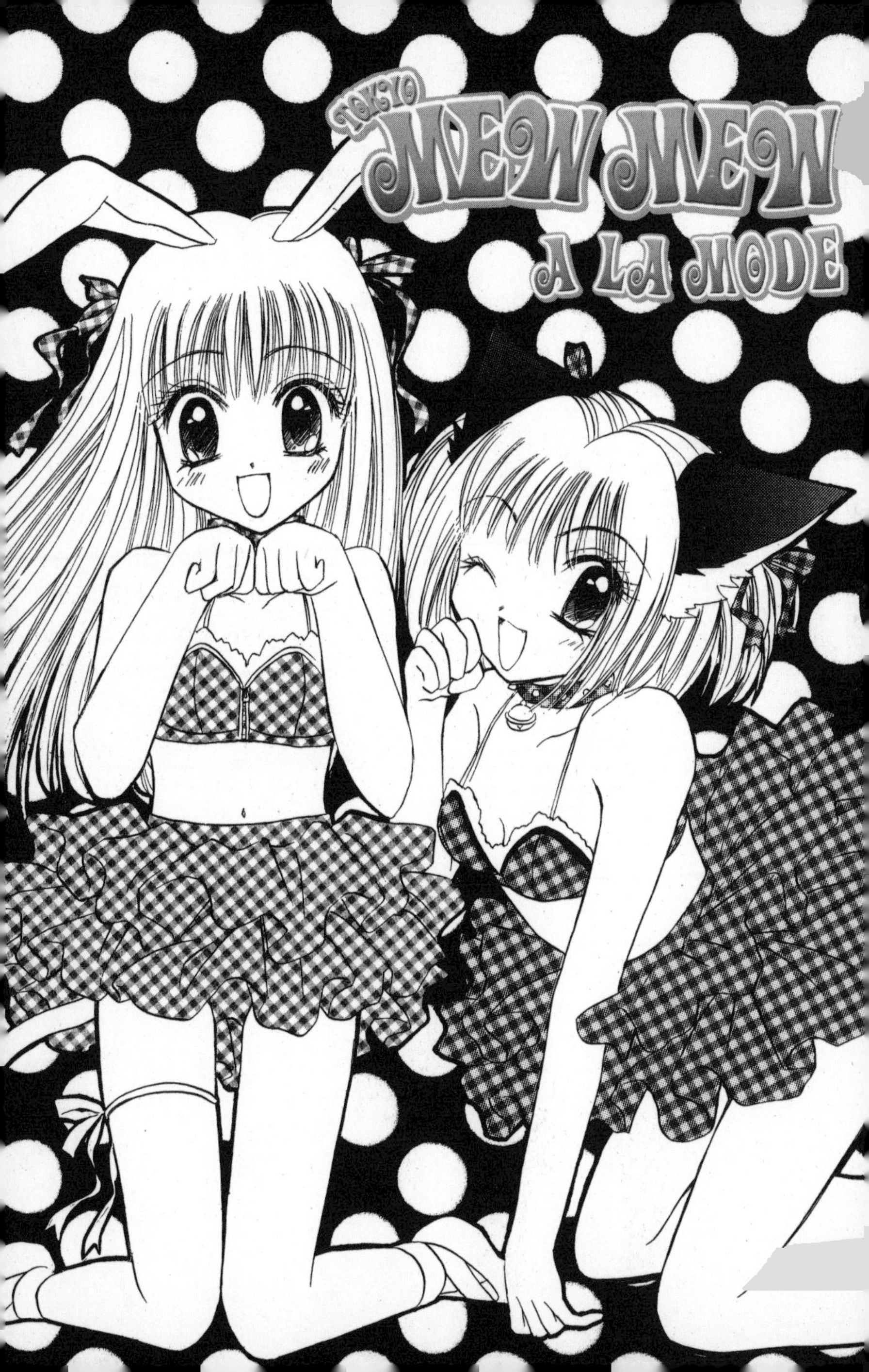
TOKYO
MEW MEW
A LA MODE

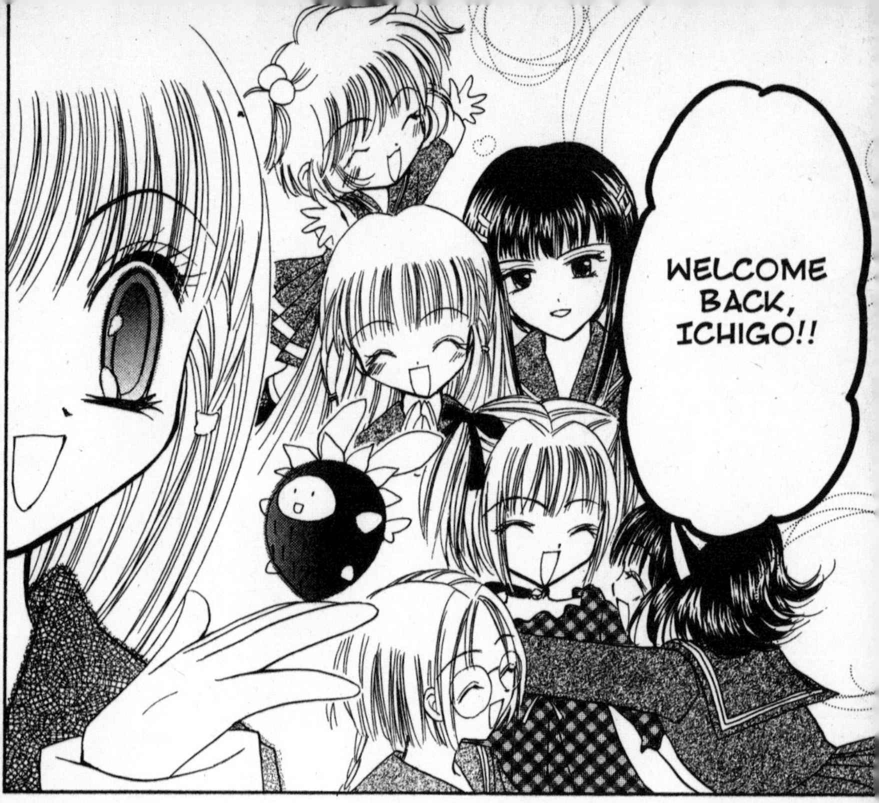
WELCOME BACK, ICHIGO!!
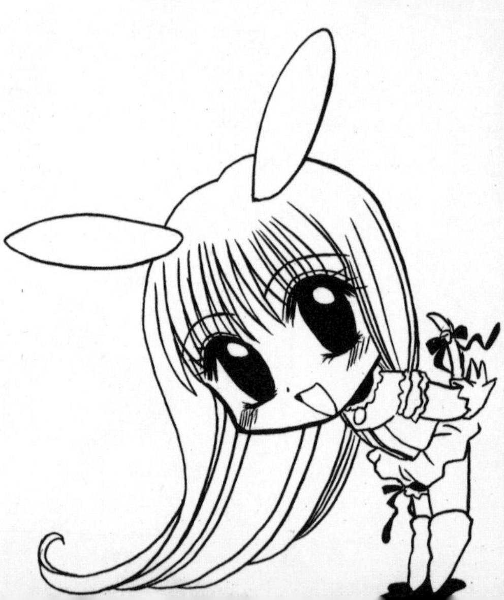

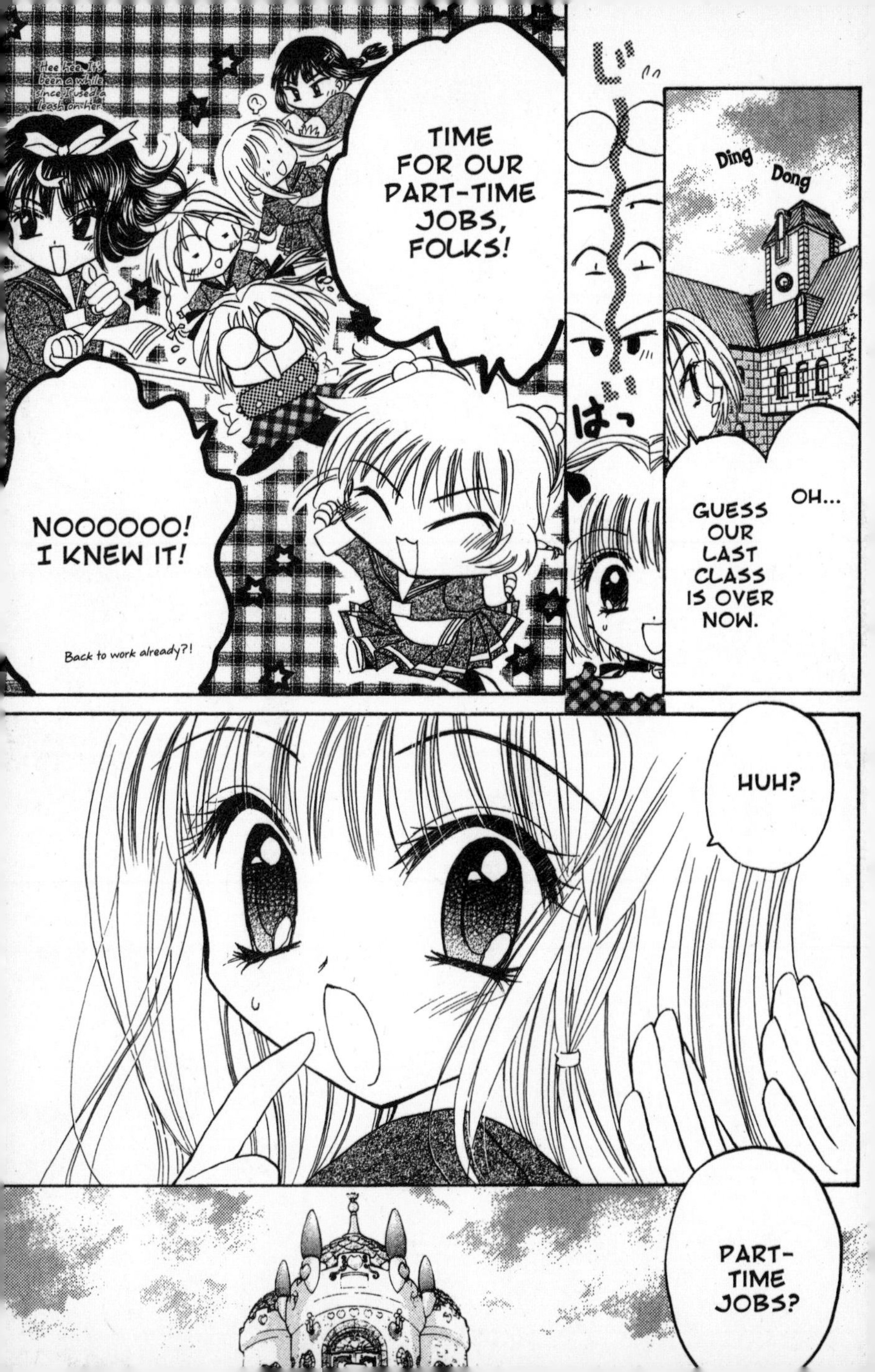

Ding
Dong
OH...
GUESS OUR LAST CLASS IS OVER NOW.
はっ
TIME FOR OUR PART-TIME JOBS, FOLKS!
Hee hee. It's been a while since I used a leash on her.
NOOOOOO! I KNEW IT!
Back to work already?!
HUH?
PART-TIME JOBS?

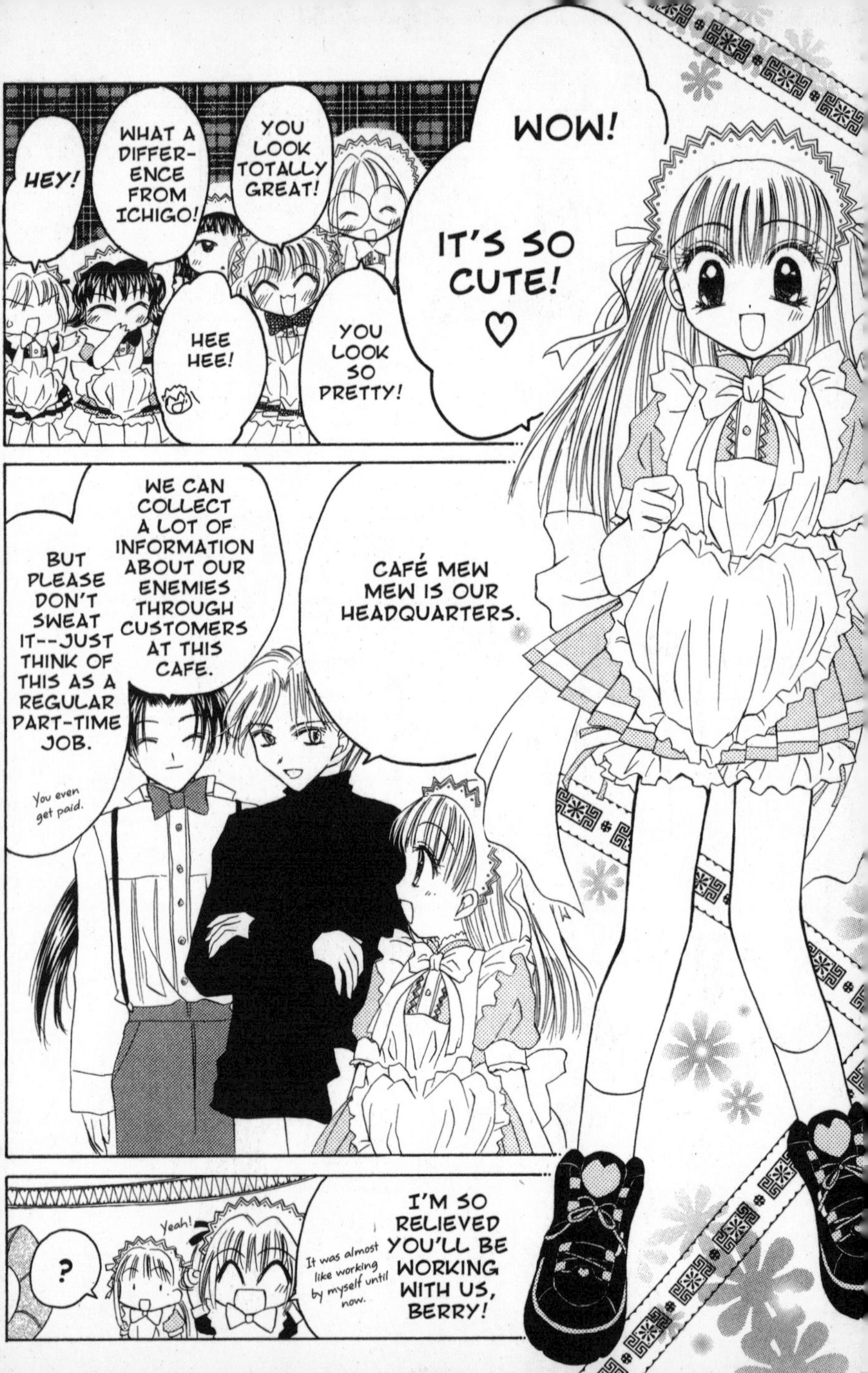
WOW!
IT'S SO CUTE! ♡
YOU LOOK TOTALLY GREAT!
YOU LOOK SO PRETTY!
WHAT A DIFFER-ENCE FROM ICHIGO!
HEE HEE!
HEY!
CAFÉ MEW MEW IS OUR HEADQUARTERS.
WE CAN COLLECT A LOT OF INFORMATION ABOUT OUR ENEMIES THROUGH CUSTOMERS AT THIS CAFE.
BUT PLEASE DON'T SWEAT IT--JUST THINK OF THIS AS A REGULAR PART-TIME JOB.
You even get paid.
I'M SO RELIEVED YOU'LL BE WORKING WITH US, BERRY!
It was almost like working by myself until now.
Yeah!
?

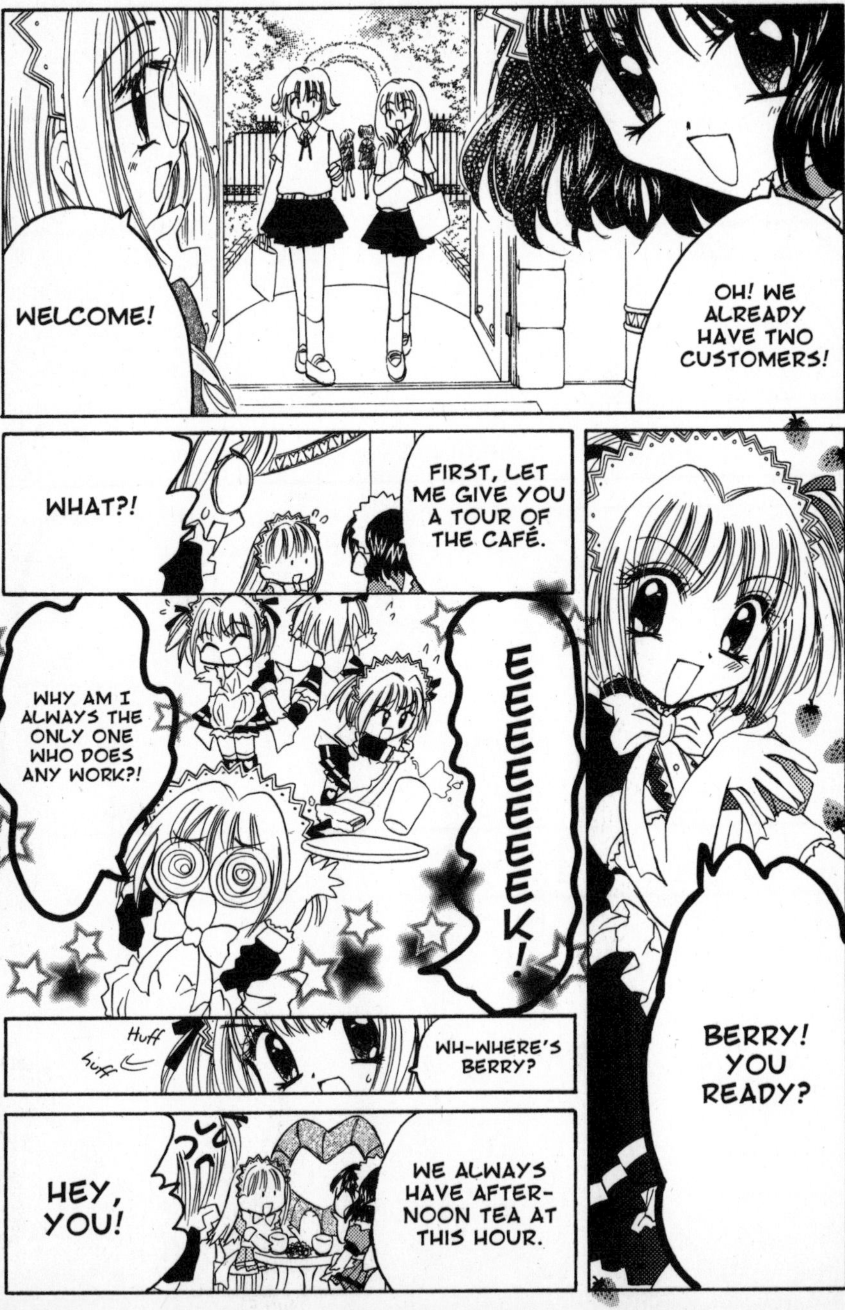
OH! WE ALREADY HAVE TWO CUSTOMERS!
WELCOME!
BERRY! YOU READY?
FIRST, LET ME GIVE YOU A TOUR OF THE CAFÉ.
WHAT?!
EEEEEEEEEK!
WHY AM I ALWAYS THE ONLY ONE WHO DOES ANY WORK?!
WH-WHERE'S BERRY?
Huff
huff
WE ALWAYS HAVE AFTER-NOON TEA AT THIS HOUR.
HEY, YOU!

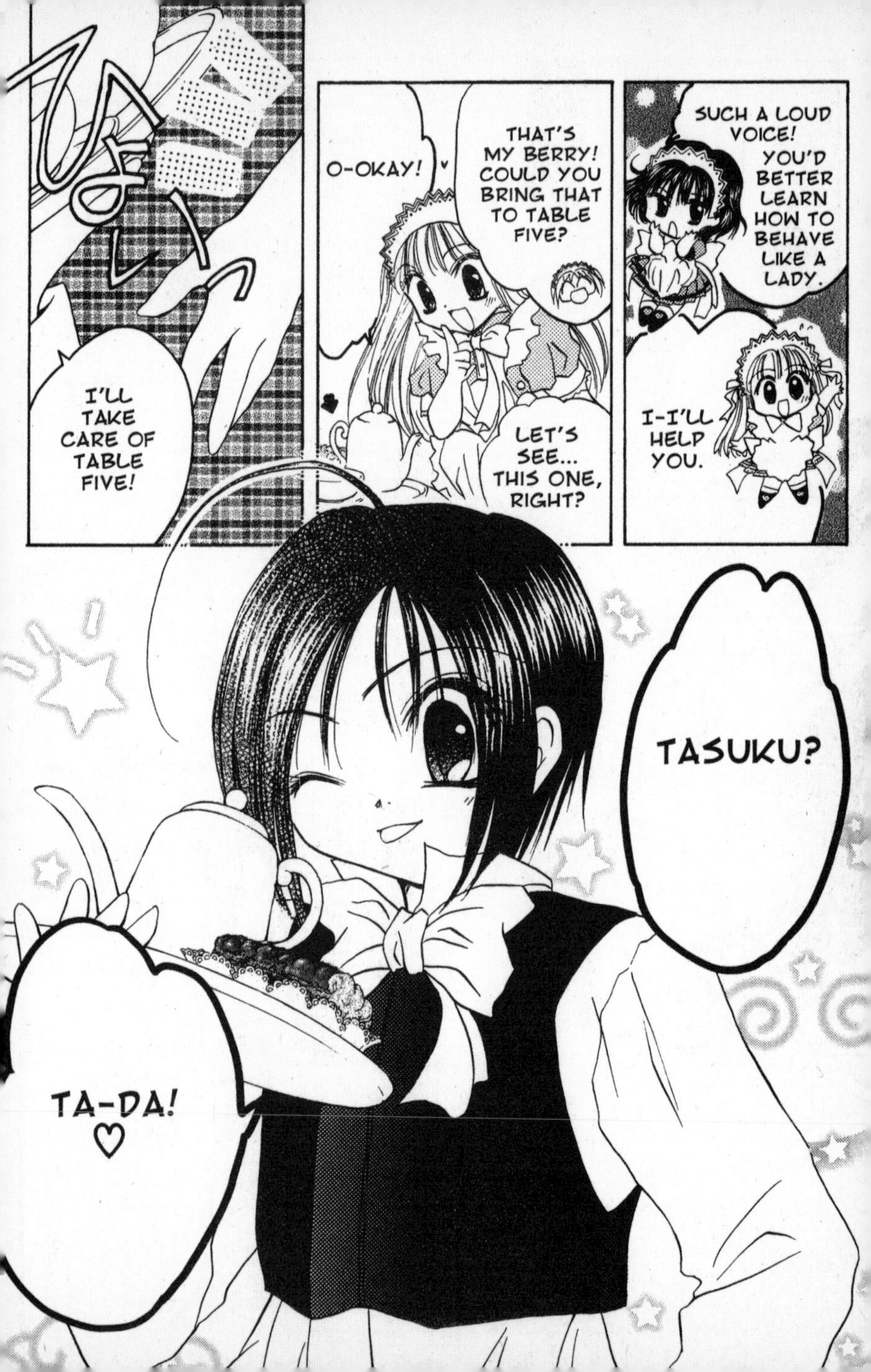
SUCH A LOUD VOICE! YOU'D BETTER LEARN HOW TO BEHAVE LIKE A LADY.
I-I'LL HELP YOU.
THAT'S MY BERRY! COULD YOU BRING THAT TO TABLE FIVE?
O-OKAY! ♥
LET'S SEE... THIS ONE, RIGHT?
I'LL TAKE CARE OF TABLE FIVE!
TASUKU?
TA-DA! ♡

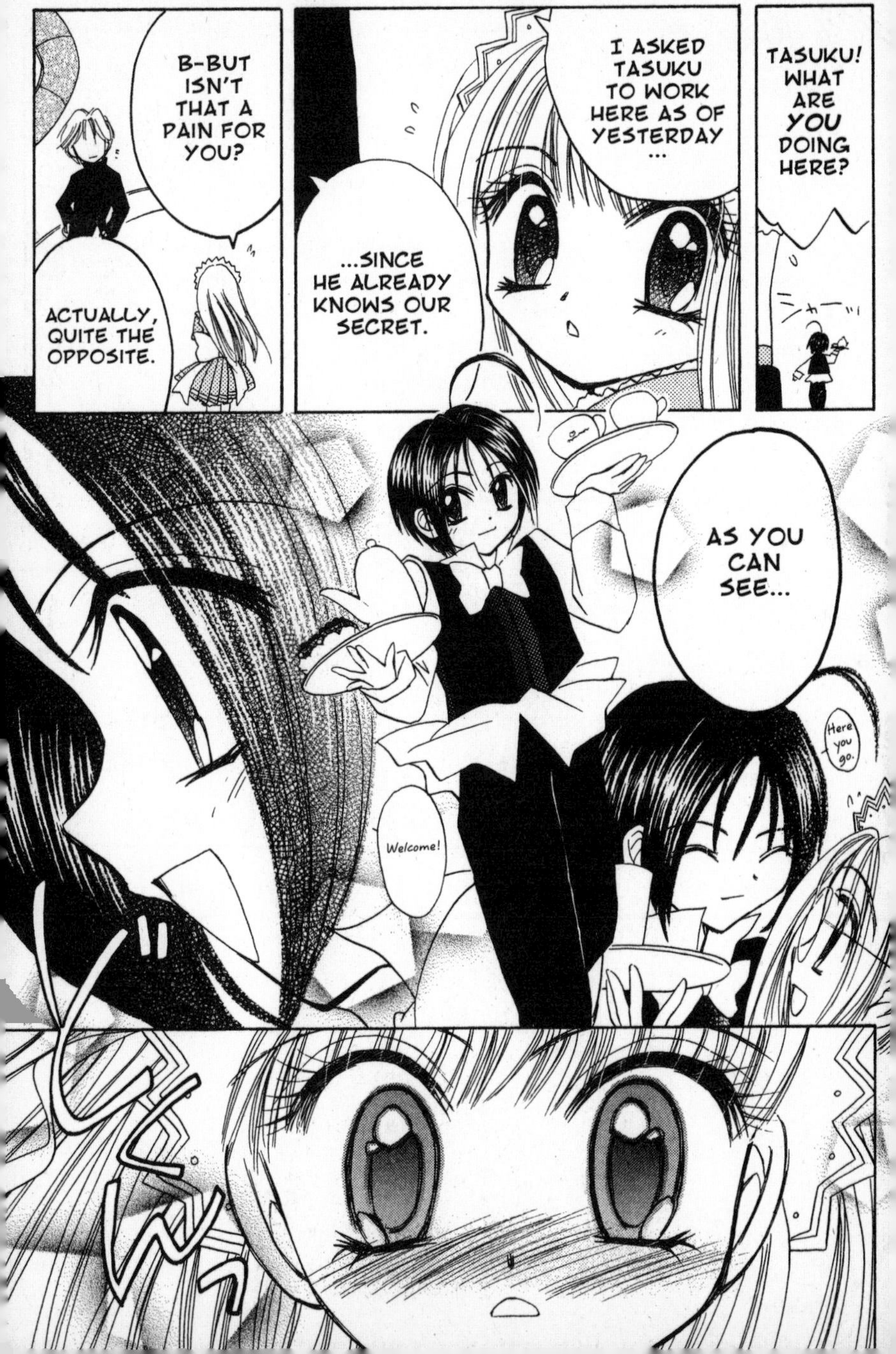
TASUKU! WHAT ARE YOU DOING HERE?
I ASKED TASUKU TO WORK HERE AS OF YESTERDAY...
...SINCE HE ALREADY KNOWS OUR SECRET.
B-BUT ISN'T THAT A PAIN FOR YOU?
ACTUALLY, QUITE THE OPPOSITE.
AS YOU CAN SEE...
Here you go.
Welcome!

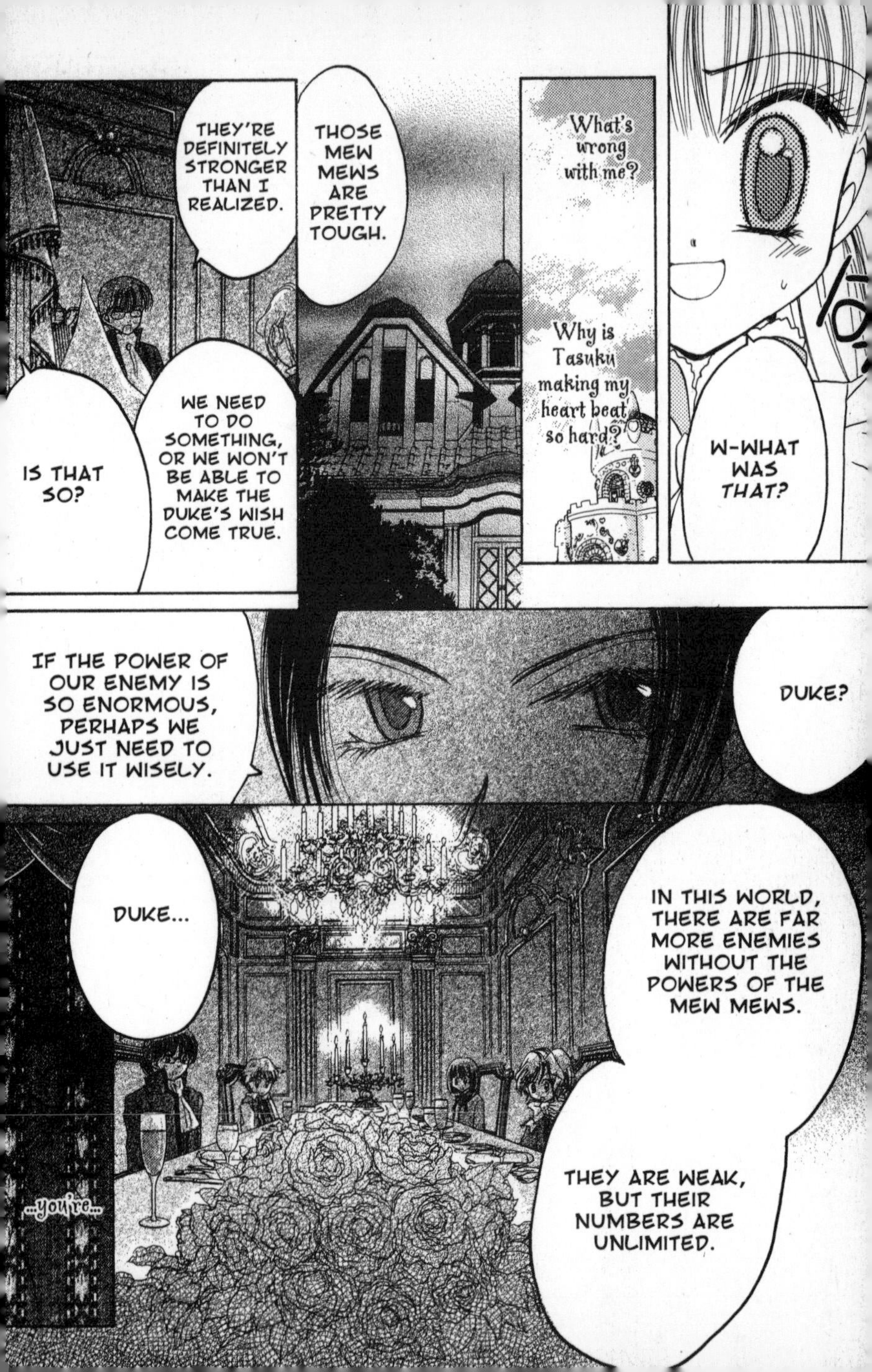
W-WHAT WAS *THAT?*
What's wrong with me?
Why is Tasuku making my heart beat so hard?
THOSE MEW MEWS ARE PRETTY TOUGH.
THEY'RE DEFINITELY STRONGER THAN I REALIZED.
WE NEED TO DO SOMETHING, OR WE WON'T BE ABLE TO MAKE THE DUKE'S WISH COME TRUE.
IS THAT SO?
DUKE?
IF THE POWER OF OUR ENEMY IS SO ENORMOUS, PERHAPS WE JUST NEED TO USE IT WISELY.
IN THIS WORLD, THERE ARE FAR MORE ENEMIES WITHOUT THE POWERS OF THE MEW MEWS.
THEY ARE WEAK, BUT THEIR NUMBERS ARE UNLIMITED.
DUKE...
...you're...

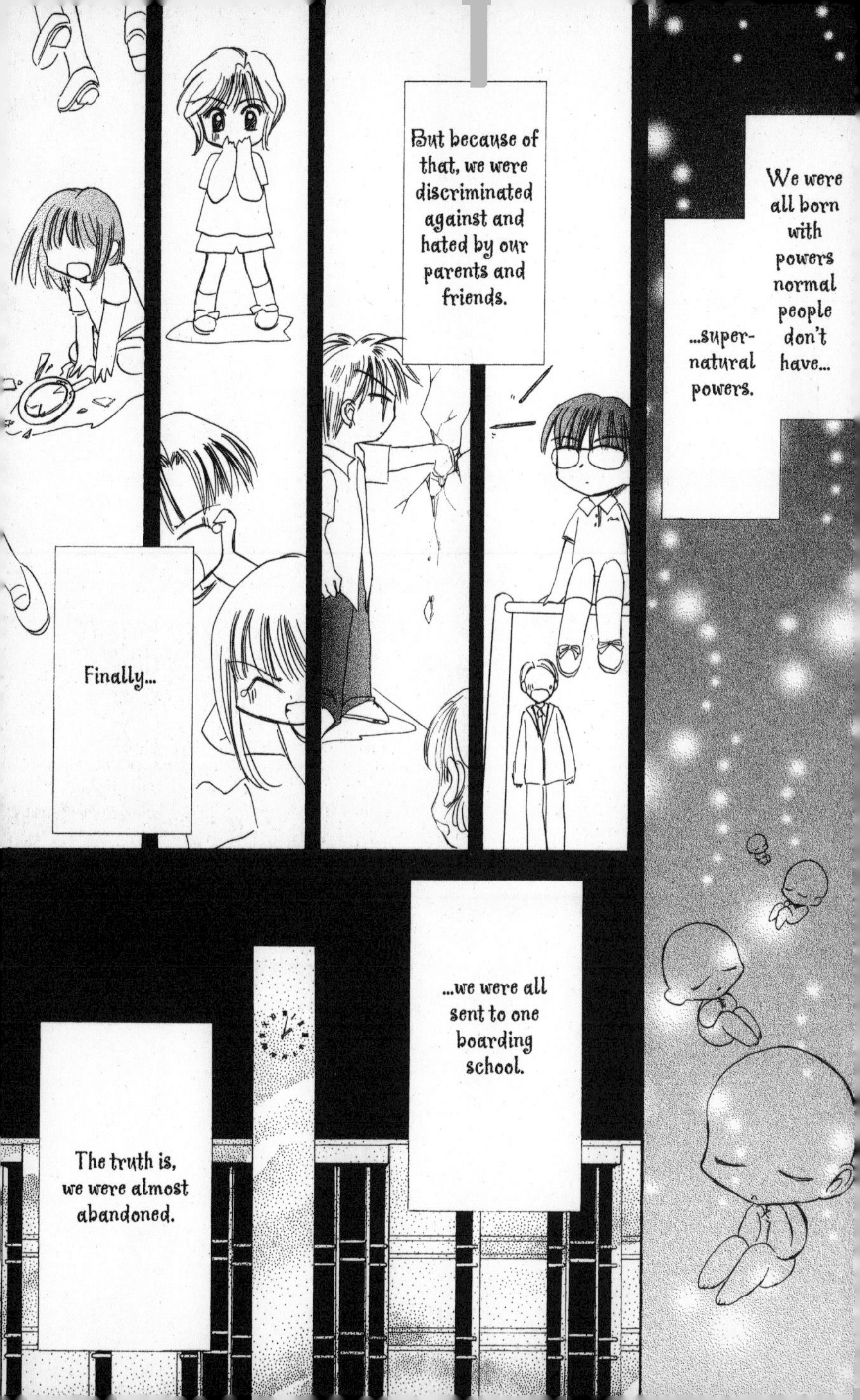

We were all born with powers normal people don't have...
...super-natural powers.
But because of that, we were discriminated against and hated by our parents and friends.
Finally...
...we were all sent to one boarding school.
The truth is, we were almost abandoned.

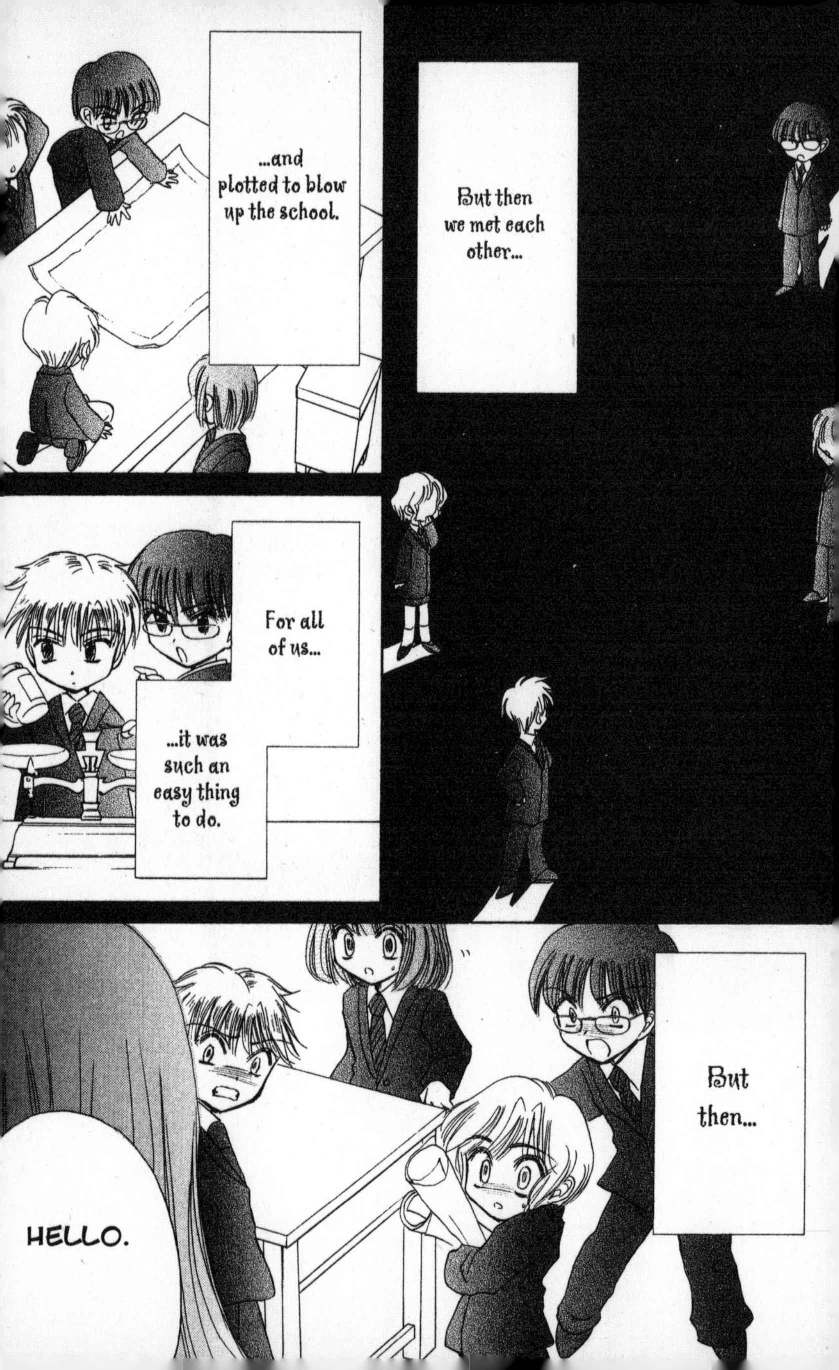
But then we met each other...
...and plotted to blow up the school.
For all of us...
...it was such an easy thing to do.
But then...
HELLO.

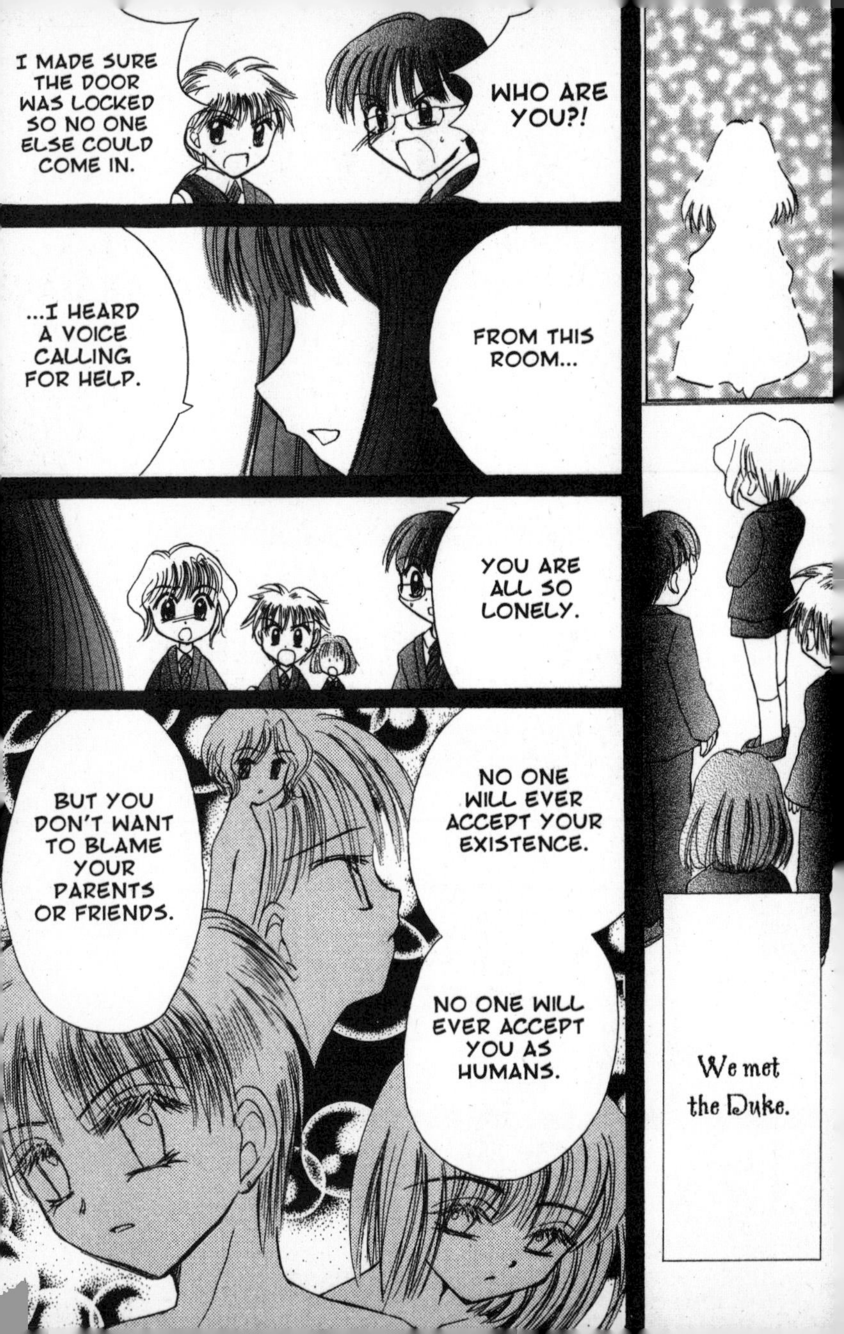
We met the Duke.
WHO ARE YOU?!
I MADE SURE THE DOOR WAS LOCKED SO NO ONE ELSE COULD COME IN.
FROM THIS ROOM...
...I HEARD A VOICE CALLING FOR HELP.
YOU ARE ALL SO LONELY.
NO ONE WILL EVER ACCEPT YOUR EXISTENCE.
BUT YOU DON'T WANT TO BLAME YOUR PARENTS OR FRIENDS.
NO ONE WILL EVER ACCEPT YOU AS HUMANS.

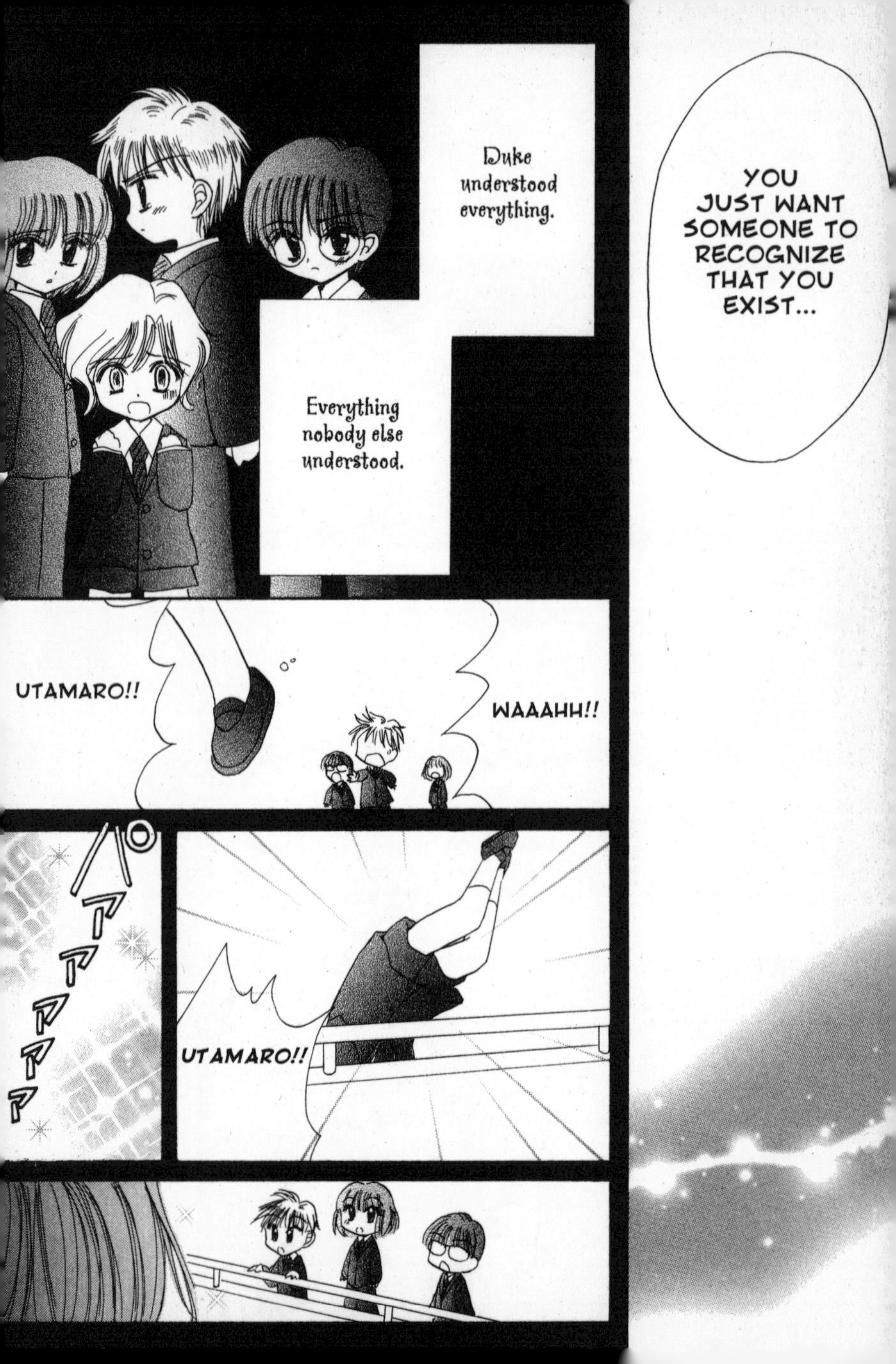
YOU JUST WANT SOMEONE TO RECOGNIZE THAT YOU EXIST...
Duke understood everything.
Everything nobody else understood.
WAAAHH!!
UTAMARO!!
UTAMARO!!
パァァァァァ

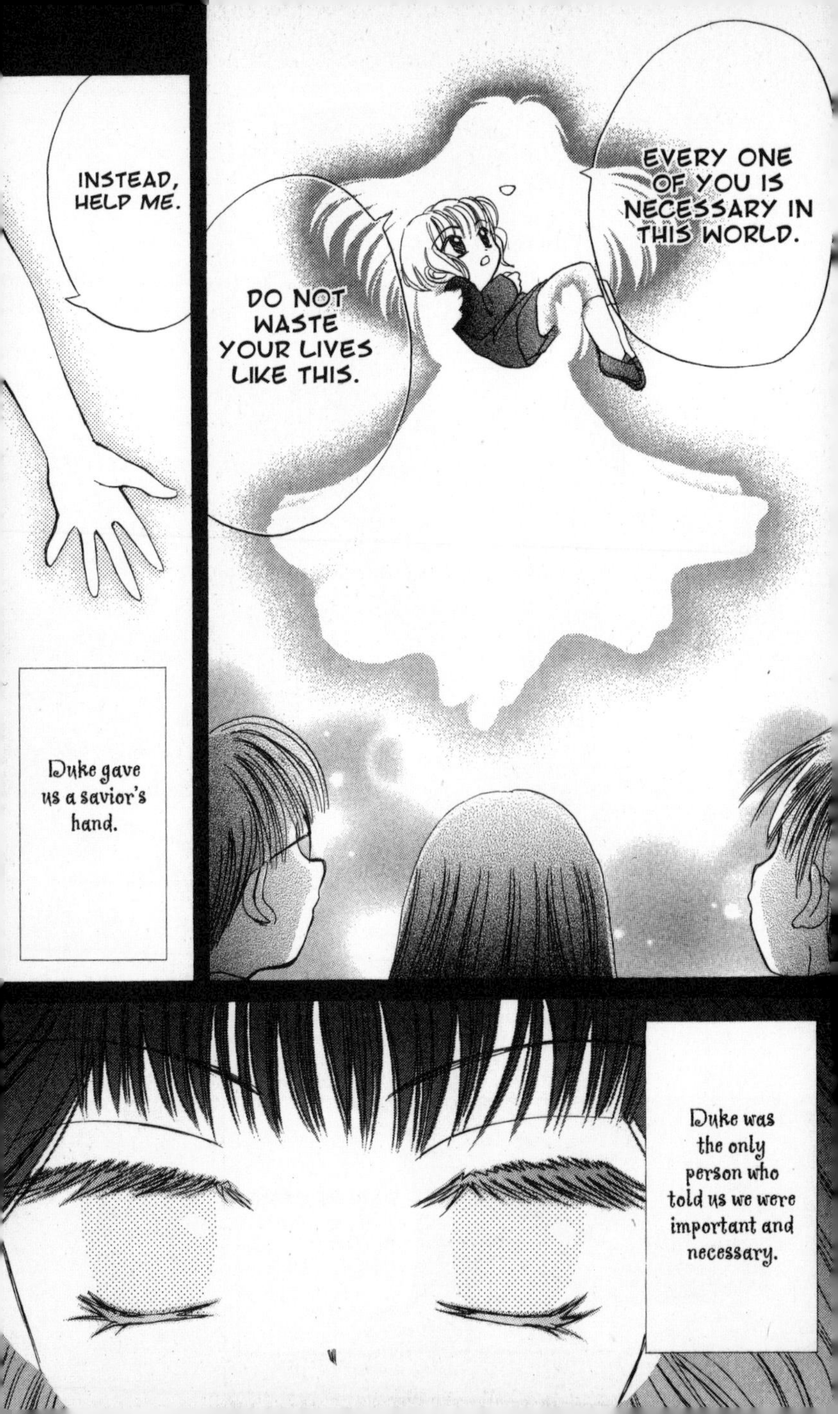
EVERY ONE OF YOU IS NECESSARY IN THIS WORLD.
DO NOT WASTE YOUR LIVES LIKE THIS.
INSTEAD, HELP ME.
Duke gave us a savior's hand.
Duke was the only person who told us we were important and necessary.

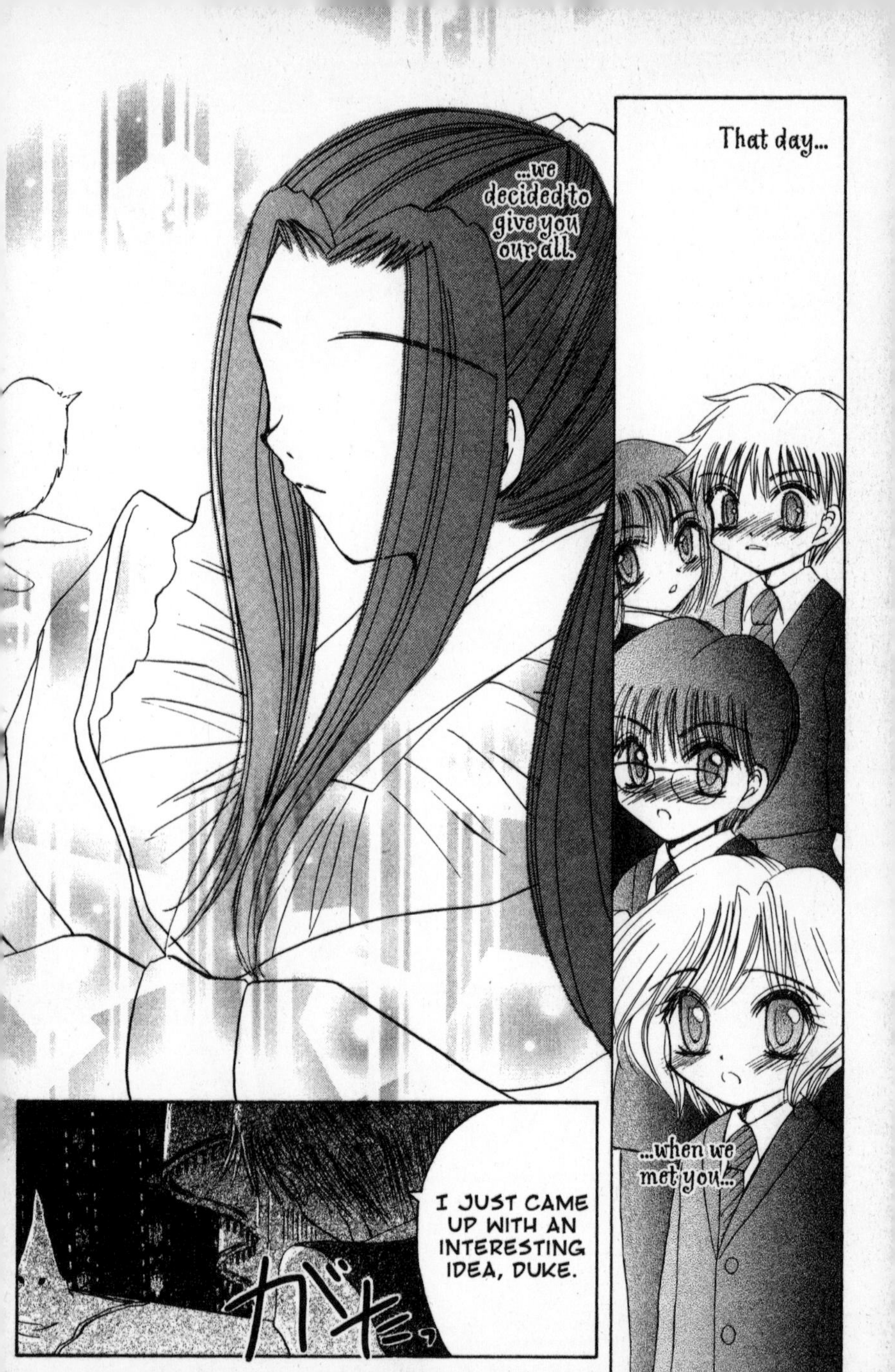
That day...
...when we met you...
...we decided to give you our all.
I JUST CAME UP WITH AN INTERESTING IDEA, DUKE.

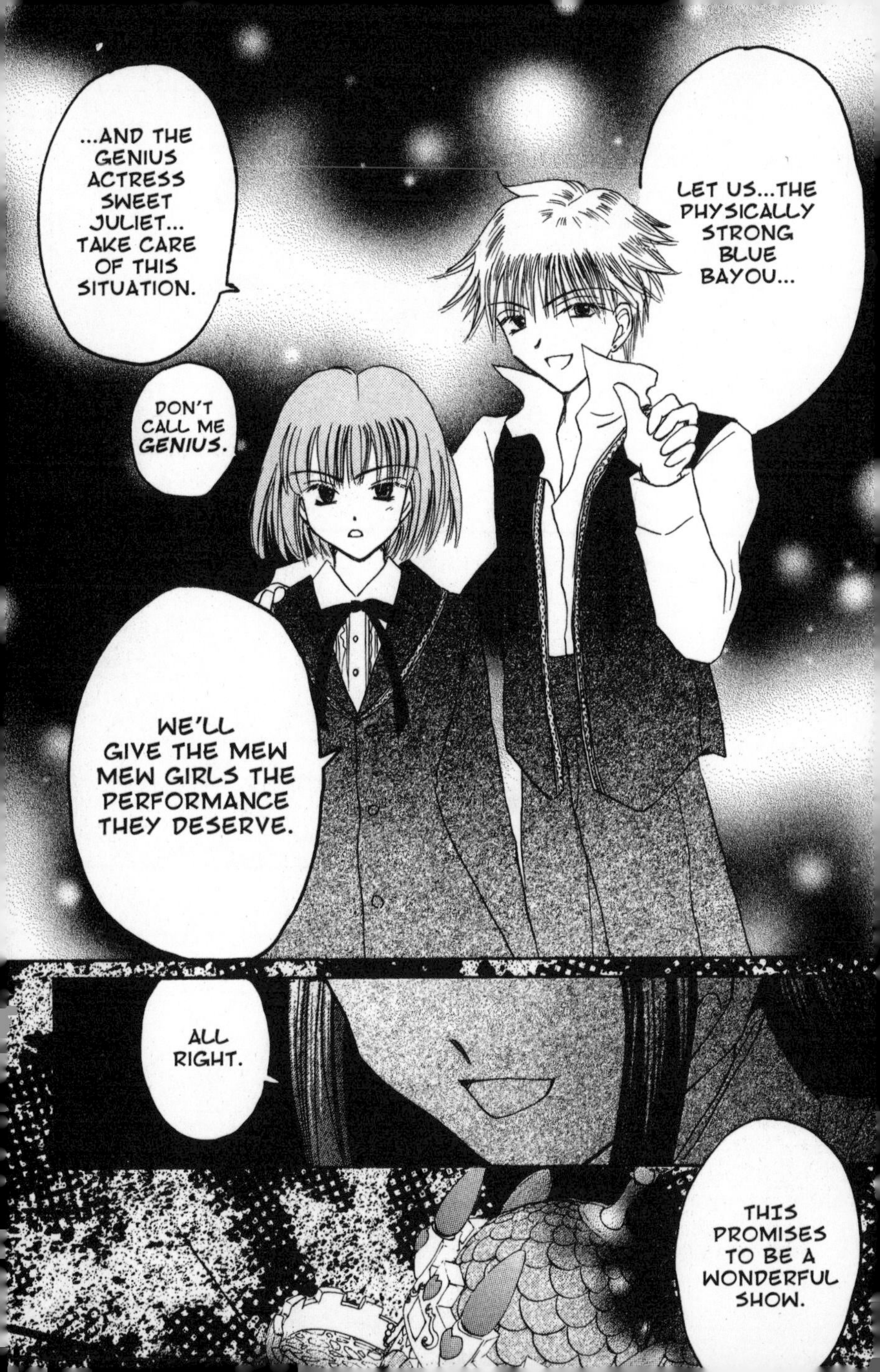
LET US...THE PHYSICALLY STRONG BLUE BAYOU...
...AND THE GENIUS ACTRESS SWEET JULIET... TAKE CARE OF THIS SITUATION.
DON'T CALL ME GENIUS.
WE'LL GIVE THE MEW MEW GIRLS THE PERFORMANCE THEY DESERVE.
ALL RIGHT.
THIS PROMISES TO BE A WONDERFUL SHOW.

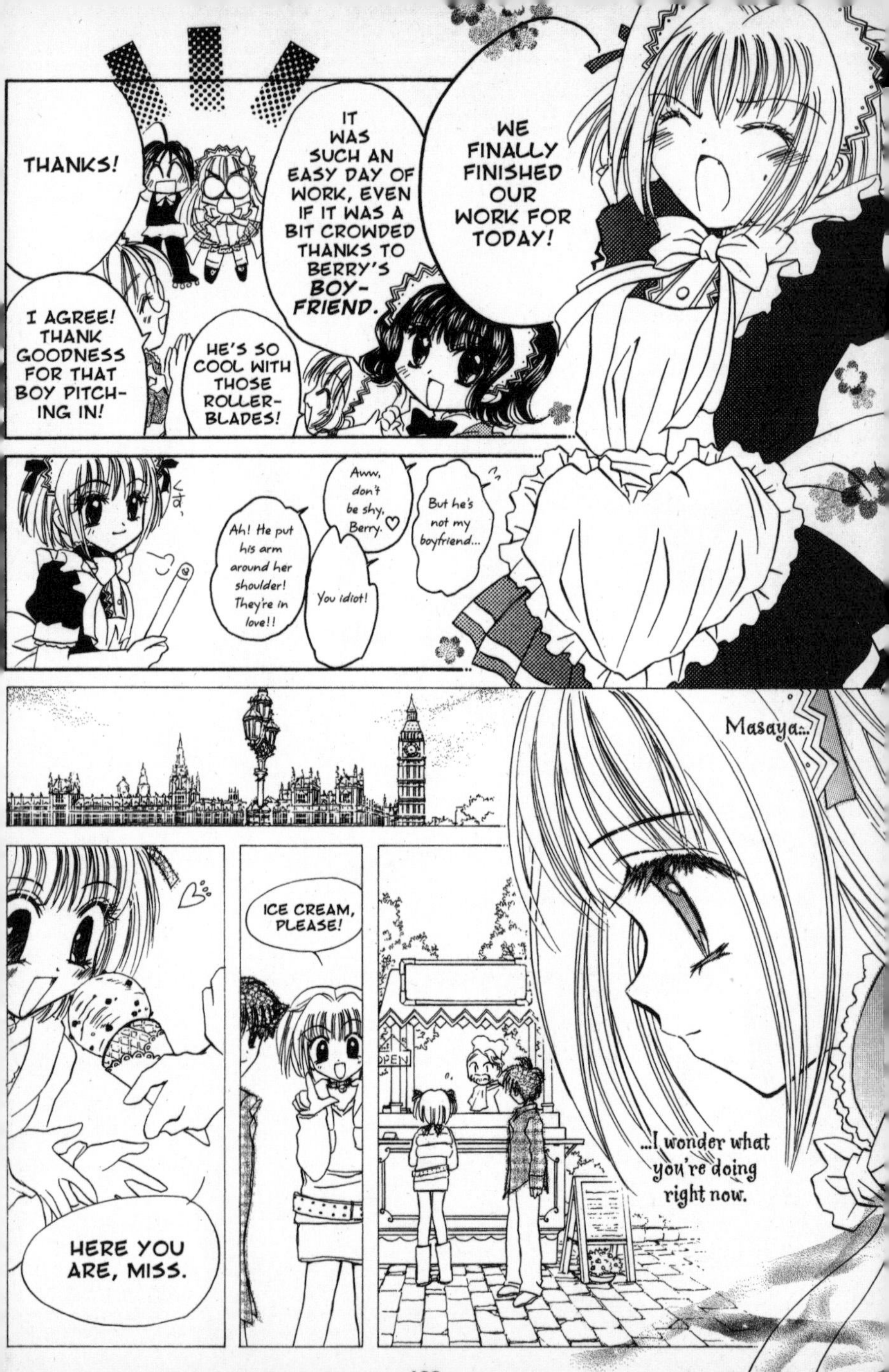
WE FINALLY FINISHED OUR WORK FOR TODAY!
IT WAS SUCH AN EASY DAY OF WORK, EVEN IF IT WAS A BIT CROWDED THANKS TO BERRY'S BOY-FRIEND.
THANKS!
HE'S SO COOL WITH THOSE ROLLER-BLADES!
I AGREE! THANK GOODNESS FOR THAT BOY PITCH-ING IN!
But he's not my boyfriend...
Aww, don't be shy, Berry. ♡
You idiot!
Ah! He put his arm around her shoulder! They're in love!!
Masaya...
...I wonder what you're doing right now.
ICE CREAM, PLEASE!
HERE YOU ARE, MISS.

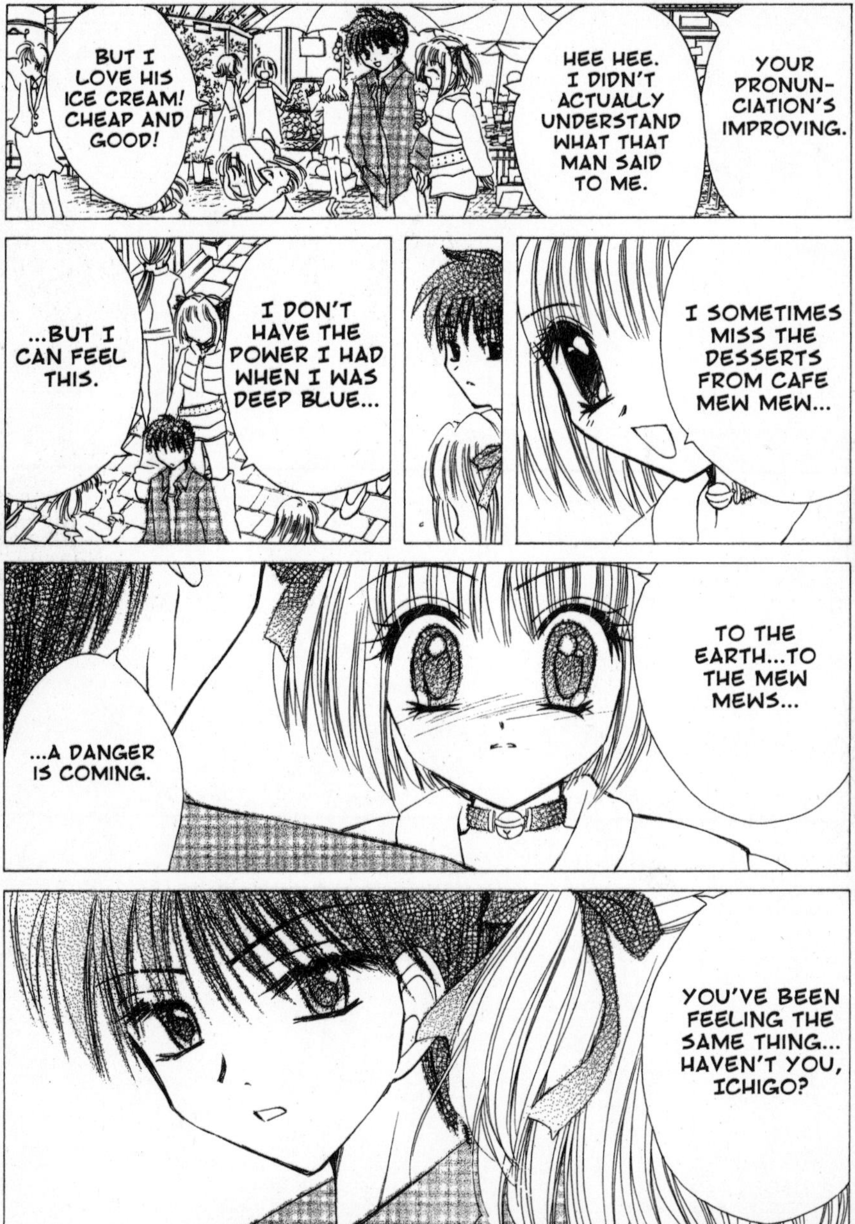
YOUR PRONUN-CIATION'S IMPROVING.
HEE HEE. I DIDN'T ACTUALLY UNDERSTAND WHAT THAT MAN SAID TO ME.
BUT I LOVE HIS ICE CREAM! CHEAP AND GOOD!
I SOMETIMES MISS THE DESSERTS FROM CAFE MEW MEW...
I DON'T HAVE THE POWER I HAD WHEN I WAS DEEP BLUE...
...BUT I CAN FEEL THIS.
TO THE EARTH...TO THE MEW MEWS...
...A DANGER IS COMING.
YOU'VE BEEN FEELING THE SAME THING... HAVEN'T YOU, ICHIGO?

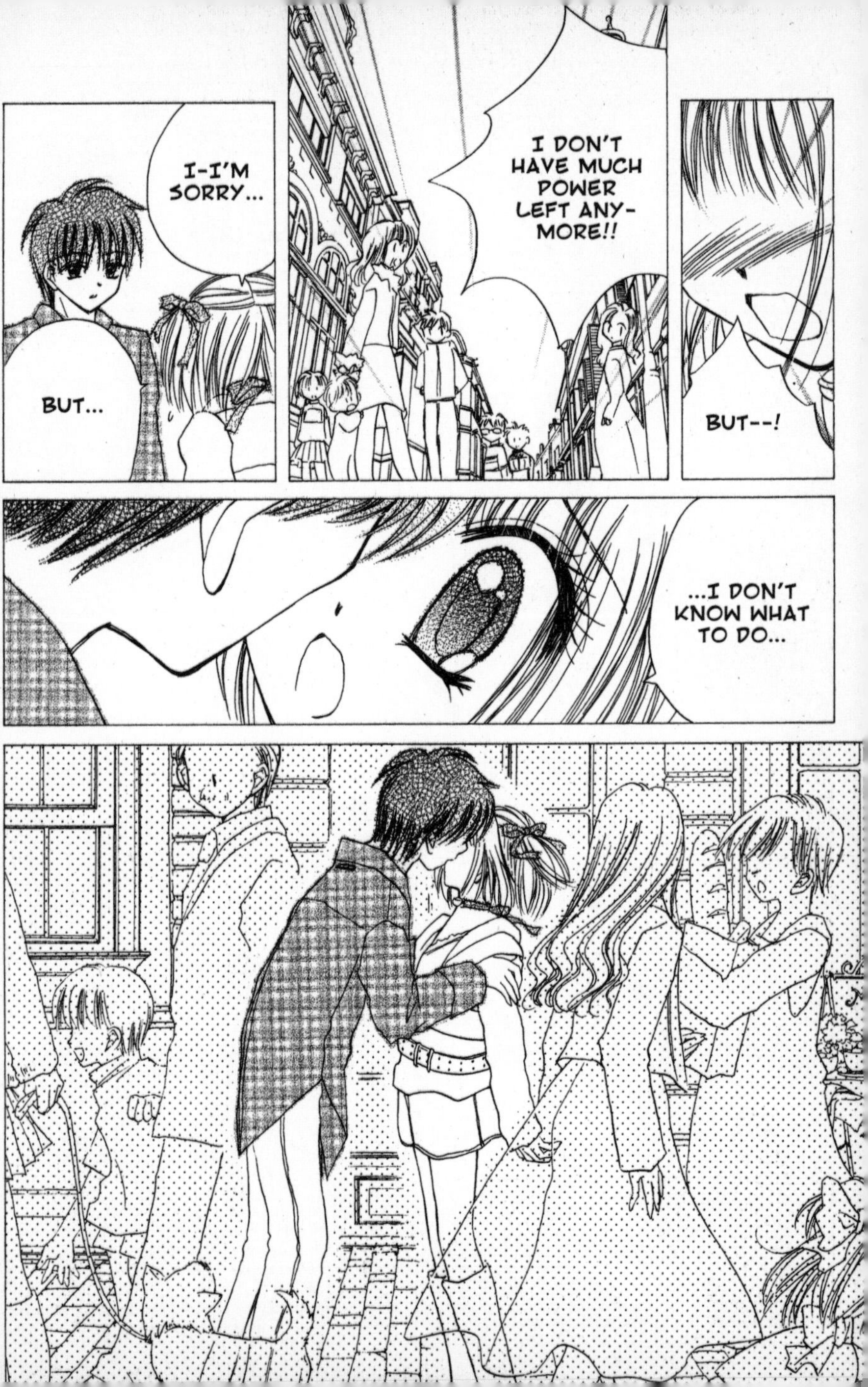
BUT--!
I DON'T HAVE MUCH POWER LEFT ANY-MORE!!
I-I'M SORRY...
BUT...
...I DON'T KNOW WHAT TO DO...

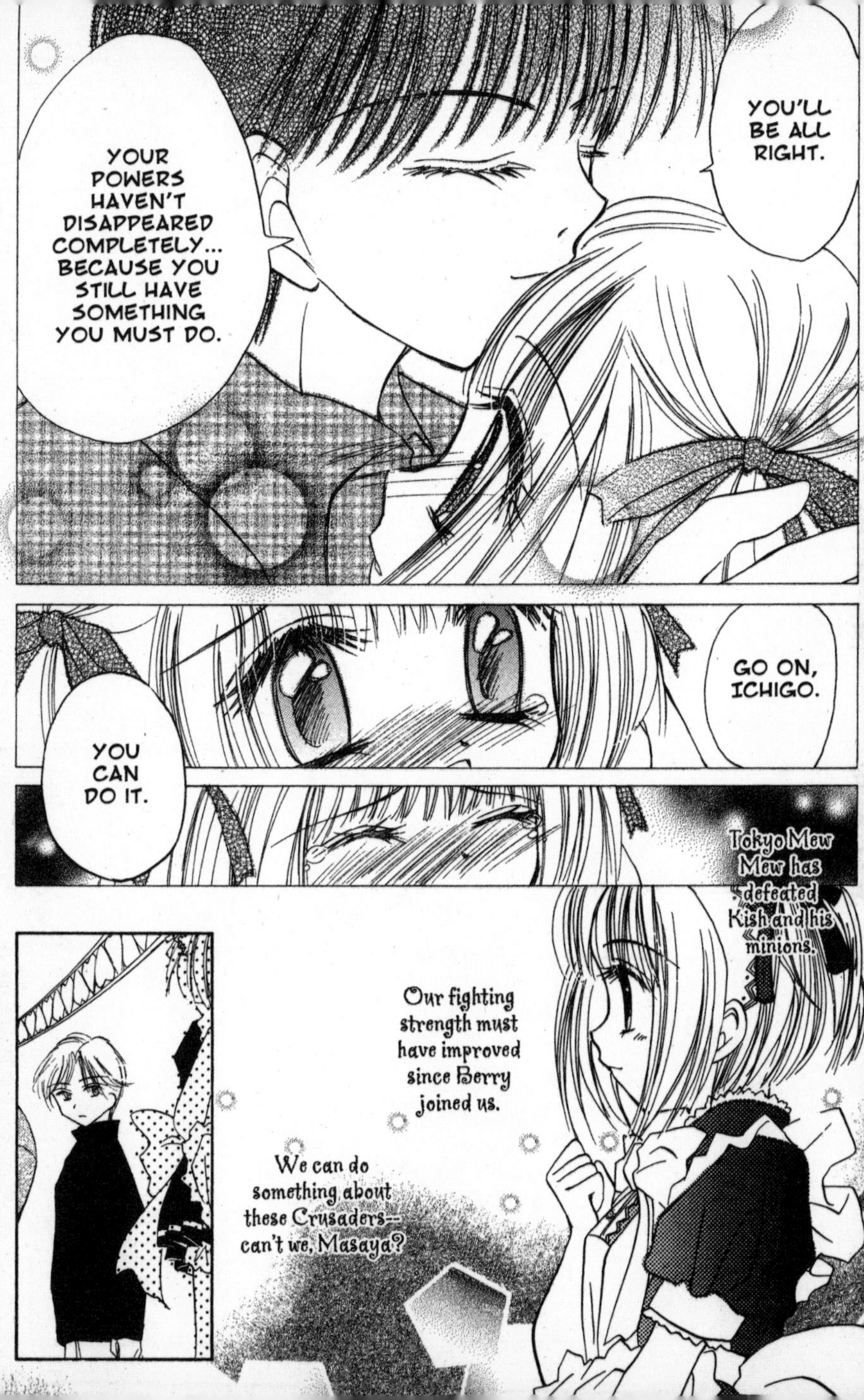
YOU'LL BE ALL RIGHT.
YOUR POWERS HAVEN'T DISAPPEARED COMPLETELY... BECAUSE YOU STILL HAVE SOMETHING YOU MUST DO.
GO ON, ICHIGO.
YOU CAN DO IT.
Tokyo Mew Mew has defeated Kish and his minions.
Our fighting strength must have improved since Berry joined us.
We can do something about these Crusaders--can't we, Masaya?

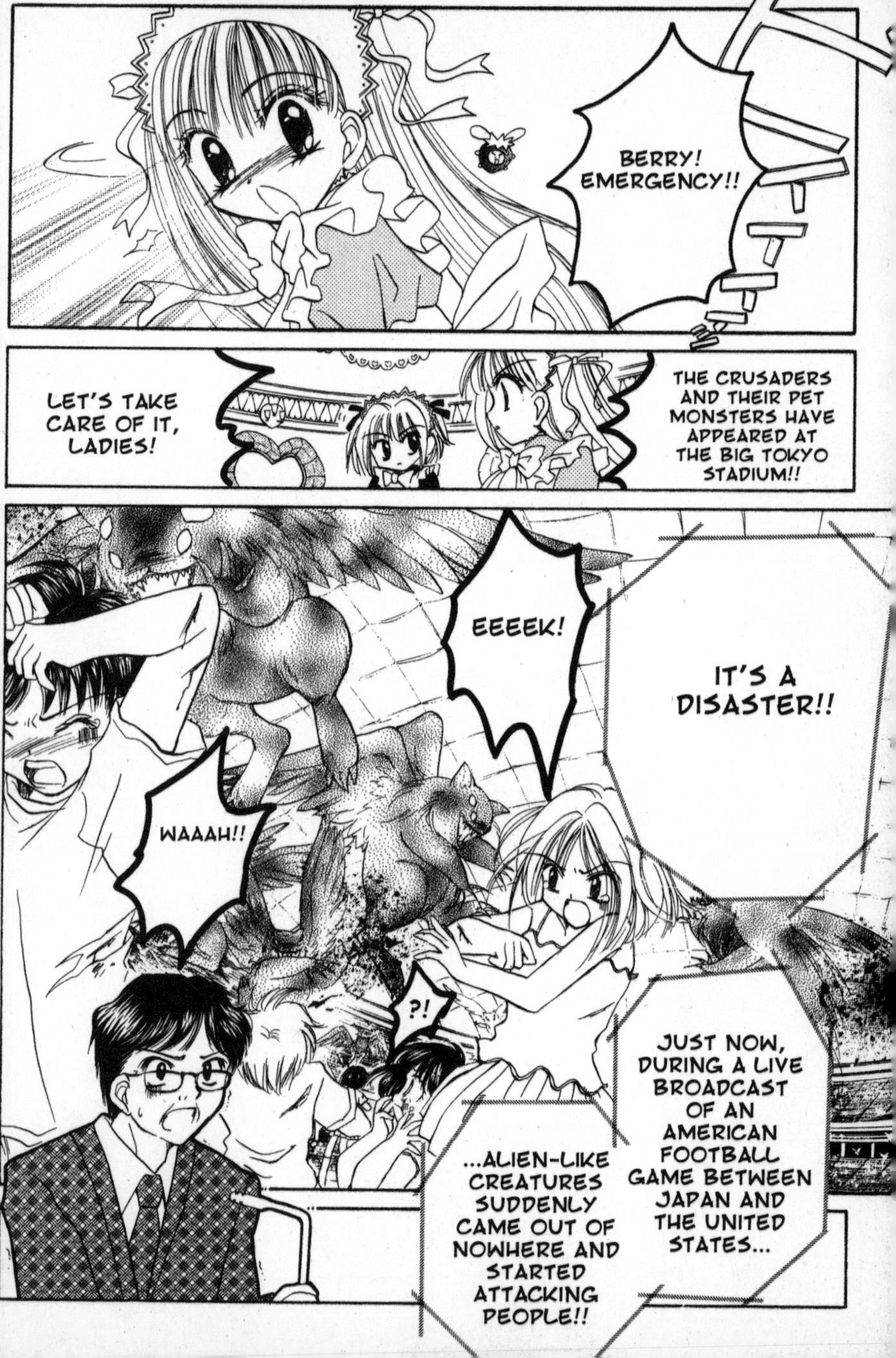
BERRY! EMERGENCY!!
THE CRUSADERS AND THEIR PET MONSTERS HAVE APPEARED AT THE BIG TOKYO STADIUM!!
LET'S TAKE CARE OF IT, LADIES!
IT'S A DISASTER!!
EEEEK!
WAAAH!!
?!
JUST NOW, DURING A LIVE BROADCAST OF AN AMERICAN FOOTBALL GAME BETWEEN JAPAN AND THE UNITED STATES...
...ALIEN-LIKE CREATURES SUDDENLY CAME OUT OF NOWHERE AND STARTED ATTACKING PEOPLE!!

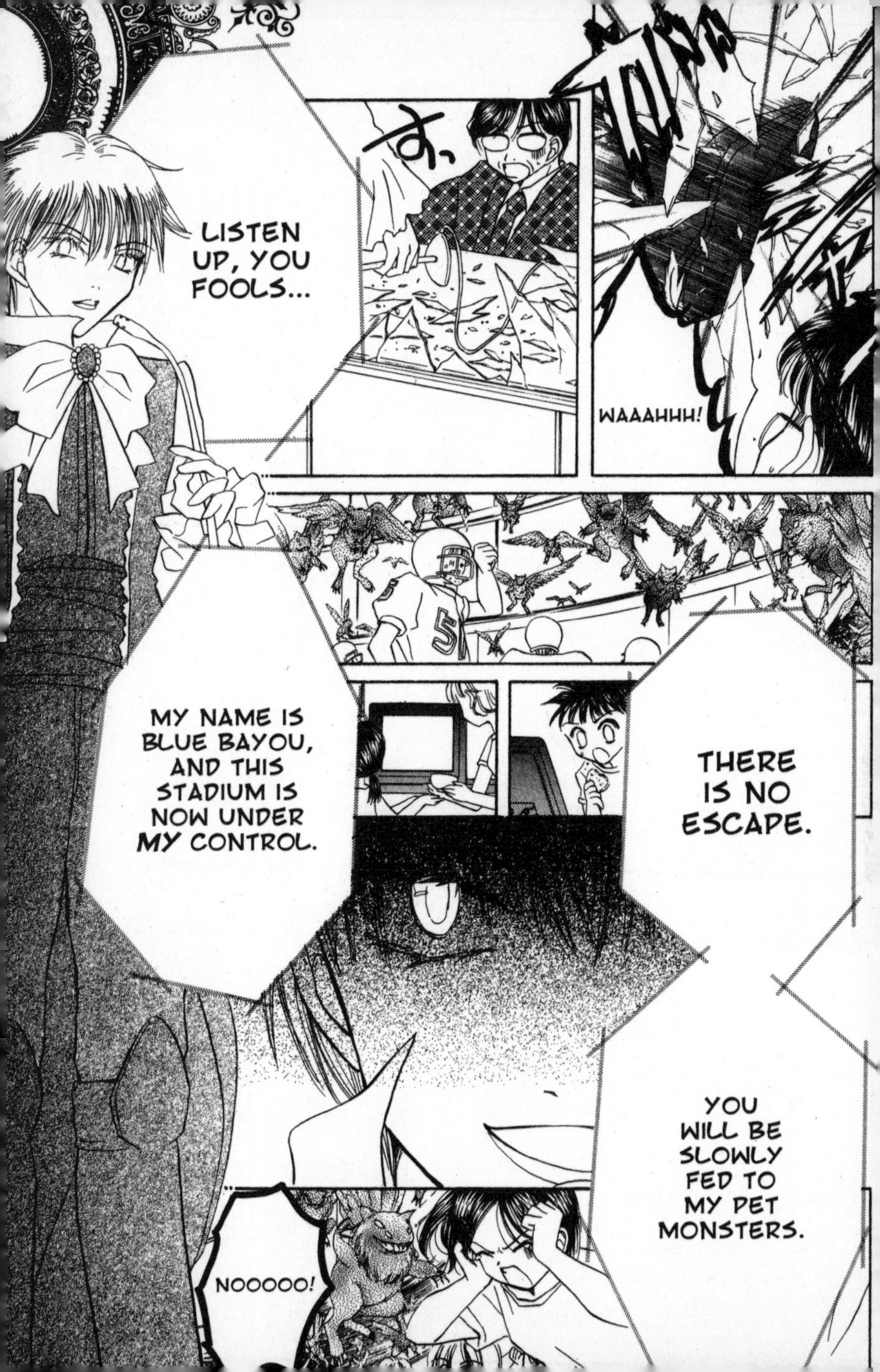
WAAAHHH!
す、
LISTEN UP, YOU FOOLS...
MY NAME IS BLUE BAYOU, AND THIS STADIUM IS NOW UNDER MY CONTROL.
THERE IS NO ESCAPE.
YOU WILL BE SLOWLY FED TO MY PET MONSTERS.
NOOOOO!

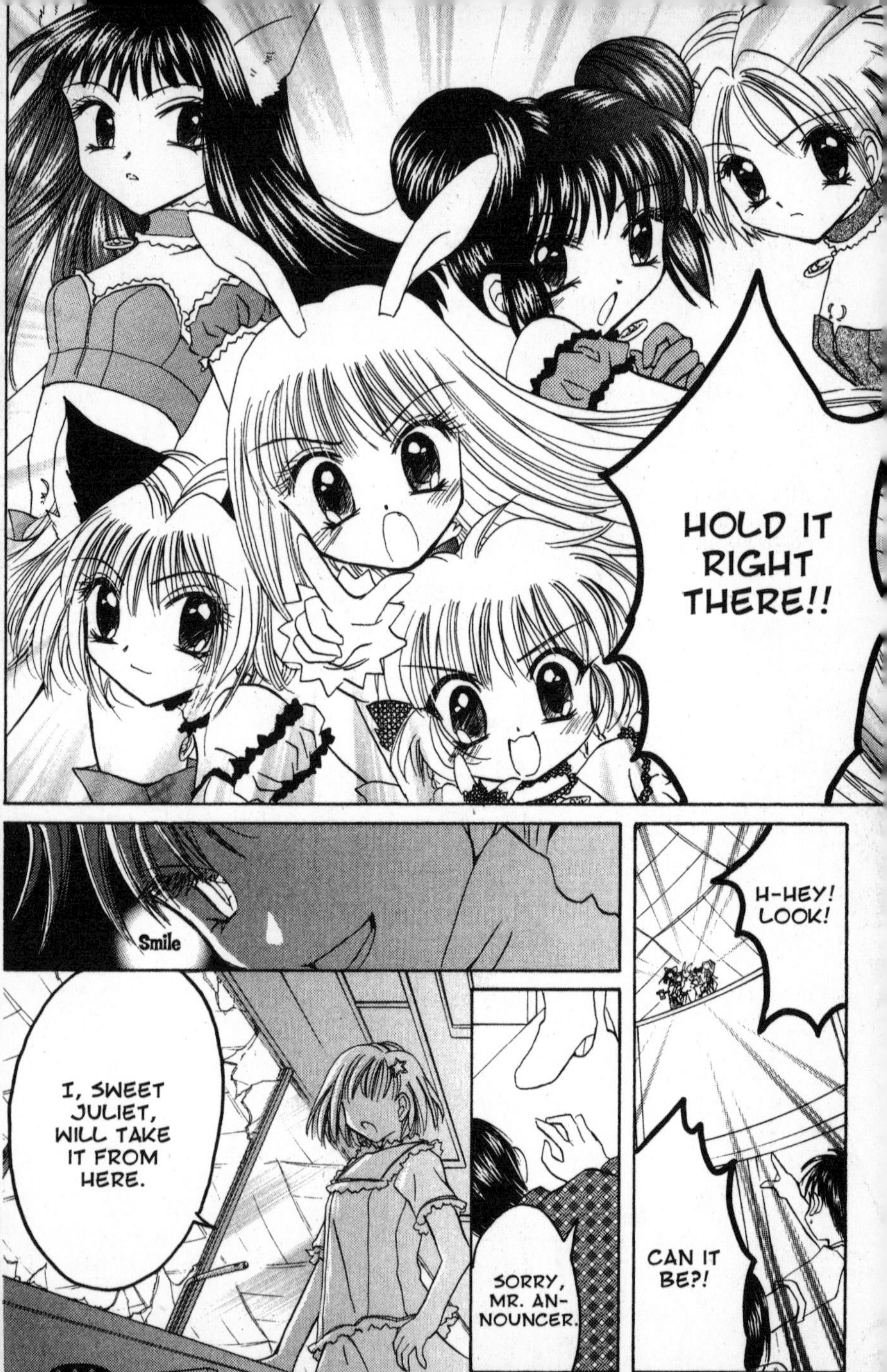
HOLD IT RIGHT THERE!!
H-HEY! LOOK!
CAN IT BE?!
Smile
SORRY, MR. AN-NOUNCER.
I, SWEET JULIET, WILL TAKE IT FROM HERE.

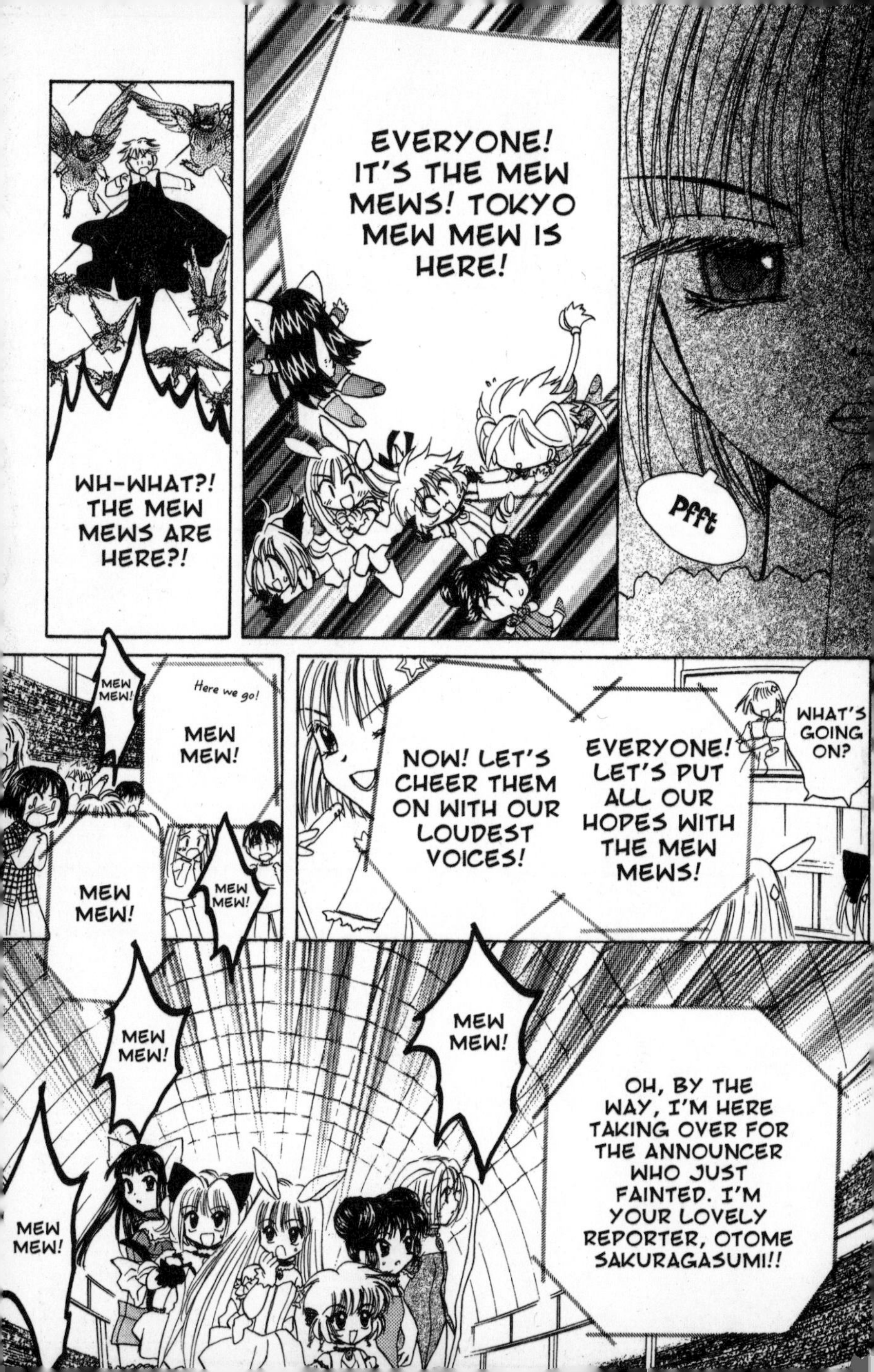
Pfft
EVERYONE! IT'S THE MEW MEWS! TOKYO MEW MEW IS HERE!
WH-WHAT?! THE MEW MEWS ARE HERE?!
WHAT'S GOING ON?
EVERYONE! LET'S PUT ALL OUR HOPES WITH THE MEW MEWS!
NOW! LET'S CHEER THEM ON WITH OUR LOUDEST VOICES!
MEW MEW!
Here we go!
MEW MEW!
MEW MEW!
MEW MEW!
OH, BY THE WAY, I'M HERE TAKING OVER FOR THE ANNOUNCER WHO JUST FAINTED. I'M YOUR LOVELY REPORTER, OTOME SAKURAGASUMI!!
MEW MEW!
MEW MEW!
MEW MEW!

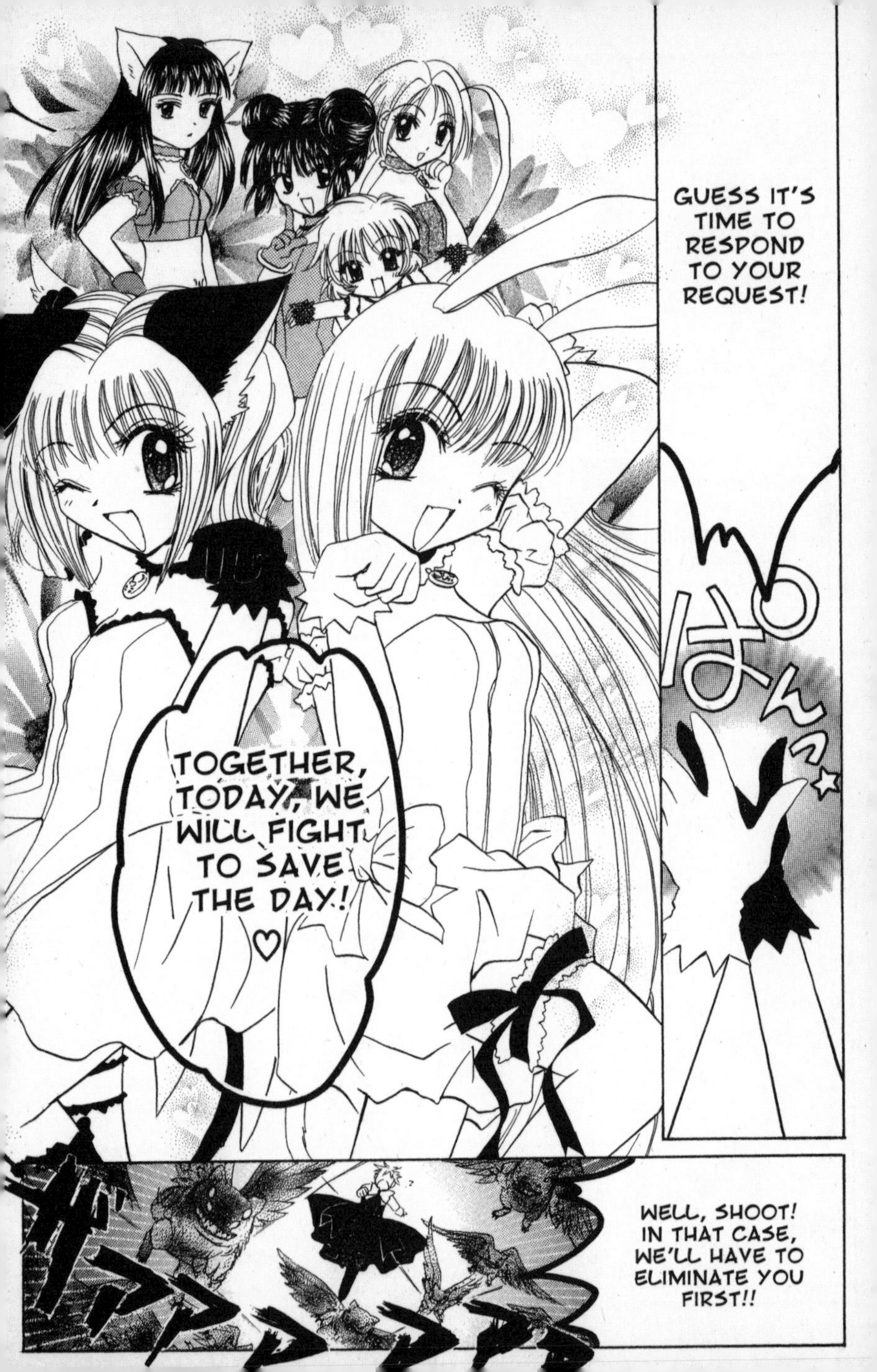
GUESS IT'S TIME TO RESPOND TO YOUR REQUEST!
ぱんっ☆
TOGETHER, TODAY, WE WILL FIGHT TO SAVE THE DAY! ♡
WELL, SHOOT! IN THAT CASE, WE'LL HAVE TO ELIMINATE YOU FIRST!!

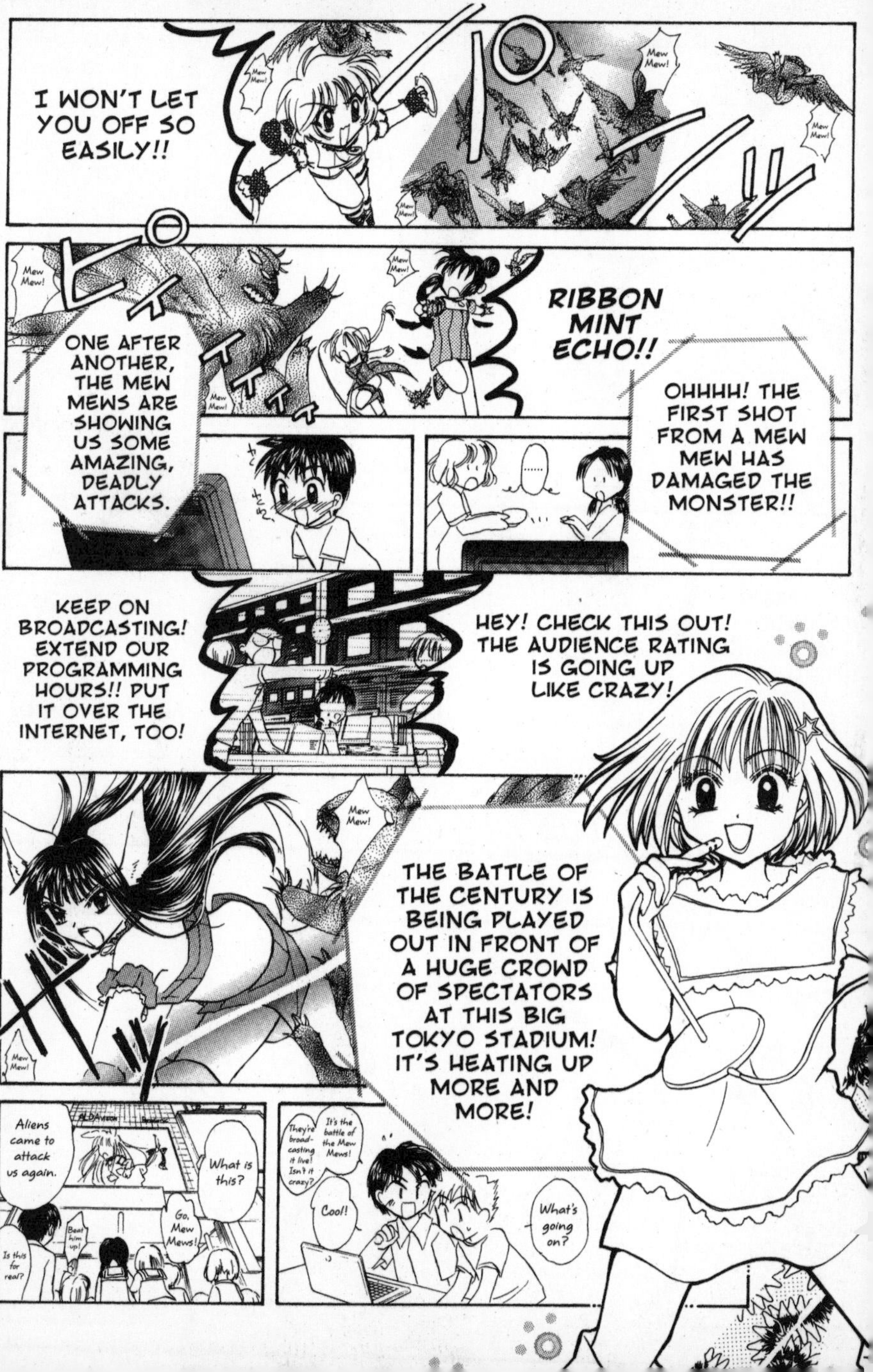

Mew Mew!
Mew Mew!
Mew Mew!
I WON'T LET YOU OFF SO EASILY!!
Mew Mew!
RIBBON MINT ECHO!!
Mew Mew!
Mew Mew!
Mew Mew!
OHHHH! THE FIRST SHOT FROM A MEW MEW HAS DAMAGED THE MONSTER!!
......
ONE AFTER ANOTHER, THE MEW MEWS ARE SHOWING US SOME AMAZING, DEADLY ATTACKS.
HEY! CHECK THIS OUT! THE AUDIENCE RATING IS GOING UP LIKE CRAZY!
KEEP ON BROADCASTING! EXTEND OUR PROGRAMMING HOURS!! PUT IT OVER THE INTERNET, TOO!
THE BATTLE OF THE CENTURY IS BEING PLAYED OUT IN FRONT OF A HUGE CROWD OF SPECTATORS AT THIS BIG TOKYO STADIUM! IT'S HEATING UP MORE AND MORE!
Mew Mew!
Mew Mew!
It's the battle of the Mew Mews!
They're broad-casting it live! Isn't it crazy?
What's going on?
Cool!
What is this?
Aliens came to attack us again.
Go, Mew Mews!
Beat him up!
Is this for real?

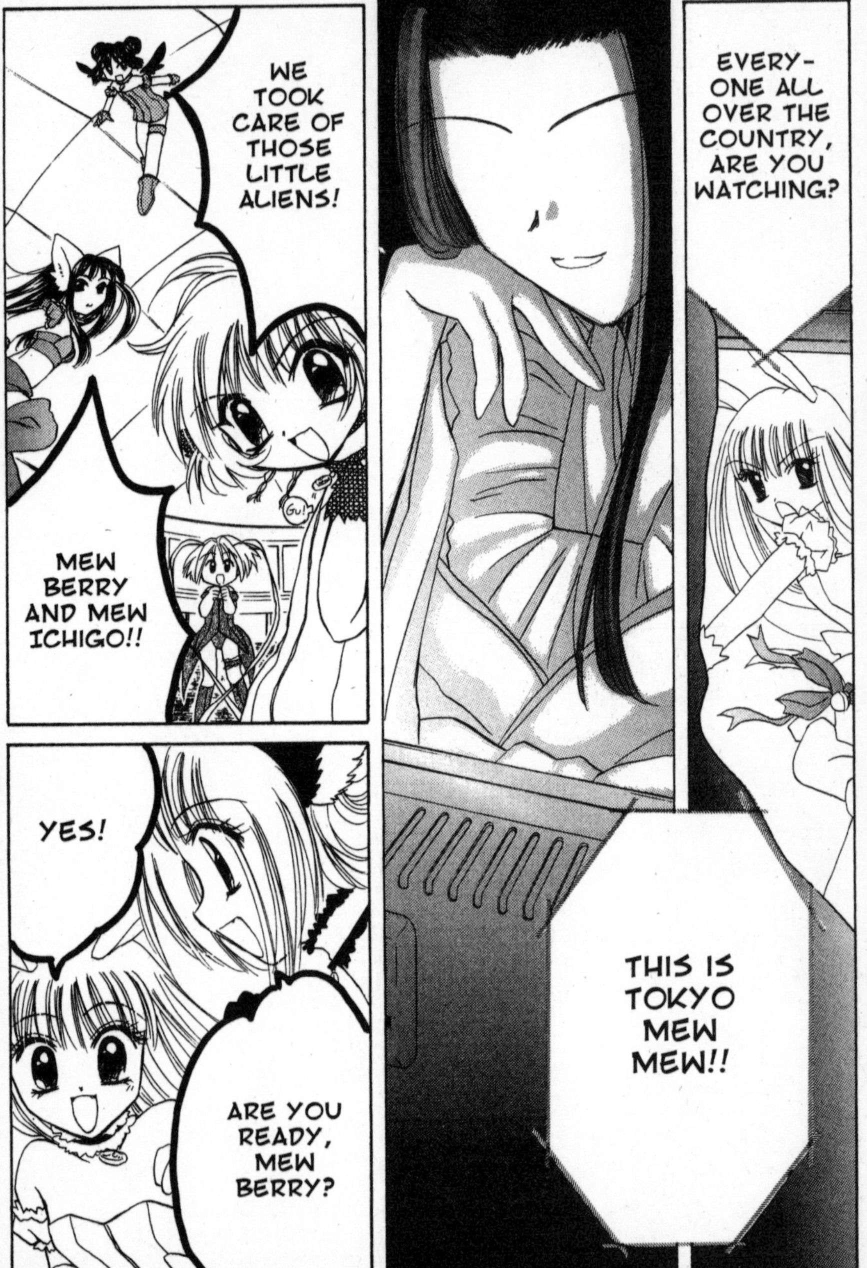
EVERY-ONE ALL OVER THE COUNTRY, ARE YOU WATCHING?
THIS IS TOKYO MEW MEW!!
WE TOOK CARE OF THOSE LITTLE ALIENS!
MEW BERRY AND MEW ICHIGO!!
ARE YOU READY, MEW BERRY?
YES!

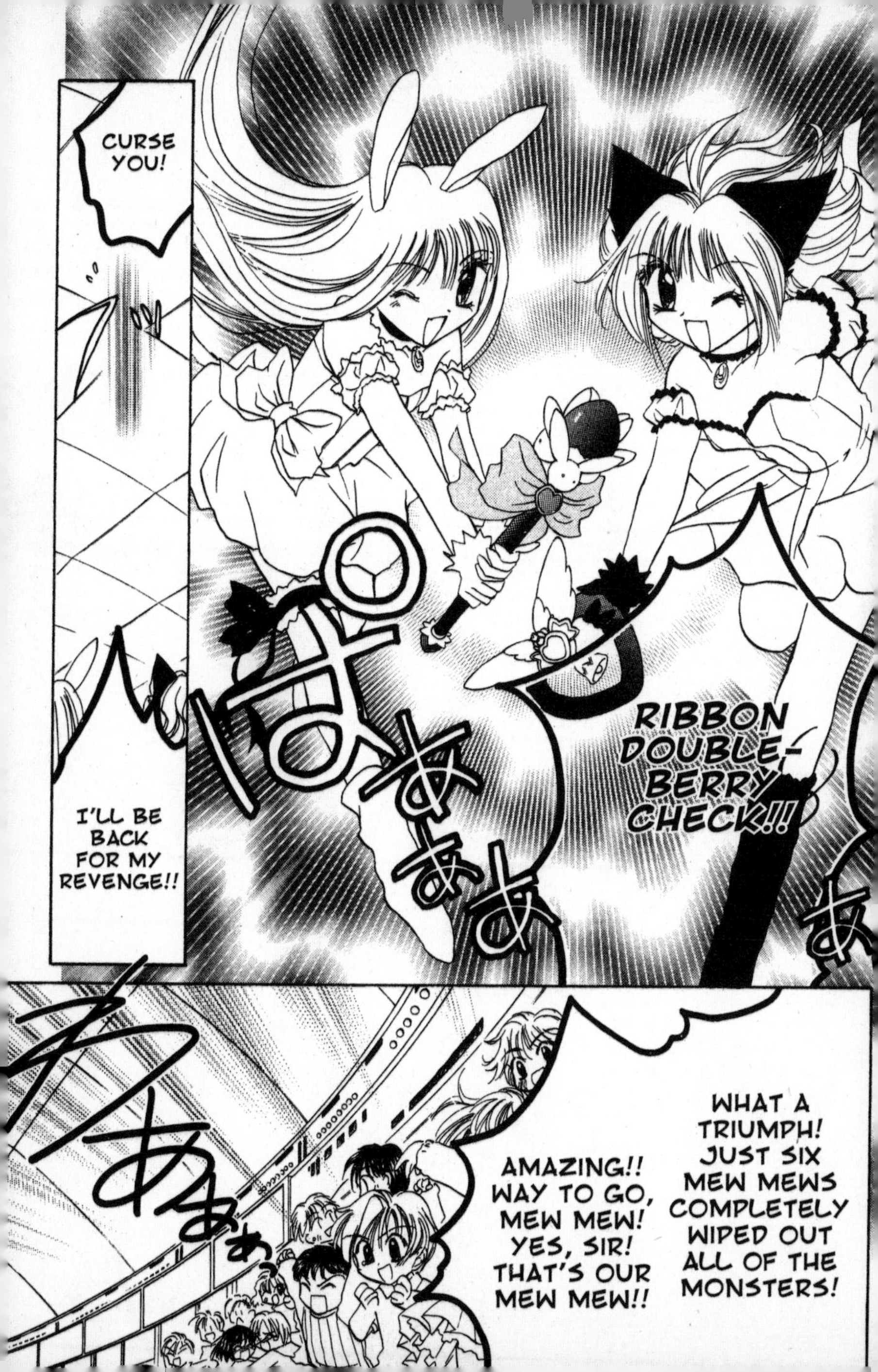
RIBBON DOUBLE-BERRY CHECK!!
ぱあああ
CURSE YOU!
I'LL BE BACK FOR MY REVENGE!!
WHAT A TRIUMPH! JUST SIX MEW MEWS COMPLETELY WIPED OUT ALL OF THE MONSTERS!
AMAZING!! WAY TO GO, MEW MEW! YES, SIR! THAT'S OUR MEW MEW!!
わああぁ

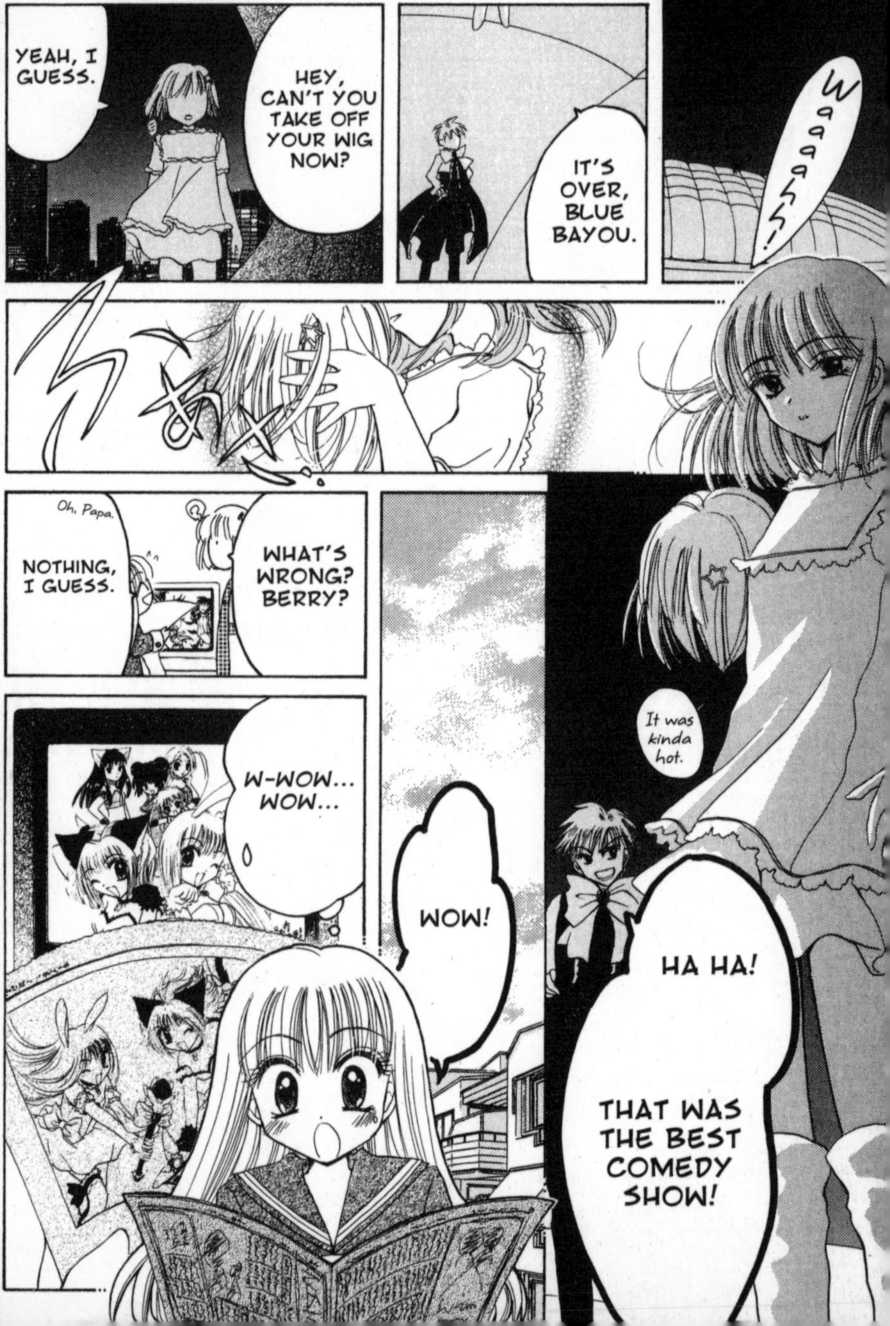
Waaaahh!
IT'S OVER, BLUE BAYOU.
HEY, CAN'T YOU TAKE OFF YOUR WIG NOW?
YEAH, I GUESS.
It was kinda hot.
HA HA!
THAT WAS THE BEST COMEDY SHOW!
WHAT'S WRONG? BERRY?
Oh, Papa.
NOTHING, I GUESS.
W-WOW... WOW...
WOW!

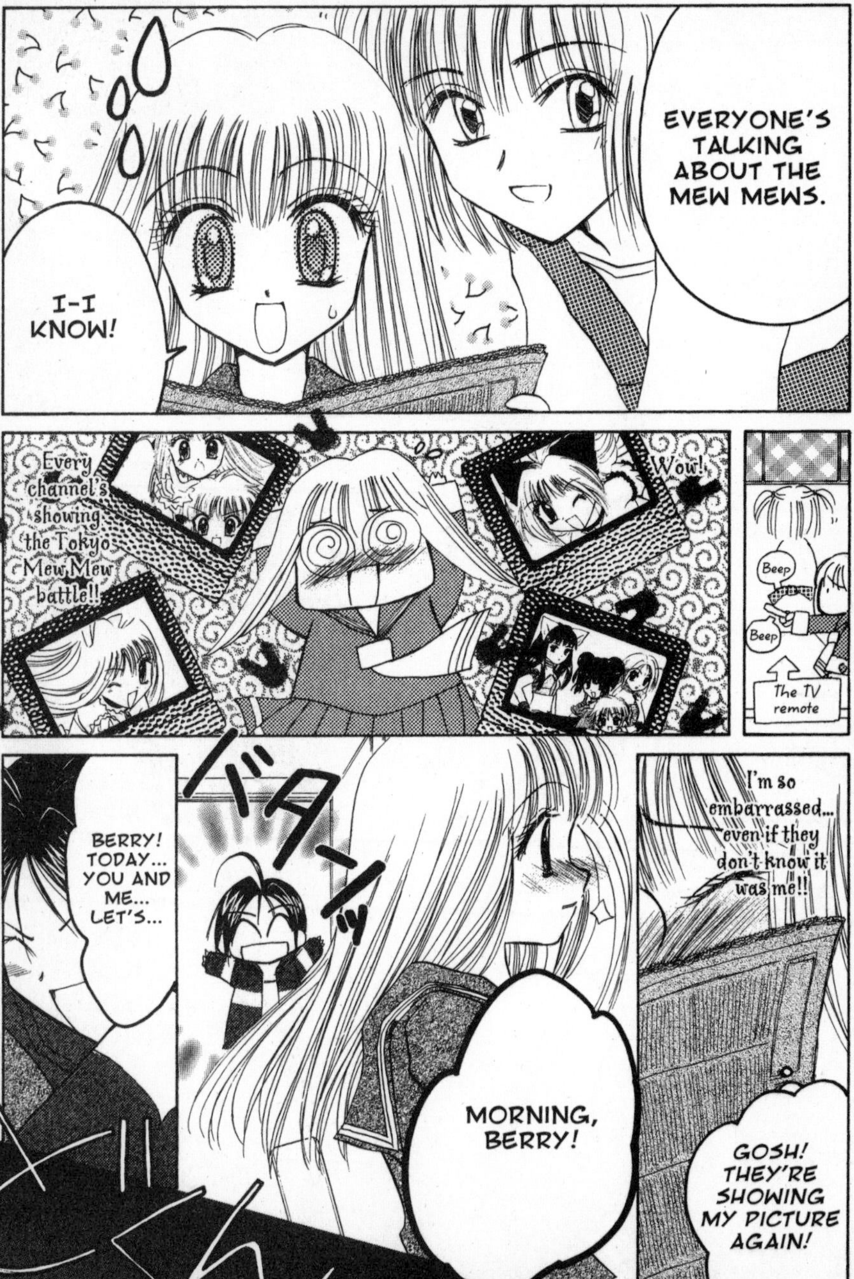
EVERYONE'S TALKING ABOUT THE MEW MEWS.
I-I KNOW!
Beep
Beep
The TV remote
Wow!
Every channel's showing the Tokyo Mew Mew battle!!
I'm so embarrassed... even if they don't know it was me!!
GOSH! THEY'RE SHOWING MY PICTURE AGAIN!
バターンッ
MORNING, BERRY!
BERRY! TODAY... YOU AND ME... LET'S...

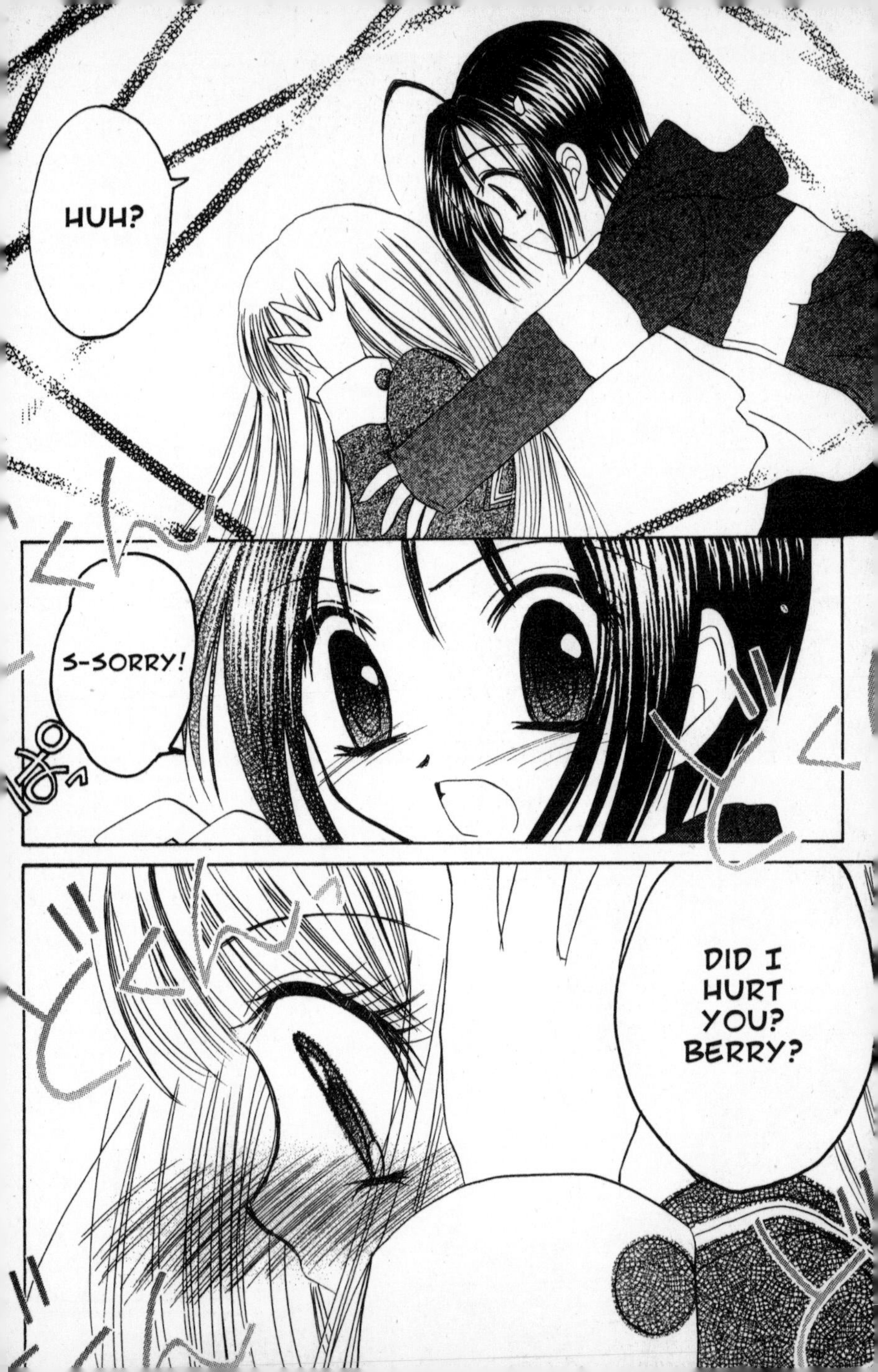
HUH?
S-SORRY!
DID I HURT YOU? BERRY?

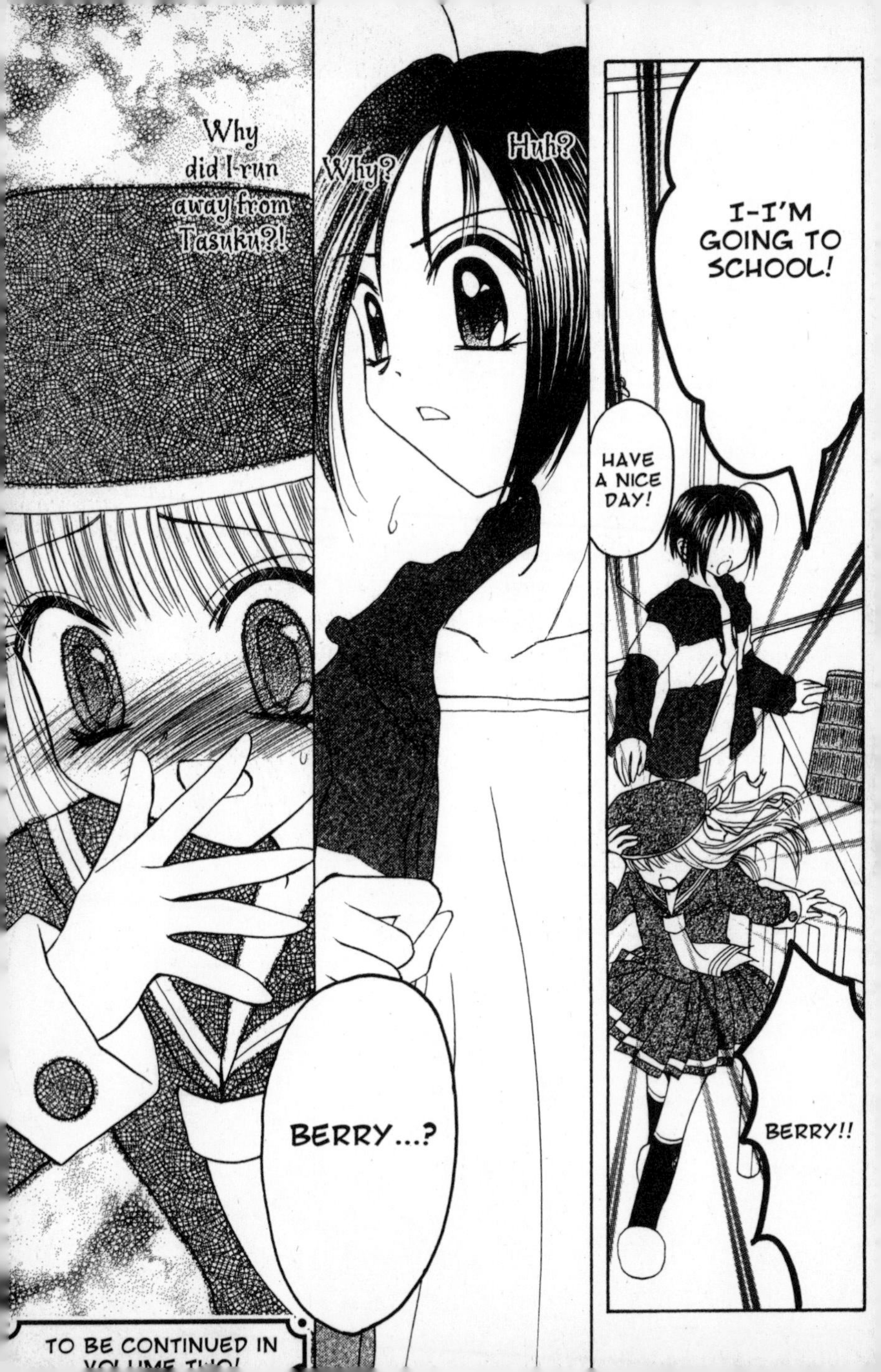
I-I'M GOING TO SCHOOL!
HAVE A NICE DAY!
BERRY!!
Huh?
Why?
BERRY...?
Why did I run away from Tasuku?!
TO BE CONTINUED IN

Killing time.

I'll just write whatever I'm feeling right now.

Number one: The Calendar
I was happy to have another book signing with my fans this year. But I was even happier about the sale of this year's 2004 Tokyo Mew Mew Calendar.☆ It will be sold for three consecutive years. I'm super-excited and drew many, many illustrations for it, since I had no time to work that much last year. ☆ I even retouched and redrew some illustrations from the past. I was sitting in front of my computer most of this time. I thought my method of drawing 13 illustrations at the same time would finish the job faster. But I haven't even finished one illustration since I started the calendar project more than a month ago (sweat, sweat). While I was working on this project, I started getting used to my new computer. I started thinking, "Hey! This illustration can be retouched and totally improved with this new technique!" or, "Oh! I really want to draw something new like this!!" But the deadline for both the calendar and this manga is only a few days away...so I'd better kick into gear soon (sweat).

Number two: Mew Mew Merchandise☆
I recently realized that I have so much *Tokyo Mew Mew* merchandise at my house. It's probably the most I'll ever have for a character I created. (And I don't even take very good care of it!! I use up so many Mew Mew dishes so I won't have to wash them, hee hee.) And I still have so many products stuck in cardboard boxes. I dream about organizing all of them one day (laugh).

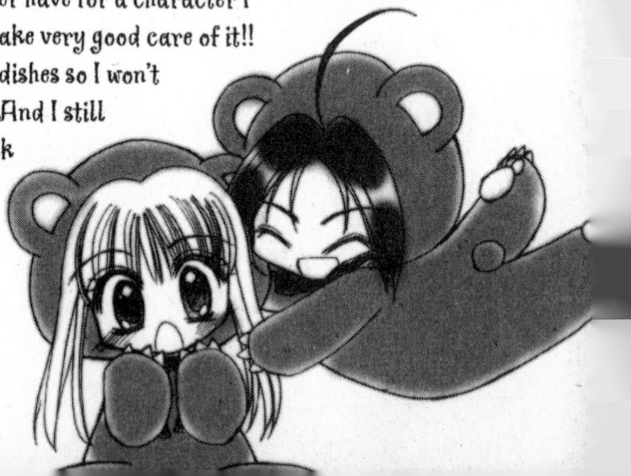

Number three: My House☆

I feel like I've found a place where I can finally live in peace. Of course, I can't live here forever, since this place is just another rental apartment. But this is the first place I have chosen on my own. Until now, I would choose a place because someone said, "Why don't you live around there?" or, "Why don't you move near my place?" And I'd always say, "Well, I guess I can." Originally I moved to Tokyo from Osaka for work, so I just thought, "The most important thing is that I can work at my place." But one day, my boss asked me, "Why don't you just live in your favorite city?" So I decided to seriously look for a new place. At first, I looked for a city I could love. And, eventually, I found this place! It's far from the train station, but the environment is great! It's a secret where I live now, though! I just want to stay here as long as I can and live happily ever after...that's my wish!

Number Four: Stuffed Animals☆

Some of the things I covet most are stuffed animals. Although I didn't use to be interested in them, I started getting into them this year. Every time I go out, I always check out the UFO Catcher (the claw) at the arcade. I know it's probably cheaper to buy it at a toy store instead of trying to catch it from the crane (since I never seem to win), but I can't stop thinking about those animals behind the glass! There was this puppet of a Panda in a commercial for some tea company that I wanted so badly and could never seem to get. (Yes, that panda that kisses!☆) By the way, I've never caught anything from that darn claw in my life. Boo hoo.

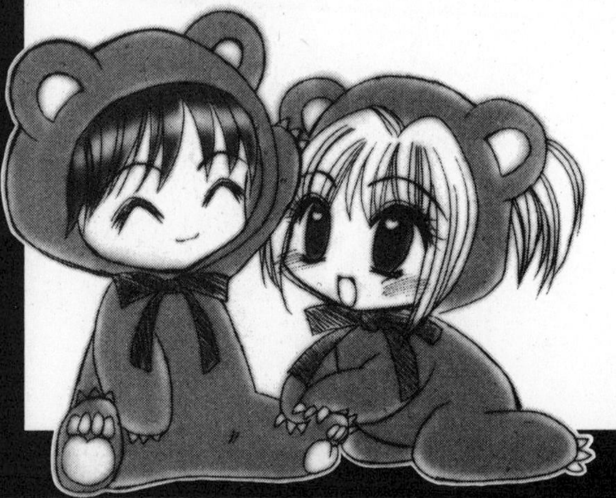

Postscript☆

Since *Tokyo Mew Mew* became a TV Anime, I have had the most hectic life, with so much work last year. I still enjoy the work, even though I'm so busy now. But even though the most hectic time has finally passed, I still don't feel like I have much free time. I guess I should appreciate that I finally have time to cook, do some laundry, and have tea with my friends.☆

Last year, it was so much work to even cook dinner while I was on a project. But I guess the reason I always felt I had no time was that I put too many different projects into my schedule. Someone actually said, "Ikumi, you are driving yourself off a cliff!" That person was right. Because even now, I still think I should be able to make some free time by working at such and such a pace—so, like a fool, I add something else to my schedule. Do you think I'm abusing myself?

I think it's great to have so many things that I want and try to do. I feel alive when I have something I can try to do my best. Even though my life is so hectic, I still have so much power to go on! Everyone, make the most of your lives along with me!

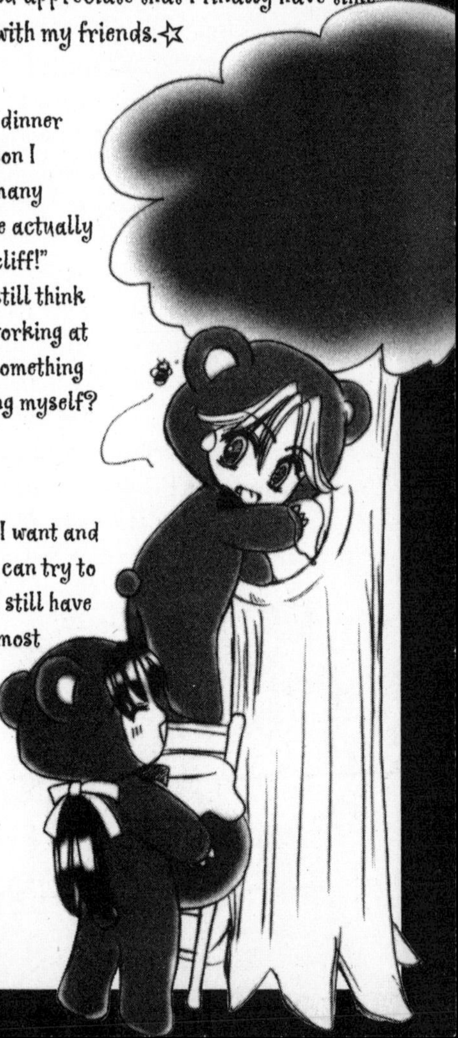

DON'T MISS THE NEXT VOLUME OF

TOKYO MEW MEW A LA MODE

The girls from Mew Mew are back with a vengeance. But this time they're up against their worst enemy ever--their fans!!! Someone is slipping subliminal messages about the Mews into television shows, the Internet and more. With not-so-friendly statements like "Down with the Mew Mew," and "Hate the Mews!" slipping into the media, everyone who watches TV is about to go into a trance where they hate anything and everything Mew! Even Mew Berry's crush buys into the Mew Mew-hating frenzy. What in the world is a Mew to do?

In conclusion...
Special thanks to the people who joined
me in the process of creating this
manga, the people who helped me to
produce it and the people who are reading it...thank you sooooo much!!

Always be positive!
5:20 P.M. 9.12.2003 Mia Ikumi

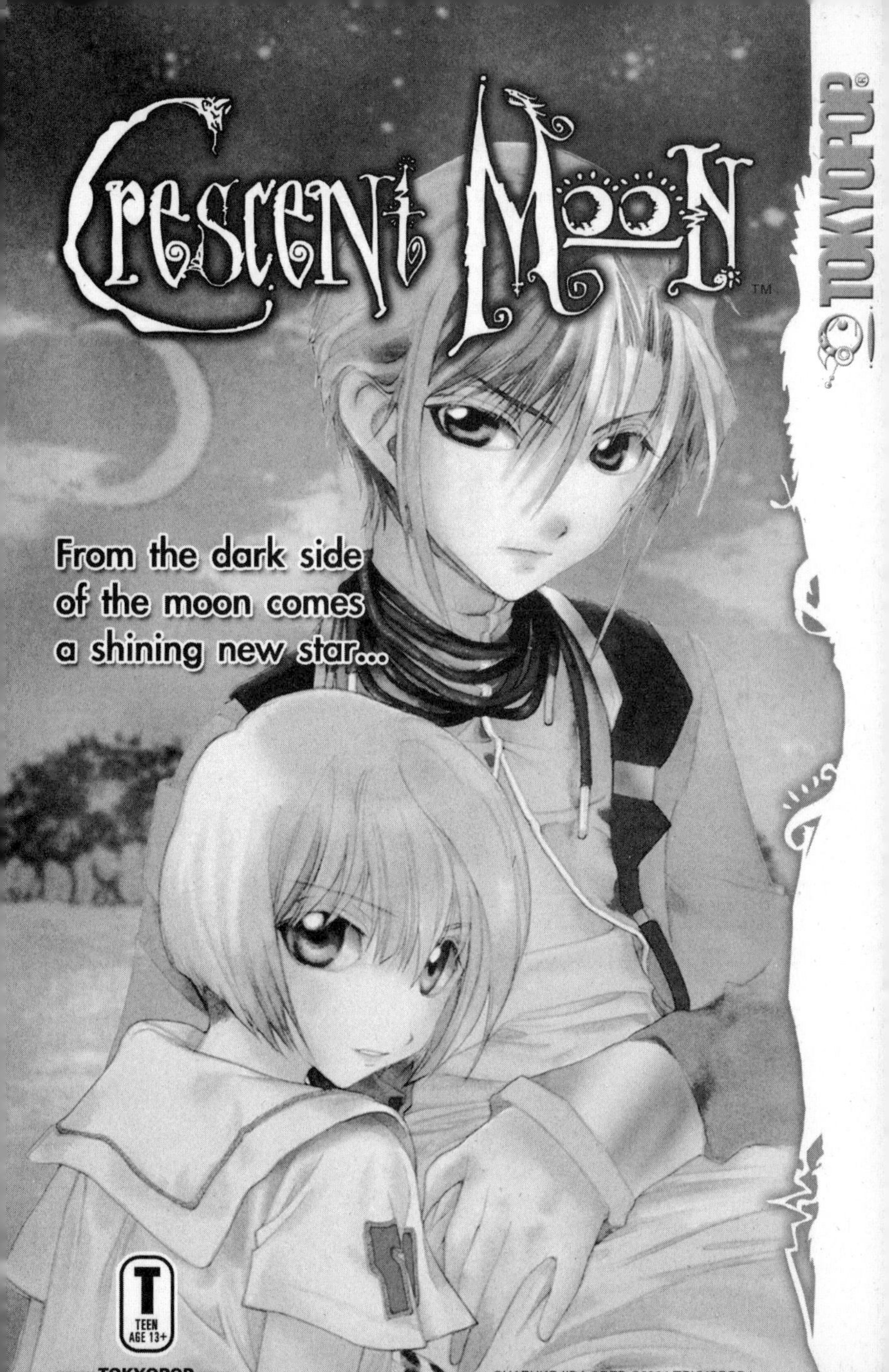
Crescent Moon™
TOKYOPOP®
From the dark side of the moon comes a shining new star...
T
TEEN AGE 13+

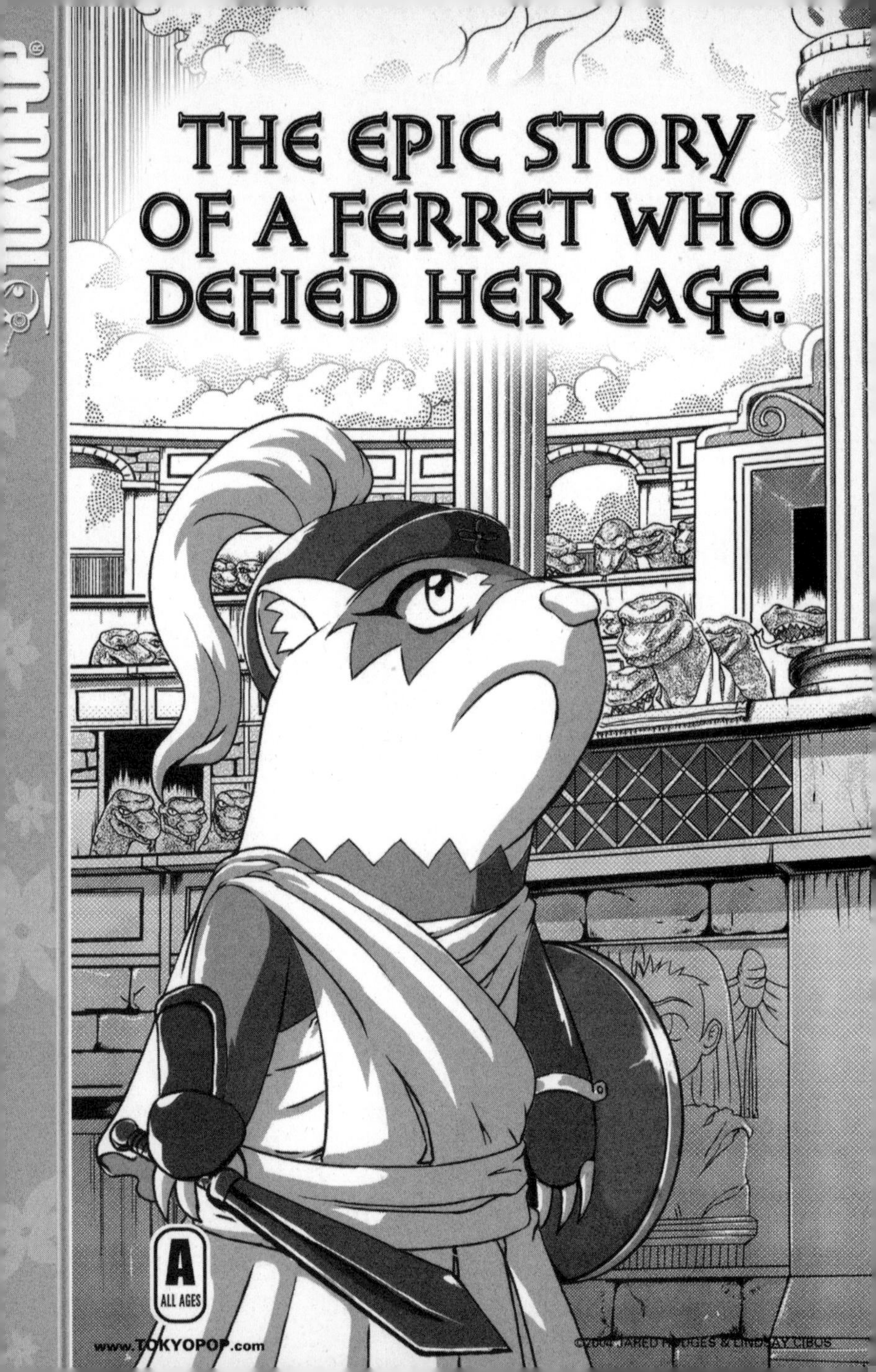
TOKYOPOP®
THE EPIC STORY
OF A FERRET WHO
DEFIED HER CAGE.
A
ALL AGES
www.TOKYOPOP.com
©2004 JARED HODGES & LINDSAY CIBOS

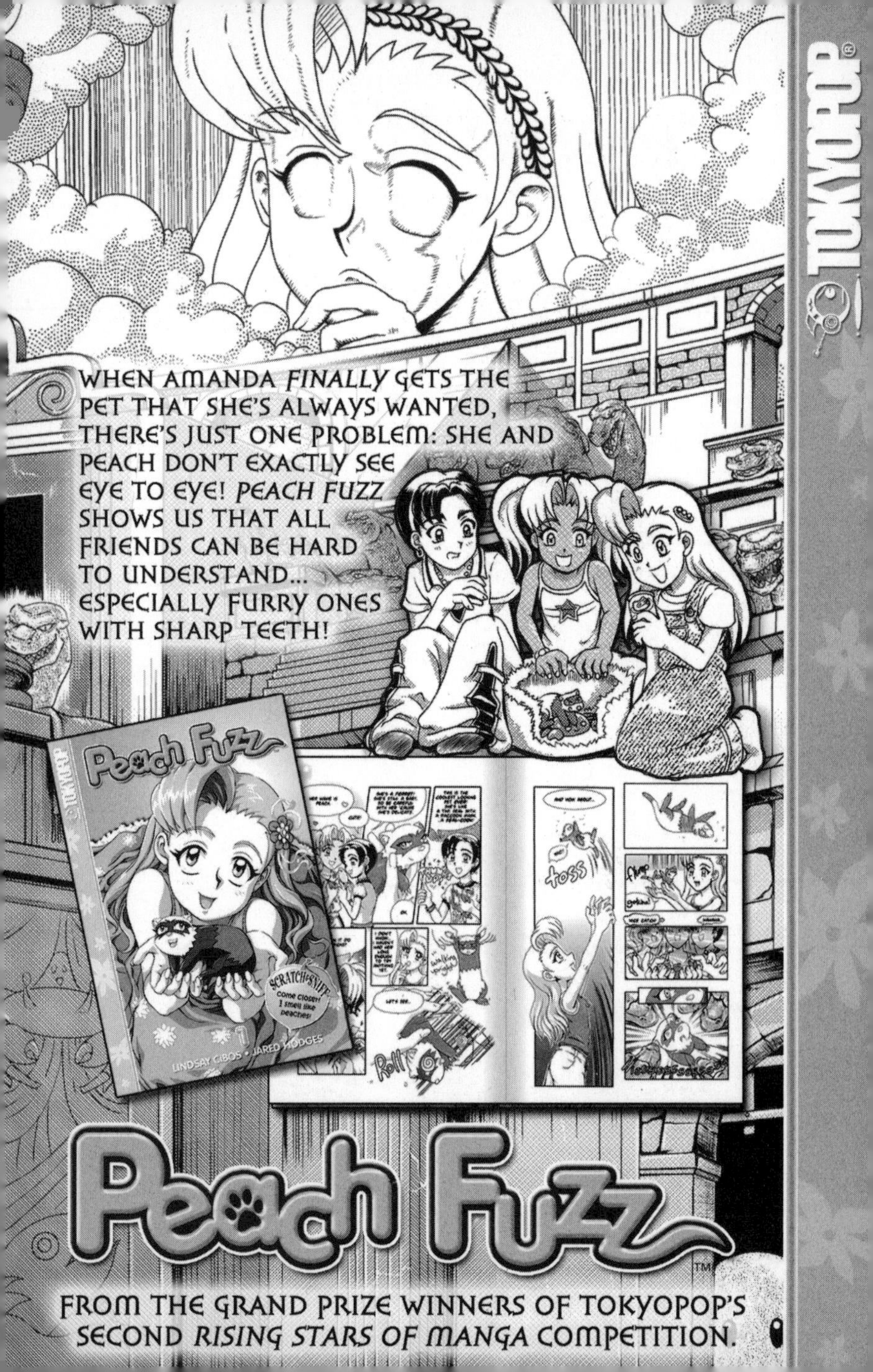
TOKYOPOP
WHEN AMANDA *FINALLY* GETS THE PET THAT SHE'S ALWAYS WANTED, THERE'S JUST ONE PROBLEM: SHE AND PEACH DON'T EXACTLY SEE EYE TO EYE! *PEACH FUZZ* SHOWS US THAT ALL FRIENDS CAN BE HARD TO UNDERSTAND... ESPECIALLY FURRY ONES WITH SHARP TEETH!
Peach Fuzz
SCRATCH & SNIFF
Come closer! I smell like peaches!
1
LINDSAY CIBOS • JARED HODGES
toss
Roll
Peach Fuzz™
FROM THE GRAND PRIZE WINNERS OF TOKYOPOP'S SECOND *RISING STARS OF MANGA* COMPETITION.

STOP!

This is the back of the book.
You wouldn't want to spoil a great ending!

This book is printed "manga-style," in the authentic Japanese right-to-left format. Since none of the artwork has been flipped or altered, readers get to experience the story just as the creator intended. You've been asking for it, so TOKYOPOP® delivered: authentic, hot-off-the-press, and far more fun!

DIRECTIONS

If this is your first time reading manga-style, here's a quick guide to help you understand how it works.

It's easy... just start in the top right panel and follow the numbers. Have fun, and look for more 100% authentic manga from TOKYOPOP®!

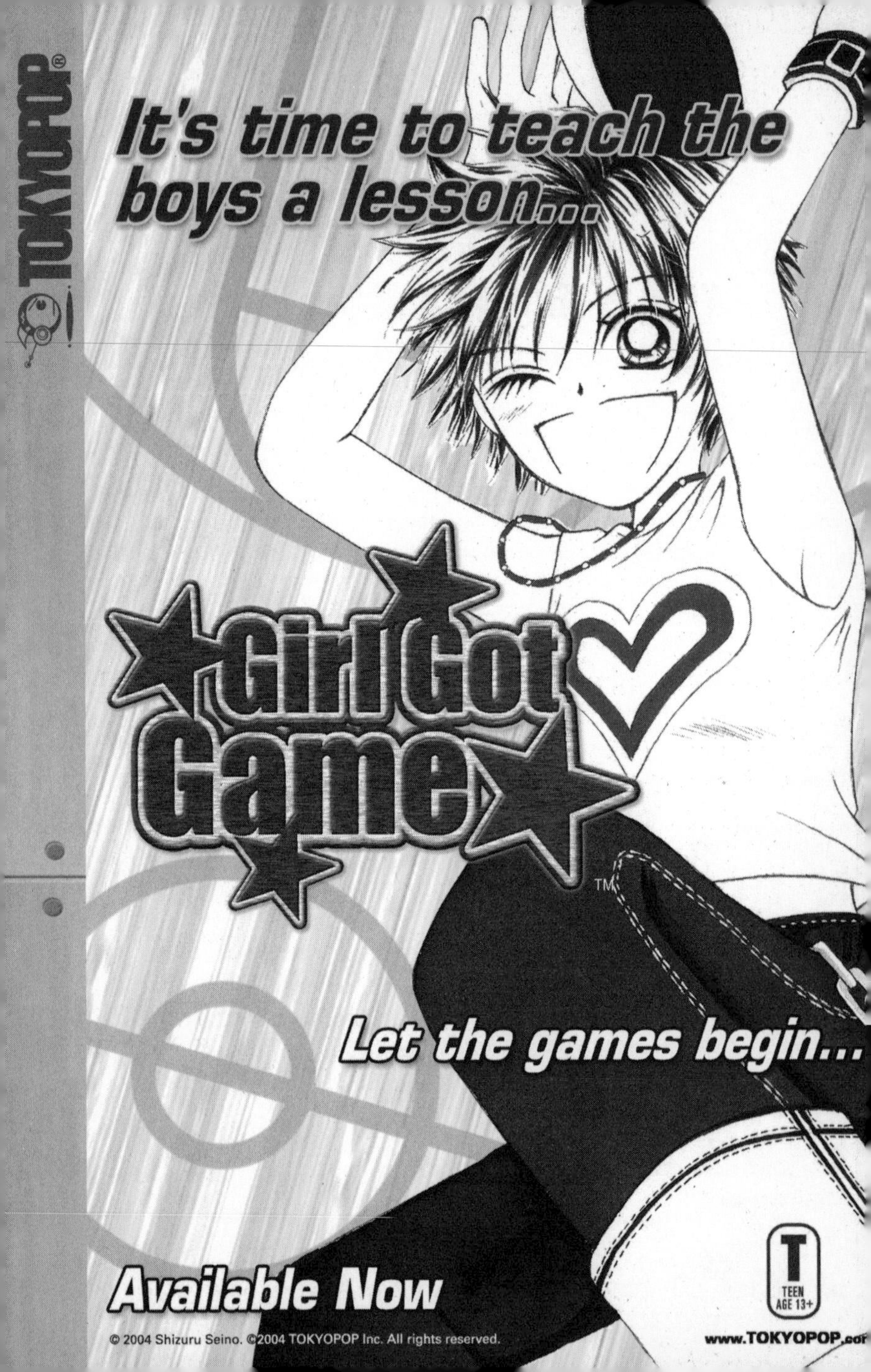
TOKYOPOP®
It's time to teach the boys a lesson...
Girl Got Game™
Let the games begin...
Available Now
T TEEN AGE 13+
© 2004 Shizuru Seino. ©2004 TOKYOPOP Inc. All rights reserved.
www.TOKYOPOP.co